GREAT CHRISTIAN JURISTS IN ENGLISH HISTORY

The Great Christian Jurists series comprises a library of national volumes of detailed biographies of leading jurists, judges and practitioners, assessing the impact of their Christian faith on the professional output of the individuals studied. Little has previously been written about the faith of the great judges and lawyers who framed and developed the English common law over centuries, but this unique volume explores how the beliefs of fourteen selected individuals were reflected in their professional functions. This comparative study, embracing ten centuries of English law, draws some remarkable conclusions as to how Christianity shaped the views of particular lawyers and judges. Adopting a long historical perspective, this volume also explores the lives of jurists whose practice in or conception of law helped to shape the Church, its law or the articulation of its doctrine.

Mark Hill QC is an associate or visiting professor at the Centre for Law and Religion, Cardiff University; the University of Pretoria; King's College, London; and Notre Dame University, Sydney. He has published widely on English ecclesiastical law and freedom of religion. He is Consultant Editor of the *Ecclesiastical Law Journal*, a Recorder of the Crown Court, Deputy Judge of the Upper Tribunal and Chancellor of the Dioceses of Chichester, Leeds and Europe.

R. H. Helmholz is the Ruth Wyatt Rosenson Distinguished Service Professor of Law at the University of Chicago. His most recent book is *Natural Law in Court*, in which he traces the role played by the law of nature in legal practice of the courts of Europe, England and the United States from 1500 to the mid-nineteenth century.

LAW AND CHRISTIANITY

Series Editor

John Witte, Jr., Emory University

The Law and Christianity series publishes cutting-edge work on Catholic, Protestant and Orthodox Christian contributions to public, private, penal and procedural law and legal theory. The series aims to promote deep Christian reflection by leading scholars on the fundamentals of law and politics, to build further ecumenical legal understanding across Christian denominations and to link and amplify the diverse and sometimes isolated Christian legal voices and visions at work in the academy. Works collected by the series include groundbreaking monographs, historical and thematic anthologies, and translations by leading scholars around the globe.

Books in the Series

Calvin's Political Theology and the Public Engagement of the Church
Matthew J. Tuininga

God and the Secular Legal System
Rafael Domingo
How Marriage Became One of the Sacraments
Philip Reynolds
Christianity and Freedom, 2 vols
edited by Timothy Samuel Shah and Allen D. Hertzke
The Distinctiveness of Religion in American Law
Kathleen A. Brady
Pope Benedict XVI's Legal Thought
edited by Marta Cartabia and Andrea Simoncini
The Western Case for Monogamy Over Polygamy
John Witte, Jr.

Great Christian Jurists in English History

Edited by

MARK HILL QC
Cardiff University

R. H. HELMHOLZ
University of Chicago

CAMBRIDGE
UNIVERSITY PRESS

CAMBRIDGE
UNIVERSITY PRESS

University Printing House, Cambridge CB2 8BS, United Kingdom

One Liberty Plaza, 20th Floor, New York, NY 10006, USA

477 Williamstown Road, Port Melbourne, VIC 3207, Australia

314-321, 3rd Floor, Plot 3, Splendor Forum, Jasola District Centre, New Delhi - 110025, India

79 Anson Road, #06-04/06, Singapore 079906

Cambridge University Press is part of the University of Cambridge.

It furthers the University's mission by disseminating knowledge in the pursuit of education, learning and research at the highest international levels of excellence.

www.cambridge.org
Information on this title: www.cambridge.org/9781316638019
DOI: 10.1017/9781108125901

First published 2017
First paperback edition 2018

A catalogue record for this publication is available from the British Library

Library of Congress Cataloging in Publication data
NAMES: Hill, Mark, editor. | Helmholz, R. H., editor.
TITLE: Great Christian Jurists in English History / edited by Mark Hill QC, Cardiff University; R.H. Helmholz, University of Chicago
DESCRIPTION: Cambridge, United Kingdom ; New York, NY, USA : Cambridge University Press, 2017. | Series: Law and Christianity | includes index.
IDENTIFIERS: LCCN 2016056469 | ISBN 9781107190559 (hardback)
SUBJECTS: LCSH: Christian lawyers – England – Biography. | Law – England – Christian influences – History. | Law and Christianity – History.
CLASSIFICATION: LCC KD620 .G74 2017 | DDC 340.092/870942–dc23
LC record available at https://lccn.loc.gov/2016056469

ISBN 978-1-107-19055-9 Hardback
ISBN 978-1-316-63801-9 Paperback

Contents

Illustrations

Biographies of Contributors

Norman Doe is Professor of Law and Director of the Centre for Law and Religion at Cardiff University. He is author of *Fundamental Authority in Late Medieval English Law* (1990), *The Legal Framework of the Church of England* (1996), *Canon Law in the Anglican Communion* (1998), *The Law of the Church in Wales* (2002), *An Anglican Covenant* (2008), *Law and Religion in Europe* (2011) and *Christian Law: Contemporary Principles* (2013). A visiting fellow at Trinity College, Oxford (2011) and visiting scholar at Corpus Christi College, Oxford (2015), he is an associate professor at the University of Paris and Catholic University Leuven. He is Chancellor of the Diocese of Bangor in the Church in Wales and a member of the editorial board of the *Ecclesiastical Law Journal*.

R. H. Helmholz is the Ruth Wyatt Rosenson Distinguished Service Professor of Law at the University of Chicago. A graduate of Princeton University, Harvard Law School and the University of California, Berkeley, he teaches the modern American law of real and personal property, including the law of oil and gas. However, most of his research interests have been devoted to the history of the European *ius commune*, with particular attention to its place in the development of the English legal system. Working from their manuscript records, he has taken a hand in tracing the history of the jurisdiction of the ecclesiastical courts in England from their beginning in the thirteenth century to their temporary abolition in the 1640s. In his most recent book, *Natural Law in Court* (Harvard University Press 2015), he traces the role played by the law of nature in legal practice of the courts of Europe, England and the United States from 1500 to the mid-nineteenth century.

Mark Hill QC is an associate or visiting professor at the Centre for Law and Religion, Cardiff University; the University of Pretoria; King's College, London; and Notre Dame University, Sydney. His publications include

Religious Liberty and Human Rights (2002), *Ecclesiastical Law* (2007), *Religion and Discrimination Law in the European Union* (2012), *Religion and Law in the United Kingdom* (2014), *Magna Carta, Religion and the Rule of Law* (2015) and *The Confluence of Law and Religion* (2016). He is Consultant Editor of the *Ecclesiastical Law Journal* and was a contributing editor for *Jowitt's Dictionary of English Law* (2010). He is a Recorder of the Crown Court, Deputy Judge of the Upper Tribunal and Chancellor of the Dioceses of Chichester, Leeds and Europe. In 2012 he was elected president of the European Consortium for Church and State Research.

James Oldham is St Thomas More Professor of Law and Legal History at Georgetown University Law Center, Washington, DC, where he teaches English legal history, contracts and labour arbitration. His major work is *The Mansfield Manuscripts and the Growth of English Law in the Eighteenth Century* (1992) and an updated one-volume abridgement *English Common Law in the Age of Mansfield* (2004). Other publications include *Trial by Jury: The Seventh Amendment and Anglo-American Special Juries* (2006) and *Case-Notes of Sir Soulden Lawrence 1787–1800* (2013). Previously he specialised in labour law with the Denver firm of Sherman and Howard, and currently he serves as the Neutral Discipline Arbitrator for the National Hockey League. During 2013–14 he served as president of the National Academy of Arbitrators.

Andrew Phang received his LLB from the National University of Singapore in 1982 and both his LLM and SJD from Harvard University in 1984 and 1988, respectively. In 1990, he was admitted as an Advocate and Solicitor in Singapore and appointed Senior Counsel in 2004. He taught at the National University of Singapore's Law Faculty from 1982 to 2000 and became Professor of Law in 1999. In 2000 he was appointed Professor of Law at the Singapore Management University. He was made the chair of the Department of Law at its business school the following year. His extensive publications include the local edition of *Cheshire, Fifoot and Furmston's Law of Contract*. He is also general editor of, and contributor to, *The Law of Contract in Singapore* (2012). He was appointed Judicial Commissioner and Judge in 2005 and became Judge of Appeal in 2006.

Norman S. Poser is Professor Emeritus at Brooklyn Law School. His most recent publication is *Lord Mansfield: Justice in the Age of Reason* (2013), the only modern biography of the great eighteenth-century British judge. Before joining the Brooklyn Law School faculty in 1980, Professor Poser served as an assistant director of the US Securities and Exchange Commission and as executive vice-president of the American Stock Exchange. He has been a consultant to the World Bank and other international financial organisations. His published writings include two treatises, *International Securities Regulation: London's 'Big Bang' and the European Securities Markets* and *Broker-Dealer Law and Regulation*, as well as numerous articles and columns. His book *Escape: A Jewish Scandinavian Family in the Second World War* (2006) is an exploration of the very different reactions of Denmark, Norway and Sweden to the Holocaust. He is a graduate of Harvard College and Harvard Law School.

Wilfrid Prest holds a BA in history from the University of Melbourne and a DPhil in modern history from Oxford, where he studied as a Rhodes Scholar, supervised by Christopher Hill. In 1966 he joined the University of Adelaide and has spent most of his academic career there, both in the Department of History and the Law School, apart from two years at Johns Hopkins University and visiting posts at Princeton, Cambridge, St Andrews and the Australian National University. His publications include *The Inns of Court under Elizabeth I and the Early Stuarts 1590–1640* (1972), *The Rise of the Barristers: A Social History of the English Bar, 1590–1640* (1986), *Albion Ascendant: English History 1660–1815* (1988) and *William Blackstone: Law and Letters in the Eighteenth Century* (2008), together with numerous edited volumes and journal articles. He is also general editor of the new Oxford edition of *Blackstone's Commentaries on the Laws of England* (2016). A fellow of the Australian Academy of the Humanities, the Academy of the Social Sciences in Australia and Queen's College, University of Melbourne, Prest has served on the Council of the Selden Society since 2010.

Russell Sandberg is reader in law and the head of the law department at Cardiff University, where he conducts research at the Centre for Law and Religion. He is the author of *Law and Religion* (2011) and *Religion, Law and Society* (2014). He is currently working on a book on English legal history for Cambridge University Press. He is co-author of *Religion and Law in the United Kingdom* (2014). He has edited or co-edited a number of collections including *Law and Religion: New Horizons* (2009), *Religion and Legal Pluralism* (2015) and *The Confluence of Law and Religion* (2016). He is co-editor of the Law and Religion and Law and History volumes in the Routledge Critical Concepts in Law Series and managing editor of the ICLARS Series on Law and Religion published by Routledge.

Charlotte Smith is Associate Professor of Law at the University of Reading. She completed her LLB and doctorate at King's College London. She has studied questions of clergy discipline and ecclesiastical judicature in the nineteenth century, particularly the intersection between secular and ecclesiastical law reform in that period. More recently, she has turned her attention to the legal treatment of the Church of England in the British Empire and to the question of the transmission of English ecclesiastical law and ideas of establishment across the empire. In 2014 she curated an exhibition on the Judicial Committee of the Privy Council at the Supreme Court of the United Kingdom. Dr Smith has also published on more modern legal controversies relating to the constitutional position of the Church of England.

David Chan Smith teaches British history with a specialisation in business history at Wilfrid Laurier University in Canada. His first book, *Sir Edward Coke and the Reformation of the Laws* (2014), examines Coke's jurisprudence from his early practice to 1616. Having published on early modern bankruptcy, common law culture and *Shelley's Case*, Smith is now publishing on the history of company law and its relationship to ideas of corporate social responsibility. His current research project examines ideas of cooperation and sociability in eighteenth- and nineteenth-century economic thought.

David S. Sytsma holds a PhD from Princeton Theological Seminary and is an assistant professor at Tokyo Christian University and research curator of the Junius Institute for Digital Reformation Research. Before moving to Japan, he taught as adjunct professor in the ThM and PhD programmes at Calvin Theological Seminary (2013–15). He is the author of *Richard Baxter and the Mechanical Philosophers* (2017); editor of the first critical edition of Matthew Hale, *Of the Law of Nature* (2015); and co-editor of *Church and School in Early Modern Protestantism: Studies in Honor of Richard A. Muller on the Maturation of a Theological Tradition* (2013). He is active in digital humanities and is project director of the Post-Reformation Digital Library. His research focuses on religious history in the early modern period.

Nicholas Vincent has published a dozen books and some hundred academic articles on various aspects of English and European history in the twelfth and thirteenth centuries. These include *Magna Carta: Making and Legacy* (2015) and *The Letters and Charters of Henry II King of England (1154–1189)*, 5 vols (forthcoming). He is Professor of Medieval History at the University of East Anglia in Norwich, and led a major project researching the background to Magna Carta to coincide with its octocentenary in 2015. Professor Vincent is a Fellow of the British Academy.

Stephen M. Waddams is Goodman/Schipper Professor of Law at the University of Toronto. He has degrees from the University of Toronto,

Cambridge University and the University of Michigan. He has authored numerous articles, notes, reviews and essays, mainly on contract law, as well as the following books: *Law, Politics and the Church of England: The Career of Stephen Lushington 1782–1873* (1992), *Sexual Slander in Nineteenth-Century England: Defamation in the Ecclesiastical Courts, 1815–1855* (2000), *Dimensions of Private Law: Categories and Concepts in Anglo-American Legal Reasoning* (2003), *Introduction to the Study of Law* (2010), *Products Liability* (2010), *The Law of Contracts* (2010), *Principle and Policy in Contract Law: Competing or Complementary Concepts?* (2011) and *The Law of Damages* (2012).

Ian Williams is a senior lecturer in the Faculty of Laws, University College London. Following undergraduate and postgraduate study at Cambridge, he was a college lecturer at Christ's College, Cambridge, and a Francis Bacon Fellow at the Henry E. Huntington Library. His work has ranged from law books to precedent, treason to the theory of the Chancery jurisdiction. He is a co-editor of *Landmark Cases in Criminal Law*, and his work on the influence of the French theorist Jean Bodin on the theory of the equity jurisdiction was awarded the Selden Society's David Yale Prize. He is a member of the editorial committee of the *Journal of Legal History*, the Council of the Selden Society and the Notaries Qualification Board for England and Wales.

John Witte, Jr. is Robert W. Woodruff University Professor, McDonald Distinguished Professor and Director of the Center for the Study of Law and Religion at Emory University. His recent publications include *The Reformation of Rights: Law, Religion, and Human Rights in Early Modern Calvinism* (2007), *Christianity and Law: An Introduction* (2008), *The Sins of the Fathers: The Law and Theology of Illegitimacy Reconsidered* (2009), *Religion and the American Constitutional Experiment*, 4th ed. (2015) and *The Western Case for Monogamy over Polygamy* (2015). He is co-editor of the *Journal of Law and Religion* and a member of the editorial board of the *Ecclesiastical Law Journal*. He is series editor of Cambridge Studies in Law and Christianity.

Foreword

Lord Mackay of Clashfern
Lord Chancellor of England and Wales (1987–97)

I was introduced to the practice of law by way of the Law of Scotland which, as part of union arrangements since 1707, has retained its separate identity. Among its foundational works one of the most important is the *Institutions of the Law of Scotland* by Viscount Stair, which contains many indications of his Christian background, so I am familiar with a legal system with Christian influence on its development. Although distinct from the English system, a practitioner of Scots law inevitably develops an acquaintance with the English law, and in my case, to my considerable surprise, I was appointed Lord Chancellor and thus became responsible for the performance of important duties in the English system. One of these, which is a special honour, is to write a Foreword to this fascinating collection of essays.

Much has been written about the lives and achievements of the many distinguished lawyers and judges who have made a lasting contribution to English jurisprudence, from the medieval times of Henry of Bratton to the present day. Much also has been written on the influence of Christianity in English society over those centuries. This collection, one of a series of national studies, is novel in that it seeks to explore the life and faith of great Christian jurists in English history. Selecting a dozen or so individuals from a span of ten centuries was evidently a difficult task, and some strong contenders have been omitted; perhaps a further volume will be needed for those who failed to make the cut.

Some, like Christopher St German, had an undistinguished career at the Bar, but are remembered for their legal writings. Several, notably Stephen Lushington and Lord Mansfield, distinguished themselves in politics as well as law. The great offices of Lord Chief Justice and Lord Chancellor are inevitably well represented by the characters in this volume. John Selden achieved notoriety through imprisonment: being deprived of his library was perhaps a greater punishment than his loss of liberty. Mansfield was haunted by the treatment of his treacherous Jacobite relations. When I was appointed Lord Advocate in 1979, I was privileged to have as a close colleague the holder of the title who lived in Scone Palace, associated with the early Scottish kings. He was a member of the English Bar, and our work was taking a Scottish criminal justice bill through the House of Lords.

For many of the characters, there is indelible evidence of their scholarship (for example, in Coke's *Institutes*), whereas Lord Denning's legacy lies primarily in his many well-crafted judgments. It is of special interest to me that the article on Lord Denning is contributed by a distinguished judge and scholar from Singapore. When I visited the Supreme Court of India in 1987, I was shown a special table in the library which at one end held the Court's copy of the Constitution of India signed by the original signatories and at the other a small pile of books, the works of Lord Denning – welcome evidence to me that Lord Denning was warmly appreciated far beyond his native land.

Whilst *Bracton* as a treatise will be familiar to English legal historians, less is known about its author and his Christian influences. In their private lives, many of these characters were noted for philanthropy and charitable works. Lushington found himself adjudicating religious controversies, whereas changes to the civil law dominated Hale's work. Some were open about the major influences on their life and work: Mansfield was a disciple of Locke, while Denning often drew on the work of William Temple. Richard Hooker, a priest and prolific Anglican writer, is reinvented in this volume as a jurist, while Maitland, who openly disavowed any Christian faith, is revealed as being shaped by the religion in which he was brought up.

There are many reasons why a study of great Christian jurists has been long in coming. There is a tendency, particularly in common law jurisdictions, to divorce the dispassionate judge from his or her personal beliefs. Indeed, in taking the judicial oath, newly appointed judges swear to 'do right to all manner of people after the laws and usages of this realm, without fear or favour, affection or ill-will'. Some years ago I took part in a seminar in Toronto with the then Chief Justices of the United States and of Canada on the selection of judges. I ventured the view that in the United States, judges were selected on the basis of their opinions while judges in the United Kingdom were selected on the basis of their ability to form opinions once they had heard full argument on the issue. My colleagues did not dissent from that view. If this distinction is correct, it would explain why in the United Kingdom the world view of a judge is irrelevant to the judicial task. But this exploration of the religious tenets of titans of English law and justice adds light and texture to our legal history and perceptive insights into the role of religion in public life today.

I commend the publishers for establishing the Cambridge Studies in Law and Christianity and creating the Great Christian Jurists series in particular. This first volume, dealing with English legal history, contains a vibrant collection of pen portraits of fourteen prominent lawyers and judges brought to life by a distinguished array of legal historians drawn from around the globe under the skilled editorship of Mark Hill and Dick Helmholz. Further national volumes over the coming years will lead to an extensive library of biographical studies of leading jurists spanning continents and centuries, and focusing on the manner in which their Christian faith is revealed in their life and work. It will become a fascinating source for stimulating comparative study in years to come.

James Mackay
Temple, London

Preface

In 2014, Cambridge University Press established Cambridge Studies in Law and Christianity, with Professor John Witte, Jr. as series editor. Its purpose is to publish cutting-edge work in Catholic, Protestant and Orthodox Christian contributions to public, private, penal and procedural law and legal theory. The Great Christian Jurists series is a part of this ambitious project, and this volume, dealing with legal titans in English legal history, is the first. Others which have been commissioned include a study on the first millennium Western church, and volumes on Nordic, Italian, Spanish, American, Welsh and German Christian jurists are already in preparation.

The task of selecting just fourteen individuals from across nearly ten centuries was invidious. The span of history needed to be fully reflected, as did England's evolution from a monolithic Christian society where religious beliefs were universally held to the rich pluralism of today's more secular world. The volume includes some very famous names and others who are perhaps a little less well known, but we are conscious that in making our selection, the pressure of space has meant that we have had to exclude many well-qualified individuals. Limiting the number has allowed the contributors the luxury of a deeper and more insightful analysis of their subject's qualifications to greatness as both a Christian and a jurist.

In producing any edited work, many debts of gratitude are incurred. We owe much to John Witte for his vision in conceiving of the series and his enthusiasm in propelling it forward, together with his erudite contribution to this particular volume. We are grateful to Emmanuel College, Cambridge and its dean, the Revd Jeremy Caddick, for hosting a symposium where early drafts of the following chapters were presented and dissected in a most convivial atmosphere. And, of course, we are indebted to the distinguished scholars who were prepared to indulge us in this unique venture and produce such thorough and perceptive biographical studies. Thanks are also due to

Dr Hester Higton for copy-editing the chapters and harmonising variations in style, and to Amy Wheeler and Anita Mann at the Center for the Study of Law and Religion at Emory University for their administrative expertise and support, and their unfaltering energy and good humour.

Generous funding for the project came from the McDonald Agape Foundation, and we are pleased and proud to record our particular thanks to Ambassador Alonzo L. McDonald, Ms Suzie McDonald and Mr Peter McDonald for their support of this publication, along with so many other projects on the vital relationship between law and Christianity.

Mark Hill QC
Temple, London

R.H. Helmholz
Chicago

St. George's Day, 2017

1

Introduction

R. H. Helmholz and Mark Hill QC

Modern law treats adherence to the Christian religion as a matter of private choice. Outside special spheres such as the internal regulation of churches and their members, texts from Scripture and other spiritual authorities rarely serve as sources of law.[1] Yet we know that this was not always so. That Christianity formed a part of the law of England was once a commonplace among English lawyers. They repeated it in many and varied circumstances. Whether the Christian religion should occupy a place in the law of the land was not even an open question. It was assumed. Recognition of its place in the common law is found in the medieval Yearbooks.[2] In the seventeenth century, Sir Edward Coke (1552–1634) wrote of the existence of a close connection between the laws of God and the laws of men. They were not identical, but he could assert, for example, that the English laws of inheritance were 'grounded on the law of God'. He then took an incident from the Bible to illustrate the point that the two were in harmony (Num. 27:6–11).[3] In the eighteenth century, Sir William Blackstone (1723–80) expressed the same sentiment, holding that secular prosecution and corporal punishment of common blasphemers was justified because 'Christianity is part of the laws of England'.[4]

[1] See the careful discussion of the question in Norman Doe, *The Legal Framework of the Church of England* (Oxford: Clarendon Press, 1996), 12–22.

[2] E.g. *Bohun v. Bishop of Lincoln* (1458), Y.B. 34 Hen. VI, Pasch, ff. 38–39, per Prysot, CJ ('car si lour ley [of the Church] soit tiel nous voulons accord ove eux en ceo case'); *Abbot of Barlings v. Pynel* (1314), in W. Bolland, ed., *Yearbooks of Edward II: 7 Edward II, A.D. 1313–1314* (London: Selden Society, 1922), 163–4, per Tondeby (adopting church's position on perpetual minority of churches).

[3] Ratcliff's case (1592), 3 Co. Rep. 37a, 40, 76 Eng. Rep. 713, 726. (Moses consulted God in order to decide on the rights of a man's daughters to inherit the father's property in the absence of male heirs. He received an affirmative answer.)

[4] William Blackstone, *Commentaries on the Laws of England* (Oxford: Clarendon Press, 1765–9), 4:59, citing Taylor's case (1676), 1 Ventr. 293, 86 Eng. Rep. 189, and *Rex v. Woolston* (1727),

Of course, the practical consequences that followed from the maxim's acceptance were not always obvious, and even its existence was occasionally contested. John Cartwright (1740–1824) once described the maxim as 'a delusion [adopted] for ill purposes'.[5] But iconoclastic views such as Cartwright's were unusual at the time he wrote. Most lawyers believed the reverse was closer to the truth. Cartwright's supposition that a sinister motive lay behind their opinion would have stirred their indignation.

We know what we do about the maxim's general acceptance because its recognition among common lawyers has been carefully investigated by modern scholars. The extent of its role in England has been confirmed by their historical accounts.[6] They have not found a perfect identity between religion and law, of course. Not all parts of the common law were based upon Christian doctrine. No one supposed that they were. Still less did English law copy the canon law. But this was never an all-or-nothing proposition. Few things in law are. The law of real property had only tenuous connections with religion, for instance, but its importance in English law did not rule out religion's presence elsewhere, and investigation has shown that in many areas of the law English lawyers did advance arguments and reach conclusions they found within the tenets of the Christian religion. If today we are not aware of the historical connection between law and religion, it is because modern lawyers have allowed the subject to 'fade into disuse'.[7] The authors of the chapters in this volume have sought to restore a balance.

They have sought to do so by taking a different approach to the subject than the one adopted by most modern studies of religion's place in law, including those just cited. It is a 'personal approach'. Most prior scholarship on the subject has focused either upon legal doctrine or the arguments advanced in decided cases. Our authors have paid more attention to people – individual people. They have sought to uncover the place that Christianity played in the lives and actions of the famous lawyers they have chosen, using points of substantive law primarily to provide readers with a fuller

2 Str. 834, 93 Eng. Rep. 881 (both cases dealing with the punishment of blasphemous speech or with writings asserting the falsity of the Christian religion).

5 John Cartwright, *The English Constitution Produced and Illustrated* (London: T. Cleary, 1823), 388. For a strong modern statement of this position, see J. H. Baker, 'Magna Carta and Personal Liberty', in Robin Griffith-Jones and Mark Hill, eds., *Magna Carta, Religion and the Rule of Law* (Cambridge: Cambridge University Press, 2015), 87.

6 See e.g. Stuart Banner, 'When Christianity Was Part of the Common Law', *Law and History Review* 16 (1998): 27–62; Bradley Chilton, 'Cliobernetics, Christianity, and the Common Law', *Law Library Journal* 83 (1991): 355–62; Jayson Spiegel, 'Christianity as Part of the Common Law', *North Carolina Central Law Journal* 14 (1983/4): 494–516.

7 Banner, 'When Christianity Was Part of the Common Law', 27.

understanding of the place of religion in the careers of these men. All of their subjects lived in centuries before our own – from the thirteenth to the twentieth, and with one possible exception, all of them professed adherence to the Christian religion.

In this respect the men described in these pages were not at all unusual or worthy of any special note. Adherence to Christianity was an accepted part of English life. These chapters seek to show what its acceptance meant in their lives and in their approach to legal questions. Two of them were civilians, the name commonly used to refer to lawyers trained in traditions of Roman law who served primarily in the courts of the Church and the Admiralty. William Lyndwood (d. 1446) and Stephen Lushington (1782–1873), who appear at opposite ends of the chapters, were the civilians. Two others, Henry of Bratton (c. 1210–68) and Richard Hooker (1554–1600), were in holy orders and do not fit neatly into either category. The rest (ten in all) were common lawyers.[8]

Each of the chapters that follow contains basic biographical information about its subject. The authors have taken account of recent scholarship, and most of the chapters contain the results of each author's own research and reflection on the contributions to English law made by the lawyer chosen. The 'personal approach' they have taken in examining the place of religion in the working lives of the jurists is what sets this volume apart from most biographical accounts. The volume does not follow exactly the lead of the *Oxford Dictionary of National Biography*, worthy though it is. The aim of each chapter is to enlarge upon religion's place in the lives of English lawyers, reflected in either general statements of principle or in treatments of the laws of the nation. Taken together, the chapters make four separate additions to our understanding of what it meant to accept and act upon the maxim that Christianity was part of the law of England.

A FULLER UNDERSTANDING OF THE LIVES AND OPINIONS OF THE LAWYERS

The first of these four grows directly out of the attention paid here to the interests and character of these fourteen jurists. It turns out that by looking primarily at individuals rather than legal doctrine, we actually learn quite a bit about what the law's connections with religion meant in practice.

[8] Lord Denning did serve briefly as a diocesan chancellor before his appointment to the High Court in 1942.

What the approach reveals is not identical for all the jurists covered in the chapters that follow. For all of them, however, the volume's authors have uncovered aspects of their views and actions that have often been left out of existing accounts of their place in English legal history. Initially it certainly might be thought that concentrating on religion would narrow or even distort our understanding of the men described – that it would create a one-sided picture. In fact, the reverse is true. Concentrating upon religion has actually enlarged what we know about them. It fills a gap in existing accounts.

In writing about John Selden or Sir Edward Coke, for example, most historians have dealt with religion's place in their lives by focusing on their subject's anti-clerical views. Selden's opposition to the clergy's claim that tithes were due *iure divino* and Coke's attempts to extend the reach of writs of prohibition at the expense of the jurisdiction of the ecclesiastical courts take centre stage in most accounts.[9] Naturally so. These were important matters in controversy at the time, and they had results that mattered in the long run. What focusing undivided attention upon them misses, however, and what the two chapters in this volume capture, is the existence of another side to the character of these two men. Not every student of the subject would have recalled that Selden 'liked the settled doctrine, liturgy and traditions of the Church of England and the settled Anglican episcopacy'.[10] And who would have remembered that week after week Sir Edward Coke sat under Richard Hooker in the Temple church on Sunday mornings carefully taking notes of the sermons he heard? The chapters that David Chan Smith and Norman Doe contribute on Coke and Hooker take careful note of this aspect of their lives.[11] In the former chapter we have a picture of Coke, a man who was regarded by his contemporaries as 'devout without being saintly'.[12] In the latter we find Selden portrayed as a Christian man impatient with some of the Church's doctrines but a 'man of simple and steady Christian piety' nonetheless.[13] This is not all the two men were, of course. The contributors to this volume do not seek to overturn conventional assessments of the efforts made by Selden and Coke as critics of

9 E.g. Allen Boyer, *Sir Edward Coke and the Elizabethan Age* (Stanford: Stanford University Press, 2003), 176–88; Stephen D. White, *Sir Edward Coke and 'The Grievances of the Commonwealth', 1621–1628* (Chapel Hill: University of North Carolina Press, 1979), 221, 273; Thomas G. Barnes, *Shaping the Common Law: From Glanvill to Hale, 1188–1688* (Stanford: Stanford University Press, 2008), 174–5.

10 See Chapter 7 in this volume.

11 See Chapters 5 and 6 in this volume.

12 See Chapter 5 in this volume.

13 See Chapter 7 in this volume.

ecclesiastical law or of then current developments within the Church led by Archbishop Laud. Their chapters describe their entry into the ecclesiastical lists of the day. But they also provide a fuller – and more balanced – account of the place of religion in the lives of the two famous men than do most accounts based on examination of the controversial side of their encounters with great issues of their day.

Even taking the lawyer whose attitude towards Christianity was the most ambivalent of the fourteen jurists covered in this volume, F. W. Maitland – a concentration on religion proves useful in enlarging our understanding of the man. In the preface to his exploration of the nature of the canon law in medieval England, Maitland described himself as 'a dissenter' from all the churches.[14] One cannot ignore this disavowal. It mattered. He ceased to attend church regularly after he reached the age of thirty, and he formed a low opinion of many parts of the law of the Church. At the same time, Russell Sandberg's chapter shows that he was no apostle of atheism. He brought up his daughters to be 'religiously literate', as he certainly was himself. His own attitude towards religion was 'more complicated' than the disavowal found in his famous preface suggests.[15] His study of the medieval canon law awakened interest and satisfaction in him. It opened a window on a subject of importance. Opinions may differ about the propriety of describing him as a Christian jurist, but following Sandberg's lead by examining the place of religion in Maitland's life and scholarship provides readers with a fuller appreciation of the importance of the subject in his scholarship than do many accounts. That much seems beyond doubt.

The identical conclusion holds true for the subjects of virtually all the chapters in this volume. For each of them, concentrating on religion teaches us something about the man. Some of what this research shows now seems interesting if trivial; Lord Kenyon's 'threadbare dress and oft-soled shoes' described by James Oldham, for example.[16] This may be regarded as a sign of his Christian modesty – a subject not discussed in most biographies of our own day. Other examples seem more consequential. It turns out that William Blackstone, whom Wilf Prest describes as a Christian habitually reluctant 'to wear his heart ... on his sleeve',[17] had taken a serious interest in theological issues as a young man. He brings to light some of the results of that interest, and only the unfortunate (and unexplained) disappearance of the unique

14 F. W. Maitland, *Roman Canon Law in the Church of England* (London: Methuen & Co, 1898), p. vi.

15 See Chapter 14 in this volume. 16 See Chapter 11 in this volume.

17 See Chapter 10 in this volume.

manuscript of his 'Select Poems' from the Law Library of the University of California, Berkeley, during the early 1950s prevents us from learning more about this part of his life.

Similarly, the theological writings of Sir Matthew Hale (1609–76) brought to light in David Systma's chapter were vitally important to the man and his work. Their extent will be quite unexpected to most readers; they even include a theological treatment of magnetism.[18] Most of these works have remained in manuscript, but they await a patient investigator in Lambeth Palace Library. The research presented by Systma's chapter makes a promising start. It allows readers to see clearly that the 'rigorous observation of the Lord's Day' which characterised Hale's activities on Sundays had definite results. Hale's adherence to the Church of England is no secret,[19] but this chapter provides a more rounded picture of the man than one that concentrates the bulk of its attention on his famous *History and Analysis of the Common Law of England*.

CONSISTENCY AND DIVERGENCE IN APPROACHES TO LAW DERIVED FROM RELIGION

Some of the conclusions about the goals and contents of English law to which the Christian religion led the men who are the subjects of these chapters were common to them all. Others were not. Religion mattered to all of the lawyers surveyed, and they sought to put what they believed into practice. But they did not always do so in the same way. They did not always draw the same lessons from it. This is a second addition to historical understanding offered by these chapters.

A theme that does recur in virtually all their lives and works, one which English lawyers sometimes called upon Christian traditions to justify and support, is the importance of making a secure place that equity could and should play in the law courts. In their eyes, its proper influence was not confined to the Court of Chancery. *Summum ius summa iniuria,* wrote Cicero,[20] and medieval jurists on the continent agreed.[21] They put it into their treatises. It was hard to deny its truth, and the same sentiment was echoed in the writings of the English lawyers. God tempers his law with

18 See Chapter 8 in this volume. 19 See e.g. Barnes, *Shaping the Common Law*, 221–36.

20 M. Tullius Cicero, *De officiis* 1.10.33, trans. Walter Miller (Cambridge, MA: Harvard University Press, 1913), 34–5.

21 Johannes Stroux, Summum jus, summa injuria. *Ein Kapitel aus der Geschichte der Interpretatio juris* (Leipzig: s.n., 1926).

mercy – a lesson taught on many pages of Scripture (e.g. Luke 6:36) – and so should earthly law. Few Christians would dispute the point. Of course, this was never a rule without exception, and it was not always obvious how far it should extend in actual cases, but these limitations did not cause the men discussed in these chapters to discard it. It was not a meaningless platitude. It was a working principle. It had results. To support the argument that judges should 'deploy mercy in many contexts', by relaxing the law's sanctions in cases where equity and strict law came into conflict, Hooker appealed to the authority of the great fifteenth-century canonist, Nicholaus de Tudeschis, known as Panormitanus (d. 1445/53).[22] Christopher St German similarly called upon the works of the French theologian, Jean Gerson (1363–1429), in defining the great duty of the English clergy to secure justice for the men and women entrusted to their care.[23] Sir Matthew Hale pointedly advised English lawyers to become familiar with examples from the Old Testament because its books 'contained eternally valid precepts of general equity'.[24]

So often did endorsements of this influence recur in the writing of English lawyers that the real question must be whether or not their endorsers consciously associated it with religion. Lord Mansfield's life and career – particularly his influence on the English law of contracts – provide a well-attested example. He made free use of 'equity' and 'natural justice' and 'conscience' to shape the law, as in the doctrine of consideration and in the scope of actions for money had and received.[25] He espoused a jurisprudence that enlarged the scope of 'natural justice and equity', describing his court as 'the custodian of the morals of the people'.[26] But he was more reticent about questions of authority and motivation that underlay his actions. Unlike Lord Kenyon, who 'preached from the Bench', Mansfield's words rarely went beyond what law and circumstance required. It may be, as Norman Poser suggests, that this apparent neglect of religion was the result of his fear that his early flirtation with the Jacobite cause would come to light. Or perhaps he was simply reticent by nature and conviction. We do not know. Only his intellectual base in morality is certain. That was a shared position – one common at the time. Mansfield had his contemporary detractors, no doubt, but it is equally important to note that in his views about the basic sources of law and justice, he was far from alone.

22 See Chapter 6 in this volume. 23 See Chapter 4 in this volume.
24 See Chapter 8 in this volume.
25 See Chapter 9 in this volume; see also Warren Swain, *The Law of Contract 1670–1870* (Cambridge: Cambridge University Press, 2015), 107–26.
26 See Chapter 9 in this volume.

The consequences that flowed from this common theme in the careers of so many English lawyers is matched by some surprises, situations in which the common opinion among jurists appears to have conflicted, or at least shifted. The career of Stephen Lushington (1782–1873) provides a notable example. By the 1830s he had come to the conclusion that human slavery was incompatible with Christianity. The chapter by Stephen Waddams makes clear that he regarded the continuation of slavery as a blot on the reputation of a professedly Christian nation – his own. He spoke and he wrote repeatedly to eradicate the institution. To him, slavery was contrary to the 'laws of God and the inalienable rights of man'.[27] One cannot doubt the sincerity of his words. To the end of his life, Lushington devoted energy and time to the promotion of emancipation. Cynicism should not creep into a fair assessment of the man, and Waddams has not allowed that to happen in his account.

So far as we can tell, however, Lushington's opinion was not shared by most other Christians described in this volume. For them, it appears not to have been a live issue. Even Lord Mansfield (1705–93), whose opinion in Somersett's case has sometimes been credited with ridding English law of the scourge of negro servitude,[28] was genuinely ambivalent about the merits of emancipation.[29] For him, the likely ill effects of freeing so many slaves at once had to be balanced against the undoubted merits of adherence to a principle of human freedom. Perhaps, he thought, the best course would be not to raise the subject at all. When we penetrate further into the evidence from prior centuries, we look in vain for champions of slavery's abolition among the lawyers whose Christian convictions are described in these chapters. No doubt most of them would have agreed that human servitude was contrary to principles of natural law, as Mansfield himself asserted in Somersett's case. They did not suppose that slavery was actually required. But its existence had been recognised in law for centuries. Slavery was part of the *ius gentium*. It seemed to have been condoned by texts in the Bible itself. Only a bold lawyer would advance the cause of emancipation in the service of the Christian religion. There were such bold men, but Lushington is the only one who appears in these pages.

The relationship between Christianity and religious freedom presents a similar example of change over time. Charlotte Smith's chapter on Roundell Palmer, first Earl of Selborne (1812–95) establishes that for him 'the principle of

27 See Chapter 11 in this volume.

28 *Rex v. Knowles ex parte Somerset* (1771–2), 20 St. Tr. 1, Lofft 1.

29 See James Oldham, *English Common Law in the Age of Mansfield* (Chapel Hill: University of North Carolina Press, 2004), 305–23.

religious liberty' went hand in hand with a belief that God's will had provided the undisputed source of the doctrines and powers of the Church of England. He meant both. He voted against continuing the disqualifications of Jews from public office, and he argued against a return to enforcement of the penal laws against Roman Catholics – stands that cost him his seat in Parliament. Yet he was not indifferent to religion's claims or to the faith of the English Church. He stood strongly against moves towards Disestablishment. He recognised the authority of the Church of England as established 'by the unchangeable laws of nature and providence'.[30]

Selborne's views of the wide scope of Christian liberty are, however, much harder to find in earlier centuries than his own. Not altogether impossible, it seems. Lord Mansfield shared them in some measure, and even the canon law contained the seeds that might have promoted freedom of religion, had they been allowed to sprout. Its texts proclaimed, for instance, that 'Where the spirit of God is, there is liberty.'[31] Hints of this sentiment are on view in the writings of Christopher St German surveyed in Chapter 4 by Ian Williams. The pity (or problem) is that these seeds did not sprout in fact, at least not until after centuries had passed. The Toleration Act of 1689 took a step in that direction,[32] but the opposite view predominated. It was this view that William Lyndwood expounded in his commentary on a provincial constitution prohibiting the translation of the Christian Scriptures into English.[33] Translations of the Bible into English from Latin must not be allowed, Lyndwood thought, because of the dangers to religious devotion translations might occasion. No doubt Lyndwood took this view out of religious conviction. It is hard to give much credit to it today, but it was a commonly held view when he composed his gloss. The halting steps towards the opposite view can be followed in several of this volume's chapters.[34]

Is this difference of views about religious liberty proof of a lack of substance in the teachings associated with Christianity? In part perhaps it is. But not necessarily. The Christian religion contains many things that have not

30 See Chapter 13 in this volume.

31 'Ubi Spiritus Dei ibi libertas', in *Decretum Gratiani*, C.19 q.2 c.2, in A. Friedberg, ed., *Corpus Iuris Canonici* (Leipzig: Tauchnitz, 1879, repr. 1959), 2:840.

32 Toleration Act, 1 Wm. & Mary, c. 18.

33 William Lyndwood, *Provinciale (seu Constitutiones Angliae)* (Oxford, 1679), 286, v. *periculosa*.

34 See John Witte, Jr., 'Introduction', in John Witte, Jr., ed., *Christianity and Democracy in Global Context* (Boulder, CO: Westview Press, 1993), 1–13; Richard Garnett, 'Religious Liberty, Church Autonomy and the Structure of Freedom', in John Witte, Jr. and Frank Alexander, eds., *Christianity and Human Rights: An Introduction* (Cambridge: Cambridge University Press, 2010), 267–82.

changed over the centuries. The rules found in the Ten Commandments have remained much the same over the years. Murder is still a wrongful act. Lord Kenyon's censorious attitude towards adultery was shared by most of the men whose views are the subjects of these pages, though few of them would have been quite so insistent in giving voice to their opinion. Coke made a joke out of it, but the laugh depended upon an assumption of a general disapproval of adultery among his hearers.[35]

In a larger perspective, perhaps even the changes in attitude towards some difficult questions, changes that have undoubtedly taken place, are best regarded as the product of a growth in human understanding. They may be the fruit of a fuller comprehension of the Gospel's intent, not simple changes of mind. Whatever the answer to this puzzling question, it is the examination of the views of individual Christian lawyers that allows it to be posed in a concrete fashion.

ADDITIONS TO UNDERSTANDING THE DEVELOPMENT OF THE COMMON LAW

Concentration on religion found in the chapters of this book does something useful in a third way. It enlarges our understanding of the common law itself. Perhaps that is an unexpected addition; most legal histories say little about the subject of religion. However, it mattered to the lawyers discussed in this volume. They carried it into legal practice in ways that illuminate some of the results of accepting the maxim that Christianity was part of the law of England. Nicholas Vincent's chapter on Henry of Bratton contains the most immediate example. Not only does it contribute to the vexed question of the authorship of *Bracton*, the treatise long and probably mistakenly associated with Bratton. It also sheds light on an important but dark corner of English legal history – the mid-thirteenth century. Clerics, such as Bratton, then sat as judges in the royal courts.[36] They were not professional canonists. They did not attempt to substitute the papal Decretals for the common law. However, finding that their professional writings shaped in part by 'a diverse range of classical or papal precedents [and] Biblical motifs' should not occasion surprise or suspicion of their motives.[37] It was a common practice of his time.

[35] See Chapter 5 in this volume.

[36] See Paul Brand, 'Edward I and the Transformation of the English Judiciary', in id., *The Making of the Common Law* (London: Hambledon Press, 1992), 135–68.

[37] See Chapter 2 in this volume.

The subject of Christianity's place in the common law goes well beyond its role during medieval centuries. The details uncovered by investigating the subject will prove interesting and meaningful even for readers whose interests lie wholly outside religion. James Oldham's exploration of the jury charges of Lord Kenyon (1732–1802), for instance, shows the influence of religion on his subject's understanding of the workings of the law. Kenyon regarded English law as 'subservient to the laws of morality and religion'.[38] He told jurors in a criminal trial for libel and blasphemy that they sat 'here in a Christian assembly'[39] and urged them to act accordingly. What he said to juries also sheds light on the contested subject of 'jury control' in the history of English law. The uncertainty arises from the question of how far English jurors were able to return verdicts free from judicial control.[40] They had the power to ignore what judges told them, but did they actually exercise it? Though Kenyon may himself have tired of dealing with cases of criminal conversation, he did not flinch from repeating his opinions on the subject, opinions based on Christian principles widely accepted at the time. They proved influential. Students of the subject of relationship between judge and jury will not soon forget the juror who had second thoughts after concurring in a verdict against a defendant whom Kenyon had described as 'hacknied in the ways of vice'. The juror later expressed his reservations about the verdict in a letter to the *Times*.[41] For his tastes, judicial control of jury discretion had worked all too well.

Modern developments in the law are also sometimes more fully understood by taking religion into account. Charlotte Smith's chapter on Selborne describes the contributions he made to nineteenth-century Parliamentary legislation. His 'spiritual sympathies' shaped at least some of the statutes,[42] and it turns out that this has not been a rare pattern. The Penitentiary Act of 1779 brought to light in the chapter on Blackstone, for example, mixed religious instruction with hard labour in seeking the proper road to amendment of life for the prisoners covered by the act.[43] From Magna Carta forwards, religious influences have mattered in shaping the contents of notable English statutes.[44]

38 See Chapter 11 in this volume. 39 See Chapter 11 in this volume.

40 See e.g. J. M. Beattie, *Crime and the Courts in England 1660–1800* (Princeton: Princeton University Press, 1986), 406–10; John Langbein, Renée Lettow Lerner and Bruce Smith, *History of the Common Law: The Development of Anglo-American Legal Institutions* (Austin: Wolters Kluwer Law & Business, 2009), 431–9.

41 See Chapter 11 in this volume. 42 See Chapter 13 in this volume.

43 19 Geo. III, c. 74; see Chapter 10 in this volume.

44 See e.g. Simon Lee, 'The Cardinal Rule of Religion and the Rule of Law: A Musing on Magna Carta', in Griffith-Jones and Hill, *Magna Carta*, 314–33; Carleton K. Allen, *Law in the Making*, 5th ed. (Oxford: Clarendon Press, 1951), 424–8.

Andrew Phang's account of contributions to the law of contracts made by Lord Denning (1899–1999) produces a similar example, one taken directly from the law courts. A popular view of Denning's approach to law holds that he was given to simply ignoring settled legal doctrine in an effort 'to achieve a fair outcome in a specific case'.[45] This essay shows that this was not so, or at least that it was not so simple. Denning did have a 'passion for justice in particular cases',[46] but he developed principles of law that were based ultimately upon religious foundations and did so in a 'coherent and systemic manner'.[47] His opinions were not based on emotion or on a disdain for either precedent or legal reasoning. Denning's approach was in accord with the latter. For instance, most thoughtful modern lawyers recognise that the strictest understanding of the requirement of bargained for consideration in contracts can lead to technicality and injustice. They admit the need for a wider enforceability of seriously intended promises and they find their way to reach that result by basing decisions on the doctrine of estoppel. Lord Denning's views of the enforcement of contracts in such situations were not, therefore, out of line with the substantive results reached in established case law. It was simply that he preferred to phrase the result 'in language which the ordinary man understands'.[48] That is the language of justice. In a way, his attitude harkens back to William Lyndwood's justification for enforcing sworn promises in the ecclesiastical courts because of the invocation of God's name that every oath involved.[49] The details are different; the impulse is the same.

A further illustration of the contribution to understanding English law made by taking a look at an individual's religious ideas, one from several centuries before the our own, emerges from an investigation of the life and work of Christopher St German. Where religion is concerned, St German is remembered today primarily as a controversialist. He was the opponent of Thomas More in the run-up to the Reformation, a critic of ecclesiastical practices that More defended. Outside the sphere of religious controversy, his contributions to English law are associated with his contributions to understanding the historical importance of the Court of Chancery, the principal court in England where conscience is commonly thought to have mattered. This contribution takes a fresh look at the subject.[50] What his

45 See Chapter 15 in this volume. 46 See Chapter 15 in this volume.

47 See Chapter 15 in this volume.

48 A. T. Denning, *The Discipline of Law* (London: Butterworths, 1979), 223, cited in Chapter 15 in this volume.

49 Lyndwood, *Provinciale*, 315, v. *perjurio*.

50 For a valuable parallel approach, see also Daniel Coquillette, *The Civilian Writers of Doctors' Commons, London* (Berlin: Duncker & Humblot, 1988), 48–57. St German was not actually a civilian member of Doctors' Commons.

examination of *Doctor and Student* shows is revealing. St German's understanding of the role of conscience in law was not confined to its place in Chancery, or indeed in any particular court. Nor was his treatment of conscience's place in law an early day argument in favour of the rights of individual interpretation of the law or of free speech. Although compliance with the dictates of good conscience was a requirement that bound all men, his principal concern about its place in law belonged within the field of professional ethics. It concerned lawyers above all. In St German's view, all men of law had an obligation to consider the ethical implications of the claims brought to them. They were to act upon those implications. His discussion was 'not directed to Chancery, but to the lawyer's own individual conscience'.[51] There, he hoped, it would take effect. It would shape the action any lawyer took. Ultimately it would shape the law itself.

Were the ethical principles St German espoused at all influential in determining the direction taken by English law in its long history? Most scholarship minimises the possibility. Today, the dominant view of the process of legal development in the English common law is that of S. F. C. Milsom. Growth of the common law, he concluded, has been the product of a 'rough free enterprise in argument of practitioners thinking about little beyond the immediate interests of a client'.[52] It is a compelling account – lawyers bending the meaning of the words of existing writs to advance the interests of their clients. They would prevail by satisfying judges that what they were asking would do no violence to existing precedents. Surely that happened. But is it the whole story? St German had other ideas – ideas based upon conscience and religion. They should have a practical effect in what lawyers did and in what they thought. He showed what some of the likely results would be.[53]

To follow this theme into the details of the common law's history would require a bold historian, perhaps even a foolhardy one. The chapter by Ian Williams does not go beyond the subject he undertook, but the possibility for carrying his theme further into the life and work of later English lawyers surely does exist. There are examples in this volume. David Systma's chapter on Sir

[51] See Chapter 4 in this volume.

[52] S. F. C. Milsom, *Historical Foundations of the Common Law* (London: Butterworth, 1969), p. xi. See also S. F. C. Milsom, *A Natural History of the Common Law* (New York: Columbia University Press, 2003), p. xvi.

[53] E.g. the laws against trespassing on another's land could give way, permitting a technical trespass if adhering strictly to the prohibition would lead to a greater injury. See T. F. T. Plucknett and J. L. Barton, eds., *St. German's Doctor and Student* (London: Selden Society, 1974), 99.

Matthew Hale describes his work as a barrister in these terms: 'If he judged a person or case to be clearly immoral, he refused to provide counsel.'[54] Are we to suppose that he was the only one who shared St German's opinion? That seems unlikely. Lord Mansfield referred to conscience's place in law repeatedly; he even credited its importance in life in his own last will and testament.[55] Norman Doe's chapter on Richard Hooker appropriately devotes a section to Hooker's views of the importance of conscience in explaining and justifying the necessity of relaxation in parts of the law of the Church.[56] Even Sir Edward Coke invoked conscience in seeking to rein in the use of the ex officio oath in the spiritual courts.[57] At the very least, the results derived from bringing St German's views on the subject to light encourage further investigation.

THE WIDE HORIZONS OF ENGLISH LAWYERS

The fourth contribution made to our appreciation of the character of the history of English law by the volume's concentration on religion is an appreciation for how far afield from many current assumptions the lawyers surveyed in its pages were willing to go in search of law. The jurisprudence of J. L. Austin (1790–1859) was not their pole star.[58] The binding force of precedents established by prior case law was not their master. That lay in the future. Nor did details about writs, mesne process and special pleading consume all their time and attention. The men depicted in this volume had wider horizons, some of them connected with their religious beliefs.[59]

The extent of their interest in the ethical norms taken from the law of nature is one of the unanticipated results that emerges from the chapters of this volume. It is not particularly controversial to say that most English common

54 See Chapter 8 in this volume.

55 *Rex v. Wroughton* (1765), 3 Burr. 1682, 97 Eng. Rep. 1045; see also Chapter 9 in this volume.

56 See in Chapter 6 the section titled 'Relaxation of Law: Equity and Conscience'. See also Will Adam, *Legal Flexibility and the Mission of the Church: Dispensation and Economy in Ecclesiastical Law* (Farnham and Burlington, VT: Ashgate, 2011).

57 See Chapter 5 in this volume; see also W. O. Hassall, ed., *Catalogue of the Library of Sir Edward Coke* (New Haven: Yale University Press, 1950), 38–41.

58 Author of *The Province of Jurisprudence Determined* (London: John Murray, 1832); Austin identified all positive law with the command, direct or indirect, of the sovereign. He therefore sought 'to dissipate the confusion between law, religion and morality which he believed had been spread by Natural Law theorists'. See H. L. A. Hart, 'Austin, John', in A. W. B. Simpson, ed., *Biographical Dictionary of the Common Law* (London: Butterworths, 1984), 21–4.

59 See also the evidence from the church's side discussed in Eric Waldram Kemp, *Introduction to Canon Law in the Church of England* (London: Hodder and Stoughton, 1957), 57–64.

lawyers knew something about natural law.[60] How much of a difference did that interest make in practice? The latter question is worth raising, and it is raised repeatedly if sometimes indirectly in the chapters of this volume. Start with *Bracton*. The introduction to the treatise begins with a large statement of law's meaning and purposes, one drawing upon what had been written by the classical Roman jurists. It includes a definition and brief discussion of natural law. It is what 'God himself [has] taught all living things'.[61] God and the law stand above the king, acting as a 'bridle' upon him.[62] Finish with Lord Denning. His approach to law can be described as 'a natural law approach that had its root source in the Christian faith'.[63] God had created what Denning called 'the right spirit' in men,[64] and they should act to make it the true measure of their laws. In between the two chapters devoted to these men, these pages contain abundant evidence of the extent of the wide horizons of the English lawyers in the centuries that separated them.

Selden and Hale, for example, both wrote treatises devoted to the law of nature. David Systma takes note of the lack of attention paid to Hale's treatise in modern historical literature. Lack of a reliable printed edition explains some of it. We await his critical edition. In the meantime, he draws a telling (if unexpected) comparison between its contents and the work of the 'Second Scholastics' in Spain. Men such as Francisco Suárez (1548–1617) sought to bring together law and theology – a long estranged couple – in order to work through enduring and contemporary moral problems.[65] Hale did the same. Conformity with 'right reason' in both spheres was the proper measure of a law's value. Reason was a necessary guide, though not an infallible one. The same blend of theology and law characterised the approach to law of Christopher St German. 'To regard *Doctor and Student* as solely a juristic work simply cannot be correct', Ian Williams reminds us.[66] Norman Doe's treatment of Richard Hooker's 'theology of law' also brings the *Laws of Ecclesiastical Polity* within the same broad category of integrative jurisprudence. The comparison of developments in England with the contribution of

60 This point is made laboriously and illustrated by examples in R. H. Helmholz, *Natural Law in Court* (Cambridge, MA: Harvard University Press, 2015), 90–2.

61 See George Woodbine, ed., and Samuel Thorne, trans., *Bracton de Legibus et Consuetudinibus Angliae*, 4 vols. (Cambridge, MA: Belknap Press of Harvard University Press, 1968), 2:26 (f. 3b).

62 See Chapter 2 in this volume.

63 See Chapter 15 in this volume.

64 See Chapter 15 in this volume.

65 See André Azevedo Alves and J.M. Moreira, *The Salamanca School* (London: Continuum, 2010).

66 See Chapter 4 in this volume.

the 'School of Salamanca' does not, therefore, seem altogether farfetched.[67] The example of John Selden only augments its credibility. John Witte describes him as 'pepper[ing] his writings with all manner of biblical citations and discussions'.[68] Today that mixture seems incongruous, but neither Selden nor his contemporaries felt any unease about it. On some issues a chasm separated these English jurists from the School of Salamanca. But not on this one. As it was for the Iberian scholars, so it was for these English lawyers on this point. Law and theology were not to be torn apart.

The enduring character of the view of all law as somehow connected with natural and divine law is one the most striking conclusion that emerges from these surveys of Christian jurists. William Blackstone also illustrates it very well. No writer on English law was more influential for a longer period of time than William Blackstone, and Wilf Prest's chapter devoted to the influence of Christianity on his subject's *Commentaries* illustrates some of the reasons for that durability. The question of the exact relationship between divine law and natural law, for example, was an old and difficult one in scholastic thought. Blackstone was abreast of it. He knew that there was an overlap between the two sources of law. That much was obvious. God was the author of both, and the Bible contained both. Yet there was a difference between them, even if both depended ultimately upon God's will. Indissolubility of Christian marriages was a textbook example. Admittedly, that doctrine formed no part of the law of nature. However, it was the subject of a divine command (Matt. 9:16). Blackstone took an interest in jurisprudential questions like this one, 'grounding his jurisprudence on God's ordinances'.[69] He had wide horizons and, for him, here was one proof of the maxim that 'Christianity is part of the laws of England.'[70]

CONCLUSION

Acceptance of that maxim produced many different results, results which are illustrated and discussed in more detail in the chapters that follow. Their cumulative effect, the subject of this introduction, is strong enough to be repeated here. One statement of its result is probably sufficient. Charlotte Smith's description of Selborne speaks of her subject in words that might with

67 See e.g. Harald Maihold, 'God's Law and Charity: Criminal Law in (Counter-)Reformation Discourse of Redemption and Retribution', in Wim Decock et al., eds., *Law and Religion: The Legal Teachings of the Protestant and Catholic Reformations* (Göttingen: Vandenhoeck & Ruprecht, 2014), 149–73; Knud Haakonssen, *Natural Law and Moral Philosophy: From Grotius to the Scottish Enlightenment* (Cambridge: Cambridge University Press, 1996), 15–30.

68 See Chapter 7 in this volume. 69 See Chapter 10 in this volume.

70 Blackstone, *Commentaries*, 4:59.

equal justice be applied to all but a few of the other jurists: his religious convictions, she discovered, 'made him a moral force' – a force strong enough to allow him to stand 'firm against any tendency or temptation to confine his faith to the private sphere'.[71] From the perspective of the twenty-first century, perhaps the most unexpected conclusion to emerge from all these chapters is their showing of just how long this attitude lasted.

[71] See Chapter 13 in this volume.

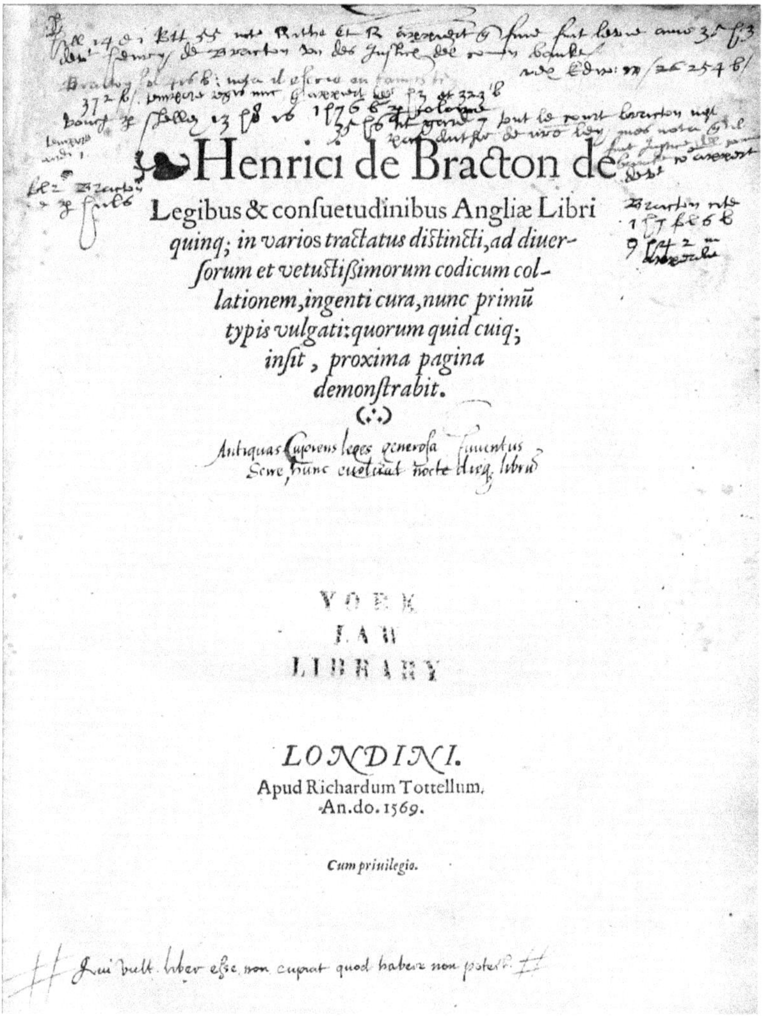

Henrici de Bracton de Legibus & consuetudinibus Angliæ Libri quinq; in varios tractatus distincti, ad diuersorum et vetustißimorum codicum collationem, ingenti cura, nunc primũ typis vulgati: quorum quid cuiq; insit, proxima pagina demonstrabit.

LONDINI.
Apud Richardum Tottellum.
An.do. 1569.

Cum priuilegio.

Qui vult liber esse, non cupiat quod habere non potest.

Henri de Bracton, *On the Laws and Customs of England*, c. 1230–50, edition of 1569: Sir Edward Coke's copy, courtesy of Georgetown University Law Library

2

Henry of Bratton (*alias* Bracton)

Nicholas Vincent

In the past half-century, Henry of Bratton has come to occupy a place in our understanding of English common law all too easily confused with that of the Wizard of Oz in the history of the Emerald City. The treatise generally attributed to him (*On the Laws and Customs of England*, commonly known as *Bracton*), was once regarded as an imposing monument written at the heart of royal government, essential to our understanding of the means by which English law was devised, administered and reformed. Bratton, identified as author of what to Maitland appeared 'the flower and crown of English jurisprudence', was described as 'England's greatest medieval legal writer'.[1] However, since the 1940s, a reaction has set in. Today, not only is Bratton viewed merely as the reviser and annotator of the work of rather more substantial predecessors, but his place in the legal firmament has been reduced to that of a second-rate camp-follower, far from the towering genius imagined by Maitland and others. *Bracton* itself has been shown to be riven with contradictions, additions of uncertain authority and simple mistakes. Rather like those luxuriously bound law reports lining the walls of up-market law firms, the medieval *Bracton* was something more to be owned than to be used.[2] In what follows, I shall suggest reasons why both Henry of Bratton and the treatise that travels under his name

1 F. W. Maitland, in F. Pollock and F. W. Maitland, *The History of English Law Before the Time of Edward I*, 2d ed., 2 vols. (Cambridge: Cambridge University Press, 1968), 2:206; C. A. F. Meekings, 'Henry de Bracton, Canon of Wells', *Notes and Queries for Somerset and Dorset* 26 (1951–4): 141–3, reprinted in C. A. F. Meekings, *Studies in 13th Century Justice and Administration* (London: Hambledon Press, 1981), ch. 7. For assistance with what follows, I am especially indebted to Sophie Ambler, Robert Bartlett, Paul Brand, David Carpenter, David Crouch, Richard Helmholz, Mark Hill, Frédérique Lachaud, John Maddicott and Magnus Ryan.

2 See P. A. Brand, 'The Age of Bracton', in J. Hudson, ed., *The History of English Law: Centenary Essays on 'Pollock and Maitland'* (Oxford: Oxford University Press, 1996), 65–89; idem, 'The Date and Authorship of Bracton: A Response', *Journal of Legal History* 31 (2010): 217–44, responding to criticisms from the late John Barton.

deserve continuing remembrance, albeit for reasons that might have shocked opinion even fifty years ago.

BIOGRAPHY

Records of the life of Henry of Bratton remain disappointingly scarce: he is mentioned by no contemporary chronicler and left no charter evidence outside the court plea rolls. Even the date of his birth remains largely unguessable. His connection to Bratton Fleming, east of Barnstable, was first firmly established by John Horace Round, who traced Bratton's possession of estates at nearby Alverdiscott and Wear in Westleigh held from the Fleming family, themselves tenants of the earldom of Cornwall.[3]

On no very secure evidence, Bratton has been credited with knightly ancestors. Of his education we know nothing, save that in his lifetime he was never assigned the title 'Master', the usual means of denoting the university graduate. This has done nothing to discourage suggestions that he attended the schools of either Exeter or Oxford (or both).[4] In this context, it is perhaps worth noting a comment by Ralph Niger (c. 1190) that the civilian lawyers of his day were increasingly refusing the title 'Master' or 'Doctor', instead preferring to style themselves 'Lord' (Latin *dominus*), rather, we may suspect, in the way that surgeons today spurn professional titles and insist on being known as plain 'Mr'.[5] 'Dominus' is certainly a courtesy title regularly applied to Bratton by his contemporaries.

Bratton himself first appears in March 1238 as party to an agreement enrolled on the plea roll of the court *coram rege*, perhaps relating to the manor of Alverdiscott, which may only recently have come into his possession.[6] Such access to the court rolls suggests that he was already

3 J. H. Round, 'Bractoniana', *English Historical Review* 31 (1916): 586–9, esp. pp. 586–8, with corrections by O. J. Reichel, *English Historical Review* 32 (1917): 160; *Liber Feodorum. The Book of Fees Commonly Called Testa de Nevill*, 3 vols. (London: HMSO, 1920–31), 2:795, where 'Aylescoth' is identified as Alscott in Alverdiscott. Neither this nor the identification as Aylescott in West Down (J. E. B. Gover, A. Mawer and F. M. Stenton, eds., *The Place-Names of Devon*, 2 vols. (Cambridge: Cambridge University Press, 1931–2), 1:39–40) is secure.

4 Maitland favoured Exeter, others Oxford: H. G. Richardson, 'Azo, Drogheda, and Bracton', *English Historical Review* 59 (1944): 40–5.

5 Ralph Niger, in H. Kantorowicz and B. Smalley, 'An English Theologian's View of Roman Law: Pepo, Irnerius, Ralph Niger', *Mediaeval and Renaissance Studies* 1 (1943 for 1941), 250 lines 31–3, although see the appearance of 'Magister' applied to a number of thirteenth-century justices, including masters Robert of Shardlow, Simon of Waltham and Richard of Staines.

6 *Curia Regis Rolls*, 20 vols. (London: HMSO, 1922–2006 [later volumes Woodbridge: Boydell Press]), 16, no. 149F; see also C. A. F. Meekings and D. Crook, *King's Bench and Common Bench in the Reign of Henry III* (London: Selden Society, 2010), 60. As pointed out to me by Paul Brand, Alverdiscott may have come to Bratton only as a gage, pending the repayment of a debt of 100 marks from Richard Fleming.

a member of the circle of William de Raleigh (d. 1250), in turn a justice of the Common Bench (1229–34), chief justice *coram rege* (1234–9), Bishop of Norwich (1239–44) and of Winchester (1244–50). Raleigh himself was a West Country man from a family associated with Raleigh in Pilton near Barnstable. In 1212, he had been presented by King John to the church of Bratton Fleming.[7] In much the same way that, twenty years later, Bratton was to rise in Raleigh's service, so Raleigh himself had prospered as clerk and confidant to the royal justice, Martin of Pattishall. By 1214, Raleigh was serving as a clerk to the justices of the bench at Westminster and was promoted as a bench justice in 1229. Through Raleigh, Bratton could thus claim connections to the heroic age of English law, stretching back via Martin of Pattishall to Martin's service as clerk to Simon of Pattishall (no certain relation), justice in the Court of Common Pleas from 1190 and in effect senior judge under both Richard I and King John.[8]

Precisely what role Bratton was performing by 1238 remains unclear, but it is more likely that he was acting as senior clerk to Raleigh in person, rather than in any more official capacity as clerk to the *coram rege* court over which Raleigh presided. Attached to the itinerant king, this was a tribunal in which many of the more serious and politically sensitive cases were tried. From the mid-1230s, its body of justices had developed their own identity as a court of 'King's Bench', distinct from the Bench of Common Pleas at Westminster. Both courts, King's Bench and Bench, had emerged since the 1190s as professional or semi-professional tribunals of justices and lawyers gradually detached from the more amorphous collection of courtiers who had previously administered the king's law.[9] The differences between Bench and King's Bench were noticed, for the first time in academic discourse, in the treatise known as *Bracton*. Here, not surprisingly, a particular stress was laid upon the justices of the King's Bench: 'major, general, permanent and of greater importance, residing at the side of the king, their duty to correct the wrongs and errors of all others'.[10]

7 *Rotuli Litterarum Patentium*, ed. T. D. Hardy (London, 1835), 93b, noting the endowment of a vicarage, in 1212 held by a man named Odo of Bratton.

8 For biographies of Raleigh, as of Martin and Simon of Pattishall, see the *Oxford Dictionary of National Biography* (Oxford: Oxford University Press, 2004); C. A. F. Meekings, 'Martin Pateshull and William Raleigh', *Bulletin of the Institute of Historical Research* 26 (1953): 157–80; 'Martin de Pateshull of Good Memory My Sometime Lord', *Bulletin of the Institute of Historical Research* 47 (1974): 224–9; Meekings and Crook, *King's Bench*, 49–50.

9 P. A. Brand, *The Making of the Common Law* (London: Hambledon Press, 1992), 86–7; R. V. Turner, 'The Origins of Common Pleas and King's Bench', *American Journal of Legal History* 21 (1977): 238–54, reprinted in idem, *Judges, Administrators and the Common Law in Angevin England* (London: Hambledon, 1994), 17–33. See also Meekings and Crook, *King's Bench*, 20–1, 49–50, esp. pp. 58–61 for Bratton as clerk.

10 G. Woodbine, ed. and trans., S. E. Thorne, *Bracton on the Laws and Customs of England*, 4 vols. (Cambridge, MA: Harvard University Press, 1968–77), 2:307.

Retained by Henry III in 1240 with an annual pension of 40 marks (just under £27), Bratton disappears from the records for five years thereafter.[11] The most likely explanation is that he supported the cause of William de Raleigh, in 1239 elected Bishop of Norwich and, against the king's wishes, promoted as candidate for the see of Winchester. This led to severe royal reprisals against Raleigh's friends and property. Bratton's close relationship with Raleigh is revealed by a series of entries on the so-called Pipe Rolls of the bishopric of Winchester, recording Bratton's entertainment at Raleigh's manors in western and southern England, throughout the late 1240s.[12] More significantly, he appears as datary to at least two of the bishop's charters, issued at Winchester 'by the hand of Henry of Bratton our clerk' on 16 April 1245.[13] This suggests that temporarily Bratton served as Raleigh's de facto chancellor. In September 1245, by which time he was rector of Gosberton in Lincolnshire, Bratton received papal dispensation to hold two further benefices with cure of souls: a standard dispensation for those considered exceptionally learned or weighed down by public affairs.[14]

Bratton's presentation to Gosberton, some time after 1230, perhaps came in reward for legal work.[15] But there are alternative explanations. One would invoke an association with Hugh of Wells, Bishop of Lincoln (d. 1235) and thence with Hugh's brother, Jocelin, Bishop of Bath and Wells (d. 1242). Certainly, the canons of Wells took an interest both in Gosberton and its one-time rector, Richard de Attebere, *alias* Master Richard of Devon, himself canon of Wells in the 1230s.[16] And Bratton's next recorded ecclesiastical promotion came as canon of Wells, where he held the prebend of Whitchurch south of Bristol from an unspecified date before July 1249.[17] An alternative would be to suggest an association with

11 *Calendar of the Liberate Rolls Preserved in the Public Record Office 1226–40* (London: HMSO, 1916), 450.

12 Meekings and Crook, *King's Bench*, 88–9.

13 Windsor, St George's Chapel MS IV.B.1 (Arundel White Book), pp. 265–6 (16 April 1245); J. Thorpe, ed., *Registrum Roffense* (London, 1769), 327–8. See also Oxford, Magdalen College Archives, MS Otterbourne Charter 75 (as 'dominus' Henry of Bratton, witnessing second, after the bishop's steward, at Marwell in September 1246).

14 E. Berger, ed., *Les Registres d'Innocent IV*, 4 vols. (Paris: Thorin, 1884–1921), 1:230, no. 1513, and see also nos. 1509–10 and 1512 in favour of others of Raleigh's clerks.

15 As implied by Meekings and Crook, *King's Bench*, 83–4, noting that Bratton's experiences at Gosberton may have inspired an *addicio* to the *De Legibus* concerning the law of gifts.

16 Gilbert de Treilly was presented to Gosberton in 1229–30 by Robert de Rye, in succession to Master Richard of Devon, *alias* Richard de Attebere, himself instituted in 1217–18 both to Gosberton and to the church of Charlton Mackrell (Somerset): W. P. W. Phillimore and F. N. Davis, eds., *Rotuli Hugonis de Welles episcopi Lincolniensis A.D. MCCIX–MCCXXXV*, 3 vols. (London: Canterbury and York Society, 1907–9), 3:172, 175; W. H. B. Bird, *Calendar of the Manuscripts of the Dean and Chapter of Wells*, 2 vols. (London: HMSO, 1907), 1:401, 404.

17 D. Greenway, ed., *John le Neve, Fasti Ecclesiae Anglicanae 1066–1300* 11 vols. (London: University of London Press, 2001), 7:75–6; Meekings and Crook, *King's Bench*, 90.

Robert Grosseteste, Bishop of Lincoln (1235–53), undoubtedly a friend and supporter of William de Raleigh, and in the 1230s found answering a request for a living for another of Raleigh's protégés.[18] Although in general opposed to entrusting the cure of souls to justices and other clerks steeped in secular affairs, Grosseteste was, as we shall see, intimately concerned in discussions that find a prominent place in *Bracton*.[19] Meanwhile, Gosberton brought Bratton an income approaching £60 a year.[20] At Whitchurch, which was worth only £8, he obtained licence from the local magnate, William Longespée, the king's cousin, claimant to the earldom of Salisbury, to enclose a rabbit warren: a clear sign of his rising position in the world.[21]

Most of what we know of Bratton's ecclesiastical career derives from the register of Walter of Branscombe, Bishop of Exeter (1258–80). By 1258, Bratton was a canon of the collegiate church of Bosham (Sussex), where the Bishop of Exeter served as dean.[22] Branscombe instituted Bratton to the church of Combeinteignhead in south Devon (worth c. £10 a year) in May 1259, and in April 1261 to Bideford (worth c. £13), close to Bratton's native stomping grounds at Bratton Fleming and Alverdiscott.[23] As a canon of Exeter, in January 1264, Bratton was promoted Archdeacon of Barnstable, but served only briefly, through to his promotion as Chancellor of Exeter that May.[24] He is assumed to have remained Chancellor of Exeter until his death in July or August 1268. Thereafter, he was commemorated with obit celebrations at both Wells and Exeter.[25]

So far, then, we have the outlines of a mid-ranking clerical career, bringing rewards in excess of £100 a year, certainly sufficient to enable Bratton to invest in the property market, as he seems to have done at Whitchurch, and in 1261, when he invested £120 in a fifteen-year, rent-free lease of Degembris in St Newlyn East, the property of Walter de Raleigh and his wife, presumably kin to William de Raleigh.[26] Into this career we must somehow fit what is known of Bratton the royal justice.

18 H. R. Luard, ed., *Roberti Grosseteste episcopi quondam Lincolniensis epistolae* (London: Longmans, 1861), 63–5, no. 17; F. A. C. Mantello and J. Goering, eds., *The Letters of Robert Grosseteste, Bishop of Lincoln* (Toronto: University of Toronto Press, 2010), 94–6, no. 17.

19 For Grosseteste's opposition to clerical judges, see R. V. Turner, 'Clerical Judges in English Secular Courts: The Ideal versus the Reality', *Medievalia et Humanistica* n.s. 3 (1972), 75–98, reprinted in idem, *Judges, Administrators and the Common Law*, 159–80.

20 Meekings and Crook, *King's Bench*, 84, 90.

21 Bird, *Calendar of the Manuscripts of Wells*, 1:487; Meekings and Crook, *King's Bench*, 90, noting that the licence must have been granted before Longuespée's departure for crusade, hence before July 1249.

22 Greenway, *Fasti*, 10:31. For his prebend at Bosham, see O. F. Robinson, ed., *The Register of Walter Bronescombe, Bishop of Exeter*, 3 vols. (Woodbridge: Boydell Press, 1995–2003), 1: no. 422.

23 Robinson, *Register of Walter Bronescombe*, 1: nos. 90, 317.

24 Ibid., 2: nos. 524, 547–8; Greenway, *Fasti*, 10:15–16, 18–19, 31, 47.

25 Meekings and Crook, *King's Bench*, 133–4.

26 Ibid., 133.

There was nothing unusual at this time about clerks also serving as royal justices. Some indeed, such as William de Raleigh, could aspire to the very highest ecclesiastical office, although their acceptance of bishoprics was considered to disbar them from further judicial service.[27] Bratton can be found as early as the summer of 1240 as a clerk offering advice in the court *coram rege*, but his first appearance as a justice came from April to July 1245, when he sat as justice in eyre at Lincoln and Nottingham, named as junior to the head of his eyre circuit, Roger of Thirkleby (another former clerk of Raleigh), but ahead of Gilbert of Preston, himself a justice for the past five years. This suggests that Bratton was already considered a lawyer of standing and experience.[28] It is also worth noting that his promotion coincided with the king's reconciliation with Raleigh, now Bishop of Winchester, and was perhaps intended as reward both for Bratton and for Raleigh as Bratton's chief patron.

After July 1245, there is a hiatus in the record of Bratton's service until August 1247 when, at Thirkleby's request, he is to be found making a search of the rolls formerly belonging to Martin of Pattishall, from the Yorkshire eyre of 1226. As has been widely noticed, this supplies proof that, as early as 1247, and perhaps for some time before this, Bratton had access to Pattishall's rolls. The rolls themselves had presumably been inherited by Raleigh as Pattishall's one-time clerk. Whether we imagine Bratton here acting as a servant of the king's court or of Raleigh, it is clear that he already had access to materials that were to prove crucial to the making of the treatise known as *Bracton*.[29] He was still in possession of the rolls of Pattishall and Raleigh in December 1257, when he was required to surrender them as part of a wider attempt by the government to recover records that the justices, until now, had treated as their own private property.[30]

It was from this period, perhaps beginning in the autumn of 1247, that Bratton began to sit for the first time as a justice *coram rege*, travelling for part of the year as a member of the king's itinerant household.[31] He appears as such in a series of final concords and in charter witness lists from November 1247 through

[27] F. Pegues, 'The "Clericus" in the Legal Administration of Thirteenth-Century England', *English Historical Review* 71 (1956): 529–59; Turner, 'Clerical Judges'; R. V. Turner, *The English Judiciary in the Age of Glanvill and Bracton, c. 1176–1239* (Cambridge: Cambridge University Press, 1985).

[28] Turner, *English Judiciary* 58–9, 83–5.

[29] H. G. Richardson and G. O. Sayles, eds., *Select Cases of Procedure without Writ under Henry III* (London: Selden Society, 1941), clxxxi–clxxxvi, esp. clxxxv for perhaps the only surviving letter issued in Bratton's name, with corrections offered by Meekings and Crook, *King's Bench*, 85–7, and a facsimile in H. G. Richardson, *Bracton: The Problem of His Text* (London: Selden Society, 1965), 42, pl. 5.

[30] G. O. Sayles, *Select Cases in the Court of King's Bench under Edward I*, vol. 1 (London: Selden Society, 1936), cliv; Meekings and Crook, *King's Bench*, 131.

[31] Meekings and Crook, *King's Bench*, 26.

to July 1251, when his retirement seems to have followed, perhaps consequentially, from the disgrace of the chief justice *coram rege*, Henry of Bath.[32] Bratton's judicial career had resumed by October 1253. Thereafter he sat *coram rege* until his definitive retirement from the court in July 1257.[33]

In retirement, he did not give up all contact with the law. Even as a justice of the King's Bench, he had been commissioned to hear assizes between 1248 and 1257 no fewer than 275 times for Somerset and Devon, and 80 times for other counties, for the most part on the road either from the West Country to London or from London to his living at Gosberton in Lincolnshire.[34] This business continued after his retirement, with further assize commissions, gradually restricted to Devon and Cornwall, the last in June 1268, only a few days or weeks before Bratton's death.[35] Although he played no discernible role in the movement of baronial rebellion and civil war that convulsed England between 1258 and 1265, from August 1259 he was among the small team of seven or eight professional justices licensed to take assizes and special commissions. In the autumn of 1260, he can be found appointed special defender and protector of Witham Charterhouse, one of the monasteries founded by Henry II after 1170 in expiation for his part in the murder of Thomas Becket.[36]

All told, Bratton enjoyed a decent but by no means remarkable judicial career. He served as a justice in eyre only once (1245), discontinuously for ten years as a justice *coram rege* (1247–51, 1253–7) and almost twice as long (1248–68) as an assize commissioner. As a justice attached to the king's itinerant court, he was close to decision-making at a very high level in government. Yet he never once served 'as sheriff or deputy in executing of judgments ... never delivered a gaol, [and] took very few special commissions apart from assizes'.[37] Above all, he never sat as a justice in the busiest of all of the king's courts, the Bench of Common Pleas.[38] Moreover, unlike Raleigh and Pattishall, he left no intellectual posterity beyond perhaps a book. We know the names of none of Bratton's clerks, and his last testament is long vanished. All we can surmise is that the treatise called *Bracton* may have been among the property that he bequeathed at his death.

Bracton, of which traces can be found as early as the 1270s, within a decade of Henry of Bratton's death, survives today in at least fifty-two medieval copies,

32 Ibid., 37–40, nos. 35–60; 45, 47, 89–90, 103. For Bath's disgrace, see ibid., 95–103.

33 Ibid., 41–4, nos. 70, 72–81, 83, 85–99; 47, 129–30.

34 Meekings, 'Henry de Bracton', 142.

35 Meekings and Crook, *King's Bench*, 132–4.

36 Ibid., 129–30. In 1259 he had been commissioned, together with the Earl of Hereford, to hold a special eyre to deal with grievances in Gloucestershire, Herefordshire and Worcestershire, although there is no evidence that such sessions were ever held: D. Crook, *Records of the General Eyre* (London: HMSO, 1982), 189–90.

37 Meekings and Crook, *King's Bench*, 139.

38 As noted by Brand, 'Age of Bracton', 88.

most of them made before 1400.[39] It is possible that this represents merely the tip of a vanished iceberg and that several hundred copies once existed.[40] The book's immense length and complexity makes the survival of even fifty copies impressive, all the more so when compared to the number of copies of the work of those who before *Bracton* had attempted a general synthesis of English law, in the so-called *Leges Henrici Primi* (six medieval copies) and the treatise known as *Glanvill* (at least forty-two medieval copies).[41] The first printed *Bracton* appeared in 1569 (excellent), and there were subsequent editions (good) in 1640 and in six volumes (atrocious, for the government-sponsored Rolls Series), between 1878 and 1883.[42] In 1895, Maitland dreamed of a new edition for the Selden Society, expected to appear in the 'not very far distant' future.[43] Instead, after Maitland's death, it was left to the American, George Woodbine, to collate the manuscripts and publish the text, in four fat volumes produced between 1915 and 1942.[44] These in turn served as the basis for what is today the standard edition, combining Woodbine's Latin text with an English translation and apparatus by Samuel Thorne, again in four volumes, published between 1968 and 1977.[45]

BRACTON, THE TREATISE

The text of *Bracton* is a sprawling mass of nearly half a million words, more than three times the length of the *Leges Henrici Primi* and *Glanvill* combined. Its opening proclaims it to be a *summa* intended to instruct those unlearned in

39 Woodbine and Thorne, *Bracton*, 1:1–20, esp. 1; 3:liii. See also J. H. Baker, *English Legal Manuscripts in the United States of America*, 2 vols. (London, Selden Society, 1995–2000), 1: nos. 89, 138 (and see also nos. 34–5).

40 H. Kantorowicz, *Bractonian Problems*, ed. D. M. Stenton (Glasgow: Jackson, 1941), 55–7, guessing a figure as high as 300 medieval copies.

41 L. J. Downer, ed., *Leges Henrici Primi* (Oxford: Clarendon Press, 1972), 45–50; Ranulf de Glanville, *De Legibus et Consuetudinibus regni Angliae*, ed. G.E. Woodbine (New Haven: Yale University Press, 1932), 1–22, citing twenty-seven copies in English collections; G. D. G. Hall, ed., *The Treatise on the Laws and Customs of the Realm of England Commonly Called Glanvill* (Oxford: Clarendon Press, 1993), viii, noting thirty-eight, to which three more are added by J. H. Baker, *A Catalogue of English Legal Manuscripts in Cambridge University Library* (Woodbridge: Boydell Press, 1996), 150. There are further exemplars elsewhere, as in Vienna, Nationalbibliothek MS 2156 (c. 1300).

42 Briefly listed by T. F. T. Plucknett, *A Concise History of the Common Law*, 5th ed. (London: Butterworth, 1956), 262–5. For Maitland's opinion of the Rolls Series edition, see C. H. S. Fifoot, ed., *The Letters of Frederic William Maitland* (London: Selden Society, 1965), 16, no. 14, as drawn to my attention by Paul Brand.

43 F. M. Maitland, ed., *Select Passages from the Works of Bracton and Azo* (London: Selden Society, 1895), 250.

44 G. E. Woodbine, *Bracton de Legibus et Consuetudinibus Angliae*, 4 vols. (New Haven: Yale University Press, 1915–42).

45 Woodbine and Thorne, *Bracton*, 1:xxiv–xxxi, with Thorne's (typically charitable) thoughts on Woodbine's edition.

the ways of the law.[46] Insofar as it can be said to have a structure, it attempts to do for the laws of England what continental jurists had already done for both Roman and canon law, most notably via Justinian's *Institutes* (whose opening words are paraphrased at the start of *Bracton*).[47] Its popularity no doubt stemmed from its blend of monumentality and systematisation. Combining the functions of a procedural treatise, a register of writs, a collection of precedents and an attempt to explain underlying causes, it seemed to supply thirteenth-century England with an equivalent to the harmonisations attempted elsewhere for Roman and civil law. At the same time, not only are many things left unresolved, inconsistent or unexplained, but a great deal that elsewhere would be referred to as written statute (as in the interplay in Roman law between *Institutes, Digest* and *Code*) here emerges only from procedural tradition and by reference to the laws of the classical past. These themselves are cited from the *Digest* and *Decretum* in ways that, very soon after, would be considered entirely alien to English practice. At any point in the work we may find ourselves confronted with a diverse range of classical or papal precedents, biblical motifs, terminology derived from Anglo-Saxon codes, case law from the 1220s and 1230s, and digressions that obscure almost as much as they illuminate. A typical example occurs in the account of the castration of rapists by outraged male kin. Here the *Decretum*, the English law of 'hamsocn', the antique Mediterranean (but hardly English) trade in eunuchs, a case heard at Windsor before William de Raleigh, and the Jewish tradition of circumcision are all brought together within a single paragraph as part of a scheme modelled ultimately on the Justinianic *Institutes*.[48]

Despite its supposed arrangement into titles and paragraphs, the work as a whole lacks anything by way of a numbering scheme to allow citation by book, let alone by individual clauses. It would thus have been fiendishly difficult to cite: a difficulty reflected both in the failure of any medieval writer to supply a gloss to *Bracton* and in the modern uncertainty as to whether to cite by folios from the 1569 'Vulgate' edition or by volume and page number from the editions by Thorne and Woodbine.[49] None of this has dampened *Bracton*'s fame. As the most systematic attempt to describe English law during a time of significant evolution, it earned the admiration of Maitland and his successors. As a treatise combining innumerable significant details, not least in its attempt to explain the relationship between God, the king and the law, it has been

46 Ibid., 2:19.

47 For an attempt to demonstrate deliberate adherence to the scheme of the *Institutes*, see Richardson, *Bracton*, 53–61.

48 Woodbine and Thorne, *Bracton*, 2:408.

49 Richardson, *Bracton*, 63–6.

mined as a crucial source not only for legal but for political and constitutional thought.

The very earliest copies seem to have circulated anonymously. Thereafter, an addition was inserted near the beginning of the treatise so that the author was made to refer to himself as 'I, Henry of Bratton'.[50] In a subsequent passage, the name 'Henry of Bratton' is used as an example of the ways in which faults in spelling could result in challenges to procedure by writ.[51] The best of the early manuscripts, now in the Bodleian Library, has been assigned the title 'the book of the lord H(enry) of Bratton (*Bratona*)', and in 1278, the Bishop of Bath and Wells, the king's chancellor, Robert Burnell, was in possession of 'a book which the lord Henry of Bratton (*Breton*) wrote (*composuit*)', perhaps recovered from among the property of Bratton's prebend in Wells Cathedral.[52] It was thus taken for granted, through to Maitland's time and beyond, not only that Bratton wrote *Bracton* but that he had composed it in a single campaign of writing, albeit extended over several years.

QUESTIONS OF ATTRIBUTION

A first great bombshell exploded in 1884 with the discovery by Paul Vinagradoff of a volume of extracts from official court records, henceforth proclaimed to be 'Bracton's Note Book'.[53] From 1884 onwards, studies of the treatise and Note Book have necessarily marched hand in hand. Maitland's edition of the Note Book, published in 1887, established both the first secure biographical sketch of Bratton and also the text and dates of some 2,000 cases reported in the Book.[54] Of these, 200 had found a place among the 500 or so cases noticed in *Bracton*. Virtually all of the Note Book cases date from the time of Pattishall and Raleigh. The cases noted in *Bracton* ranged rather later, with a flurry from the very end of Bratton's judicial career, the last of them datable to 1262.[55] Maitland therefore concluded that *Bracton* was a work of the mid-1250s, albeit drawing on materials that reached back, via the Note Book, to cases reported in the rolls of Pattishall and Raleigh, at least

50 Woodbine and Thorne, *Bracton*, 2:19, 3:li. 51 Ibid., 3:79.

52 Brand, 'Age of Bracton', 74–5, noting the loan of Burnell's book to Robert of Scarborough, archdeacon and future Dean of York (d. c. 1291: see Greenway, *Fasti*, 6:12, 43). See also Richardson, *Bracton*, 36n.

53 Now British Library, Add. MS 12269.

54 F. W. Maitland, *Bracton's Note Book*, 3 vols. (London: Clay, 1887), reprinting Vinogradoff's initial announcement of the discovery (1:xvii–xxiii), with a forensic table (1:146–71) showing not only which cases were cited in *Bracton* but which of these were also to be found in the Note Book.

55 Ibid., 1:161; Meekings and Crook, *King's Bench*, 132; Woodbine and Thorne, *Bracton*, 2:447, noted as an early 'addicio' (ibid., 1:391, marginalia in the best of the early copies).

one of them as early as the reign of King John, most of the others to be dated between the reopening of the Bench after the civil war of 1215–17 and the mid-1230s.[56] The treatise, it was agreed, was composed before the baronial rebellion of 1258, taking no account of the significant reforms achieved in the so-called Provisions of Oxford (1258) or Westminster (1259). The assumption remained that *Bracton* was written by Henry of Bratton in the 1250s and that Bratton's draft had then been revised over a number of years between the 1250s and his death in 1268. Such revision led to the insertion of various afterthoughts and additions (the notorious *addiciones*, of which more below).

Having dealt with date and authorship, Maitland tackled a more sensitive issue. Nobody reading *Bracton*, either in the thirteenth century or later, could doubt that its author was as much a civilian as a common lawyer. Indeed, *Bracton* describes actions and procedures in the English common law in language borrowed from the Romano-canonical tradition. Thanks in large part to the Protestant Reformation and the consequent suspicion of all things Roman, the English common law was supposed by its eighteenth- and nineteenth-century admirers to be something ancient and Anglo-Saxon, entirely uncontaminated by the traditions of either the Roman Empire or the Roman Catholic Church. By the seventeenth century, indeed, not only had Roman law come to be stained with the red rag of popery, but the civilian lawyers themselves were viewed as aiders and abettors of a distinctively 'Catholic' tradition of absolutism and the divine right of kings.[57] It was against such filthy foreign ways that the English Civil Wars were fought and that, both before and after the 1640s, common lawyers such as Coke or Blackstone championed the traditions of Magna Carta, Parliament, habeas corpus and the rest of England's ancient constitutional baggage.[58]

Against what was widely regarded as the triumph of the common law, *Bracton* appeared a dangerous and retrograde anomaly. Since at least the 1860s and the work of Carl Güterbock, it had been acknowledged not only that *Bracton* used Roman law but that large parts of it were lifted wholesale from the *Summa Codicis* of Azo of Bologna, by the 1220s the leading Roman law textbook.[59] Sir

56 Maitland, *Bracton's Note Book*, 1:146–7, 162; Woodbine and Thorne, *Bracton*, 4:145, and, for another case that perhaps dated from the time of King John, ibid., 2:152 (Maitland, *Bracton's Note Book*, 1:169).

57 See here especially B. P. Levack, *The Civil Lawyers in England 1603–1641* (Oxford: Clarendon Press, 1973), with a wide-ranging review by C. Donahue, *Yale Law Journal* 84 (1974): 167–81.

58 Classic here remains J. G. A. Pocock, *The Ancient Constitution and the Feudal Law* (Cambridge: Cambridge University Press, 1957; 2d ed. 1987). See also G. Burgess, *The Politics of the Ancient Constitution* (Basingstoke: Macmillan, 1992); R. J. Smith, *The Gothic Bequest* (Cambridge: Cambridge University Press, 1987).

59 C. Güterbock, *Henricus de Bracton und sein Verhältniss zum römischen Rechte* (Berlin: Springer, 1862), with an English translation and additions by B. Coxe, *Bracton and His Relation to the Roman Law* (Philadelphia: J. B. Lippincott, 1866).

Henry Maine, writing in 1861, and as yet unaware of *Bracton*'s indebtedness to Azo, had already been inclined to dismiss *Bracton* as an outrageous plagiarist who passed off as 'pure English law a treatise of which the entire form and a third of the contents were directly borrowed from the Corpus Juris'. This, Maine concluded, was 'among the most hopeless enigmas in the history of jurisprudence'.[60] Similar sentiments persuaded William Stubbs, the father of the modern study of England's medieval past, that England was a land closed not only to the *Corpus Iuris Civilis* but to the continental tradition of canon law. Works such as the *Decretum* or Gregory's IX's *Liber Extra*, he argued, were not considered to be 'authoritative' in England.

As Maitland was among the first to point out, this was pure nonsense.[61] Not only had the *ius commune* been widely taught in England from the twelfth century onwards, but at precisely the time that Henry of Bratton was prospering in royal service, the University of Oxford divided its law faculty into distinct schools of Roman and canon law – the consequence not of neglect but of a burgeoning interest perhaps provoked by the publication of Gregory IX's *Liber Extra* (September 1234).[62] As early as the 1190s, voices raised in protest against the proliferation of Roman lawyers touting for business in the English courts could be heard at Oxford and elsewhere. Such civilian 'experts' were derided as medieval equivalents to the modern ambulance-chaser or MBA. Then as now, the targets of such attacks were clearly enjoying a success envied by their critics (for the most part, members of the more cerebral faculty of theology).[63] Even *Glanvill* (c. 1188), in many ways the foundational text of English common law, owed its prologue and at least part of its arrangement to Justinian.[64] Just as there could be no doubt that the author of *Bracton* knew *Glanvill* and had borrowed from *Glanvill*'s civilian prologue, so Maitland acknowledged *Bracton*'s awareness of both Roman and canon law.[65]

60 H. S. Maine, *Ancient Law* (London: John Murray, 1861), 48.

61 See C. Donahue, 'Roman Canon Law in the English Medieval Church: Stubbs vs. Maitland Re-Examined after Seventy-Five Years in Light of Some Records from the Church Courts', *Michigan Law Review* 72 (1974): 647–716.

62 See here the chapters on civil and canon law by J. L. Barton and L. E. Boyle in J. I. Catto, ed., *The History of the University of Oxford, Vol. I: The Early Oxford Schools* (Oxford: Oxford University Press, 1984), 519–64, esp. 535 on the possible influence of *Liber Extra*.

63 J. L. Barton, review of F. De Zulueta and P. Stein, *The Teaching of Roman Law in England around 1200* (London: Selden Society, 1990), *Journal of Legal History* 14 (1993): 53–8; Kantorowicz and Smalley, 'An English Theologian's View of Roman Law', 237–51; R. V. Turner, 'Roman England before the Time of Bracton', *Journal of British Studies* 15 (1975): 1–25, reprinted in idem, *Judges, Administrators and the Common Law*, 45–69.

64 Hall, *Glanvill*, with a guide to further reading by M. T. Clanchy, xxxvi–xxxviii, lxi; see also E. H. Kantorowicz, 'The Prologue to Fleta', *Speculum* 32 (1957): 231–49.

65 Maitland, *Select Passages from Bracton and Azo*.

The problem, as Maitland saw it, was that *Bracton* was the work of an expert common lawyer entirely out of his depth when it came to the *ius commune*. Why else, he demanded, should *Bracton* have so hopelessly muddled a large number of the citations and concepts that he had borrowed from Azo? *Bracton*'s Romanism was freakish and therefore dismissable: foreign varnish applied incompetently to the good old English oak of *Bracton*'s common law.

BRACTON: REVISIONISM AND RE-EVALUATION

Following Maitland, there was no significant revolution in Bractonian studies before the late 1930s, even though there were those prepared to question whether *Bracton*'s Romanism was really as superficial or poorly mastered as Maitland had suggested.[66] In 1934, Doris Stenton revisited the question of sources for the Note Book, demonstrating that numerous rolls of the king's law court, some of them as early as 1200, had been marked up by clerks, apparently under the supervision either of Bratton or of some other individual concerned with establishing a collection of precedents. Stenton believed that this strengthened Bratton's claim to authorship of the Note Book.[67] On the contrary, it tended to suggest that Bratton was not alone in referencing the early plea rolls and that the Note Book was therefore by no means the unique record that it had once been supposed to be. Against this background, Woodbine's edition was brought to completion between 1915 and 1942.

Even before the final volume of Woodbine had appeared, however, a further series of mines were detonated beneath the Bractonian enterprise. All were Nazi engineered, albeit to England's great gain. The rise of fascism forced many German intellectuals to seek exile overseas.[68] Hermann Kantorowicz (1877–1940), already a target of suspicion in his homeland as an advocate of German 'war guilt' for 1914, was sacked as professor at Kiel on anti-Semitic grounds in 1933, and spent the next seven years in exile. Not to be confused with his better-known namesake, Ernst (to whom he was unrelated, despite both of them being born in Posen, both as assimilated Jews, both as the sons of distillery owners), Kantorowicz first gave a seminar series on *Bracton* at

66 G. E. Woodbine, 'The Roman Element in Bracton's *De Adquirendo Rerum Dominio*', *Yale Law Review* 31 (1922): 827–47; P. Vinogradoff, 'The Roman Element in Bracton's Treatise', *Yale Law Review* 32 (1923): 751–6.

67 D. M. Stenton, ed., *Rolls of the Justices in Eyre . . . for Lincolnshire 1218–9 and Worcestershire 1221* (London: Selden Society, 1934), xi–xv.

68 J. Beatson and R. Zimmermann, eds., *Jurists Uprooted: German-Speaking Émigré Lawyers in Twentieth-Century Britain* (Oxford: Oxford University Press, 2004), 105–204, 271–89, for studies of Fritz Schulz (by Wolfgang Ernst) and Hermann Kantorowicz (by David Ibbetson).

Oxford in 1937, repeated at Cambridge in 1939.[69] His lecture notes were written up and published posthumously by Stenton in 1941.[70]

Kantorowicz showed that the author of *Bracton* was an expert civilian lawyer and not at all the blundering amateur portrayed by Maitland. He also scorned Woodbine's edition, taken from manuscripts that were in all cases so hopelessly corrupt that *Bracton*'s Romanism could be recovered only after a laborious process of amendment and textual criticism. This, let it be recalled, from a compatriot of Mommsen, deeply versed in the tradition by which much nonsense foisted upon Ulpian, Theodosius or Justinian had been transformed by the critics into meaningful Latin prose.[71] Finally, there was the question of date. So much of *Bracton*, Kantorowicz demonstrated, drew upon the rolls of Pattishall and Raleigh, and so little upon law as it was practised in the 1250s or 1260s that it made more sense as a book written in the 1230s or 1240s. In his view, it was written between 1240 and 1245, ten or fifteen years earlier than the date suggested by Maitland. It had subsequently been revised, perhaps under Henry of Bratton's direction, more likely under the guidance of an anonymous 'redactor'. This 'redactor', Kantorowicz suggested, was a barely competent Romanist, lacking the civilian expertise that had informed the treatise as originally compiled.[72]

In 1934, Kantorowicz's friend and long-term collaborator, Fritz Schulz (1879–1957) was forced into retirement from the University of Frankfurt am Main. In England, he took up Kantorowicz's lead to investigate *Bracton*'s sources. In a series of masterly articles, the most important of them published in 1945, Schulz revealed that those parts of *Bracton* devoted to kingship and the relationship between law and society, previously assumed to be the thoughts of Henry of Bratton himself, represented little more than a chain of quotations compiled from such sources as the Vulgate Bible, John of Salisbury's *Policraticus*, Azo, the *Decretum* and *Liber Extra*.[73]

There is magnificent irony to the work of Kantorowicz and Schulz. In the midst of the Second World War, with England more isolated from continental Europe than at any time since the seventeenth century, the study of the

69 Ibbetson, 'Kantorowicz', 281. For confusion between Hermann and Ernst, see C. M. Bowra, *Memories 1898–1939* (London: Weidenfeld and Nicolson, 1966), 286, reporting a mistaken invitation made by the Fellows of New College, Oxford, in 1934 to Ernst, whom they had confused for Hermann, 'who was no relation and whom [Ernst] did not much like'.

70 Kantorowicz, *Bractonian Problems*.

71 Kantorowicz and others have stressed the comparisons to be drawn between *Bracton* and the text of Manilius, thinking of the work of Scaliger and specifically of the achievements of the Cambridge scholars Richard Bentley and A. E. Housman, the closest rivals to Mommsen that England can boast.

72 Ibid., 78–127, 127–33, 22–36, 36–76 respectively.

73 F. Schulz, 'Bracton on Kingship', *English Historical Review* 60 (1945): 136–76.

common law was quietly revolutionised by the discovery of *Bracton*'s dependence upon a host of Roman or Romano-canonical texts. Its use of Azo, the *Decretum* and William of Drogheda's *Summa Aurea* (c. 1239) had been acknowledged since before the First World War. To these, between 1943 and 1945, were added Tancred's *Ordo iudiciarus* (c. 1216), the *Summa de Casibus* (before 1228) and *Summa de Matrimonio* (c. 1234) of Raymond de Peñafort, and, in all likelihood, John de Sacrobosco's *Computus Ecclesiasticus* (c. 1236). *Bracton*'s dependence upon these sources was for the most part first disclosed by Schulz.[74] Indeed, between them Schulz and Kantorowicz did for English legal scholarship what wartime performances of Brahms or Beethoven achieved on a rather wider front: reminders of that other, far greater Germany, for the past decade concealed behind the leering mask of fascism.

Unfortunately, the extent of Kantorowicz and Schulz's achievement was appreciated only after a series of counter-manoeuvres had muddied the waters they laboured so hard to clear. Kantorowicz's study had been posthumously published, criticising the Woodbine edition in words that Kantorowicz himself might have tempered and that guaranteed a response from Woodbine's friends and admirers. Foremost into the lists stepped H. G. Richardson, a scholar of considerable learning but more adept at fashioning plough shares into swords than in establishing truths universally to be acknowledged. Beginning in 1944, and continuing for the next twenty years, Richardson published a series of papers intended to dish his opponents. On the positive side, he carried forwards the exploration of *Bracton*'s sources, drawing into debate a group of texts including the *Leges Edwardi Confessoris* and the *Instituta Cnuti* (apocryphal Anglo-Saxon texts of the twelfth rather than the eleventh century), and revisiting the *Summa Aurea* of William of Drogheda (d. 1245) which, in contradiction to Kantorowicz, Richardson demonstrated must have served as a source for *Bracton* (rather than Drogheda copying *Bracton*).[75] At the same time, obsessed with disproving Kantorowicz and Schulz's theory of a 'redactor' rewriting *Bracton* in the 1250s or 1260s, Richardson defended Maitland's position, not only by questioning *Bracton*'s essential expertise in Roman law, but by insisting that the treatise was composed in the mid to late 1250s. Its errors and *non sequiturs*, he suggested, represented the thoughts

74 F. Schulz, 'Critical Studies on Bracton's Treatise', *Law Quarterly Review* 59 (1943): 172–80; idem, 'Bracton and Raymond de Peñafort', *Law Quarterly Review* 61 (1945): 286–92; idem, 'Bracton as Computist', *Traditio* 3 (1945): 265–305.

75 Richardson, 'Azo, Drogheda and Bracton', 22–47; H. G. Richardson, 'Tancred, Raymond and Bracton', *English Historical Review* (1944): 376–84; idem, 'Studies in Bracton', *Traditio* 6 (1948): 61–104; idem, 'Studies in Bracton: An Addendum', *Traditio* 14 (1958): 399–400.

of an author who, in true English fashion, wrote what he meant to write, not what foreign intellectuals now insisted he must have intended be written. In this reading, indeed, Henry of Bratton emerged as one and the same as the incompetent 'redactor' whom Kantorowicz and Schulz claimed had so muddled *Bracton*.[76]

BRACTON AND BIBLICAL KINGSHIP

Where Richardson prowled, even angels feared to tread. Rather than tackle the still undecided issues of date and authorship, most scholars preferred instead to pursue Schulz into the exploration of *Bracton*'s theocracy. There thus followed a series of studies, some of more clarity than others, in which *Bracton*'s understanding of kingship was examined and rethought.[77] The outcome here was to show that *Bracton* had no very clear understanding of kingship, or at least could not be easily pigeon-holed into some camp either of proto-absolutists or proto-constitutionalists. On the one hand, citing Romano-canonical sources, *Bracton* was adamant that the king served as God's vicar on earth. Following a line of argument known both in twelfth-century Bologna and in the England of King John, kings were declared to be the equivalent to emperors within their own lands.[78] They might therefore consider themselves above any law save the judgment of God. At the same time (here quoting both Bede on the Virgin Mary and, perhaps via the Sarum liturgy for Christmas Day, St Leo the Great on Christ's determination to defeat the devil through incarnation and death), *Bracton* required that kings live under the law, albeit as a matter of virtue and the public good, rather than as an obligation enforceable by human agency.[79] Just as a criminal could not claim the protection of a law that he had defied, so *Bracton* implied, only

76 Richardson, *Bracton*, 45–52, esp. 48, 52.

77 Following Schulz, 'Bracton on Kingship', see S. J. T. Miller, 'The Position of the King in Bracton and Beaumanoir', *Speculum* 31 (1956): 263–96; B. Tierney, 'Bracton on Government', *Speculum* 38 (1963): 295–317; E. Lewis, 'King Above Law? "Quod Principi Placuit" in Bracton', *Speculum* 39 (1964): 240–69. Among the more opaque, see G. Post, 'A Romano-Canonical Maxim, "Quod Omnes Tangit", in Bracton', *Traditio* 4 (1946): 197–251; E. Kantorowicz, *The King's Two Bodies: A Study in Mediaeval Political Theocracy* (Princeton: Princeton University Press, 1957), 143–92.

78 For the king as emperor, see Schulz, 'Bracton on Kingship', 150–1, citing *Rotuli Litterarum Patentium*, 18 (King John, 8 September 1202).

79 Leo, *Sermo*, 22:3, a citation first identified by Peter Kelly SJ: Woodbine and Thorne, *Bracton*, 2:33, n. 9. For its use as a Christmas Day lection, unnoticed by Thorne, see F. Procter and C. Wordsworth, eds., *Breviarium ad usum insignis ecclesiae Sarum*, 3 vols. (Cambridge: Cambridge University Press, 1879–86), 1:clxxx–clxxxi. For *Bracton* on the Virgin Mary, unidentified by Schulz or Thorne, see Bede, *Homilia* 1.18 (in D. Hurst, ed., *Bedae venerabilis opera Pars 3/4: Opera homiletica. Opera rhythmica* (Turnhout: Brepols, 1955), 129).

a king who operated under the law could claim the privileges of the law-giver.[80] *Bracton* thus followed the wider trajectory from an early medieval tradition of 'Christ-centred kingship' to an ideology in which kings, to a greater or lesser extent became 'law-centred' servants of the public good.[81] At the same time, through his very submission to law and virtue, the Bractonian king retained distinctly Christ-like qualities.[82]

Against a wicked or erring king, subjects might complain. But in the end all should be left to God's judgment. There are direct echoes here of John of Salisbury's insistence that, although it might be right to kill a tyrant, such things should ultimately be left to divine rather than human agency.[83] Citing a definition that perhaps came to him from the London collection of laws – a compilation generally attributed to the circle of King John's critics around 1210 – *Bracton* declared that kings (Latin *reges*) were so called because of their obligation to rule well (Latin *bene regendo*).[84] Elsewhere, *Bracton* cited the text of the English coronation oath, for one of the first times in English history drawing this text directly into political debate as a means of defining royal obligation.[85]

A number of themes here invite more general comment. The first is that none of the sources – biblical or patristic, juridical or scholastic – that *Bracton* used to discuss kingship would have seemed in any way out of place at the Plantagenet court.[86] Even the blend of biblical and juristic language was nothing new. The prologue to *Glanvill*, for example, had mixed together Justinian, Scripture and the Roman Missal.[87] *Bracton* nonetheless seems caught rather awkwardly in a transition between two schools of thought. Critics of kingship in the reign of King John had regularly resorted to biblical

80 For the tag 'sine lege pereant qui secundum legem viuere recusauerunt', see Woodbine and Thorne, *Bracton*, 2:354, 363, derived ultimately from Romans 2:12, familiar in the centuries before Bracton (e.g. *Patrologia Latina*, 103, col. 580d). See also Woodbine and Thorne, *Bracton*, 2:408 ('non est dignus habere pacem qui non vult obseruare eam'). All this is directly relevant to (although not noticed in) the otherwise useful discussions by Lewis, 'King Above Law?', 240–69, and especially Tierney, 'Bracton on Government', 295–310, criticising both the super-refinement of Schulz and the crude assumptions made by other authorities, keen to find in *Bracton* a proto-republican.

81 Kantorowicz, *King's Two Bodies*, ch. 4.

82 See Schulz, 'Bracton on Kingship', 144 (A4, A6).

83 J. van Laarhoven, '"Thou Shalt Not Slay a Tyrant!" The So-Called Theory of John of Salisbury', in M. Wilks, ed., *The World of John of Salisbury* (Oxford: Blackwell, 1984), 319–41.

84 Woodbine and Thorne, *Bracton*, 2:305; see also Schulz, 'Bracton on Kingship', 140 (A24).

85 Woodbine and Thorne, *Bracton*, 2:304; see also Schulz, 'Bracton on Kingship', 137 (A2).

86 The very latest of *Bracton*'s identified sources, the *Summa Aurea* of William of Drogheda, seems to be datable to *c.* 1239: J. E. Sayers, 'William of Drogheda', *Oxford Dictionary of National Biography*, and references there cited.

87 Hall, *Glanvill*, 1–2, citing Psalm 18 and (in describing Henry II as 'author and lover of peace') the Roman Missal.

analogies. Indeed, the entire school of biblical exegesis in which Stephen Langton (Archbishop of Canterbury 1207–28) and his fellow English bishops operated was one in which typological similarities were sought between biblical and modern affairs. Thus comparisons could be drawn between wicked kings of Judea and the tyrants of a later age, between kings who refused their people justice and a written law code, and those kings of the Old Testament who suffered God's wrath for their failure to consider the public over private good.[88] Some of this language persists into *Bracton*, but restructured in accordance with the thinking and processes of the learned law.

A famous passage, generally considered an *addicio* to *Bracton*, although by Kantorowicz declared to be 'more genuinely Bractonian' than anything else in the treatise, is directly relevant here. This, the so-called 'addicio de cartis', allowed that a king who failed to redress injuries might be placed under the bridle of the law by his earls and barons:

> The King has a superior, namely God, and also the law by which he is made King. Also his court (*curia*), namely the earls and barons, because if he is without bridle (*frenum*), that is without law, they ought to put the bridle on him. That is why the earls are called the companions, so to speak, of the King, since he who has a companion has a master.[89]

Despite demands by Richardson and others that *Bracton*'s words on 'bridling' the king be assigned to the 1260s or even later, there is nothing in this passage inappropriate to the 1230s or 1240s.[90] The idea of the earl (Latin *comes*) as a 'companion' can be found in embryo in Horace and Cicero, and occurs fully fledged in the *De instructione principis* of Gerald of Wales (c. 1200).[91] The word for companion used by *Bracton* (Latin *socius*) also carried a technical meaning in Roman law as a member of a business partnership, itself implying equality between partners.[92] Long before *Bracton*, Gerald had rehearsed at least

88 N. Vincent, 'Stephen Langton, Archbishop of Canterbury', in L.-J. Bataillon, N. Beriou, G. Dahan and R. Quinto, eds., *Étienne Langton: prédicateur, bibliste, théologien* (Turnhout: Brepols, 2010), 51–123, summarising the work of Beryl Smalley, John Baldwin and Philippe Buc. See also J. Baldwin, 'Due Process in Magna Carta: Its Sources in English Law, Canon Law and Stephen Langton' in Robin Griffith-Jones and Mark Hill, eds., *Magna Carta, Religion and the Rule of Law* (Cambridge, Cambridge University Press, 2015), 31–52.

89 Woodbine and Thorne, *Bracton*, 2:109–10; see also Kantorowicz, *Bractonian Problems*, 52.

90 For suggested dating to the 1260s, see Schulz, 'Bracton on Kingship', 172–3; G. Lapsley, 'Bracton and the Authorship of the "Addicio de Cartis"', *English Historical Review* 62 (1947): 1–19; Richardson, *Bracton*, 31–5.

91 Gerald, 'De Instructione', in J. S. Brewer et al., eds., *Giraldi Cambrensis Opera*, 8 vols. (London: Longmans, 1861–91), 8:106: 'Comes dicitur a comitando, quia multi eum comitari debent', drawn to my attention by David Crouch. Among classical precedents, see e.g. Horace, *Carmina*, 1, 7, 25 ('O socii comitesque nil desperandum!').

92 C. M. Radding, 'The Origins of Bracton's "Addicio de Cartis"', *Speculum* 44 (1969): 242–3, citing *Digest* 8.3, 4; 17.2. For the Roman law of partnership, see P. Stein, 'The Mutual Agency of Partners in the Civil Law', *Tulane Law Review* 33 (1958–9): 595–606; R. Zimmermann,

two authorities that directly foreshadow the 'addicio de cartis', one from Isidore of Seville subsequently repeated in the twelfth-century *Decretum* ('Laws are made so that through fear of them ... the opportunity for doing harm may be bridled by fear of punishment') and another from Sidonius Apollinaris, familiar to Gerald via the collection of sayings and citations known as the *Florilegium Angelicum* ('Just as the people are placed under arms, so are such arms bridled by laws').[93] This same language of bit and bridle also occurs in Seneca's *De Clementia*, an authority said by Gerald to have been rarely out of the hands of Henry II, as early as the 1180s.[94]

The starting point for the 'addicio de cartis' was the king's obligation to warrant his own charters, an issue that had loomed large in English history between 1232 and 1234 and whose resolution first brought William de Raleigh to prominence in the court *coram rege*.[95] Not only did these disputes of 1232–4 find a place in *Bracton's Note Book* but, as Brian Tierney long ago pointed out, the idea that the king, or any other ruler acting with counsel, exercised an authority superior to that of the ruler acting alone, was widespread for many years before 1234, not least among glosses to the *Decretum*.[96] By such means, a Pope acting in council was considered a particularly powerful combination: a fact that should surely remind us of English involvement in attempts made first by Gregory IX in 1240, and thereafter by Innocent IV in 1244–5, to summon councils in which it was intended that Emperor Frederick II be deposed. The Council of 1245, indeed, witnessed the deposition not only of Frederick II but of the king of Portugal, judged to be incapable of rule.[97]

The Law of Obligations: Roman Foundations of the Civilian Tradition (Oxford: Oxford Clarendon Press, 1996), 451–65.

93 Both in the same passage of the 'De Instructione', in Brewer, *Giraldi Cambrensis Opera*, 8:32, the second truncated in the Victorian edition, as drawn to my attention by Robert Bartlett.

94 Seneca, *De Clementia*, 1.24.2; see also Gerald, 'Topographica Hibernica', iii.48, in Brewer, *Giraldi Cambrensis Opera*, 5:191, and Gerald, 'Retractiones', in ibid., 1:427, where, late in life, and attempting to be fairer to Archbishop Hubert Walter, Gerald refers to him as 'principis frenum et tyrannidis obstaculum'.

95 N. Vincent, *Peter des Roches: An Alien in English Politics, 1205–1238* (Cambridge: Cambridge University Press, 1996), esp. 312, 334–7, 464; see also D. A. Carpenter, *The Reign of Henry III* (London: Hambledon Press, 1996), 39–40.

96 Tierney, 'Bracton on Government', 310–17. For notice of the King's disseisins 'per voluntatem' that had first provoked the crisis of 1232–4, see Richardson, *Bracton*, 33–4, citing Maitland, *Bracton's Note Book*, 2:664–7 no. 857, 3:126–8 no. 1108. For further echoes of the chief test case of 1232–4, involving the Wiltshire manor of Upavon, see Woodbine and Thorne, *Bracton*, 2:337 (obligation to respect counsel), 358 (outlawry), 3:43 (restraint), as drawn to my attention by David Carpenter.

97 E. M. Peters, '"Rex Inutilis": Sancho II of Portugal and Thirteenth-Century Deposition Theory', *Studia Gratiana* 14 (1967): 255–305.

LEGITIMACY AND INHERITANCE

If we were looking for further historical conjunctions, it would be worth remarking an exchange of letters between Henry of Bratton's patron, William de Raleigh, and the Bishop of Lincoln, Robert Grosseteste, generally dated to 1235. The issue at stake here was the Church's ability to legitimise bastards by marrying the parents of children born outside wedlock. According to canon law, the offspring of such marriages were henceforth legitimate and entitled to inherit their parents' property. According to English law, they remained without rights of inheritance. *Bracton* first expresses the canon law position, citing Raymond of Peñafort's *Summa de Casibus* quoted from *Liber Extra* (1234), but then gives exceptions to demonstrate English departure from the canonical tradition.[98] In his letters to Raleigh, using an impassioned series of scriptural quotation, Grosseteste argued the case for the Church. To judge from a subsequent letter, Raleigh poured scorn on the bishop's attempt to argue points of law using theology and the Bible, instead citing an otherwise unrecorded opinion of Henry II's justiciar, Richard de Lucy (d. 1179), that marriage by no means legitimised offspring born outside wedlock. Certainly it was English custom rather than canon law that subsequently found acceptance in the provisions issued at the Council of Merton, in January 1236.[99] *Bracton*, with its mixture of theology and jurisprudence, occupies a position midway between Raleigh and Grosseteste. This balancing act was accomplished only at the cost of awkwardness and self-contradiction.

LAW AND DOCTRINE

Whatever else it may have achieved, the post-war discussion of *Bracton*'s political theory has undoubtedly reconciled the Bractonian thought world to that of the theologians. As revealed more generally over the past sixty years, kings, barons and bishops of the thirteenth century had ideas as well as policies, an intellectual hinterland as well as immediate needs or

98 Woodbine and Thorne, *Bracton*, 2:185–6; see also Richardson, *Bracton*, 96–101.

99 Luard, *Grosseteste epistolae*, 76–97, nos. 23–4 (trans. in Mantello and Goering, *Letters of Robert Grosseteste*, 108–25, nos. 23–4). For the provisions of Merton more widely, see F. M. Powicke and C. R. Cheney, eds., *Councils and Synods with Other Documents Relating to the English Church II 1205–1313*, 2 vols. (Oxford: Clarendon Press, 1964), 1:198–201; R. W. Southern, *Robert Grosseteste: The Growth of an English Mind in Medieval Europe* (Oxford: Clarendon Press, 1986), 252–7. The provisions of 1236 are set out at length in Woodbine and Thorne, *Bracton*, 4:294–300. Richard de Lucy was perhaps cited from a lost annotated copy of *Glanvill* similar to those in which authorities are occasionally cited in the margins: see Hall, *Glanvill*, xliv–xlvii, 78n.

grievances.[100] Moreover, as Richard Helmholz has shown, *ius commune* continued to echo in the thinking of English common lawyers long after the common law had in theory become divorced from its continental equivalents.[101] To cite just one instance, William de Raleigh's statutes for the Diocese of Winchester (1247) answered a particular query over the status of mortuary offerings that had long troubled canonists and common lawyers.[102] Raleigh's election to Winchester provoked litigation before the royal and papal courts in which the great canonist Henry of Susa ('Hostiensis') involved himself in English affairs.[103] Set in the context of Langton, of the canonists or of Grosseteste's arguments with Raleigh, *Bracton* once again appears a text entirely appropriate to the 1230s or 1240s, redolent of a time when lawyerly debate was still infused with the language of Scripture and when attempts could still be made to systematise the common law using the methods of Constantinople, Bologna or Rome.

Samuel Thorne, in revising and translating Woodbine's edition, himself arrived at very similar conclusions, albeit from deductions made according to law rather than context. Maitland, and later Richardson, had argued that the text of *Bracton* as received in the Middle Ages was not corrupt, as Kantorowicz and Schulz suggested, but pretty much as Bratton had left it, its confusions and errors testifying to Bratton's own lack of expertise in Roman law. On the contrary, Thorne now declared, the text was so contaminated with misreadings, both in its Roman and English parts, that it could not be translated without heavy correction to grammatical and jurisprudential sense.[104] While praising Woodbine's efforts to publish the text in its definitive albeit corrupted state, Thorne set about precisely the programme of restitution and textual amendment that Kantorowicz and Schulz had been urging since the 1930s.

Up to this point, Thorne appears to have believed that he was dealing with a text produced as a single work, by the man known as Henry of Bratton. By 1977, even this certainty had vanished. Instead, Thorne now argued, so much of the text referred to the 1220s and 1230s – indeed, so much of it would have been obsolete as a description of English law in the 1240s let alone the 1250s – that it had to be assumed to be the work of several hands: one or more

100 See, in particular, J. W. Baldwin, *Masters, Princes and Merchants*, 2 vols. (Princeton: Princeton University Press, 1970); B. Smalley, *The Becket Conflict and the Schools* (Oxford: Blackwell, 1973); P. Buc, *L'Ambiguité du livre: prince, pouvoir, et peuple dans les commentaires de la Bible au Moyen Age* (Paris: Beauchesne, 1994).

101 R. H. Helmholz, *The Ius Commune in England: Four Studies* (Oxford: Oxford University Press, 2001); see also idem, 'Magna Carta and the "Ius Commune"', *University of Chicago Law Review* 66 (1999): 297–371.

102 Helmholz, *Ius Commune in England*, 165–6. 103 Ibid., 31.

104 Woodbine and Thorne, *Bracton*, 2:v–vii, repeating the analogy with Manilius.

authors who first assembled the basic subject matter, and then one or more 'redactors', including Henry of Bratton, who attempted, later, but before 1257, to insert further precedents and to some extent to bring the work of their predecessors up to date.[105] In this process, not only was the original work so mangled that later copyists could produce the nonsense repeated in all subsequent copies, but parts of the original, at one time marked for deletion, were reinserted, perhaps as marginalia, perhaps on distinct slips of parchment. In this way, a large number of the passages that Maitland and others had assumed to be 'addiciones', incorporated within an older pre-existing text, were in fact not additions but 'restituciones', restoring passages that an editor had at first considered deleting. As a text, *Bracton* had not grown in size between the 1240s and 1260s. On the contrary, the text had originally shrunk, as parts were cut away, only to be reintroduced subsequently as marginal 'addiciones'. In this way, many of the 'addiciones', not least the 'addicio de cartis', previously assigned to the 1250s or 1260s were instead ripe for rediscovery as work of the 1230s or 1240s.[106]

Meanwhile, the association between *Bracton* and the Note Book began to fray. As Thorne demonstrated, the author of the treatise, although using many of the same cases found in the Note Book, cited them not from the Note Book copies but either from their original locations among the various plea rolls of Pattishall and Raleigh or from some other source, perhaps personal memory, independent of either the Note Book or the plea rolls. Not only was there a less than perfect match between Note Book and treatise (with the later rehearsing only 200 of the nearly 2,000 cases in the Note Book), but any attempt to explain why the additional 300 cases cited in the treatise did not also occur in the Note Book tended to devolve into nonsense and special pleading.[107]

Despite a rearguard action fought by John Barton, it is Thorne's arguments, now greatly strengthened by Paul Brand, that have won the day. Thanks to a technically challenging but nonetheless entirely convincing discussion of the form of writs and actions reported in *Bracton*, Brand has demonstrated that large parts of the treatise, although good law in the 1230s, would have been to a large extent obsolete twenty years later. Thorne had already shown that *Bracton*'s account of the 1236 provisions of Merton read like a series of afterthoughts, introduced to a text substantially completed. Brand has extended this to show

105 Ibid., 3:xiii–xxxiii.

106 Ibid., 3:xliv–l, developing ideas first expressed by Thorne as early as 1941: S. Thorne, review of Woodbine, *Bracton*, in *Speculum* 16 (1941): 266, and see also idem, 'The Text of Bracton's "De Legibus Angliae"', in idem, *Essays in English Legal History* (London: Hambledon, 1985), 93–110, esp. 93–4, 93–7. See also the review of Woodbine and Thorne, *Bracton*, by Paul Hyams, *English Historical Review* 93 (1978): 864–6.

107 Woodbine and Thorne, *Bracton*, 3:xxxiv–xxxix.

that *Bracton*'s version of the 1236 provisions derived not from the provisions as officially published but from drafts of writs composed in the circle of William de Raleigh. Such access to drafts rather than to official copies not only re-emphasised the close association between *Bracton* and Raleigh, but helps to explain why the processes described in the treatise could at no point in time have corresponded precisely to law as practised in the king's courts.[108]

CONCLUDING REFLECTIONS

Where does this leave us? We might appeal here to *Bracton* itself, writing on the Roman law of 'confusio'. With his Roman training, the author knew that there comes a time when certain things are so intermixed that they cease to represent the property of two or more individuals but instead combine into a new substance. *Bracton*, following Azo, applied this to such materials as honey and wine, iron and lead, distinguishing their fusion from a simple mixture of parts, say of grain or sheep, that might still be assigned as the property of two or more owners.[109] We might just as easily apply this same law to the attribution of authorship of a book in which one writer's words have become indistinguishably overlaid with those of another. The way in which *Bracton* itself adapts the words of earlier writers represents an inherent tendency towards combination, or what the *prooemium* to the *Institutes* refers to as *consonantia* ('harmonisation'), inherent in *Bracton*'s wholesale adoption of the words and organisational principles of the *Institutes* or Azo of Bologna.

How, then, was *Bracton* written? There now seems little doubt that the bulk of it was composed before 1245, probably before 1240. It may first have emerged as a series of tractates on various aspects of the law, some written as early as the 1220s, by Pattishall or by Raleigh as Pattishall's clerk. There are alternative possibilities. It might still be accepted as a through-composed work of the 1230s or early 1240s by Henry of Bratton working under Raleigh's guidance and from Raleigh's rolls. Perhaps it was begun by Pattishall, continued by Raleigh and then passed on for revision by Bratton through to the 1250s. In all of this, we should nonetheless notice its resonance (*consonantia*, indeed) with the tradition of politico-theological exegesis championed by Stephen Langton and his pupils. One of the ambitions of the exegetes had been to supply the community of the faithful with a Deuteronomy: a book of written laws to which the king and his justices could be held accountable.[110] *Bracton* provided just such a text. Certainly, it

108 Brand, 'Date and Authorship of "Bracton"', 217–44, esp. 219–23.
109 Woodbine and Thorne, *Bracton*, 2:47; see also Kantorowicz, *Bractonian Problems*, 119–21.
110 D. d'Avray, 'Magna Carta: Its Background in Stephen Langton's Academic Biblical Exegesis and Its Episcopal Reception', *Studi Medievali* 3rd series 38, part 1 (1997): 423–38.

bears a closer resemblance to the modern Deuteronomies imagined by Langton than any of its immediate predecessors, such as *Glanvill* or the various registers of writs establishing due process but with no real exploration of underlying causes. To this extent, *Bracton* was precisely the sort of text that might have appealed to Raleigh and his circle, heirs to the turmoil of English politics both during the civil war of King John's reign and again in 1232–4, serving the king, convinced of the majesty of kingship and of the king's sovereign right to rule, yet aware that the person, as opposed to the office of kingship, was in need of guidance from both clerical and baronial counsellors, themselves properly instructed in the mysteries of the law.

Similar thoughts continued to circulate throughout the period of political crisis after 1258. They can be found reflected in the pro-Montfortian *Song of Lewes* (c. 1264), with its insistence that the king take counsel with his greater men and that the king must be ruled by the laws that he himself decrees, since 'He cannot rule who fails to serve the law.'[111] They appear in the commentary on Deuteronomy by the Oxford Franciscan Thomas Docking (d. 1270). Here an older tradition of the king's obligation to take counsel with the priesthood rubs shoulders with more radical ideas, not just on the obligation for law to be administered by due process, but that, *in extremis*, men of God were entitled to seize power in the interests of their fellow subjects.[112] Without fully coalescing into a political 'philosophy', such thoughts continued to circulate throughout the fourteenth century. *Bracton*, with its remarks on God, kingship and the law, had some role to play here. Certainly, it was mined by the authors of later legal treatises, most notably by 'Britton', which enjoyed a popularity almost equal to that of its progenitor.[113] Even thereafter, *Bracton* was not entirely forgotten. It can be found cited occasionally in early Tudor readings in the Inns of Court, especially with relation to criminal law.[114] Together with Magna Carta, it then enjoyed an apotheosis under Sir Edward Coke. Ignoring its Roman elements, Coke referred to *Bracton* as yet another proof of the 'Ancient Constitution': a fantasy very largely of Coke's invention, intended to preserve the English common law against the threat of Stuart absolutism.[115]

111 C. L. Kingsford, ed., *The Song of Lewes* (Oxford: Clarendon Press, 1890), esp. 15, lines 443–60; 25–7, lines 759–826.

112 F. Lachaud, 'Autour des sources de la pensée politique dans l'Angleterre médiévale (XIIIe–début du XIVe siècle): la contribution de Thomas Docking, William de Pagula et Roger de Waltham à la réflexion sur les pouvoirs', *Journal des Savants* (2015), 29–45.

113 Plucknett, *Concise History*, 265–6.

114 S. Tullis, '"Glanvill" after Glanvill', in S. Jenks, J. Rose and C. Whittick, eds., *Laws, Lawyers and Texts: Studies in Medieval Legal History in Honour of Paul Brand* (Leiden: Brill, 2012), 330–1.

115 D. E. C. Yale, '"Of No Mean Authority": Some Later Uses of Bracton', in M. S. Arnold et al., eds., *On the Laws and Customs of England: Essays in Honor of Samuel E. Thorne* (Chapel Hill: University of North Carolina Press, 1981), 383–96.

To those of the seventeenth century, including John Milton, in search of precedents for the binding of a tyrant king, *Bracton* seemed to supply constitutional justifications for rebellion. It was in such circumstances that the 'addicio de cartis', originally framed in response to the crisis over royal warrants in 1234, came to be cited by John Bradshaw, presiding at the state trial of Charles I.[116] Like Magna Carta, *Bracton* then crossed the Atlantic, exported to the American colonies as part of the birth-right of all free-born Englishmen. Interpreted as a text insisting that kings be subjected to law, it was cited in *Marbury v. Madison* (1803), a crucial case in establishing the principal of judicial review. As an authority demanding rule under God and the law, *Bracton* was still an aspect of American political discourse as recently as the Watergate prosecutions of the mid-1970s.[117]

To this extent, we can perhaps at last begin to reconcile Henry of Bratton the man with the treatise *Bracton* that travels under his name. Maitland and his predecessors saw no difficulty in such reconciliation. By means entirely foreign to Victorian understanding, we have been shown in the twentieth century that the difficulties are in fact immense and can be resolved only by a fully European understanding of English law. The final word here should be left to the two scholars who between them did most to revolutionise understanding of *Bracton* in the century since Maitland. The first, the American Samuel Thorne, describes *Bracton* as deserving a 'place in the mainstream of European development: the last English law book of which that can be said'.[118] The second, the German-Jewish exile Hermann Kantorowicz, expressed the same thought in rather more elaborate terms, in 1941, at a time when many Europeans were obliged to reconsider their own ideas both of legality and of national allegiance:

> The chief superiority of the Civil law over the various national systems was that it had become a subject of scientific research through the work of the glossators, and thereby a treasure house in which the solution of almost any legal problem could be found ready made for all who might care to enter. In England alone the legal profession had become equipped with the methods, terms, concepts, and classifications, distinctions and maxims necessary for the rational elaboration and application of their national law. If [*Bracton*] the first great book on English law had contained less Civil law, the later books would have contained much more, and the fate of England's law might have been similar to that of England's language. Rome was again defeated by men trained in Roman arts and arms.[119]

116 Richardson, *Bracton*, 31; C. J. Nederman, *Lineages of European Political Thought: Explorations Along the Medieval/Modern Divide from John of Salisbury to Hegel* (Washington, DC: Catholic University of America Press, 2009), ch. 7, esp. 315–16 for Milton.
117 Gaines Post Jr., *Memoirs of a Cold War Son* (Iowa City: University of Iowa Press, 2000), 181–2.
118 Thorne, *Essays in English Legal History*, 78.
119 Kantorowicz, *Bractonian Problems*, 126–7.

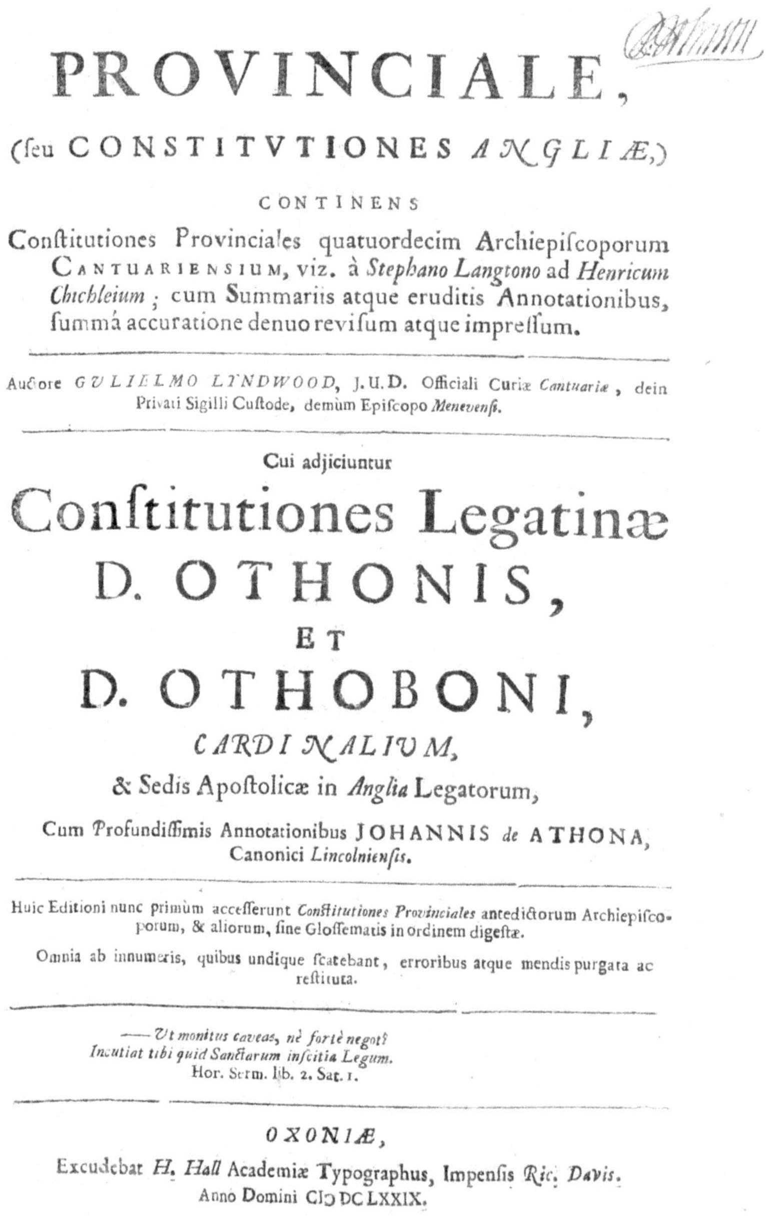

PROVINCIALE,

(seu CONSTITVTIONES *ANGLIÆ*,)

CONTINENS

Constitutiones Provinciales quatuordecim Archiepiscoporum CANTUARIENSIUM, viz. à *Stephano Langtono* ad *Henricum Chichleium*; cum Summariis atque eruditis Annotationibus, summâ accuratione denuo revisum atque impressum.

Auctore *GULIELMO LYNDWOOD*, J.U.D. Officiali Curiæ *Cantuariæ*, dein Privati Sigilli Custode, demùm Episcopo *Menevensi*.

Cui adjiciuntur

Constitutiones Legatinæ D. OTHONIS, ET D. OTHOBONI,

CARDINALIUM,

& Sedis Apostolicæ in *Anglia* Legatorum,

Cum Profundissimis Annotationibus JOHANNIS *de* ATHONA, Canonici *Lincolniensis*.

Huic Editioni nunc primùm accesserunt *Constitutiones Provinciales* antedictorum Archiepiscoporum, & aliorum, sine Glossematis in ordinem digestæ.

Omnia ab innumeris, quibus undique scatebant, erroribus atque mendis purgata ac restituta.

——*Ut monitus caveas, nè fortè negoti*
Incutiat tibi quid Sanctarum inscitia Legum.
Hor. Serm. lib. 2. Sat. 1.

OXONIÆ,

Excudebat *H. Hall* Academiæ Typographus, Impensis *Ric. Davis*.
Anno Domini CIↃ DC LXXIX.

William Lyndwood, *Provinciale (seu Constitutiones Angliae)*, courtesy of Special Collections, The University of Iowa Law Library

3

William Lyndwood

R. H. Helmholz

INTRODUCTION

By most estimates, William Lyndwood was medieval England's leading canonist. With very few exceptions, however, acknowledgement of his pre-eminence in this field has not been matched by exploration of the contents of his famous work, the *Provinciale (seu Constitutiones Angliae)*. A partial explanation for the imbalance is that historians of the canon law have long been thin on the ground in English academic circles. Until Brian Ferme undertook an examination of Lyndwood's contributions to the law of last wills and testaments in the 1990s,[1] study of this eminent ecclesiastical lawyer's contributions to canonistic scholarship had a been 'no go' zone in modern scholarship.

Walter Ullmann, one of the most knowledgeable students of the subject among historians active during the second half of the twentieth century, did once call attention to this gap. Born in Austria in 1910, Ullmann came to England soon after the *Anschluss* of 1938. He settled in his adoptive land and, after having held a number of minor academic posts, became professor of history and fellow of Trinity College in Cambridge. He died in 1983, having written many books and taught many future historians. Trained as a lawyer in his native land, Ullmann lost his taste for the law's intricacies in favour of a slightly schematic interest in political theory, using the works of medieval jurists primarily to describe large trends in that subject's history. All along, he nonetheless retained a thorough familiarity with the canon law itself, and it is significant that in a general treatment of its history – one he must have been commissioned to write – he expressed the view that the *Provinciale* contains

[1] See Brian Ferme, *Canon Law in Late Medieval England: A Study of William Lyndwood's Provinciale with Particular Reference to Testamentary Law* (Rome: LAS, 1996).

'plenty of unquarried material ... that needs detailed exploration'.[2] Ullmann himself went no further with the subject, either in that book or in what he wrote after it had appeared, but in my opinion, he was entirely right to speak of the worth of material to be uncovered in Lyndwood's great work. What follows is one such an attempt. It is meant to show that perusal of the *Provinciale* helps deepen our understanding of the work of a Christian jurist in England during the last century of the Middle Ages.

LYNDWOOD'S LIFE AND CAREER

Like the majority of even the most successful men within the ranks of the medieval clergy, the early years of William Lyndwood's life are traceable only in outline.[3] We know that he was born in Linwood, a village near Market Rasen in Lincolnshire, probably near the start of the last quarter of the fourteenth century. His father, John Lyndwood (d. 1419), was an active and successful wool merchant. About Alice, his mother, virtually nothing is known but her name, and this is also true of Lindwood's own siblings. A monumental brass in the Linwood parish church depicts the family together, but its value as anything more than an indication of the fame of William is doubtful. The brass depicts him as a child, but already dressed in the robes of a Doctor of Law.

The first step in Lyndwood's education we can be sure about was his matriculation as a commoner at Gonville Hall, Cambridge. An inscription beside a window in the old library of Gonville and Caius College enjoined viewers to offer prayers on his behalf. However, he seems to have left no other enduring mark there, and only the outlines of his subsequent academic career are visible. He is reported to have become a fellow at Pembroke College, Oxford. At some point during these early years he moved there from Cambridge. Fuller's *Worthies* records that he 'proceeded doctor of laws (probably rather by incorporation than constant education' at the older university.[4] He was BCL by 1403 and DCnL and DCL by 1407. Lyndwood himself referred to his having lectured in Oxford on the canon law. He also

2 Walter Ullmann, *Law and Politics in the Middle Ages: An Introduction to the Sources of Medieval Political Ideas* (Ithaca, NY: Cornell University Press, 1975), 175.

3 The fullest account of his career is A. Compton Reeves, 'The Careers of William Lyndwood', in J. S. Hamilton and Patricia Bradley, eds., *Documenting the Past: Essays in Medieval History Presented to George Peddy Cuttino* (Woodbridge: Boydell, 1989), 197–216. The best guide to the textual history of the *Provinciale* is C. R. Cheney, 'William Lyndwood's *Provinciale*', *The Jurist* 21 (1961): 405–34, reprinted in his *Medieval Texts and Studies* (Oxford: Oxford University Press, 1973), 158–84.

4 Thomas Fuller, *History of the Worthies of England*, ed. John Freeman (London: s.n., 1952), 332.

took holy orders at about the same time; he was made deacon on 15 February 1404 and priest on 12 March 1407.

Only a little more than a year after Lyndwood's receipt of his final degree, he was commissioned to serve as official (judge) of the consistory court at Salisbury. In itself this rapid appointment was not an unusual event. There were many such offices in English dioceses; they were often in need of the talents of graduates in law, and recent graduates were frequently appointed to act as judges within them. In Lyndwood's case, this initial appointment was merely the first step in a judicial career that led remarkably quickly to the highest judicial offices in the English Church. In 1414 Archbishop Henry Chichele, whom Lyndwood had known at Oxford and who was later the dedicatee of the *Provinciale*, nominated him as chancellor and auditor of causes in his own court of audience. Three years later Lyndwood became the official principal or Dean of the Court of Arches in London. Court documents issued in his name have been preserved in contemporary formularies. The position was no sinecure.

Besides handling the ecclesiastical litigation routinely dealt with in these courts, he was delegated from time to time to judge a number of maritime cases, and he also took part in some of the prosecutions of Lollards that occurred during these years. Lyndwood served as prolocutor for the lower clergy at provincial convocations in 1419, 1421, 1424, 1425 and 1426, and in January 1431 he acted in the place of an indisposed Archbishop John Kemp of York, delivering a sermon devoted to the blessings of unity within the realm at the opening of Parliament. He enjoyed the full confidence of his archbishop, Henry Chichele, and the great variety of administrative tasks he was called upon to perform followed from that trust.[5]

Such an administrative and judicial career was not then thought incompatible with the accumulation of ecclesiastical benefices, at least if obtained with the necessary dispensations, and Lyndwood held a considerable number of them over the course of his life. In a purely economic sense, they were the base of his career, providing him with a stream of income without requiring performance of the duties associated with the cure of souls. The first recorded benefice came to him even before he had been ordained deacon. On 30 November 1396, through royal patronage he was preferred to the wardenship of St Nicholas' Hospital, Scarborough. To this benefice, he added the wardenship of St Mary's Chapel in Scarborough Castle on 25 January 1399. In November 1403 he became Rector of Walton on the Wolds, Leicestershire. He had surrendered this rectory by March 1410, when

[5] See E. F. Jacob, *Archbishop Henry Chichele* (London: Nelson, 1967), 26–7, 110.

he was collated to the benefice of Winfrith Newburgh, Dorset, a benefice he later surrendered in exchange for the parish of St Mary in Romney Marsh, Kent. In September of 1411 he had received a papal dispensation allowing him to hold an additional incompatible benefice with or without cure of souls for seven years, a dispensation that was made perpetual in 1421. Following this grant, he became Rector of Shoreham in Kent with the dependent chapel of Otford in October 1415 (vacated by August 1425), Rector of All Hallows, Bread Street, London (vacant by August 1433 when he became Rector of Wimbledon), and in 1424 Rector of Tring in Hertfordshire (occupied until he became a bishop), a parish he remembered with the gift of a book in his will. In addition to these benefices, Lyndwood held prebends in what now seems an astonishing number of England's cathedral churches: Exeter, where he was canon and prebendary from 1419 to 1442; Hereford, where after a dispute with Thomas Berkeley in the 1420s he occupied the prebend of Hunderton until 1442; Lincoln, where he was archdeacon of Stow between 1434 and 1442; St David's, where he was canon and prebendary of Llanwrthwl from 1421 to 1442; Salisbury, where he held the prebend of Ruscombe Southbury from 1412 to 1424 and that of Bishopstone from 1424 to 1434; and Bath and Wells, where he was prebendary of Taunton from 1419 until 1433.

As was true for many prominent civilians, Lyndwood's talents also found an outlet in diplomacy and other service to the Crown. In July of 1417 he accompanied Henry Ware, Keeper of the Privy Seal, to Calais to negotiate the extension of the truce with the duke of Burgundy. In 1422 he was sent to Portugal to help negotiate a treaty with that land, and in the following year he accompanied John Kemp on a diplomatic mission in France. In 1431 he was chosen to be a member of the retinue that attended the coronation of Henry VI as King of France on 16 December; when he returned to England early the following year, he was appointed Keeper of the Privy Seal. Then a kind of secretariat to the King's Council, the Office of the Privy Seal allowed Lyndwood to assume a leading role in diplomatic efforts. He was involved, for example, in the negotiations that led up to the congress of Arras in 1435, and he was also active in the formulation of several agreements with the Hanseatic League and other German interests. He helped negotiate commercial treaties in the Low Countries, and in 1438 he acted to secure a truce with the Scots.

Despite these responsibilities in temporal affairs, Lyndwood did not neglect his duties as an ecclesiastic. Besides the continuing and active part he took in convocation, he was called upon to give articulate voice to English interests at the Council of Basel (1431–2). He played a part in the foundation of Eton College and was also appointed one of the commissioners responsible for drafting the statutes of King's College, Cambridge. Finally, and rather late in life for so prominent an ecclesiastic, he was given the Welsh bishopric of St David's after the death of Thomas Rodeburne in 1442. Provided to the see by the pope on 27 June, he received the temporalities on 14 August and was consecrated on 26 August. Lyndwood held the see until his death, which occurred towards the end of October of 1446. His will was proved a month later, and his body was buried in St Stephen's Chapel in the palace of Westminster, following the desires expressed in the will. The later history of the burial spot is uncertain, but in 1852 a body with a crosier thought to be Lyndwood's was discovered in the crypt. The body was then reinterred in Westminster Abbey in the north wall of the north cloister, a short distance from the east entrance door. The black marble ledger, under which it rests, is unfortunately now invisible because of construction carried out at a later date around the cloister door.

LYNDWOOD'S REPUTATION AS A LAWYER

Lyndwood's reputation among lawyers can most accurately be described by surveying how his work was regarded by his successors in both the English temporal and spiritual laws. Any such evaluation must begin by surveying the attention paid to and uses made of the *Provinciale* in later cases and legal treatises. By that standard, he passes any tests of contemporary importance or continuing relevance with flying colours.

Legal Authority of the Provinciale

In the English ecclesiastical courts, Lyndwood's glosses to the provincial constitutions long remained one of the most widely recognised authorities on the ecclesiastical law. This was true at the time he wrote and, because the medieval canon law did not disappear from the courts of the Church with the coming of the Reformation, it continued long afterwards. Although the Church's law was subject to modification by parliamentary statute and in the end also by the common law's writs of prohibition, the system Lyndwood described in his glosses continued to be followed in most of its particulars. The basic law of procedure and proof remained much the same, and Lyndwood's treatise informed practice in that area even into the nineteenth century.[6] The *Provinciale* was used more widely in court decisions too. It served, for example, to prove that the sacrament of baptism, once

6 See e.g. *Titchmarsh v. Chapman* (Arches 1844), 3 Curt. 840, 863.

administered under its canonical form, was under no circumstances to be repeated.[7] It was also invoked to justify treating the customary payment made to a parson on the occasion of a marriage as a purely voluntary offering, rather than an unlawful sinful reimbursement for spiritual services.[8] Centuries after his death Lyndwood was still being described as one of only two who were the 'ancientest and the best of our canonists'.[9] He was 'a most learned and sound expositor of the law' of the English Church.[10] In litigation, the *Provinciale* continued to be a widely recognised authority on English ecclesiastical law for centuries after its compilation.

Authors of treatises that analysed English ecclesiastical law after the Reformation were just as likely to base their conclusions on Lyndwood's glosses as were judges and lawyers in framing decisions and arguments for their clients. His opinions were relevant in defences of the scope of ecclesiastical jurisdiction over the laity.[11] They provided both rules of law and theoretical justification for the English Church's law of last wills and testaments.[12] They gave essential guidance for understanding the Church's complex procedural law.[13] They mattered for financial matters such as the law of tithes and enjoyment of ecclesiastical revenue. For English civilians who wrote about the subject of their own work, Lyndwood stated the relevant law. The *Provinciale* even served the purposes of controversialists who wished to rid England of its separate ecclesiastical jurisdiction.[14]

Recognition of Lyndwood as an authority on the Church's law was also not limited to the civilians. The *Provinciale* was long looked to and treated with respect by English common lawyers. Of course, that respect did not necessarily mean treating the conclusions found in it as 'binding precedent' in the modern sense. Indeed, the common lawyers in later centuries rejected outright some of the conclusions Lyndwood reached, treating them as outdated or worse. But that rejection would have been close to opinions held by common

7 *Kemp v. Wickes* (Arches 1809), 3 Phill. Ecc. 264, 280.

8 *Patten v. Castleman* (Arches 1753), 1 Lee 387, 393.

9 *Miller v. Bloomfield* (Delegates 1823), 1 Add. 499, 516.

10 *Mastin v. Escott* (Arches 1841), 2 Curt. 692, 734.

11 Richard Cosin (d. 1597), *Apologie for Sundrie Proceedings by Iurisdiction Ecclesiastical* (London, 1593), pt. I, ch. 10.

12 Henry Swinburne (d. 1624), *Brief Treatise of Testaments and Last Wills* (London, 1590), pt. VI, pt. 2. See also John Goldolphin (d. 1678), *Orphan's Legacy or A Testamentary Abridgment* (London, 1701), pt. I, ch. 10, no. 2 (on the ability of married women to bequeath their property by will).

13 Henry Conset, *Practice of the Spiritual or Ecclesiastical Courts* (London, 1685), pt. V, s. 2, no. 5.

14 See Edmund Hickeringill, *The Test or Trial of the Goodness and Value of Spiritual Courts in Two Queries* (London, 1683), pt. I, c. 9, citing the *Provinciale*, 23, v. *Nullus*, and objecting on legal grounds to the fees customarily paid for ecclesiastical services.

lawyers active at the time when Lyndwood himself wrote, and it was a disagreement members of both professions somehow lived with. It should not obscure the many areas of agreement. In both periods, the law of the Church remained relevant, even in the royal courts, and the clear exposition found in Lyndwood's *Provinciale* made it a natural choice for understanding and interpreting the laws of the English Church.

The law of last wills and testaments provides the best example of the work's continuing value. Primary jurisdiction over succession to personal property rested in the hands of the English Church at the time when Lyndwood described it, and much of it remained there until the late nineteenth century. The extent of that jurisdiction was always subject to customary exceptions, periodic obstruction by common lawyers and poaching by the Court of Chancery, but the law administered in the spiritual tribunals remained the starting point and the basic legal guide. Lyndwood's great work was often used in the secular courts to describe and interpret testamentary law.[15] Outside that corner of law, common lawyers also cited the *Provinciale* to describe many customary practices that had hardened into law and were accepted by their own courts.[16] For instance, many rules relevant to the basic law of tithes – important through the nineteenth century and still of occasional use today – were also taken from the *Provinciale* by English common lawyers.[17]

The dates of publication of Lyndwood's great work support the story of its continuing relevance that is apparent in later case law. The *Provinciale* was quickly and frequently printed in England once printing became an option. Sir John Baker's treatment of Lyndwood in *Monuments of Endlesse Labours* (1998) establishes that it appeared in print only two years after the first common law treatise, Littleton's *Tenures*, was printed in 1481. This canonical experiment proved to be a success (as did Littleton's), and other editions of both works soon followed in profusion. Sweet and Maxwell's *Legal Bibliography of the British Commonwealth* (1955) lists twenty different printings of Lyndwood's work between 1483 and 1589, some of them from continental presses. The standard edition of the *Provinciale* was the text printed in Oxford in 1679 together with John of Atho's *Constitutiones legatinae*.[18] Its use became so automatic that for the sake of convenience, its

15 E.g. *Marriot v. Marriot* (Exch 1725), 1 Str. 666, 669–70.

16 E.g. *Rex v. Ragsden* (KB 1734), Cunn. 54, 61.

17 E.g. *Barnard v. Garnons* (HL 1797), 7 Bro. P.C. 105, 113.

18 The authentic texts of the provincial constitutions glossed by Lyndwood are now collected in a modern edition: F. M. Powicke and C. R. Cheney, eds., *Councils & Synods with Other Documents Relating to the English Church II: A.D. 1205–1313* (Oxford: Clarendon, 1964) [hereafter *C&S*]. The earlier standard edition, covering a longer period and a larger area, was David Wilkins, ed., *Concilia Magnae Britanniae et Hiberniae* (London, 1737).

pagination have been retained and used as the point of reference in modern scholarship, including this chapter. Its date of publication ought also to be underlined. That a text written in the fifteenth century should have been considered worth printing more than two centuries later – after the Restoration of the monarchy and the re-establishment of ecclesiastical jurisdiction – is as worthy of note as is its modern usage by historians.

Today, at least a modicum of respect continues to be paid to Lyndwood by most scholars and writers. The 1679 text of the *Provinciale* was reprinted by a commercial press in 1968. Mark Hill's fundamental work on the contemporary law of the Church of England mentions his work as the standard resource for English canonists in its own time,[19] and the relevant Oxford survey includes at least a brief entry devoted to the work's place in English church history.[20] Few legal historians today doubt that the *Provinciale* is one of the best places to find answers to questions about the nature of ecclesiastical jurisdiction in medieval England, a subject that has enjoyed a certain renaissance of interest in recent years.

Nineteenth-Century Controversies and the Provinciale

Lyndwood's reputation as a lawyer is still affected today, however, by the character of the use that was made of his work in the late nineteenth-century controversy over the extent of papal authority in England during the Middle Ages: the so-called Stubbs–Maitland Dispute.[21] The position associated with William Stubbs (1825–1901), bishop of Oxford and a constitutional historian of high repute, was maintained in a *Report* to the Ecclesiastical Courts Commission (1883). Stubbs took the view that 'the canon law of Rome, though always regarded as of great authority in England, was not held to be binding on the courts'. In other words, his contention was that the English Church had maintained a degree of independence from papal control even during the Middle Ages when papal claims to control over the Christian world reached their height. The breach with Rome in the sixteenth century simply broadened an already existing gap. For this argument, the *Provinciale* seemed to offer some support. It covered national laws and provincial constitutions, not decisions taken by the papal court. It also dealt with several areas of the law where English practice diverged in significant ways from the law set forth in

19 M. Hill, *Ecclesiastical Law*, 3d ed. (Oxford: Oxford University Press, 2007), § 1.10.

20 *Oxford Dictionary of the Christian Church*, 3d ed. rev. (Oxford: Oxford University Press, 2005), 1018.

21 See Chapter 14 on Maitland in this volume.

the *Corpus iuris canonici*. Testamentary law was the obvious example. So, Stubbs concluded, in matters of law the Church of England had always had some degree of choice. It could go its own way.

F. W. Maitland (1825–1906), a contemporary of Stubbs, was Downing Professor of the Laws of England in Cambridge University. His name still commands instant respect among historians of the law. He took the directly opposite view. Indeed, he turned the example of Lyndwood's *Provinciale* against those who had used it to illustrate the freedom of the medieval English Church. In a series of articles published in the *Law Quarterly Review* and the *English Historical Review*, Maitland set out to prove that in the opinion of English canonists such as Lyndwood, papal decretals were not only to be regarded with respect. They were regarded as binding statute law. In an article entitled 'William Lyndwood', Maitland concluded melodramatically that, in his subject's own opinion, '[t]o dispute the authority of a decretal is to be guilty of heresy at a time when obstinate heresy is a capital crime'.[22] In other words, papal decretals bound the English Church prior to the Reformation. Lyndwood himself was an avowed and thorough-going papalist.

Maitland's witty and confident treatment won the day. Stubbs himself halfway recanted his earlier opinion, and it has only been in the last few years that a more balanced view has emerged from careful research. It has begun by recognising that some of the assumptions on which the argument rested were quite anachronistic. The controversies of the nineteenth century were not those of the fifteenth. Neither were many widely shared juridical assumptions identical. Recent research has more fully recognised the strength of custom in the medieval canon law, even in the face of specific papal decretals, and it has also established the early importance of goals in ecclesiastical jurisprudence other than the enforcement of papal sovereignty. Among them were avowedly religious aims such as the promotion of social harmony, the avoidance of scandal and the protection of the *salus animarum*. In legal practice, these goals might prevail over decretal law.

Research has also shown that the medieval canonists themselves did not treat papal decretals as binding in a sense that accorded with the tenets of Austinian jurisprudence. They had greater freedom. In particular, Lyndwood's position has been better understood by virtue of Brian Ferme's careful examination of his treatment of testamentary law.[23] Ferme showed that the commentator's object was to describe English practice correctly and

22 F. W. Maitland, *Roman Canon Law in the Church of England* (London: Methuen, 1898), 17.

23 See Ferme, *Canon Law*.

also 'wherever possible' to 'hold [it] consistent' with the *ius commune*.[24] Attempting to demonstrate that English testamentary practice was not out of step with the formal law did lead Lyndwood into some 'complex academic flourishes', as Ferme expressed it. Some of these flourishes bent the sense of papal decretals, but this technique was consistent with common canonical learning of its time. We return to this subject in the final section of this chapter, which attempts to assess the extent of religion's influence on Lyndwood's legal thought.

Ferme's vindication of Lyndwood's abilities as a medieval canonist does, however, raise a different question – an issue related directly to his reputation among scholars – that is, the neglect of his work in the continental literature devoted to the history of the European *ius commune*. Neither Lyndwood nor his *Provinciale* is mentioned in standard handbooks on the history of the canon law. His name is not found in the famous *De claris legum interpretibus* compiled by Guido Panziroli (d. 1599). Van Hove and von Schulte, authors of the basic modern manuals on the history of the law of the Church, do not mention him at all,[25] and even the comprehensive seventeenth-century bibliography published by Martin Lipen (d. 1692) limits its recognition of his work to a single entry under the heading 'English law'.[26]

The surprising picture of neglect brightens a bit today, probably because of works such as Ferme's and the firm place the *Provinciale* has come to occupy in English legal history. Understanding legal history today all but requires some knowledge of law that existed beyond one's own national boundaries, and a listing for the *Provinciale* appears in some of the general works on the *ius commune* written on the continent in recent years.[27] However, they are quite brief. What they contain comes to little more than a mention of Lyndwood's existence and a notation of the title and coverage of his great work. They say little about that work's contents or about its author's standing within the learned literature of European law.

Two explanations for this neglect present themselves. One is that the later medieval period has attracted much less attention among historians of the

24 Ibid., 142.

25 A. van Hove, *Prolegomena ad Codicem iuris canonici* (Mechlin: Dessain, 1945); J. Friedrich von Schulte, *Die Geschichte der Quellen und Literatur des canonischen Rechts* (Stuttgart: Enke, 1875).

26 Martin Lipenius, *Bibliotheca realis iuridica*, 2 vols. (Hildesheim: Olms, 1970–1), 1:58.

27 Knut Nörr, 'Die kanonistische Literatur', in Helmut Coing, ed., *Handbuch der Quellen und Literatur der neueren Europäischen Privatrechtsgeschichte, vol. 1 Mittlelalter (1100–1500)* (Munich: Beck, 1973), 382; Brigitte Basdevant-Gaudemet, *Histoire du droit canonique et des institutions de l'église latine: XVe–XXe siècle* (Paris: Economica, 2014), 601.

learned laws than has the period during which the Decretals were being written and collected – that is, the time before the appearance of the *Liber sextus* at the very end of the thirteenth century. Stephan Kuttner's renowned exploration of the medieval canonistic literature went no further forward,[28] and few have taken up the challenge of extending what he began further in time.[29] What came afterwards has thus come to seem somehow anti-climactic, a tired repetition of what had come before. That has become a common assumption. For instance, the chapter in a handbook on the subject devoted to the time period when Lyndwood wrote is entitled 'Decline'. The following chapter is called 'Mediocrity'.[30] Scholarly recognition of Lyndwood's importance has suffered by being associated with this characterisation of the years when he wrote.

The second explanation for neglect of Lyndwood's contribution is less obvious but more interesting. It is that the subject of his *Provinciale* had no established place within the accepted categories of treatises and commentaries on the medieval Roman and canon laws. The glossing it contains was, of course, the standard way in which the basic texts of the learned laws were interpreted. Lyndwood did not invent a new method. What may have been new on his part was to apply that method to a source that was not ordinarily subject to it. Providing a gloss for local statutes and diocesan decrees was not a common practice during the Middle Ages.[31] Probably for this reason, the leading French canonist of the last generation, Jean Gaudemet, had to conclude in his survey of the canon law's history that the workings of diocesan and provincial legislation in earlier centuries were '*mal connues*'.[32] They did not attract scholarly attention in earlier centuries, and that has had an effect on modern accounts of the literature of the canon law. It may have been for this reason that Professor Gaudemet found no occasion to mention Lyndwood at all; there was no obvious place to put him in the ordinary classification schemes covering the literature of the European *ius commune*.

28 Stephan Kuttner, *Repertorium der Kanonistik (1140–1234)* (Vatican City: Biblioteca Apostolica Vaticana, 1936).

29 See e.g. Wilfried Harmann and Kenneth Pennington, eds., *History of the Medieval Canon Law in the Classical Period, 1140–1234* (Washington, DC: Catholic University of America Press, 2008). Martin Bertram, *Kanonisten und ihre Texte (1234 bis Mitte 14. Jh.)* (Leiden and Boston, MA: Brill, 2013) has made a promising start in exploring developments during the later period.

30 J. A. Clarence Smith, *Medieval Law Teachers and Writers: Civilian and Canonist* (Ottawa: University of Ottawa Press, 1975), 83–114.

31 It was later attempted at least occasionally, e.g. Michael Pontich, *Constitutiones synodales dioecesis Gerundensis* (Gerona, 1691).

32 Jean Gaudemet, *Les Sources du droit canonique VIIIe–XXe siècle* (Paris: Les Editions du Cerf, 1993), 73.

In a way, this omission is surprising. Collections of *synodalia* were widely made throughout Europe in earlier centuries. They were useful and important. However the *Provinciale* did not fit neatly into that category. Collection of synodal statutes in Lyndwood's hands was a small part of what he intended; bringing this legislation together for the province of Canterbury was not the reason for his efforts. It was only the starting place. The true purpose (and value) of the *Provinciale* was to comment on the meaning of the constitutions, to clarify their relationship with the *ius commune* and to describe what they meant in practice within the English courts. It was much more than a collection of diocesan or provincial statutes. Any look at the work itself shows this. Throughout, the glosses dwarf the texts of the legislation. It was the glosses that counted. They were Lyndwood's real contribution.

The *Provinciale* thus did not fit very well within the ordinary classification schemes that were familiar then and that remain familiar today to historians of the canon law. Works such as Lyndwood's did not constitute one of the recognised categories of literature within the *ius commune. The Provinciale* was not a *Lectura* or a *Summa*. It was not an interpretive gloss on the texts of the various parts of the *Corpus iuris canonici*. It took the formal law for granted, citing its texts when appropriate but not commenting directly upon them. Nor is the *Provinciale* a monograph on a particular subject matter dealt with by the medieval canon law. Many such works were written – on marriage, on tithes, on testamentary succession and so forth. They find a place in modern manuals. But Lyndwood's work does not fit there. It is also not at all like the collections of *Consilia* or *Decisiones* that filled the shelves of sixteenth-century libraries, works that are just coming into their own in the work of legal historians. Both dealt with legal practice, but Lyndwood's text began with the texts, not with individual cases.

What the future holds for Lyndwood's reputation today we do not know. A sober prediction ought, I think, to depend in part on the extent to which the *Provinciale* makes a connection with current interests of scholars – among whom should be counted those who look with attention to the subject of the following section, the role within it played by the Christian religion.

CHRISTIANITY IN LYNDWOOD'S *PROVINCIALE*

What influence did spiritual concerns and other specifically religious influences have on Lyndwood? He was a clergyman and he became a bishop. It would not be surprising to discover that he was interested in religion. He suggested ways to encourage attendance at church,[33] and he interested himself in the minutiae of double feast days.[34] He shared the common clerical desire to stamp out religious dissent at all costs.[35] However, Lyndwood was also a lawyer and a lifelong administrator. He served both Church and Crown. Avowedly 'spiritual themes' usually fit awkwardly within the daily concerns of such men. That makes it sensible to inquire further – to ask what effect religion had on the content of his professional work. Happily, we can confront the question with more than guesses and generalisations. Concrete conclusions emerge from a consideration of four examples drawn from within the *Provinciale*.

Education of the Parochial Clergy

The first example comes from a famous enactment Lyndwood chose to include even though it did not fit naturally within the order of titles he took from the Gregorian Decretals. It was Archbishop Pecham's constitution known from its incipit as *Ignorantia sacerdotum*. A provincial statute meant to govern the clergy in the southern province of England, it was adopted as a remedial measure at the Council of Lambeth in 1281.[36] As its title suggested, it began by stating a source of special concern among the English bishops – clerical ignorance. In strong terms, the decree bewailed the low state of knowledge of theological matters among incumbents of English parish churches, and on the lamentable level of learning said to prevail, the archbishop's decree did not mince words. From its recital of the reasons compelling its enactment, one might suppose that the great majority among parochial incumbents knew nothing or little about the religious doctrine they were expected to understand and teach. Today, its lament seems hyperbolic. Moralists exaggerate. However, there must have been some truth in what the decree described. At the time, no special training in theology or canon law was required of candidates for ordination. Literacy was necessary, but requiring a university degree was out of the question. Some knowledge of the duties of a cleric, coupled with a good character, seems to have sufficed.

Ignorantia sacerdotum was meant to provide a partial remedy for the state of clerical ignorance that resulted from the absence of educational requirements. It went on to provide a summary of the rudiments of knowledge expected of

33 William Lyndwood, *Provinciale*, 238, s.v. *lectum Evangelium*.

34 Ibid., 103, s.v. *officio duplici*.

35 See Reeves, 'Careers of William Lyndwood', 203.

36 See C&S, 2: 900–5.

the parochial clergy, requiring them to acquire at least a working acquaintance with what they needed. They must, for instance, understand and communicate to their flock what was found in the Nicene Creed, the Ten Commandments, the seven deadly sins and the seven sacraments. They must know enough law and theology to hear and respond to the confessions of their parishioners.

Issuing such a decree was not an original idea. What it touched was not even a special English problem. Much of its content was in fact taken almost verbatim from a continental source – so much so that one twentieth-century commentator described it as 'a clumsy pastiche of a somewhat uninspired work'.[37] But no matter the modern reaction to its apparent lack of originality; in its time it was taken to be a vital constitution. It remained so for many decades afterwards. Lyndwood had a good deal of company among medieval contemporaries in his decision to take special note of it.

And take special note of it he did,[38] even though the constitution's impact on ordinary practice within the ecclesiastical courts was small. The most natural reading of the evidence is to take this as an indication of Lyndwood's own interest in spiritual matters. In his glosses on it, he raised and discussed matters which we would regard as purely theological in nature – predestination, for example, and the importance of prayer for salvation in addition to receipt of the sacraments. He often called upon 'proof texts' from the Bible for support, as was common among medieval canonists, and he also cited passages from the works of saints and theologians: Augustine of Hippo, Ambrose of Milan and Thomas Aquinas were the most familiar names. He even raised and discussed the perennial question of the comparative virtue of a purely contemplative life, though this could scarcely have been a required topic in outlining the need for learning among the clergy.

It would be a mistake to give the impression that Lyndwood's reading of *Ignorantia sacerdotum* turned out to be a spiritual meditation. It was a work of the Schools. It was written by a lawyer who had absorbed what the Schools taught. Accordingly it included the distinctions, the divisions and the learned citations that were common fare among medieval academics. In discussing the Church's prohibition on repeating the sacrament of baptism, for example, he recited the six reasons for the ban that were commonly given in the scholastic literature. Similarly, in glossing a provincial statute on sacramental confession, he discussed at length the nature of (and the exceptions from) the

[37] Decima Douie, *Archbishop Pecham* (Oxford: Clarendon Press, 1952), 135.
[38] See Lyndwood, *Provinciale*, 42–5.

requirement that it be made to one's parish priest.[39] This was a matter of legal as well as pastoral moment, and Lyndwood dealt with it appropriately.

In his choice and much of his discussion of *Ignorantia sacerdotum*, Lyndwood did nevertheless raise religious themes that were not necessarily required in a work of canon law. This was not an invariable rule for him, and the line between 'religious' and 'legal' concerns was not fixed in the fifteenth century. It is not fixed today. What we can say is that Lyndwood did raise spiritual themes even though they were not required by some of the texts he glossed. Sometimes he went beyond specific legal to theological subjects. Sometimes he did not. His viewpoint was wide enough to encompass both.

Duties of the Clergy

A second example illustrative of the role religion played in the treatise is Lyndwood's treatment of a constitution of the Council of Oxford (1222) referred to as *Statuimus*.[40] This enactment required several things of the English bishops. Most notably they were to provide almoners to help support the poor – part of their duty as pastors. They were also to observe the duties of hospitality, to do justice to those subject to them, to keep residence in their cathedrals at least during the Church's great festivals and to hear at least some confessions in person. Lyndwood placed his treatment of this constitution under the heading *De officio judicis ordinarii*, not in the title *De excessibus praelatorum*, where it would have been at least equally at home.

It is difficult to assign a reason for this, but its placement may have suited his own purposes. Its title described exactly some of the duties that bound Lyndwood in the courts of his archbishop. There, he was the *judex ordinarius*. He exercised the jurisdictional powers of the archbishop, and some (but not all) of what he wrote under this title seems rather like a discussion of the requirements that were important for that office, together with some further advice for all ecclesiastical administrators.

The extent of its coverage as Lyndwood understood it is immediately apparent in his gloss. Of course, he read the word 'prelates' in its text to mean bishops, but he added that it also covered those who were not bishops. Other clerics could appropriately be put within the category of 'prelates', at least for purposes of this provision. If they were left out, the purposes of the provision might fail in practice. In discussing the requirement that an almoner

39 Ibid., 331, s.v. *Sacerdos*. 40 *C&S*, 1: 108.

be appointed, for instance, he asserted that its true intent was to ensure that services to the poor were provided as widely as possible. The constitution required not simply that an official be named, it required that the term 'works of mercy' should extend to spiritual needs as well as physical needs. That was the true 'mind' *(mens statuentis)* of the provision.

In glossing the duties stated in this constitution, Lyndwood again gave the text a broad reading, one seemingly motivated by religious concern. It included a duty to provide a lawyer if one was needed, particularly if the person involved was a woman, a minor, a weak or mentally deficient person. In glossing the phrase *justitiam exhibendam*, he added that the judge's duty extended to doing right to the rich as well as to the poor, citing a biblical passage (Exod. 23:3) in support. He finished his coverage with a brief discussion of penitential practices. Efforts should be 'tailored to' the person subject to discipline – rich or poor, young or old, cleric or lay, and so forth. His coverage ended with an injunction to his readers to take notice of the discussion of the subject in the *Summa aurea* of Hostiensis,[41] an example of his consistent effort to bring provincial constitutions within the general law of the Church, but specifically religious concerns appeared in most of Lyndwood's gloss to it.

In interpreting this constitution, Lyndwood looked for specific things that could be brought within its words in the interests of religion. Statutes, he must have thought, ought to be interpreted in a sense that would bring spiritual benefits or at least promote the beneficial purposes of the Church's laws. That seems to have been the law's true goal, and in this thought, of course, he was not alone. The approach was consistent with traditional ways of thought among many of the jurists. Even so, it does not require a stretch of the imagination to describe his efforts in dealing with this constitution as 'spiritual in character'. He took a consistently wide view of what spiritual duties were included in its words, apparently because the purpose of the canon law included the protection of the weak.

Testamentary Jurisdiction in England

A third example – to which this chapter will devote particular attention because of its importance in understanding Lyndwood's approach to morality and law – is his treatment of important aspects of the law of charity as they related to the law of last wills and testaments. As Brian Ferme has shown, his

41 See Henricus de Segusio, *Summa aurea* (Venice, 1574, repr. 1965), Lib. V, tit. 38.

Provinciale offers an important perspective on the subject as it was understood at the time and as it affected practice in the English ecclesiastical courts. Lyndwood's coverage dealt with the provincial constitutions that authorised and controlled several aspects of the English Church's jurisdiction, including the law of testamentary succession. It also provided a natural 'home' for his discussion of the canon law of charity. The *Provinciale* contained no separate section for pious causes. Neither did the Decretals. However, Lyndwood dealt with the concept of pious causes at length in outlining the sources and nature of the English Church's testamentary jurisdiction.

The immediate problem for him was the following: the medieval canon law did not claim exclusive jurisdiction over last wills and testaments. Proof and enforcement of testaments belonged to the secular forum. The most ecclesiastical courts could claim under law found in the Decretals was a subsidiary jurisdiction over specifically charitable bequests. Where the temporal courts failed to act, the Church could step in to secure enforcement of charitable gifts and bequests. That was a bishop's special duty. In England, however, custom had established a different regime. Nothing depended upon failure by the secular authorities to protect charitable bequests. In the absence of special custom, the dividing line depended upon subject matter. Succession to real property was dealt with by secular courts; succession to goods and chattels was handled by the courts of the Church.[42] Charitable bequests were not treated as a special case, and ecclesiastical jurisdiction in England therefore seemed out of step with the general canon law.

Lyndwood sought to explain this system and to bring it into tolerable harmony with the Church's general law. One possibility open to him was to treat it simply as a matter of local custom. Custom could be a legitimate source of jurisdiction under the medieval canon law, although limits were put on its scope (X 1.4.11). Lyndwood did make this choice as one way of dealing with the problem raised by English jurisdictional practice. Citing the opinions of Hostiensis and well as other papal decretals, he asserted that the English system was based on a custom valid under existing canon law.[43] It did not, he held, directly contradict any canon or papal decretal. It did not violate natural or divine laws. Hence it passed the test of reasonability in addition to that met by its long observance in practice.

42 For an attempt to trace the obscure process by which this division of jurisdiction was reached, see M. M. Sheehan, *The Will in Medieval England* (Toronto: Pontifical Institute of Mediaeval Studies, 1963), 164–76.

43 Lyndwood, *Provinciale*, 174, s.v. *approbatis*.

However, Lyndwood was not content to leave it there. Perhaps he himself was dissatisfied with custom as a full justification for this deviation from the law found in the Decretals. He also sought to show that the English system came within the jurisdictional exception made within that law for episcopal responsibility to secure enforcement of charitable bequests.[44] He did so by invoking claims based upon the Christian religion. He sought to fit English practice within the canonical claim to allow the Church to intervene when a matter of piety was involved, and he did so by expanding the meaning of the words 'charitable' and 'pious'.

The terms 'charitable' and 'pious' were not self-defining. Obviously they included testamentary gifts to one's parish church, but in contemporary jurisprudence they were not necessarily limited to that purpose. In fact, they had no fixed meaning in the canonical texts, and it might even be said that a testamentary gift in favour of one's children could be described as 'pious' in the larger sense of the term. The law of nature recognised a parent's duty to support one's offspring as aligned with the fundamentals of any system of justice. Fulfilment of that duty might be regarded as a pious act. And if one's children, why not others? Was it not also a charitable act to secure performance of the last wishes of a dying man who had directed that his property pass in a certain way but had died before he could make certain that it happened? And was it not an equally pious act to see to it that his debts were paid so that the debtor could appear unspotted before the Final Judge?

An affirmative answer to questions such as these seemed plausible. So, at any rate, ran the argument Lyndwood made.[45] In support, he offered more than speculation. He offered citations to one Roman law text (Cod. 1.2.1), three papal decretals (X 3.24.2, X 3.24.6 and X 3.24.17), commentaries on the latter by Hostiensis and Innocent IV, and also one text from the *Liber sextus* (Sext 3.11.2). None of these citations provided unambiguous support for his argument, but they did count in its favour. They spoke, for example, of the work of a testamentary executor as a quasi-sacred duty. In the fashion of the day, they also provided grist for legal argument, raising the possibility of an understanding of the canons based upon their assumed intent. In this instance, they allowed Lyndwood to argue that the canon law's special solicitude for charitable bequests counted in support of the legitimacy of the English

44 See Brian Ferme, 'The Testamentary Executor in Lyndwood's *Provinciale*', *The Jurist* 49 (1989), 644, speaking of 'Lyndwood's reluctance to rely merely upon the authority of English custom' as a general trait running throughout his great work.

45 Lyndwood, *Provinciale*, 169, s.v. *residuis*.

Church's own testamentary jurisdiction. That jurisdiction might be supported as something more than a local custom. It might fall within the legitimate definition of the Church's duty to promote and secure pious bequests. This was a stretch, but it was not wholly out of line with what other canonists and civilians did with the texts at their disposal.

What of the law of charity itself? There was a potential danger in this expansive justification for ecclesiastical jurisdiction. If payment of debts owed by decedents could be thought of as falling under the rubric of pious causes, so could almost any lawful activity. Lyndwood's argument proved too much. Potentially, it might have opened the jurisdiction of the Church's tribunals to litigation well beyond a reasonable understanding of the clergy's proper role in society, not to speak of the jurisdictional rules of the English common law's writ of prohibition. It would have twisted the concept of charity out of shape, making it perform tasks for which it was ill suited. The definition of charity might then have been stretched to cover virtually every part of human life, allowing canon lawyers to claim jurisdiction in every situation where the Church's law sought to do what was right. Such a prospect and problem was not entirely unknown in other parts of the medieval canon law; for instance, the concept that the courts of the Church could take cognisance of any sort of human behaviour because it was sinful (X 2.11.13). Here the same danger existed: a claim potentially so extensive that it far overstepped widely accepted boundaries between temporal and ecclesiastical authority. It was a danger the medieval canonists themselves recognised. Perhaps it was prudent to leave the jurisdictional question to custom – which is what in fact happened in English law. When that jurisdiction was at last removed from the ecclesiastical courts, it could be treated as merely an adjustment to a customary practice.

From our perspective, however, the example shows how far the concept of religious influence on the law might extend in the hands of a canonist such as William Lyndwood. Was the argument here no more than the product of a lawyer's ingenuity? Or did he really think that Christian piety provided a proper basis for the English Church's testamentary jurisdiction? It is hard to be sure.

Jurisdiction over Contracts

A fourth example of the recognition of religion's place in Lyndwood's treatise, not dissimilar to the third, existed in what we would today call the law of contracts. In the fifteenth century, the subject became a matter of contention between the temporal and the ecclesiastical courts in England, and it is a measure of its importance at the time that Lyndwood discussed it more than once. He did so in glossing two provincial constitutions of the Council of Lambeth of 1261.[46] These constitutions asserted the jurisdictional claims of the Church in the strongest terms, objecting to the use of royal writs of prohibition to restrict their exercise and threatening users with excommunication. Writs of prohibition were employed by those cited to appear before an ecclesiastical tribunal in order to prevent ecclesiastical courts from proceeding. They forbade the hearing of cases common lawyers regarded as beyond the limits of ecclesiastical jurisdiction. The writs thus restricted the jurisdictional rights of the Church, and in the Lambeth constitutions the bishops sought to strike back. They threatened anyone who acted in violation of the Church's jurisdictional rights with excommunication, asserting that this result was required by Magna Carta itself. The Great Charter had recognised and protected the liberties of the English Church, as Lyndwood noted.[47] Aggressive use of writs of prohibition violated the charter's guarantee of freedom for the Church, the bishops argued, and in these constitutions they imposed excommunication on anyone who employed prohibitions to diminish the Church's sphere of freedom.

Lyndwood placed his gloss to these constitutions under two separate titles, both appropriate. The first is found under the title *De foro competente*, the second under the title *De poenis*.[48] In them he discussed in detail the matter of contention of the greatest moment – the enforcement of contracts accompanied by a pledge of faith. Large numbers of such cases were being brought before the English consistory courts at the time, and most of them involved quite ordinary obligations – a promise to pay a commercial debt, an agreement to do construction work or a pledge to accept an arbitration award, for example. At least in part, deficiencies in the common law's own writ of debt were responsible for the popularity of the ecclesiastical forum at the time, but to the common lawyers that did not matter. To them, bringing such cases before a spiritual court was contrary to a long-established jurisdictional rule: that enforcement of temporal obligations belonged within temporal courts. Their view was supported by a long-established royal provision of 1286,[49] and even by specific texts in the formal canon law itself (X 2.2.10). Their view made practical sense.

The canon law, however, left an opening for ecclesiastical jurisdiction. A sworn promise might be distinguished from an ordinary promise. The oath made the difference. A separate title in the Decretals was devoted

46 *C&S*, 1: 660–84. 47 Lyndwood, *Provinciale*, 315, s.v. *chartas*. 48 Ibid., 92–6, 314–18.
49 The royal writ 'Circumspecte agatis', found in *C&S*, 2: 974–5.

to it (X 2.24.1–36); the title established that all licit oaths were specifically enforceable; to hold otherwise would risk God's wrath. Under this view, violating an oath was different from violating an ordinary promise, because oaths belonged to the realm of the spirit. At least they could be so understood. This mattered under the canon law itself, which was itself restricting the misuse of the sanctions of the Church for purely secular purposes such as the recovery of simple debts (Ext. Com. 5.10.2), but nevertheless put oaths into a different category. It was a complicated question. Current deficiencies in the common law's writ of debt were not irrelevant. The courts of the Church could with some reason be said to have been filling a gap in existing secular law by providing a remedy. Justice was what mattered and the ecclesiastical courts were entitled to step in to deal with deficiencies in its provision (X 2.1.13).

Lyndwood stepped directly into this controversy in glossing the constitutions of the Lambeth council. Obviously, the claims of religion were involved. He saw this. However, some of his comments seem to have recognised the practical difficulties in what might be called the 'High Church' position. In glossing the first Lambeth decree, he began by confessing his treatment would be brief because, as he said, 'the constitution was little respected in practice'.[50] Similarly he later remarked that 'in this realm the laws of the world prevail'.[51] He even admitted that the libels used in courts Christian routinely omitted any mention of the nature of the underlying obligation, mentioning only breach of an oath, in order to minimise the possibility that a writ of prohibition would be introduced.[52] In other words, here Lyndwood seems to have spoken to his readers with the voice of a hard-headed lawyer.

Others of his glosses, however, seem to point in the opposite direction. They accepted and seemed to defend the position that the cases brought to enforce contracts in English ecclesiastical courts belonged there, finding in the Christian religion strong support for that placement. Violation of an oath was perjury, Lyndwood noted, and 'perjury directly concerns irreverence towards God'.[53] In this stated view, interposition of the oath – even mild words such as 'by my faith' – was sufficient to support the conclusion that the speaker had meant to invoke God's name.[54] The faith being called upon was evidently the Christian faith. If the man who had made such a studied promise failed to fulfil it, he had committed an offence against God. When

50 Lyndwood, *Provinciale*, 92, s.v. *Contingit aliquando*.

51 Ibid., 97, s.v. *curia Christianitatis*. 52 Ibid., 315, s.v. *perjurio*. 53 Ibid.

54 Ibid., 315, s.v. *fidei transgressione*.

that happened, the spiritual courts could and should intervene to put things right.

Moreover, when temporal lawyers objected to this as an encroachment upon their own sphere of jurisdiction (as they did), Lyndwood regarded it as an overreaction on their part. What the Church's jurisdiction offered was simply an example of what was then called the 'accumulation of forums'.[55] Plaintiffs who sued to enforce contracts under the rubric of breach of faith were doing so by making a legitimate election among the resources at their disposal. It was no attack on the king's rights for them to choose a spiritual path. In Lyndwood's view, they were doing no more than exercising a choice the canon law expressly allowed. He cited several decretals in support of this view (X 1.34.1, X 4.17.13), together with the opinions of Joannes Andreae (d. 1348) and Antonius de Butrio (d. 1408). In other words, his view was that here the canon law was making no exclusive claim to jurisdiction. The royal courts were free to offer an adequate remedy. The English ecclesiastical courts were not interfering with temporal jurisdiction if the common law failed to provide one. The Church's law merely offered litigants a choice, one tied to their religion. There was nothing wrong if litigants chose to invoke a religious understanding of the law. And many of them did so when they had a choice.

From a modern perspective, Lyndwood's defence of the ecclesiastical jurisdiction nevertheless raises the same issue his interpretation of the English Church's testamentary law does. Putting it strongly, one can ask whether his invocation of religion was not a thin cloak to cover a 'power grab' by the men who administered the Church's courts in England. Common lawyers of his own time came very close to taking that view of the matter. That the men who served in the spiritual forum profited by this jurisdiction over what could be seen as simple debt collection is not open to doubt. It could not have been a secret. Was Lyndwood therefore complicit in giving a religious cover to what was at bottom a hunt for profit? Or is posing such a question itself misplaced modern cynicism? As with the prior example, this is an easier question to raise than it is to answer.

CONCLUSION

We know that Lyndwood's basic position on matters such as the nature of the canon law of testaments and sworn contracts was shared among canonists of his time. What counts as 'religious' in nature is often a matter of contention today,

55 Ibid., 315, s.v. *perjurio*.

and similar disagreements were not unknown in fifteenth-century England. The logical course is surely to see Lyndwood's position in this light. The importance of the Christian religion in his career and commentary on the laws of the province of Canterbury is manifest. That he carried it into jurisdictional controversies is to be expected. We may not share fully in his perspective on Christianity's requirements, but we ought to recognise its exsitence.

The fyrste dyaloge in Englysshe/with newe addycyons.

Christopher St German, *Doctor and Student* (1531), courtesy of HeinOnline

4

Christopher St German
Religion, Conscience and Law in Reformation England

Ian Williams

Christopher St German, a barrister and writer, has attracted considerable attention from historians. His work known as *Doctor and Student* provides evidence of common law practice and rules around 1500, but for legal historians is usually more significant as a serious attempt to provide a coherent and complete theory of English law. In particular, St German seems to have introduced the language of equity into English law and provided a theory of the equity jurisdiction based around conscience. This set the parameters for future discussions of the nature of equity in the common law tradition.

St German has also been of considerable interest to non-legal historians. *Doctor and Student* and St German's later writings are associated with the Henrician Reformation and the controversy it engendered. St German is sometimes seen as providing important intellectual support for the developments of the early 1530s, especially the break from Rome itself. From this perspective, St German may be considered more as a political thinker, concerned with the relations between Church and state.

This chapter focuses on *Doctor and Student* as St German's principal juristic writing. However, a new perspective shall be put forward, arguing that we should see *Doctor and Student* not just as a juristic and political work, but much more as a religious one. The argument here is that to focus on St German as a jurist is to overlook important aspects of his work. *Doctor and Student* had juristic content and clearly a juristic afterlife, but that was not St German's primary purpose in writing and printing it.

My thanks to the participants in this volume's symposium held at Emmanuel College, Cambridge, in September 2015 for their comments on an earlier draft of this chapter.

ST GERMAN'S LIFE

Christopher St German lived longer in obscurity than many of the other individuals in this volume lived at all. He was probably born around 1460 to a minor gentry family in Warwickshire, and details of St German's life until the late 1520s are lacking.[1] No evidence of his legal or non-legal education exists. He made his way to London, probably in his mid–late teens, became a member of the Middle Temple (perhaps after membership in an Inn of Chancery) and a barrister. His (extended) family and fellow Templars seem to have comprised most of his social and other contacts for most of his life. John Guy has painstakingly drawn together the very limited evidence about St German's life.[2]

St German's career as a barrister was undistinguished. The first mention of St German in any historical sources is in the records of the Middle Temple for 1502, when St German was probably already in his early forties. He was still an 'utter barrister' and he never progressed to membership of the Bench of his Inn. There is sparse evidence for St German's legal practice. Status as an utter barrister denied lawyers audience rights in the Court of Common Pleas, the most important of the central common law courts, and so it is no surprise that St German does not appear as a lawyer in any contemporary law reports.

Some aspects of his practice can be traced in other records. In 1505, St German was involved in the Court of Requests in a dispute between family members about inherited property. It is not clear whether St German was counsel for one of the parties or appointed as an independent actor – together with another barrister he was to gather all the family's relevant deeds and other documents and distribute them to those family members best entitled to them. In 1508 and 1510 he was involved, with other Middle Templars, as one of several feoffees of land, to hold to the use of others. By the early sixteenth century, placing land in use (the precursor to the trust) was a means by which landowners could avoid some of the undesirable financial consequences of English feudal land law, and groups of lawyers were frequently appointed as the feoffees (legal owners) for these purposes. All of the evidence of St German's practice, like that of many other lawyers, suggests a regional component. These three records

[1] St German's birth around 1460 is inferred from Bale's claim that St German was about eighty when he died (John Bale, *Scriptorum illustrium maioris Brytannie* (Basel: Johannes Oporin, 1557–9), 660). However, various aspects of Bale's biography are questionable, and the known evidence of St German's legal career is not incompatible with his birth being up to a decade later.

[2] For the biographical material in this chapter, see generally J. A. Guy, *Christopher St German on Chancery and Statute* (London: Selden Society, 1985), 1–55.

relate to land in Staffordshire, Warwickshire and Nottinghamshire, all in the Midlands and no more than 40 miles from St German's birth parish of Shilton.

St German disappears from the records of the Middle Temple after 1511, and a remark in a 1539 letter suggests that he left the Temple before about 1515. There is no evidence of further remunerated legal practice, although St German did continue to provide some services for family members, such as acting as an executor. He also lent money to a cousin's widow. St German seems not to have inherited his family's property in Shilton, eventually renting and then owning land in Alvechurch, Worcestershire (again, less than 40 miles from Shilton). For much of his life he lived in London, and from 1527 the Alvechurch property was rented to a cousin. By 1540 he was living in a rented house in Old Fish Street in London, a little south of St Paul's.

That location must have been desirable for St German. Although some distance from the Inns, the area around St Paul's was an important one for the early modern English book trade, and St German was described by John Bale as leaving most of his wealth in books. St German certainly was a keen reader, especially of religious works. In a 1539 letter to Thomas Cromwell, Henry VIII's chief minister, the nearly eighty-year-old St German apologises for his inability to visit Cromwell personally, observing that 'I am not able to it'. While the elderly St German could not manage that journey, he remained a bibliophile. The letter is directed to a matter of business, but St German's final, telling, remark concerns his ongoing search for books, 'And I can not gette any of the bokes of Erasmus de Sarcerio *de Locis Communibus*.'[3] This is a reference to the *Commonplaces of Scripture*, translated by Richard Taverner, whose Protestant leanings can be seen by his role as a lay preacher during the reign of Edward VI.[4] St German regarded his books as both his most valuable and most desirable possessions. In his will, he directed his executor to sell assets from the estate to pay his bequests, a typical instruction. Very unusually, the executor was first directed to sell St German's books, together with the right to take books from St German's collection for himself, paying a fair price.

St German was not just a reader of books, but a producer of them. His first foray into the world of publishing was in the first decade of the sixteenth century when, in combination with two other Middle Templars, he entered into an agreement with the printer Richard Pynson for the reprinting of Pynson's *Abridgement of the Statutes*, a work of almost 200 folios which

3 The National Archives [hereafter TNA], PRO SP 1/152, f. 249.

4 Erasmus Sarcerius, *Common places of Scripture ordrely and after a compendious forme of teachyng set forth*, trans. Richard Taverner (London: John Byddel, 1538).

arranged statutes under alphabetical subject-matter titles.[5] The arrangement did not proceed as well or as happily as planned, and ended in litigation in the common law courts and the Chancery. No outcome to the dispute is known, and no copies of this printing of the *Abridgement* are known to exist.

It was not as a publisher, and certainly not as a lawyer, but as a writer that St German became famous. Despite his seeming retirement in the second decade of the sixteenth century, St German embarked on a new career as a prolific author a few years before turning seventy. His first book, and the one on which his description as a 'jurist' is principally based, is known as *Doctor and Student* and was first printed in 1528.[6] It seems to have been sufficiently impressive to lead Cardinal Wolsey to appoint St German to a role in the Court of Requests in 1529, although there is no evidence St German ever sat. He continued to write until at least 1537 (the last year for which extant writings survive), dying in London in 1541.

ST GERMAN'S RELIGIOUS VIEWS

Our knowledge of St German's religious views is drawn principally from four sources: two unpublished manuscripts which he sent to Thomas Cromwell in 1537, St German's comments on the 1537 *Bishops' Book* (solicited by Thomas Cromwell), and his will.[7] All of these are from late in his long life. The first manuscript, a 'Discourse of the Sacraments' relates to debates in England in 1537 about the number of sacraments.[8] The second manuscript continues the dialogue between the Doctor of theology and the Student of the laws, begun in *Doctor and Student*, now as a 'Dialogue showing what we be bound to believe as things necessary to Salvation, and what not'.[9]

In 1536, predating all of these sources, St German's writings were described in the articles of the Pilgrimage of Grace as 'heresies' needing to be 'annulled and destroyed'.[10] St German's books were associated with Tyndale, and other heresies identified in the article include those of Wycliffe, Huss, Luther and Zwingli. From the perspective of the Protestant tradition, St German was

5 *Abbreuiamentum statuorum* (London: Richard Pynson, 1499).

6 T. F. T. Plucknett and J. L. Barton, eds., *St German's* Doctor and Student (London, Selden Society, 1974) [hereafter *Doctor and Student*]. There are persistent claims of a 1523 edition, but there are no known copies or contemporary evidence for this.

7 Christopher St German, *The institution of a Christen man, conteynynge the exposition or interpretation of the commune Crede, of the seuen sacramentes, of the x. commandementes, and of the Pater noster, and the Aue Maria, justification and purgatorie* (London: Thomas Berthelet, 1537); TNA, PRO PROB 11/28/511.

8 TNA, PRO SP 6/8, pp. 1–20.

9 TNA, PRO SP 6/2, pp. 89–168.

10 James Gairdner, ed., *Letters and Papers, Foreign and Domestic, of the Reign of Henry VIII*, vol. 11 (London: HMSO, 1888), 506 (no. 1246).

keeping impressive company. It seems likely St German would have been disappointed with these associations. Although the sources from late in his life present a somewhat mixed picture, there were clear differences between the views of St German and those of people identified as Protestants, such as Luther and Zwingli.

St German was clearly not an ardent follower of Luther. His written works show considerable reliance on the *Summa Angelica*, a work which Luther had burned in December 1520.[11] More significantly, the two 1537 manuscripts show that St German rejected the Lutheran idea of a priesthood of all believers. For St German the priesthood continued to have a vital sacramental role, and priests were in that way different to other people. No one else, not even the king, could exercise certain sacramental roles, such as consecration. St German also retained a firm belief in transubstantiation, rejecting alternatives presented by Protestants. Prayers for the souls of the dead were effective, and St German made provision for such prayers for his soul and those of his parents in his own will. The saints also continued to have an intercessory role, although St German was concerned that this should not be amplified.[12] These beliefs, together with a belief in the Trinity, the perpetual virginity of Mary and the contents of the Apostles' Creed were all within medieval orthodoxy.

A parliamentary draft attributed by Guy to St German also supports a vernacular New Testament. This was not a particularly Protestant position and had support within the Catholic Church too. St German's support was also not unequivocal. A vernacular New Testament was only to be supported if the demand for it flowed from 'meekness and charity', reflecting contemporary concerns that vernacular Scriptures could be used to undermine existing beliefs and authority.[13]

St German rejected any role for religious tradition in determining what was necessary for salvation and largely rejected the Church Councils of the past. Instead, St German regarded Scripture alone as the basis for determining Christian doctrine, and Scripture was only to be interpreted literally.[14]

11 Letter to George Spalatin, 10 December 1520, in Gottfried G. Krodel, ed. and trans., *Luther's Works*, vol. 48: *Letters I* (Philadelphia: Fortress Press, 1963), 186–7.

12 St German disagreed here with Henry VIII. The *Bishops' Book* referred to Christ as the only mediator, but this did not preclude the intercession of saints. Henry wished to change this to the 'mediation' of saints, while St German wished to maintain the original 'intercession' on the basis that Henry's amendment would set 'the saints in more estimation' (Guy, *St German on Chancery and Statute*, 54).

13 Guy, *St German on Chancery and Statute*, 127.

14 TNA, PRO SP 6/2, p. 117; TNA, PRO SP 6/8, pp. 13–16 (where literal interpretation is the basis for St German's belief in transubstantiation).

Doctrine could be found not just from the words of Scripture, but also what 'may be derived out thereof in a probable consequence'.[15] St German's justification for relying on Scripture but not the views of doctors of the Church for determining doctrine was not like most Protestants. It was not normative but evidential; he thought that it could not be certain whether or not writings attributed to doctors were actually their work.[16] St German recognised a need for someone to be able to determine doctrine authoritatively and he seems to have accepted that even allowing only literal interpretation might not achieve this. He changed his views on how a single correct interpretation of Scripture was to be achieved over the 1530s, locating that authority in various groups (although consistently away from the clergy alone).[17] While a rejection of tradition was a strand within late-medieval Catholic theology, by 1537 St German's religious views were importantly heterodox.[18] Crucially, he denied the status of marriage and penance as sacraments.[19]

ST GERMAN THE AUTHOR

By the time of his death, nine of St German's works had been printed. A parliamentary draft, two religious manuscripts and a work on the Chancery all survived in manuscript, with the Chancery work being printed in 1787 as *A Little Treatise Concerning Writs of Subpoena* and his parliamentary draft in 1985. St German may also have been the author of another manuscript, seemingly written in reply to St German's own work on conscience.[20] For a man in his eighth decade of life, this is an impressive display.

Several of St German's publications in the 1530s were printed by the King's Printer, Thomas Berthelet, and this suggests a link with the government, even that St German was working for Henry VIII's government in forming opinion about the developments of the 1530s. However, St German seems to have retained his independence from the government. He declined a request for assistance from writers working for Thomas Cromwell in 1534. It seems more

15 TNA, PRO SP 6/2, p. 89. 16 Ibid., p. 90.

17 The most detailed account is Daniel Eppley, *Defending Royal Supremacy and Discerning God's Will in Tudor England* (Aldershot: Ashgate, 2007), 80–119.

18 The links between St German's views and late medieval theology have not yet been investigated. For example, St German's views on the role of tradition seem to indicate a departure from a reliance on Gerson in his thinking (for Gerson, see Heiko Oberman, *The Harvest of Medieval Theology: Gabriel Biel and Late Medieval Nominalism* (Cambridge, MA: Harvard University Press, 1963), 385–7).

19 TNA, PRO SP 6/8, p. 2 (marriage) and p. 4 (penance).

20 For these publications, see Guy, *St German on Chancery and Statute*, 16–17.

likely that he was someone whose learning Cromwell respected and whose ideas Cromwell found useful. This is corroborated by Cromwell seemingly soliciting St German's views about the *Bishop's Book*, suggesting that it was Cromwell who sought the link with St German, rather than the other way around.

Although there are close links between many of St German's writings, his place in this volume is based on his more legal writings. These appeared at the beginning of his career as an author and in many respects laid the foundations for future works. The First Dialogue of what would come to be known as *Doctor and Student* appeared in Latin in 1528 (an English version appearing in 1531), the Second Dialogue in 1530 and the *New Additions* to the dialogue in 1531. *Doctor and Student* went through eleven printings of the combined two dialogues in the sixteenth century and a further eleven in the seventeenth, with handfuls in the eighteenth and nineteenth centuries. By way of comparison, there were nine printings of Edward Coke's *Commentary on Littleton*, a rapidly accepted authoritative work, in the seventeenth century.[21] In early modern legal publishing terms, *Doctor and Student* was a bestseller. It was also read. Citations of *Doctor and Student* in court can be found into the 1670s, almost a century and a half after its initial publication.[22] Its availability in English made *Doctor and Student* an accessible student work. St German's intellectual contribution in these works will be considered later in this chapter.

Not all of St German's writings were so well received. His *Treatise Concerning the Division between the Spiritualty and Temporalty* provoked a response by the later canonised Thomas More, leading to what has been described as a 'battle of the books' between the two closely connected men.[23] After St German was answered by More, St German responded with a new dialogue, *Salem and Bizance*, to which More replied; St German composed *The Addicions of Salem and Bizance* as a further response.[24] The battle then

21 See Chapter 5 on Coke in this volume.

22 *Haughton v. Wilson* (1673) 3 Keble 203, 204; 84 ER 677.

23 Christopher St German, *A treatise concernynge the diuision betwene the spiritualtie and temporaltie* (London: Thomas Berthelet and Robert Redman, 1532); modern edition in J. B. Trapp, ed., *The Complete Works of St. Thomas More, vol.* 9 (New Haven: Yale University Press, 1979), 173–212; John Guy, 'Thomas More and Christopher St German: The Battle of the Books', in Alistair Fox and John Guy, *Reassessing the Henrician Age: Humanism, Politics and Reform 1500–1550* (Oxford: Basil Blackwell, 1986), 95–120. More's brother-in-law was John Rastell, a lawyer who had been appointed as a feoffee with St German in 1508 and who later became a law printer, printing the 1528 edition of *Doctor and Student.* The Rastell family was connected with Coventry, near St German's own family home.

24 Christopher St German, *Salem and Bizance* (London: Thomas Berthelet, 1533); modern edition in J. Guy, R. Keen, C. H. Miller and R. McGugan, eds., *The Complete Works of St. Thomas More, vol. 10* (New Haven: Yale University Press, 1987), 325–92. Christopher St German, *The addicions of Salem and Bizance* (London: Thomas Berthelet, 1534).

petered out, but St German is one of a few authors whose works can accurately be described as having tried the patience of a saint.

The publications to which More took exception were anti-clerical. St German attacked what he perceived to be clerical abuses, both in performing their religious functions and in the church courts. A particular target was the investigation, trial and punishment of heretics, St German complaining about the use of inquisitorial process. For St German, the underlying problem was that men of God were men, with all the flaws and fallibility that implied. As men, priests were capable of sin, vulnerable to conflicts of interest and capable of abusing their power. More responded forcefully, not just to defend the Church, but also his own reputation; More had been a vigorous participant in the detection of heretics while Lord Chancellor. These works by St German were not directly juristic, although his claims of procedural unfairness in, and understanding of, inquisitorial process probably reflect the views of someone more familiar with common law process than the nuances of *ius commune* procedure.

ST GERMAN THE JURIST

Although the main use of St German's writings in court was to provide cases for lawyers to put in the same manner as actual curial discussions and decisions, his principal contributions to English law were more jurisprudential. St German not only set out a theory of English law, he also provided the first theory to justify both the intervention of the Chancery in what came to be known as 'equity' in general, and its application in specific cases.[25]

St German's legal theory was in many respects unoriginal. He used widely accepted ideas from European legal theory. St German explained that the laws of England were several: the law of God, the law of reason (which seems to have been the same as the law of nature) and the various types of human law (general customs and maxims, as well as legislation).[26] These various types of law were generally compatible. St German was very clear that human law could not be incompatible with either the law of God or the law of reason. Any human law incompatible with these higher laws would be void. There was nothing controversial in this in terms of late-medieval European legal theory.

St German's discussion of equity was derived from the French theologian Jean Gerson, who made considerable use of Aristotle's discussion of *epieikeia*, although often used the Latin *aequitas* (equity) interchangeably with it.

25 For what follows, see especially J. L. Barton, 'Introduction' in *Doctor and Student*, xi–lxvii.

26 Although St German's language of 'maxims' might have been less comprehensible to civilians – he did not use the familiar civilian language of *regulae iuris* (*Doctor and Student*, 57).

In fact, St German's discussion in *Doctor and Student* is often taken more or less verbatim from Gerson's work,[27] and it is the conflation of *epieikeia* and *aequitas* which leads to descriptions of the Chancery as a court of 'equity'.

The medieval theory of *epieikeia* which St German used in *Doctor and Student* was premised on the observation, taken from Aristotle, that human laws framed in general terms would inevitably fail to achieve their objects in the infinite variety of circumstances to which they might be applied. In such cases, the failings of human law could be redressed by application of the intention of the legislator. Medieval theologians applied this to the laws of God and nature. Gerson, and through him St German, took this further in its application to human laws. Human law-makers would not have intended for their creations to be contrary to the law of God or the law of nature (or reason, on the Student's description of English law) – no law-maker would have intended to create void law. If a human law therefore caused an outcome contrary to the law of God or the law of nature in a particular case, it followed that this was not what the law-maker intended. To apply the outcome mandated by the law of God or nature would be to reach the result intended by the law-maker.

St German was clear that in some cases, at least, just such an approach could be taken in common law courts. But in many instances the common law judges were required to follow the common law, law which was generally compatible with the laws of God and nature, but might produce an incorrect outcome in a particular case before the judges. In such cases, recourse could be had to the Chancery, via a subpoena. In such cases, the Chancery would be fulfilling the underlying intention behind the common law. Chancery provided equity to support, not undermine, the law.

Before St German, the Chancery is normally described as proceeding according to 'conscience'.[28] St German's work did little to change this, instead bringing the two concepts of equity and conscience together, so that the Chancery as a provider of equity would be acting in accordance with conscience. While St German justifies the role of the Chancery in general in terms of equity, the Chancery's interventions in specific cases are described as the application of conscience.

St German's theory of conscience, like the components of his legal theory, was also derived from orthodox medieval theology. According to this theology, all human beings had the faculty of *synderesis*, 'moving and steering it to good and abhorring evil'.[29] Although *synderesis* itself could never be extinguished, its

[27] Zofia Rueger, 'Gerson's Concept of Equity and Christopher St. German', *History of Political Thought* 3 (1982): 1–30.

[28] (1469) YB Trin 9 Edw. 4, f. 14, pl. 9, per Stillington LC.

[29] *Doctor and Student*, 81.

exercise might be overcome by error (such as someone incorrectly believing evil to be good) or obstinacy. Good and evil were not subjective, but determined by revelation and reason. Identifying what was good or evil therefore required knowledge of law. The laws of God and nature would often identify what was good or evil. Because the temporal authorities 'have received of god power to make laws', their laws were also considered to 'be made by god'.[30] As the Doctor later observed, 'all laws made by man which be not contrary to the law of god must be observed and kept and that in conscience. And he that despises them despises god.'[31]

Conscience, in the strict sense, was not this knowledge of good or evil, but the application of this knowledge to particular facts to generate rules of conduct. Conscience was applied knowledge, 'the judgement of practical reason judging on the particular acts of man'. As St German noted on several occasions, in combination with his understanding of *synderesis*, 'conscience must always be grounded upon some law', whether divine, natural or human.[32] This meant that human law took effect in conscience, unless, on particular facts, the laws of God or nature (themselves both coming directly from God, and therefore demanding obedience) required a different outcome.

St German described this mode of reasoning in conscience in the terms of formal logic:

> the syllogism of conscience in this manner: *synderesis* ministers the major thus: Rightwiseness is to be done to every man. Upon which major the law of England ministers the minor thus: the inheritance belongs to the son born after spousals. The conscience makes the conclusion and says therefore the inheritance is in conscience to be given to the son born after spousals. And so in other cases infinite may be formed by the law the syllogism or the right judgment of conscience.[33]

As with all formal logic, provided the premises and reasoning were correct, the correct conclusion in conscience would inevitably follow. St German recognised, however, that conscience, like *synderesis*, was not infallible. Conscience could err, 'led astray by passion, or through ignorance, or through a wrong and evil disposition'.[34] Such erring consciences would need to be corrected. This had long been a justification for the church courts' activities in various spheres, but the role of human law meant that secular courts would also be involved in the regulation of conscience.

St German's model of conscience brought together the theory of equity and that of conscience. Equitable intervention occurred where human law would

[30] Ibid., 111. [31] Ibid., 147. [32] Ibid., 133, 163, 207. [33] Ibid., 129. [34] Ibid., 91.

lead to an outcome contrary to the laws of God or nature (or reason) on particular facts. Identifying what the laws of God, nature or man required on particular facts was an act of reasoning that was conscience. The Court of Chancery was a court of equity because it used conscience to ensure that the human law of the common law did not lead to outcomes contrary to the laws of God or nature, outcomes which the common law wished to avoid but sometimes could not.

Within this theory, St German, like Gerson, defined the law of God narrowly, denying that much of the law of the Church was in fact divine law.[35] He was also clear that the entire law of property, and all law affecting property, was ultimately human law. There was no divine or natural law of property. This was not an especially controversial premise. Aquinas recognised that while natural law recognised the need for a law of property, it did not determine that law, which was a matter for human regulation.[36] St German's position was the same. It followed that property rights were governed by human law and courts applying that law. For St German, this also meant that contract was similarly governed by human law, as contracts were about distributing property and so could not have existed without human property law. As the Doctor observed, 'contracts be not grounded upon neither of those laws but upon the law of man'.[37] This did not mean that the Chancery was not involved with contractual matters, but that its intervention in this context was not about fulfilling the laws of God or nature.

The example which came to be the paradigm for early modern explanations of the Chancery jurisdiction was the first specific case of conscience discussed by St German and did in fact relate to the law of contract.[38] At common law, if one party entered into a sealed bond (an obligation) saying that they owed money to another (perhaps if certain circumstances were fulfilled), the debtor was strictly liable on the debt. The only available defences once the money was due were either to show that the bond itself had been cancelled or to produce another sealed document stating that the debt had been paid (an acquittance). This meant that if a debtor paid the creditor, but failed to obtain (or lost) an acquittance, the creditor could sue the debtor and at common law the debtor would be required to pay again. Common lawyers knew this was not the desirable outcome; had the case been brought for a debt owed on an informal contract, prior payment would be a good defence. However, they were

[35] St German's law of reason secondary also introduced human law as an element in the law of reason, again limiting the scope for an independent law of reason to act as the basis for Chancery intervention.

[36] Thomas Aquinas, *Summa Theologiae*, 2a2ae.66.2.

[37] *Doctor and Student*, 133.

[38] Ibid., 76–9.

constrained by the evidential rules of the common law to require the debtor to pay twice where there was a sealed bond.

This was an excellent demonstration of the role of *epieikeia*. As the Student observed, in general the requirement of strong evidence of the discharge of a debt was a good one, given that the debt was also proved by strong evidence. The common law here 'sets a general rule which is good and necessary to all the people'. After explaining this, the Student said that the debtor can be aided by conscience. It is this discussion which begins St German's discussion of the nature of conscience itself. According to the Doctor, double payment was contrary to the law of reason and therefore also contrary to conscience.[39] The Student agreed, but also made it very clear that 'it is not the law of England' that double payment is required, as that would be contrary to the law of reason. Chancery intervention not only satisfied conscience, it also fulfilled the underlying intention behind the common law, as the doctrine of *epieikeia* would suggest.

St German's theory of equity and conscience had several important consequences. In the context of the Reformation, St German's model was a challenge to claims by the Church and its courts to adjudicate matters of conscience. For many such issues, at least when connected with St German's broad view of what constituted purely temporal matters, conscience could only be determined through an understanding and application of English law. Limitations similar, but not identical, to those St German advocated had in fact largely been achieved (at least from the point of view of common lawyers) in the late fifteenth and early sixteenth centuries.[40] More generally, and advocated more strongly in the *New Additions* and his other writings, St German's theory developed into a strong claim for secular control over many issues previously addressed by the Church.

Within the context of English legal history, St German's model led to a Chancery which was not an arbitrary court. It applied law of various types, all of which people could learn, and a reasoning process which was theoretically available to all human beings to produce entirely predictable outcomes. Crucially, the role of human law in determining conscience in many cases also meant that the Chancery's role was limited. If the laws of God and nature were indifferent as to the outcome of a particular scenario, conscience was determined by the law of man, for St German the common law. In those situations, there was no justification for Chancery intervention; indeed, such intervention would be illegitimate. St German's theory therefore explained

39 Ibid., 77.

40 J. H. Baker, *Oxford History of the Laws of England, Vol. VI: 1483–1558* (Oxford: Oxford University Press, 2003), 237–43.

the need for the Chancery as a court of conscience, but circumscribed it. Equity and conscience could not extinguish the common law; indeed, they were predicated upon its existence. Equity was to remain an ancillary to the common law.

THE ROLE OF RELIGION IN ST GERMAN'S JURISTIC WORK

The influence of Christianity on *Doctor and Student* is both obvious and profound. First, St German's principal sources for his legal theory, including his theories of equity and conscience, are medieval theology, principally the writings of the early fifteenth-century French theologian Jean Gerson and Thomas Aquinas. There is also considerable use of the *Summa Rosella* and the *Summa Angelica,* books written for confessors to aid in confession and absolution.

Second, *Doctor and Student* is in the form of a dialogue, a dialogue which itself reveals more about the interaction between law and religion in St German's thought. A point which is obvious, but perhaps so obvious that it is usually overlooked, is that *Doctor and Student* is a dialogue between a Student of the common law (meaning a barrister) and a Doctor of theology. A useful comparison is William Fulbeck's *Parallele*.[41] The *Parallele* is another dialogue about law involving a barrister which discusses various issues casuistically. The participants in Fulbeck's dialogue, however, are all lawyers: a common lawyer, a civil lawyer and a canon lawyer. The only comparable work to *Doctor and Student* as a dialogue which moves beyond the world of law in a narrowly conceived way is Thomas Hobbes's *Dialogue ... of the Common Laws of England,* where a common lawyer and a philosopher (no longer a theologian) engage in debate.[42] St German's work is consequently not narrowly legal and law is not a discipline strongly separated from others.

Crucially, in *Doctor and Student,* it also becomes apparent that law and theology are sufficiently similar that the Student and the Doctor can understand one another and can reach conclusions in the other's discipline. The two disciplines were not identical, but were related. For example, when discussing the law of reason in England, the Doctor explains that he wishes to know about the law of nature in English law. The Student explains that English lawyers do not use the language of the law of nature, instead 'when anything is grounded upon the law of nature: they say that reason will that such a thing be done'.

41 William Fulbeck, A *Parallele or Conference of the Civill Law, the Canon Law, and the Common Law of This Realme of England* (London: Thomas Wight, 1601).

42 Thomas Hobbes, *Writings on Common Law and Hereditary Right,* ed. Alan Cromartie and Quentin Skinner (Oxford: Oxford University Press, 2005).

The Student considers this difference to be essentially terminological, a question of what common lawyers say, rather than what they mean, and the Doctor does not disagree. The Doctor subsequently asks for an example of the law of reason secondary particular. The Student poses a case and asks for the Doctor's view. Having heard this, the Student informs the Doctor that 'you have given a true judgment'.[43] The Student can communicate English legal theory to the Doctor, and the Doctor can reach conclusions in English law when provided with the relevant information. If lawyers are priests, as the *ius commune* and John Fortescue claimed, for St German priests could equally be lawyers.

These observations make clear that religion was clearly an influence on *Doctor and Student*. However, a better understanding of *Doctor and Student* views the work as a more thoroughly religious one, even a work with a religious purpose, containing juristic elements. This is best seen by examining aspects of the work which are largely overlooked or ignored, as not directly relevant to legal historians or those concerned with the Henrician Reformation.

Doctor and Student *as a Religious Work*

Several aspects of *Doctor and Student* suggest that we should understand the work as one directed to religious ends, rather than secular ones.

What Was Doctor and Student?

The first, neglected, issue is what we mean by *Doctor and Student*. It is conventional to identify as *Doctor and Student* three works: the 1528 Latin dialogue on the grounds of the laws of England and conscience and its subsequent English versions, when it is described as the 'First Dialogue'; the 1530 Second Dialogue; and the 'New Additions' to the Second Dialogue, printed in 1531. However, there is a fourth work by St German which continues the dialogue between the Doctor of Theology and the Student of the Common Law. This unprinted work was sent by St German to Thomas Cromwell and is entitled 'A Dialogue showing What we be bound to believe as things necessary to salvation and what not'.[44] This last work is clearly directed to religious ends and is really a work of theology, in which St German sets out his religious epistemology and conclusions on various matters of faith.

If all four of these works are what St German would, near the end of his life, have regarded as the complete *Doctor and Student*, then to regard *Doctor and Student* as solely a juristic work simply cannot be correct. The final dialogue

43 *Doctor and Student*, 31–7. 44 TNA, PRO SP 6/2, pp. 89–168.

shows a clearly religious purpose directed not to this world, but the next. The Student here is concerned not with the laws of England, but with his soul.[45]

It may be that this premise is wrong and that St German would not have treated these works as related. On this analysis, St German presumably reverted to the dialogue with which he was familiar and by which he seemed to have made his name in one of his final works. But such an analysis seems weak. First, St German did treat *Doctor and Student* as an ongoing work in the early 1530s, making additions to the Second Dialogue after its initial publication. It is quite plausible to see subsequent work using the Doctor and the Student to be taking the original dialogue further, rather than a new departure. Second, St German's more controversial writings from the 1530s show a willingness to write outside the dialogue form; in *Salem and Bizance*, St German wrote a dialogue with new characters to frame the work itself. The choice to go back to a dialogue between the Doctor of theology and the Student of the laws of England was a deliberate one, and the inference has to be that St German saw his final dialogue as related to the earlier discussions between those characters. That points to an understanding that those earlier discussions were not simply directed to worldly concerns, a conclusion which is supported by aspects of the earlier dialogues.

St German's Sources

It is well known that St German's principal sources for his theory, and much of the content of parts of *Doctor and Student*, derives from religious and theological works: the writings of Jean Gerson and Thomas Aquinas; the *Summa Angelica* and the *Summa Rosella*. These were not the only sources, but they are the dominant ones in both the First and Second Dialogues.

Historians have spent considerable time and energy tracing these influences on St German, but have not considered what the choice of these sources tells us about the purpose of St German's work. He did not, for example, look to civil or canon law literature for his work. If St German was writing a juristic work, such juristic sources would seem a more likely reference. All of St German's religious sources did contain canon and civil law material, but St German chose to read and cite religious books, not legal ones. The titles of the works of Jean Gerson which particularly interested St German are revealing: *Moral Rules* (*Regulae Morales*); *The Book on the Spiritual Life of the Soul* (*Liber de Vita Spirituali Animae*); and *On the Carthusian Rule of Abstinence*

45 It is tempting to view St German as modelling this dialogue on Luke 10:25, where a lawyer asked what was necessary for eternal life. In the dialogue, the Student of the law asks what it is necessary to believe for salvation.

from Meat (*De Non Esu Carnium apud Carthusienses*).[46] These are works which evidently have legal content but are directed to non-legal purposes, to morality, the spiritual life and the soul.

If St German began his reading before conceiving of *Doctor and Student* as a project, then St German's interest was in religion, not law. If St German conceived of his project and then began research, he thought that religious works would provide what he needed. Either of these positions, and anywhere between them, suggests religion was a crucial element in St German's view of his project.

A related consideration is the extent of St German's use of Jean Gerson. Gerson was a considerable and reputable theologian, so in that sense St German's reliance upon him is uncontroversial. But literature by theologians was not in short supply in late-medieval Europe, so why did St German choose this particular theologian as his principal theoretical source? One possibility, which cannot be discounted, is that Gerson's generous use of equity in his theology was suitable for St German's juristic project.[47]

Another possibility places St German into a different historical context. St German is often treated by historians as providing a theory for the Chancery or as an important element in the Henrician Reformation, his writings providing intellectual legitimacy to the break from Rome. Rather than focusing on how St German's work has been received or on what occurred after the publication of the First Dialogue in 1528, looking at the situation before and at the time of the production of the First Dialogue gives a very different perspective. St German, seemingly a quite conservative individual, had the misfortune to live in interesting times. The obvious context is the European Reformation. England was not isolated from continental developments, and there was English knowledge of the religious turmoil on the continent. The Church was divided. There clearly was some anti-clericalism in Henrician England, particularly visible in the Richard Hunne affair and its aftermath, an event with which St German may have had a tenuous personal connection.[48]

Richard Hunne was sued in the church courts by the priest who had buried his five-week-old son. The priest claimed the baby's christening robe as a customary payment, a mortuary, in the church courts. Hunne, who was

46 Rueger, 'Gerson's Concept of Equity', 8, 11–12, 16–19.

47 Aquinas, for example, had a more restricted view of the acceptable use of equity, limiting it to exceptional situations and placing it under the control of the ruler (Rueger, 'Gerson's Concept of Equity', 14).

48 The wardship of Richard Hunne's daughters was granted to John Rastell (Alan Harding, 'Rastell, John (by 1468–1536), of London', in S. T. Bindoff, ed., *The House of Commons 1509–1558*, 3 vols. (London: Secker and Warburg, 1982), 3: 177), who was linked with St German (see note 23 in this chapter).

already involved in litigation with the Church, began proceedings for *praemunire* in the King's Bench, alleging that the church court was the imposition of a foreign power in England. The Church responded by investigating Hunne for heresy. Hunne was imprisoned, found hanged in his cell and a coroner's jury found foul play, rather than suicide. The case was an extreme example, but allegations of praemunire in relation to cases arguably concerned with secular rights were not unusual in the common law courts in the late fifteenth and early sixteenth centuries.[49] The common law courts could be a route for voicing dissatisfaction with and challenging the Church.

For someone who clearly was concerned about religious matters, these issues would have mattered to St German. His own anti-clericalism is quite clear, but so is his sincere religious belief. St German may have been concerned, quite plausibly, that divisions between the laity and the clergy might pave the way for division in the Church. St German did seek to address this issue in other writings; his *Treatise concerning the Division* is directed to the causes of – and solutions to – just such a division. If this interest existed before the early 1530s, as is perfectly plausible, an interest in and reliance upon Gerson becomes very readily explicable. Gerson was in many ways a theologian of the Great Schism, many of whose writings were directed at identifying a way to resolve the divide in the Church. Gerson's prescriptions included an accurate understanding of legal theory with the consequence that many aspects of canon law were not divine law.[50] Just such a theory could address some of the dissatisfaction in England, curbing what St German perceived as clerical abuses. For example, Gerson and St German would both reject questions of payment, such as that sought by the priest when claiming the mortuary in Hunne's case, as being subject to spiritual sanction, as when the priest brought proceedings in the church courts. *Doctor and Student's* discussion of Chancery provided legitimacy for the jurisdiction of the clerical Chancellor, provided that Chancery kept within certain bounds.

Equity and Conscience in Doctor and Student

The discussion of equity and conscience in *Doctor and Student* has typically been associated with the Chancery jurisdiction, which came to be known as equity. Relief from the Chancery had increased in importance through the fifteenth century, and Wolsey's tenure as Chancellor was controversial. St German's elaboration of conscience in the First Dialogue clearly had the potential to provide a theory for that jurisdiction and explain why clerical

49 Baker, *Oxford History*, 237–43.

50 See generally, Louis B. Pascoe, *Jean Gerson: Principles of Church Reform* (Brill: Leiden, 1973), 49–79.

chancellors needed to respect the common law and in many instances allow the decisions of common law courts.

However, this focus on the Chancery does not easily flow from *Doctor and Student* itself. The Chancery is considered, but is rarely the focus of the discussion. As John Guy has observed, for St German's detailed consideration of the Chancery and its activities we need to look at his *Little Treatise on Writs of Subpoena*, not *Doctor and Student* itself.[51] The *Little Treatise* was first printed in 1787, and although it is dangerous to infer too much from the unprinted state of any early modern work, the fact that St German printed several other works at around the time the *Little Treatise* was written may indicate that he could have printed it, had he wished to do so. Legal printing in the reign of Henry VIII was dynamic, and a successor to the frequently reprinted *Doctor and Student* would probably have sold well. Market explanations for the manuscript status of the text seem improbable. Guy suggests that the manuscript was unprinted because St German 'became involved in other things'.[52] This does not seem especially convincing; St German had not become so involved elsewhere that he was uninterested in writing on the topic. An alternative explanation may be that St German did not think the Chancery debate was that important – interesting, but not important. He was interested in Chancery as a court of conscience, but his principal concern was not the practice of the Chancery itself.

This provokes consideration of why St German was interested in conscience. There are good reasons for believing that St German's predominant concern was not with conscience as applied in the Chancery, but individual conscience, perhaps as affected by confession and even the church courts.

Most obviously, the English version of *Doctor and Student* sometimes uses the language of 'conscience' when the Latin equivalent, *conscientia*, is absent. Instead, the original Latin of the First Dialogue suggests a concern with the internal forum, rather than any application of conscience in the courts. Where the English at one point refers to laws made by men binding 'and that in conscience', the Latin is *etiam in foro anime*, suggesting a concern with the individual's soul.[53]

Doctor and Student also includes discussions of situations where Chancery provides no remedy. This is obviously important when considering the jurisdiction of any court. But St German goes on to consider what ought to happen despite the absence of a Chancery remedy. At such points St German is not concerned with conscience in Chancery, but the conscience of the

51 Guy, *St German on Chancery and Statute*, 64. 52 Ibid., 57.

53 *Doctor and Student*, 146–7. The weight of evidence suggests that St German was the composer of the original English text, although this is disputed (see Barton, 'Introduction', xvi–xviii).

individual. Simply because the Chancery does not intervene on the grounds of conscience does not mean conscience has no role.

A particularly good example of this is found in the Second Dialogue, where three questions by the Student are directed not to what the outcome in conscience of facts ought to be, but whether a lawyer, knowing all the facts and understanding that the outcome in conscience would be different to that in law, could in conscience 'be of counsel' for the party right in law but wrong in conscience.[54] These are not questions of Chancery remedies, but of professional ethics. They are not about correcting the conscience of the litigant, but ensuring conscientious action by lawyers.[55]

In one of the cases, while the Chancery is mentioned, the real issue is the conscience of the lawyer placed in the invidious position of a difference between law and conscience, asked to act at law: 'whether may a man with conscience be of counsel with the plaintiff in an action at the common law knowing that the defendant has sufficient matter in conscience whereby he may be discharged by a subpoena in the Chancery which he cannot plead in the common law or not'.[56] St German clarifies the example as that of the paradigmatic case of double recovery of a debt on a bond. Could a lawyer, for example, act to recover a debt in the common law courts which had already been paid, but where there was no written acquittance, the only acceptable proof of that payment?

As with the other cases, it is clear that the lawyer should not act against conscience. In this particular instance, however, the Student replies by observing that serjeants at law were 'sworn to give counsel according to the law . . . it seems he is bound to give counsel according to the law, for else he should not perform his oath'. Conscience required this lawyer not to act, but his sworn oath seemed to require him to do so. Oath-taking and breaches of oaths were taken very seriously in Henrician England as a matter of individual conscience, with breaches of oaths placing one's soul in jeopardy.[57] This lawyer was consequently in a particularly difficult position. The difficulty, however, was not one for any court. This was a matter for the internal forum, the individual's own conscience and perhaps ultimately sin, repentance and penance through the Church. The Doctor finds a solution to the problem; the serjeant's oath to give

54 *Doctor and Student*, 187–92.

55 See also ibid., 215–17, concerning inaccurate legal advice, and 285, where St German refers to the conscience of judges.

56 Ibid., 189–90.

57 See e.g. Jonathan Michael Gray, *Oaths and the English Reformation* (Cambridge: Cambridge University Press, 2012).

counsel according to law includes according to the 'law of god and the law of reason', both of which the Student had earlier enumerated as part of the laws of England. Acting to claim the debt for a second time would contravene both of these laws and so the serjeant is not bound by his oath to do so; indeed, he is bound by his oath not to act.

This discussion is clearly not directed to the Chancery, but to the lawyer's own individual conscience. Similarly, in the First Dialogue, St German elaborates several situations where someone 'shall not be punished ... by the law'. Instead he is 'bound in conscience to reform if he will save his soul', that judgment applying only 'to his conscience'.[58] Like the discussion of the lawyer, conscience here is personal, directed to the conscience of the wrongdoer, not conscience as applied in the Chancery. St German's analysis of these situations seems to reduce the need for the Chancery. If lawyers acted in accordance with conscience, then cases where they knew of reasons for Chancery intervention would not be brought in the common law courts at all.[59] The Chancery would then not need to intervene. If individuals acted in accordance with their conscience, there would be no need for Chancery intervention. For St German, attention to individual conscience therefore obviates the need for Chancery.

This concern with individual conscience in the internal forum, rather than the imposition of conscientious outcomes through courts is identifiable in other aspects of *Doctor and Student*. Most obviously, this can be seen in the neglected prologue to the 1528 Latin printing, a text which was not included in the English editions. St German explains that one of his purposes in the First Dialogue (perhaps the only part then written) was 'to incite others to collect and put into writing additional cases in English law upon which conscience ought to be based'. St German wanted more English law cases to be written, because conscience ought to be based on such cases. He then explained that 'the knowledge of which is necessary not only for the rendering of justice in the king's courts, but also for leading all those who heed them *in the internal forum* to a good and healthy conscience' (emphasis added).[60] St German makes it quite clear here that his work is not simply directed to the courts, but to the internal forum too.

In fact, the internal forum was probably more important. According to St German in the preface, the First Dialogue was published in Latin 'for the greater ease of those who know that language'.[61] Assuming this is true, it is safe

58 *Doctor and Student*, 113.

59 This does not, of course, address the situation where a lawyer is unaware of the reasons for Chancery intervention when acting in the common law courts.

60 *Doctor and Student*, 3. 61 Ibid., 3.

to infer that St German sought a wider audience than common lawyers, whose literature was usually in law-French. A Latin text would be available to the clergy (including the clerical Chancellor) and educated laypeople. Such audiences did not need to know the intricacies of common law for their own purposes, and most did not need to know about the Chancery. But they did need to know about conscience and about sin.

Once St German reached the conclusion, which he states in the preface, that English law informs, even governs, many aspects of conscience, then English law in its relation to conscience does need to be published 'for the good direction of conscience in this realm'. The preface makes it clear – *Doctor and Student* began as a book about directing conscience. That conscience was relevant to lawyers and it was relevant to the Chancery, but it was also relevant to everyone else in England. St German even ends the Latin First Dialogue making just this point. The final word goes to the Doctor, who says, 'I will make a greater effort than I have so far made to gain a fuller acquaintance with English law, for it is clear that a knowledge of it is highly necessary, even in matters of conscience, to clerks and laymen, and to all who dwell within this realm.'[62]

The Second Dialogue continues this theme. Out of fifty-five chapters in the Second Dialogue, twenty raise issues which are taken explicitly from the *Summa Angelica* and *Summa Rosella*, confessional manuals concerned with sin, albeit with considerable legal influences.[63] These confessional questions were also legal, ranging from the rules about appointments of priests to benefices (the right to appoint being a type of property right known as an advowson in medieval English law), to whether a landowner can seize animals trespassing on his land and doing damage to it or who should bear the loss if without fault a house falls on a borrowed horse.[64]

An obvious question is why St German chose to discuss these questions. He could simply have been identifying differences between the common law and the *ius commune* tradition, much in the way that Fulbeck did in his later *Parallele*. But St German was doing much more than this. He seems to have been concerned that people may be reading the *Summae* to provide them with guidance as to what they ought do in conscience or what they as confessors should do in relation to the consciences of their charges. This was not implausible: Thomas More was able to use St German's reliance on the

62 Ibid., 153.

63 Ibid., 237–79. The last of these chapters (ch. 45) is itself a list by the Student of more than forty further questions from the *Summae* which require reconsideration.

64 Ibid., 239, 243–5, 254–9 (all on presentments), 240–1, 259–61.

Summa Rosella in his later anonymous writings to suggest that the author was a parish priest, rather than a barrister.[65]

From St German's perspective, because the *Summae* relied upon the incorrect temporal law in answering these questions, they gave the wrong answers to questions of conscience which depended upon matters of law. As St German's Student observed, there was no fault on the part of the authors of the *Summae*,

> for they have thereby given a right great light in conscience to all countries where the law Civil and the law Canon be used to temporal things. But as for the laws of this realm they knew them not . . . if they had known them it would little have helped for the countries that they most specially made their treatises for.

Conscience was in many cases governed by the temporal law of a particular jurisdiction, so St German instead marvelled:

> greatly that none of them that in this realm are most bound to do that in them is to keep the people in a right judgement and in a clearness of conscience: have done no more in time past to have the law of the realm known than they have done.[66]

The Second Dialogue, printed in English, served to correct this failing on the part of the English clergy to explain English law in relation to English conscience. Comparative law became comparative conscience and thinly-veiled anti-clericalism. St German, a layman and lawyer, provided a guide to conscience in English to the people of England. This criticism of the clergy's failure suggests a lay audience; this is confirmed by the introduction to the Second Dialogue.[67] St German's guide to conscience was not for confessors, but the laity – the prevention of sin rather than the cure of souls.

This analysis of St German's purpose in *Doctor and Student* suggests greater coherence with his other works appearing shortly after 1530 than an understanding focused directly on the Chancery or the break from Rome. It is evident in the *New Additions* and the Parliamentary Draft that St German was interested in Parliament's role to intervene in Church matters not for its own sake, but to ensure that priests better performed their roles. This is precisely the concern which lay behind his discussion of conscience and is raised expressly in the Second Dialogue.

St German's discussion of conscience, directed to the laity, had a further, dramatic consequence. It fundamentally undermined any claims by the

65 J. B. Trapp, 'Introduction', in Trapp, *Complete Works of St. Thomas More, vol. 9*, xxxix.
66 *Doctor and Student*, 275; similarly 131. 67 Ibid., 176–7.

European Church to knowledge and expertise in conscience. The Church could claim such expertise in relation to St German's narrowly defined laws of God and nature, but many questions of conscience, as St German showed, were determined not by universal law but by local law. Conscience had become geographically diverse. For St German, writing in the midst of the Reformation, there was no unity of Christendom in questions of conscience, and for the Church to claim such universality risked leading people into error and sin.

CONCLUSION: ST GERMAN THE CHRISTIAN JURIST

Doctor and Student contains much that was relevant for equity and Chancery and for the Henrician Reformation. Such material appears in much of the text. The pervasiveness of religion to medieval and early modern life and thought means that religious works were also often works of law or political theory. The argument is that substantial parts of *Doctor and Student* are best understood through a religious lens, and that religion, in particular the guidance of the conscience of individuals, was a prominent purpose in the text. Whatever his later importance and reputation, in much of *Doctor and Student* St German was more concerned with the soul than the subpoena.

Sir Edward Coke (1552–1634) (19th century) / private collection / Ken Welsh / Bridgeman Images

5

Sir Edward Coke
Faith, Law and the Search for Stability in Reformation England

David Chan Smith

INTRODUCTION

When he was an old man writing his testament in 1623, Coke wrote of his faith by quoting words from the book of Job: 'whose patience by God's merciful goodness I have endeavored to follow'.[1] Coke had also been tested by adversity during the arc of his life. He had risen quickly in the legal profession, his capacity for hard work and clever reasoning bringing him recognition as a talented student at the Inner Temple (1572) and then as a practising lawyer (1578). Success at the bar attracted the notice of Queen Elizabeth I, who took him into her service as solicitor-general in 1592 and then attorney-general (1594). James I, the next monarch, raised Coke higher still, elevating him to the bench as Chief Justice of the Common Pleas (1606) and then the King's Bench (1613). Coke declared in his notebook that he had attained these positions 'neither by entreaty or purchase', and even the king later admiringly observed that Coke was in 'no way corrupt'.[2] But whether out of a virtuous attachment to principle or a granitic devotion to the authority of his own court, he alienated James I in a line of cases that seemed to undermine the royal prerogative. The king dismissed Coke in 1616. The episode was humiliating: the chief justice was forced to defend his legal decisions and review his own writings for errors (he found only a few). Coke was briefly restored to favour and reappointed to the Privy Council (1617), but he never returned to judicial duty in the Westminster Courts.

Instead, he became a leader in the stormy parliaments of the 1620s as constitutional debates flared over the extent of the royal prerogative in matters of taxation and security. He had much experience to draw upon and to share with younger members, having first been elected to Parliament in 1589 and serving as the

[1] The National Archives [TNA], PROB 1/6 (a copy), citing Job 19:25–7.

[2] British Library [BL] Harley MS 6687A, f. 18v; Norman McClure, ed., *The Letters of John Chamberlain*, 2 vols. (Philadelphia: American Philosophical Society, 1939), 2:3.

speaker of the Commons in 1593. In the 1620s he was among those who revived impeachment proceedings against royal officials, and he took a leading role in the drafting of documents that asserted the fundamental rights and privileges of the subject, culminating in the Petition of Right (1628). These efforts again provoked royal displeasure. After he defended parliamentary privileges against the king in 1622, he was imprisoned in the Tower and his manuscripts seized. From these experiences of dismissal and arrest grew a sense of humiliation and anger. When in 1628 he joined the debate in the Commons over illegal search and seizures, he objected that three of his confiscated manuscripts had never been returned to him. He added that he had known first-hand the stigma of a sudden arrest by order of the king: 'the commitment is fearful. All men's mouths are open against the party, and our friends afraid as well to come to us.'[3] The parliament of 1628 would be the last in his lifetime. After its abrupt dissolution by the king, another would not be summoned until 1640 after rebellion in Scotland had opened the crisis that would lead to civil war in Britain (1642–60).

Approaching his death in 1634, Coke could look back on a remarkable, if turbulent, career. His achievements included the publication of eleven volumes of law *Reports* (1600–15) and his first volume of the *Institutes* (1628), a comprehensive, if confusing, guide to English law, as well as several minor works. Two more volumes of *Reports* and three of the *Institutes* would appear posthumously in print. These texts influenced generations of students and their understanding of the common law. Nor was his influence limited to the common law. Coke remains an authority in ecclesiastical law on the consecration of buildings, and his report of *Corven v. Pym* (1612) established the heir-at-law's enduring rights over funerary monuments.[4] Posterity remembers him as an 'oracle' of the law who popularised Magna Carta as a statement of fundamental liberties and had the knack of turning legal principles into memorable phrases: 'a man's house is his castle'.

Though the subject of many biographies and well known for his contributions to the shaping of the English constitution, Coke's religious beliefs remain enigmatic. Only one of his biographers has probed his faith in any depth.[5] Most writers have emphasised instead Coke's devotion to common law

3 Robert C. Johnson et al., eds., *Commons Debates, 1628*, 4 vols. (New Haven: Yale University Press, 1977) [hereafter *CD 1628*], 3:150.

4 Kenyon Homfray, 'Sir Edward Coke Gets It Wrong? A Brief History of Consecration', *Ecclesiastical Law Journal* 11 (2009): 36–50; J. H. Baker, 'Funeral Monuments and the Heir', in *The Common Law Tradition: Lawyers, Books and the Law* (London: Hambledon, 2000), 349–64.

5 Allen Boyer, *Sir Edward Coke and the Elizabethan Age* (Stanford: Stanford University Press, 2003); Stephen D. White, *Sir Edward Coke and 'the Grievances of the Commonwealth', 1621–1628* (Chapel Hill: University of North Carolina Press, 1979), 14.

learning, ancient custom and the authority of the law's reason as the leading influences on his thinking. This approach has tended to secularise Coke's thought and minimise the impact of faith on his jurisprudence. Yet he lived during a period when religious ideas and imagery shaped every secular activity. In the opening page of Coke's law notebook, he wrote his name with a flourish underlined with 'Serve God'. Biblical references frequently appear in his writing. When convinced that he was in the right in debate, he sometimes cited the phrase from the Apocrypha, 'Great is truth and it will prevail.' Reminders of God's influence were often at hand: sometimes literally, at other times more figuratively. When he was out riding in the spring of 1632, his horse took a 'strange stumble backward and fell upon me', and Coke's head came to rest near 'sharp stubbes'. He gave thanks to 'the providence of almighty God though I was in the greatest danger yet I had not the least hurt, nay not hurt at all . . . the Angels of the lord turneth round about them that fear him and delivereth them'. He wrote of the influence of the Lord in the manner of a habit. Instructing another about the investigation of a woman accused of poisoning her husband, he wrote encouragingly, 'And I doubt not but god (who is the Author of truth) assisting your painful and discrete labour herein, the truth will appear.' Coke surrounded himself with images of those who had been tested in their faith, like Job, but had not always been found true. In his chambers at the Inner Temple he hung tapestries depicting the story of Solomon, and he owned a portrait of Cardinal Thomas Wolsey.[6]

These exemplars suited not only a man facing the temptations of high office, but living through a tempestuous period of religious controversy. The very frame of the state had been transformed during the Reformation when Henry VIII declared himself head of the Church of England, melding even more closely the civil and ecclesiastical spheres. Religious commitment could be a test of political loyalty, as those who opposed Henry VIII discovered to their loss. By Coke's lifetime, Europe was divided between Catholics and Protestants, and he well knew the threat to political stability posed by their differences. Three years after his birth in 1552, John Rogers was burnt at the stake in Smithfield for his Protestant beliefs as he resisted the Catholic regime of Mary I, and other Protestant martyrs followed him. Norfolk, the county of Coke's upbringing, was riven by discord in his youth. After the Duke of Norfolk was executed for his involvement in the Ridolfi Plot to assassinate Elizabeth I (1571), the county's patronage system fragmented, leaving the gentry to pursue their fractious quarrels. Neither was the confessional situation

[6] Yale University, Beinecke Library, Osborn MSS 184, no. 392; BL, Harley MS 6687A, f. 17r; 1 Esdras 4:41; BL, Harley MS 6687A, f. 16r, citing Psalm 34:7; Holkham Hall MS 748c, unpaginated.

in the region settled. Chief Justice Wray reported to the government in 1576 that Norfolk and Suffolk were the most disordered counties in England, observing a high level of non-conformity among 'obstinate Papists, but the most of them willful and undiscreet precisians [i.e. Puritans]'.[7] When Edmund Freke, Bishop of Norwich, began a campaign to discipline the puritans in his diocese, he was strongly resisted and, exhausted, he was translated to the See of Worcester in 1584. Sharp theological disagreement intruded even into the Temple Church. On Sundays at the Temple, Coke carefully took notes on the sermons of Richard Hooker in the morning and Walter Travers in the afternoon.[8] Travers' public criticisms of Hooker's orthodoxy in 1586 led to the former's suspension from preaching at the Temple and an unsuccessful appeal to the Privy Council. At the other end of his life, as Coke lay dying in 1634 at his country house in Stoke Poges, Buckinghamshire, the combatants in the Thirty Years War were decimating central Europe.

Yet contemporaries regarded Coke as devout without being saintly, a conscientious gentleman with secular cares. Thomas Fuller, his contemporary biographer, recorded that '[h]e constantly had prayers said in his own house, and charitably relieved the poor with his constant alms'.[9] His eldest daughter Anne Sadleir pointedly closed a letter to Roger Williams, the Puritan founder of Rhode Island and Coke's erstwhile clerk, by

> putting you in minde how deare a lover and great an admirer my father was of the liturgie of the church of England, and would often say no reformed church had the like. He was constant to it both in his life and at his death.[10]

Coke often flashed humorous comments and, despite his devotion to the Church, he was not beyond making a slightly irreligious joke. During a debate in 1628 over a bill for the punishment of adultery and fornication, the preceding speaker had warned, '[E]very man that was guilty of the sin would speak against the committing [of the bill]: the rest, whoever not guilty, would speak for it.' Coke replied that he 'wished that the old man would explain himself what he meant by the words of "Commit it"; for there were many young men might mistake thinking he meant commit the sin, not the bill'.[11] But Coke also attended to more serious matters to protect the Church. He was counsel to

7 Boyer, *Sir Edward Coke*, 59–65; quote in A. Hassell Smith, *County and Court: Government and Politics in Norfolk, 1558–1603* (Oxford: Clarendon Press, 1974), 201.

8 Thomas Fuller, *The Church History of Britain*, ed. J. S. Brewer, 6 vols. (Oxford, 1845), vol. 5, 184. See also Chapter 6 on Richard Hooker in this volume.

9 Thomas Fuller, *The History of the Worthies of England*, 3 vols. (London, 1840), vol. 2, 453.

10 Glenn LaFantasie, ed., *The Correspondence of Roger Williams: 1629–1653*, 2 vols. (Providence, RI: Brown University Press, 1988), 1:379.

11 *CD 1628*, 3:30.

and a benefactor of Norwich Cathedral. With great skill he defended the dean and chapter against a legal challenge to their estates from those who argued that the cathedral had been improperly re-founded in 1538 and 1547. He observed (suggestively) in his report of the legal case that the same reasoning would extend to protect all cathedral lands throughout England.[12] In fact, Fuller, whose conservative uncle Robert Townson had been Coke's chaplain, explicitly denied that the chief justice was a 'back-friend to the church and clergy'.[13]

Despite this evidence, a suspicion that Coke opposed the Church of England has attached to him since his own lifetime. Certainly a mild anti-clericalism appeared in his occasional jabs that, 'small cures preach, great cures are dumb'.[14] While he was chief justice, his contests with the church courts over the scope of their jurisdiction raised the ire of the clergy and other lawyers, as well as bringing the frowning attention of the king. Lord Chancellor Ellesmere, certainly no friend, once accused Coke of malice towards the Church: 'he hath as it were purposely Laboured to derogate much from the Rights of the church and dignitye of churchmen'.[15]

Historians have been divided in their interpretations of Coke's motives for these challenges to the ecclesiastical courts. Charles Gray thought Coke was 'an ardent Erastian . . . with a thoroughly Anglican respect of the privileges of the church and little use for puritans'.[16] Others have differed. Allen Boyer has recently provided renewed support for Coke's inclination towards moderate puritanism, arguing his 'bias against prelates shaded into a preference for Puritans'. Boyer notes Coke's support of such Puritan ministers as his brother-in-law George Leedes and his nephew Edmund Stubbes in their search for livings. He has also painstakingly traced the puritanism of Anne Stubbes, Coke's godly sister.[17] Resolving the mystery of his religious commitments can, as this chapter will explore, reveal the underlying springs of important aspects of Coke's legal thought.[18]

12 Ralph Houlbrooke, 'Refoundation and Reformation, 1538–1628', in Ian Atherton, ed., *Norwich Cathedral: Church, City and Diocese, 1096–1996* (London: Hambledon Press, 1996), 528–9; Jeremy Collier, *An Ecclesiastical History of Great Britain*, new ed., 9 vols. (London: William Straker, 1852), 7:238. *The Case of the Dean and Chapter of Norwich* (1598), 3 Co. Rep. 73.

13 Fuller, *Worthies of England*, 451.

14 *CD 1628*, 3:439.

15 'The Lord Chancellor Egertons Observacions upon Ye Lord Cookes Reports' (1615), in Louis Knafla, *Law and Politics in Jacobean England: The Tracts of Lord Chancellor Ellesmere* (Cambridge: Cambridge University Press, 1977, repr. 2008), 297.

16 C. M. Gray, 'Reason, Authority, and Imagination: The Jurisprudence of Sir Edward Coke', in Perez Zagorin, ed., *Culture and Politics from Puritanism to the Enlightenment* (Berkeley, 1980): 59, n.36.

17 Boyer, *Sir Edward Coke*, 182, 184–6, 163–5, 173–5.

18 It is instructive that David Little, 'Differences over the Foundation of Law in Seventeenth- and Eighteenth-Century America', in R. Griffith-Jones and M. Hill, eds., *Magna Carta, Religion and the Rule of Law* (Cambridge: Cambridge University Press, 2015), 141, notes that Coke

ANTI-POPERY

There is one irrefutable characteristic of Coke's religious thinking: he strenuously opposed 'popery'. Popery was a perception of Catholicism as a distortion of true religion, an idolatrous practice of human invention. Popery was shorthand for a corrupt, Catholic Church whose clergy preferred the pursuit of temporal riches rather than their pastoral duties. The Roman pontiffs, who similarly lusted for earthly power, had pursued universal monarchy and authority over kings. Popery was thus equated with tyranny.

Anti-popery was an elemental force in early modern English Protestantism. When Protestants discovered 'popery' in ceremony or doctrine, they objected – sometimes violently.[19] Disputes over which religious practices remained corrupted with popery after the Reformation, however, divided Protestants. Controversy erupted within the English Church over such issues as the appropriate vestments that a minister might wear during service, the authority of bishops and the placement of the communion table. The sharp edge of anti-popery was the belief held by many English Protestants in a 'popish plot' by papal agents in England and abroad to undermine the nation and return it to Catholic tyranny.

Coke was among them. Throughout his life, he vehemently declared his opposition to popery, which he believed to be an existential threat to the state. His feelings animated him to combat the popish threat to political stability in England, as he wrote, 'The commonwealth does flourish when religion does flourish, and they do live and die together.' The law was Coke's tool to protect religion, and he was mindful that they strengthened each other. He summed up this belief in a favourite phrase drawn from the Roman *Digest*: 'The highest principle ("ratio") is that which serves religion, for which there is no worthier law.' He believed that good law was anchored in higher forms of law – the law of reason or as Coke once declared in Parliament: 'The grounds of the common law are grounded upon the law of God.'[20]

roundly attacked radical Puritans and others whose 'endeavors strive to shake in sunder the whole frame of our Imperial government ... [including] our Common Law'. Those 'that would have no Bishops among us, do by their desires strive ... to pluck the right hand of government, and ... to break in sunder, the golden frame of just authority, for if no Bishops, then no Lawes, no King': *The Lord Coke His Speech and Charge*, delivered at the Norwich Assizes, 1607, no pagination.

19 Peter Lake, 'Anti-Popery: The Structure of a Prejudice', in Richard Cust and Ann Hughes, eds., *Conflict in Early Stuart England: Studies in Religion and Politics 1603–1642* (Harlow: Longman, 1989), 72–106.

20 *CD 1628*, 4:173; Norfolk Record Office, DCN 28/11, paraphrasing *Digest*, 11.7.43; *CD 1628*, 2:205, 209.

In contrast, Catholicism, with its assertion of the pope's temporal supremacy, undermined the natural harmony of the political order. Coke's opposition to popery focused on its corrosion of the natural ties of allegiance that bound subject and monarch, and which he believed were necessary for political stability. Allegiance was a natural duty, 'a true and faithful obedience of the subject due to his Sovereign'. Brought before Elizabeth I on his appointment as solicitor-general, Coke described in his notes how he felt 'a wonderful natural fear and love which god hath grafted in a subject's heart towards his natural sovereign . . . that my heart shaked within my body and all the parts of my body trembled'. Coke's report of *Calvin's Case* (1608) emphasised that allegiance was a duty that a subject owed by birthright to the person of the king by the law of nature: 'that which God at the time of creation of the nature of man infused into his heart, for his preservation and direction'.[21]

Though the Reformation had re-united the religious and secular spheres under the authority of the monarch, Rome still meddled, seeking to return the pope to the headship of the English Church. According to Coke, the root of the political troubles in England was a papal bull in 1570, *regnans in excelsis*, in which Pope Pius V had declared Elizabeth I a heretic and deposed her from the throne. Coke believed that the bull had transformed an obedient Catholic community into a source of potential rebellion.[22] The bull had placed individuals in a terrible bind. They had to choose either to obey the pope and by doing so break their allegiance to their queen, or risk being 'accursed who should yield any obedience unto her'. Like many Elizabethan Protestants, especially those in government, Coke distinguished between recusants who sought to undermine royal authority and quietist Catholics who went about their business and remained loyal. For example, Edmund Plowden, a noted common lawyer whose *Commentaries* served as a model for Coke's own law reports, was a Catholic. Yet Coke described him thus: 'excepting his recusancy he was otherwise a learned and good man'. This approach was consistent with the pragmatic strategy of the Elizabethan government not to 'make window's into men's hearts and secret thoughts, except the abundance of them did overflow into overt and express acts'. In Coke's view, if Catholics objected to the government

[21] *Calvin's Case* (1608), 7 Coke Report 13 a, 77 ER 382, 392; BL Harley MS 6686A ff. 34–5 and see also ff. 86–87v; D. M. Jones, 'Sir Edward Coke and the Interpretation of Lawful Allegiance in Seventeenth-Century England', *History of Political Thought* 7 (1986): 325–30.

[22] Henry Foley, ed., 'Life of Father Henry Garnett', in *Records of the English Province of the Society of Jesus . . . in the Sixteenth Century*, vol. 4 (London, 1878), 168.

and its Protestantism, as loyal subjects their weapons should not be arms, but rather 'prayers and tears'.[23]

The principal agents of popish subversion were found in the Jesuit mission to England. Rome's support of the English College at Douai and the infiltration of seminarians trained there and elsewhere into England, provided further evidence of the means by which popery corrupted the natural bonds of fidelity and allegiance. In reality, the Elizabethan Catholic community as a whole, by and large, chose quiescence over resistance. But from Coke's perspective, the series of events beginning with *regnans in excelsis* and climaxing in the Spanish Armada (1588) and the shocking discovery of the Gunpowder Plot (1605) suggested the determination of the forces of the Counter-Reformation and their threat to 'bring a final and fatal confusion upon the state'.[24]

The Elizabethan regime passed treason laws in response to these dangers. As attorney-general, Coke was tasked with enforcing them and he did so with a luciferous passion. A series of notorious treason cases followed, including the trial of Dr Lopez, the queen's physician; the Jesuit Father Henry Garnett and the Gunpowder Plotters. These experiences primed him to sense popery in even the faintest rustle of conspiracy. When Coke prosecuted Sir Walter Raleigh for treason (1603), he attempted to connect Raleigh with the Main and Bye plots and notoriously declared that the accused 'hast an English face, but a Spanish heart'. During the trials for the poisoning of Sir Thomas Overbury (1615), Coke suggested from the bench (incorrectly) that Sir Thomas Monson was part of a vast popish conspiracy that would soon be uncovered. In Parliament in 1621, after the first Protestant defeats in the Thirty Years War, Coke warned ominously of the 'great Resort of Recusants' to London and other cities and their 'insolent and proud carriage especially of late'. Urging that the king forbid the hearing of Mass in Catholic homes or foreign embassies, he argued for the strict execution of the laws against priests, 'lest the contagion of their corrupt Religion do yet run further'. Like many others, Coke feared that the Jesuits directed a fifth column within England that was prepared to overthrow the state: 'our state is so settled and established, as neither strength nor stratagem can prevail, unless there be a party made in England'.[25]

23 T. B. Howell, *A Complete Collection of State-Trials*, 34 vols. (London, 1814–28), 2: col. 222, 228; Foley, 'Life of Father Henry Garnett', 168–9; James Spedding, ed., *The Letters and the Life of Francis Bacon*, 7 vols. (London: Longmans, Green, and Co., 1890), 1:98.

24 Howell, *Complete Collection of State-Trials*, 2:179, 233.

25 Ibid., 2:7, 237, 949–50; Wallace Notestein, Frances Helen Relf and Hartley Simpson, *Commons Debates, 1621*, 7 vols. (New Haven: Yale University Press, 1935), 5:458–9.

DEFENDING ROYAL SUPREMACY AND THE CHURCH OF ENGLAND

By prosecuting treason, Coke used the law to safeguard the state, but he also defended the royal supremacy in academic controversy. His treatise, *Of the King's Ecclesiastical Law*, laid out the legal case for the royal supremacy and the rejection of papal authority in England. The treatise was included in Coke's *Fifth Reports* as a commentary on *Cawdrey's Case* (1591) and developed a narrative that was frequently stated in differing forms among Protestant writers, including Christopher St German.[26] The church courts, so Coke's account ran, had usurped legal authority in England prior to the reign of Henry VIII in order to promote papal authority. But the common law and the king had staunchly resisted these encroachments. As a consequence, even 'in the very midnight of popery' the English kings had not feared the pope's bulls, fortified as they were by the municipal law. Coke's belief in this narrative illuminates some of his constitutional statements. His assertion that the law 'protected His Majesty in safety and peace' has been understood within a secular context as a declaration that even the king was under the law.[27] But set within the frame of the religious history outlined in the *King's Ecclesiastical Law*, these assertions meant precisely what Coke said. The common law had protected the king from his enemies, had safeguarded his succession to the throne, and had protected him against claims that he was subservient to the pope. And the common law was a powerful defender: the law had been accepted and refined from time immemorial to suit the English people. It was, as Coke liked to write, the 'perfection of reason'.

The specific source for many of these arguments was a book that had first been published in 1538 during the heat of Henry VIII's Reformation. Coke had in his possession a manuscript copy of the *Treatise Proving by the Kings Law, that the Bishops of Rome had Never Right to any Supremacy within this Realm*, and made notes throughout the text. The anonymous author constructed the legal case for the prince's sovereign authority over the English Church. He insisted that Rome had never had complete jurisdiction in England and that independence had been maintained 'as well by the common laws of this realm, as by diverse statutes'.[28] The *King's Ecclesiastical Law* follows many of the same themes as the *Treatise*, most importantly in Coke's assertion that

26 See Chapter 4 on Christopher St German in this volume.

27 Howell, *Complete Collection of State-Trials*, 2:236; *Prohibitions*, 12 Coke Report 65, 77 ER 1343.

28 Anon., *A treatise prouynge by the kynges lawes, that the byshops of Rome, had neuer ryght to any supremitie within this realme* (London, 1538), STC 24248, f. 3v, sig. Aiii; Coke's copy is in Yale University, Beinecke Library, MS G R 24, 84–117.

the canon laws were 'allowed' to have force by the king and commons as the 'King's Ecclesiastical Laws'.[29] This implied that the ecclesiastical law was dependent on the king for its binding authority, thereby promoting the idea of the royal supremacy.

But the *King's Ecclesiastical Law* differs from its sources in one aspect of its analysis. Even a careful reader might miss recognising the Reformation as a pivotal event. The 'break with Rome' appears in the *King's Ecclesiastical Law* as part of the text's ongoing survey of legislation and royal acts that defended the liberties of the English Church and people from the predations of Rome. The *King's Ecclesiastical Law* emphasised the continuity of resistance to papal usurpation rather than stressing the Reformation as a point of sudden change. This argument for continuity downplayed papal influence in England throughout history while locating the central action of the resistance to papal authority in the present day. Just as English law had operated in the past to protect the liberties of the subject and the prince, so the common law was doing so in the present. As Coke observed during the trial of the Jesuit Father Henry Garnet, the 'antient common lawes of England . . . if they were exactlie looked unto, would restrain our Romish Catholickes from growing anie more to parts'.[30]

Coke and other Protestants understood themselves as participating not in a post-Reformation history following a sharp break with Rome, but as part of the ongoing struggle of the true Church against the forces of popery. This conflict was apparent in the temporal events that revealed the insidious efforts by papal forces, especially the Jesuits, and temporal princes such as the Spanish king, to snuff out the Reformed churches. At one assize, Coke told his audience that 'we may be sure that peace shall be opposed so long as there is a Pope in Rome, a devil in hell, [and] mischief in a Jesuits head'. During the trial of the Gunpowder Plotters, Coke gave a full rehearsal of the history of conspiracy beginning with the entry into England of 'Campion the Jesuit and many others of his profession with him, purposely to make a Party in England for the Catholick cause'. These Jesuits were the 'fore-runners' of the Armada and having failed in this attempt, they turned to secret plots to murder the queen through poison or violence.[31] This contest was the stuff of dramatic visual and written commentary by English Protestants.

As Coke and his co-religionists well understood, continuity was a critical argument supporting the legitimacy of their Church. Catholics asserted that

29 Edward Coke, 'Of the King's Ecclesiastical Law', 5 Coke Report 9a, 77 ER 11.

30 Foley, 'Life of Father Henry Garnett', 179; see also Howell, *Complete Collection of State-Trials*, 2:179.

31 Society of Antiquaries, MS 291, f. 12v; Howell, *Complete Collection of State-Trials*, 2:223–30.

Protestantism was an innovation, a recently sprung error. In contrast, the universal Catholic Church could trace its ancient existence through apostolic succession and the antiquity of the Roman see. Coke adopted the conventional Protestant response that an invisible church had existed alongside, even mixed into, the visible, Catholic Church:

> But you will ask, perhaps, where our Church lurked before Luther's cominge ... but I say it makes no great matter where it was, so that I am certain it was, for as a wedge of gold if it be dissolved and mixed with a mass of brasse, tynn, and other metals does not lose its nature, but remainethe gold still ... soe though our Church hath ever byn since Christ's tyme in the world, yet being mixed and covered with innovations and errors wee cannot tell in what parte it was.[32]

Coke's efforts in *Of the King's Ecclesiastical Law*, in particular, to bolster the royal supremacy involved him in a polemical exchange with the English Jesuit, Robert Persons. Among the English Catholics in exile, Persons was a leader and he energetically involved himself in a number of print debates, including those over the succession of James I and Catholic recusancy. His fulsome *Answer to the Fifth Part of Reports* (1606) and another publication attacked not only Coke's arguments for the royal supremacy, but the integrity of the common law itself. In Persons' polemics we can see the inverse of the arguments that Coke had made: the English monarch did not have ultimate jurisdiction over the Church and never had – this was merely an innovation.[33] The common law, far from being the perfection of reason as Coke liked to claim, was instead marked by change and corruption. Persons emphasised discontinuity, making clear the Reformation under Henry VIII had marked an abrupt shift into error.

Whereas Coke had attempted to present the common law as the bulwark of the royal supremacy against papal claims, Persons heaped scorn on the very authority of the law: 'our Common Lawes at this day are not so excessively ancient, entire, and excellent, as Syr Edward Cooke would have us thinke'. The common law had instead been frequently altered, especially by William the Conqueror, 'who like a Conquerour indeed tooke that liberty to himself, as to change and alter at his pleasure all laws'. Indeed, the deficiencies of the common law were manifold from the failure to provide adequate counsel in

32 Foley, 'Life of Father Henry Garnett', 167–8; Howell, *Complete Collection of State-Trials*, 2:223.

33 Robert Persons, *An Answere to the Fifth Part of Reportes Lately Set Forth by Syr Edward Cooke* (St. Omer, 1606?), STC 19352; Robert Persons, 'A Piece of a Reckoning with Syr Edward Cooke', in *A Quiet and Sober Reckoning with M. Thomas Morton* (St. Omer, 1609), STC 19412, 538–9, 541, 591.

cases of life and death to a lack of recognition of the inheritance rights of younger brothers.[34]

Instead Persons proposed an alternative history whereby the Reformation had changed and sullied the common law and led lawyers such as Coke to fictionalise its past. Persons sought to capture the argument for antiquity when he appealed to common sense by reminding his readers of 'the old, ancient honour, that was wont to be borne to Rome and Romanists, by our English Common Lawes'. Coke's representation of the past and his own arguments about the common law in the present were in fact the real corruptions. In time, Coke's deviations would be removed and the old law restored: 'For [Coke's *Reports*] must once againe be cast of[f] and forgotten, as novelties, when our old course of Commonlaw [sic] must returne to follow her ancient streame againe.'[35]

Rather than engaging in an extended debate, Coke simply dismissed Persons' objections. But the exchange reveals several insights into Coke's thinking about law, government and the political order. First, he sought to defend the royal supremacy to protect political stability and the Protestant Church. The sovereign had a natural claim on the allegiance of his or her subjects, and popery poisoned this tie. Second, Coke interpreted papal influence in England prior to the break with Rome as a form of legal usurpation, by which the clergy insinuated their claims in jurisdictional form. His historical narrative in *Of the King's Ecclesiastical Law* explicitly linked the common law as an instrument to defend royal authority against those who sought to question the legal sovereignty and very legitimacy of the crown. Lastly, this narrative and Coke's many statements in treason trials implied a contest between English liberty and popish tyranny. This comparison revealed a nationalistic tinge to his thinking.[36] Coke's pride in the common law, often remarked upon as a consequence of a narrow-minded provincialism, served him in his confessional disputes to put distance between England and Rome.

COKE AND PURITANISM

Coke's belief that the conflict with anti-popery continued into his own time suggested the dynamic of clerical corruption persisted. This perspective is crucial to understanding his debates with the Church of England. Just as Coke could see

34 Persons, 'Piece of a Reckoning', 566, 563, 567–70.

35 Ibid., 621, 622; Persons, *Answere to the Fifth Part*, sig. a2v.

36 See also Richard Helgerson, *Forms of Nationhood: The Elizabethan Writing of England* (Chicago: University of Chicago Press, 1995), 65–104.

himself in the ongoing struggle against popery, the logic of encroachment and corruption could be turned inward against the English Church itself. The clergy who had once amplified their jurisdictions in their own interests might do so again, as Coke wrote, 'for the temporal courts must always have an eye that the ecclesiastical jurisdiction usurp not upon the temporal'.[37]

This suspicion prepared Coke to pursue his quarrels with the church courts. During his time on the bench (1606–16), Coke clashed with the ecclesiastical courts by using the writ of prohibition to review their proceedings. Three areas were specifically contested by the civilians and common lawyers: the jurisdiction of the court of High Commission and its use of the oath ex officio, the cognisance of tithe litigation and the granting by the Court of Common Pleas of prohibitions based on the statute of 23 Henry VIII, cap. 9. A series of conferences (1608–11) involving the king, canonists, churchmen and common lawyers followed a complaint to the king from the Archbishop of Canterbury about Coke's interference in these issues. These meetings revealed that James I and Coke shared very different understandings of the common law's role in controlling other courts. The king believed that jurisdictional squabbles among his judges should be referred to him for resolution.

There also emerged five treatises that Coke wrote to defend the common law position.[38] Perhaps best known for their assertion of the privilege against self-incrimination, these treatises also illustrate Coke's conception of the role of the common law as a restraint on the Church's jurisdiction. They asserted the common law's power to review the proceedings of the ecclesiastical courts and remedy their proceedings if they trenched on the rights of the subject or the prerogative of the prince. Coke also asserted that the common law judges were the ultimate arbiters of statute, even those related only to ecclesiastical matters.

Some clergy represented these claims as a fundamental threat to the autonomy and even survival of their courts. Archbishop George Abbott wrote to Coke in 1612 to ask him to cease issuing prohibitions to his courts, which he hyperbolically claimed were 'almost utterly overthrown'. Others with equal spleen warned that Coke 'endeavored to bring upon the Church a servitude, far exceeding the Egyptian or Babylonian servitude . . . to overthrow the church of England, yea Christianity it self'. Coke stridently denied these charges, explaining that 'I acknowledge my self to be filius Ecclesiae and not of any foreign or metaphysical church, but of the church of England.'[39]

37 'Certain Articles of Abuses', Holkham Hall, MS 677, f. 347v.

38 Holkham Hall MS 677, f. 321r.

39 Holkham Hall MS 677, 316r; 'A Conference . . . touching prohibitions on the 28 of May 1611', Inner Temple, MS 511/16, 225, 226.

Despite Coke's protestation about his commitment to the English Church, the tendency has been to view his opposition to the ecclesiastical courts as motivated by his sympathy for puritanism. Puritanism is a concept that is difficult to define with precision. Catholic polemicists used the term in the 1560s as a pejorative for Protestants, and Protestants applied the term to themselves as well as to their overly zealous co-religionists. Although the stereotypical Puritan existed on stage and in literature as an uptight busybody, as Patrick Collinson has written, a puritan was 'in the first instance … in the eye of the beholder'.[40] 'Puritanism' captures a spectrum of opinion, practices and beliefs that could be moderate or radical, could be comprehended within the Church or were viewed as heretical or even schismatic by the authorities. Some of the self-styled 'godly' aimed to reform the Church from within, while others, whose consciences were especially pricked, refused to attend Church of England services. Some of these groups eventually chose to emigrate from a spiritually corrupt England, most notably the congregation that sailed on the *Mayflower* (supposedly taking with them a copy of Coke's *Commentary on Littleton*). Perhaps one unifying thread was a shared assumption that significant corruptions remained in the Church of England and must be reformed.[41] Agreeing upon how far reform should proceed, however, divided puritans.

Calibrating an assessment of Coke's relationship with Puritanism, therefore, requires great care. While he was apprehensive about corruption in the English Church, his attitude towards expansive reform was conservative, and he rejected doctrines or arguments that would detract from the royal supremacy or unity of the Church. Much of the evidence of Coke's 'puritanism' is inferential. Although puritan divines praised him, they may have done so in recognition of Coke's efforts to punish irreligiousness and to suppress popery, as Richard Rogers seemed to have alluded in the dedication of his sermon to the chief justice.[42] Coke encouraged sabbatarianism, often taken as a marker of puritanism, urging his audiences that 'the Sabbath being well observed we have better success in all our actions'. Yet such respect for the day of rest was, in fact, widespread. Nor did Coke always interpret the Sabbath observance strictly, mentioning in one letter to Robert Cecil that the press of business had

40 Patrick Collinson, 'Antipuritanism', in John Coffey and Paul Lim, eds., *The Cambridge Companion to Puritanism* (Cambridge: Cambridge University Press, 2008), 19.

41 Patrick Collinson, *Elizabethan Puritan Movement* (Oxford: Oxford University Press, 1990), 25–8, 36, 364–71.

42 Richard Rogers, *A commentary upon the whole booke of Iudges* (London, 1615), STC 1186, sig. B; similarly Francis Bradley, *A godly sermon preached before the right worshipfull Edward Cooke* (London, 1600), STC 1128.

forced him to work on a Sunday.[43] One of Coke's sisters and his nephew were towards the more radical end of puritanism, but he had six other sisters.

Reading confessional belief from associations is challenging during a period when many people had friends and family members across the spectrum of religious belief. This problem is clear from Coke's employment of Roger Williams as his clerk. His patronage of the young man has suggested Coke's implicit support of radical puritanism, but Williams himself did not think so. In a letter (1652) to Anne Sadleir, Coke's daughter, Williams recounted his decision to leave England for America and the parting from his beloved mentor that was 'as bitter as Death'. Williams wrote that he left due to his radical opinions about the Church, which were not shared by Coke: 'Laud pursued me out of this Land and my Conscience was perswaded ag[ain]st the Nationall Church and Ceremonies and B[isho]ps beyond the Conscience of your deare Father'. Riding past Coke at Stoke House on his way to Bristol, Williams did not inform his master of his intentions nor of his more radical beliefs: 'I then durst not acquaint him with my Conscience and my Flight.' In this decision, Williams probably chose well: Anne did not believe her father would have been sympathetic, scribbling on the letter from Williams, 'Full little did [Coke] think he would have proved such a rebel to god the king and his country.'[44]

Of the King's Ecclesiastical Law also implies Coke's suspicious attitude towards puritanism. The text, which is ostensibly a defence of royal authority against papal pretensions, is annexed to a case about a zealous Protestant minister Robert Cawdrey, whose deprivation the judges ultimately supported. Coke, in fact, prosecuted radical puritans, such as Thomas Bywater, when they challenged the royal supremacy. In 1604 Bywater had presented a manuscript to James I, probably in the form of religious advice, that contained 'very treasonable & seditious Contentes' that proposed reform of the Church. His papers were then searched, and evidence was discovered revealing his strong opposition to prelacy and the authority of bishops, including a copy of a libel against Archbishop Whitgift. Bywater was arrested and Coke accused him of a conspiracy to undermine the royal supremacy by attempting to 'stirre the people to a desyre of reformacyon' that would take the form of a general council. Coke interrogated Bywater and later wrote to

43 '[W]hosoever departs from the unity of the Church must be found among the heretics' (translation mine); Kenneth Parker, *The English Sabbath: A Study of Doctrine and Discipline from the Reformation* (Cambridge: Cambridge University Press, 2010), 108–10; Royal Commission on Historical Manuscripts [RCHM], *Calendar of the Manuscripts of the Most Honourable the Marquess of Salisbury*, 24 vols. (London: HMSO, 1883–1976), 9:74.

44 LaFantasie, *Correspondence of Roger Williams*, 1:358–9.

Cecil to summarise his investigation into 'the cause why he turned Puritan'. In the letter he speculated that Bywater had other associates, and he enclosed as evidence a letter by the accused written to a 'Puritan preacher, of whom I must say that *quicunque ab unitate ecclesiae decesserit necesse est ut inter haereticos inveniatur*'.[45]

Coke emphasised this commitment to the unity of the Church during his assize charges. After one speech in 1608, a listener understood that Coke expected his audience to follow Church practices that some puritans believed were popish: 'his audience gathered that we should show some obedience at the name of Jesus by yielding a cap or bowing a knee or such other'. In the same charge he tied conformity to church proceedings with obedience to the king, again sounding the theme of religion and allegiance, and again emphasised practices that some had critiqued as popish:

> Also he said those that did not show outward reverence to that in the Church which the king hath commanded to doe, and god hath not forbidden, it doth show that they want there inward obedience, both to god and the king, because god sayth that the king is such a one that every soul should submit themselves . . . .[46]

Coke's conservatism, did not, of course, prevent criticism of the Church or its courts. But the background to Coke's challenge to the ecclesiastical jurisdiction was his fear that the spiritual judges were repeating the pattern of its pre-Reformation predecessors. These objections grew from the framework of Protestant history that Coke had developed to such effect in his treason prosecutions. During the time before the Reformation, the ecclesiastical judges had worked to enlarge their jurisdictions at the expense of the rights of the subject and the prerogative of the prince. Historical example sensitised Coke to the illegitimate expansion of jurisdictional power. This mode of thinking could spill out beyond the religious into the secular sphere in many forms. For example, in Coke's writings on Chancery, he quoted the complete articles of *praemunire* against Wolsey, a not so subtle threat to the chancellors who might exceed their authority.[47]

45 A copy of the tract is Oxford University, Bodleian Library, Rawlinson MS B 151, f. 95r; discussed in David Colclough, *Freedom of Speech in Early Stuart England* (Cambridge: Cambridge University Press, 2005), 226–33; John Hawarde, *Les reportes del cases in Camera Stellata, 1593 to 1609*, ed. W. P. Baildon (London, 1894), 223–4; RCHM, *Salisbury*, 17:104; in manuscript as BL, Add. MS 6177, f. 200r.

46 BL, Sloane MS 1664, ff. 47v–48r.

47 Edward Coke, *Fourth Part of the Institutes of the Laws of England* (Union, NJ: Law Book Exchange, 2002, repr. 2009), 88–9; Holkham Hall, MS 677, 'Cardinal Wolsey's Praemunire', f. 111r; ibid., 'Precedents for Praemunire', ff. 112r–115r and ff. 496r–497v.

The issue for Coke and many other lawyers of his day was to determine the boundaries of the Church's jurisdiction and to identify those popish corruptions that remained in the canon law and needed to be restrained. Coke noted that the Elizabethan Act of Supremacy (1559), which had restored the royal supremacy, had extinguished all jurisdiction that was 'either ungodly or repugnant to the prerogative or the ancient law of the crown of this realm'. It followed, therefore, that the temporal courts might review and would prohibit any repugnancy in the canons or the ecclesiastical courts. Coke warned that 'where such incroachments or usurpations have been made, they have been the seeds of great trouble and inconvenience'.[48] The challenge was to identify these repugnancies and the limits of the ecclesiastical law.

There was much room for debate. The long-running dispute over the powers of the High Commission for Causes Ecclesiastical exposed this problem. Coke observed that the Elizabethan High Commission (tribunals composed of laymen and clergy) was authorised by the Act of Supremacy as an instrument to reform the ecclesiastical state since 'all bishops and clergy of England being then popish it was necessary to raise a commission to deprive them that would not deprive themselves'. The Commission was also intended to protect the Protestant settlement by punishing heresy, schism and other 'enormities'. The Act of Supremacy granted the Commission an extraordinary authority to fine and imprison. The language of the statute was broad, and Coke feared that a general construction of its 'cloudy words' might lead to the 'forfeiture of lands, confiscation of goods, nay corporal punishment, loss of member and life also for inconveniency, solicitation of chastity, working on a holy day or any other inferior offence'. Coke responded with more circumscribed interpretations of the Commission's jurisdiction. The tribunal should hear only 'enormous crimes' such as schism and heresy. Coke would prohibit its proceedings for lesser offences, such as adultery.[49]

The procedure of the Commission also presented opportunities for abuse, especially the court's use of the oath ex officio. As early as 1591, Coke, along with the judge Francis Wyndham, supposedly gave a charge at the Norfolk quarter-sessions that the church courts should not summon persons to answer questions put to them by oath ex officio.[50] Coke made clear throughout his career that he opposed the use of the oath ex officio by the High Commission except in cases limited to clergy and laymen examined in testamentary or

48 Coke, 'Of the King's Ecclesiastical Law', 5 Coke Report 8a, 77 ER 10. See 25 Henry VIII c. 19, § 3, *SR*, vol. 3, 461; 1 Elizabeth I c. 1, § 8, *SR* vol. 4, 352; Coke, *Fourth Part of the Institutes*, 321.

49 Inner Temple, MS 511/16, 125, 126, 128; Holkham Hall, MS 677, f. 321r.

50 A. Hassell Smith and Gillian Baker, eds., *The Papers of Nathaniel Bacon of Stiffkey, 1586–1595* (Norwich: Norfolk Record Society, 1990), 118.

matrimonial matters. Coke perceived several dangers. Laymen ignorant of the reasons for their summons and who were under oath might be forced to admit matters that would expose them to temporal penalties or commit perjury in desperation. Deponents might also be drawn to accuse themselves, a violation, Coke and the common law judges believed, of the principle drawn from the *ius commune* and canon law, *nemo tenetur prodere seipsum*. Since the common law judges did not strictly insist on the application of the rule in their own courts, Coke's citation of the maxim may instead suggest his insistence that the ecclesiastical courts should not innovate from the traditional body of church law.[51] But behind Coke's thinking was also the concern that the examination would be used to intrude into the 'secret thoughts' of individuals. They might be summoned and required to answer whatever questions the Commission asked them.[52] The Commission's jurisdictional creep and use of the oath bore the hallmarks of popery: the imposition of temporal punishments by clerical judges, the assertion by spiritual courts of ever wider jurisdiction and the use of the oath ex officio to 'ransack' the consciences of the accused. No wonder then that Coke was willing to prohibit their proceedings.

Coke's willingness to support the Commission's work to enforce religious conformity is perhaps more illuminating.[53] The tension is demonstrated by *Burrowes et al. v. The High Commission Court* (1615). John Burrows and others had been imprisoned by the High Commission for contempt for refusing to be examined by oath ex officio. The judges in the case acted to protect due process while preserving the authority of the Commission to investigate serious matters of schism and heresy. The case had come before Coke and the King's Bench on habeas corpus, Burrows and others claiming that their imprisonment for refusing to take the oath was illegal. But as the High Commission responded, these were 'wicked schismaticks ... speaking against all church-government'.[54] The Commission had intended to examine whether they had conformed themselves to the Book of Common Prayer or sought its alteration, possibly catching them within the operation of the statute of 1 Elizabeth I, which carried temporal penalties. At stake, the Commission argued, if they 'shall not be suffered to question them, this land will then overflow with blasphemous and wicked persons'.

51 R. H. Helmholz, 'The Privilege and the Ius Commune: The Middle Ages to the Seventeenth Century', in R. H. Helmholz et al., *The Privilege against Self-Incrimination: Its Origins and Development* (Chicago: University of Chicago Press, 1997), 17, 21–4, 29, 35–6, 43–4.

52 *Of Ex Officio Oaths before an Ecclesiastical Judge*, 12 Coke Report 26, 77 ER 1308; *Edwards's Case* (1608), 13 Coke Report 11, 77 ER 1422.

53 C. M. Gray, 'Self-Incrimination in Interjurisdictional Law: The Sixteenth and Seventeenth Centuries', in Helmholz et al., Privilege against Self-Incrimination, 68, 80.

54 *Burrowes Cox Dyton v. High-Commission Court* (1615), 3 Bulstrode 52, 81 ER 44.

Coke agreed with the Commission that Burrows and the others might be investigated if they spoke against the king or kept conventicles.[55] But, as he pointed out, these matters had not appeared in the return. Instead the issue before the court was whether the Commission had imprisoned Burrows for refusing the oath ex officio. Coke urged, 'We will not here encourage any sectaries', and John Dodderidge joined him on the bench in this sentiment: 'We do all of us agree with you in the due punishing of these sectaries; and in this we will rather strengthen than weaken you.' But Coke explained that the Commission should not force a person to accuse him- or herself within the reach of a temporal law. The deponent should, in any event, have the articles delivered to them. Rather than joining in sympathy with Burrows, however, Coke remarked, 'I do much dislike of these sectaries' and encouraged them to conform to the Commission by 'receiving the Communion kneeling'. The court only agreed to bail Burrows and the others instead of discharging them. When Burrows and his co-defendants appeared again before the King's Bench, they were asked whether they had conformed themselves, but they declined to answer. The court then recommitted them and allowed the Commission to proceed against them for heresy.

Coke's prohibitions also reveal his commitment to preventing the ecclesiastical courts from drifting into consideration of temporal matters. Tithe litigation clearly demonstrated this pattern, though many prohibitions were simply a consequence of the pattern of litigation and forum shopping. Many areas of the law related to tithes were squarely within the ecclesiastical jurisdiction, and yet tithe cases raised the most disputed prohibitions.[56] The common law courts asserted jurisdiction in the case of a tithe that was commuted by custom or perpetual agreement in a *modus decimandi*. Where a *modus decimandi* existed, the common law would try the custom because 'customs extending to a temporal inheritance shall be tried by the common law'. The basis for this claim partly drew upon the language of the Reformation statutes, Coke noting that since the *modus decimandi* 'is due by custom' and 'the lawe is that no canon or constitution etc that is contrary to any custom of the realm shall be put in use, And therefore the custom of England shall not be tried by the ecclesiastical law'.[57]

This distinction between temporal and spiritual matters shaped Coke's position on the more fundamental issue of the interpretation of statutes.

55 *Burrowes Cox Dyton v. High-Commission Court*, 3 Bulstrode 53, 81 ER 45.

56 C. M. Gray, *The Writ of Prohibition: Jurisdiction in Early Modern English Law*, 2 vols. (New York: Oceana, 1994), 1:xxxiii.

57 'An Answer to the Chief Points … Touching the Modus Decimandi', Inner Temple, MS 511/16, 175.

Coke claimed that the common law judges should determine the meaning of a statute as it applied to ecclesiastical matters. The issue emerged most clearly over the interpretation of the statute of 23 Henry VIII, c. 9, which required (with some exceptions) that individuals could not be cited outside their diocese and included a penalty against the offending ecclesiastical judge. By the early seventeenth century, there may have been a move among litigants to begin their litigation in the provincial courts. The debate over the application of the statute began under Coke in the Common Pleas.[58] Although the civilians argued that the ecclesiastical judge should interpret the statutes touching their jurisdiction, Coke and the common law judges argued otherwise and asserted their authority over the final interpretation of statutes. Their reasoning provided that the breach of a statute was always a temporal matter: 'the breach or not performance of that statute is temporal, and is punishable by the temporal law, and thereupon a prohibition lieth, and therefore the exposition of such a statute doth belong to a temporal judge'. Among others, Ellesmere found this argument unconvincing.[59] Coke's fall in 1616 calmed the acrimony between the jurisdictions and curbed, but did not eliminate, these prohibitions.

CONSTITUTIONALISM AND JURISPRUDENCE

Coke's statement in his *Institutes* that 'the law is the surest sanctuary, that a man can take, and the strongest fortresse to protect the weakest of all' was characteristic of his commitment to the rule of law and equality before the law.[60] The complex of Protestant thought about the Reformation deeply impacted Coke's thinking about the law as a protection against arbitrary power. Anti-popery remained a powerful influence on his thinking, providing the very example of tyranny in papal monarchy, a government in which religion and law failed to conjoin. His efforts to defend the religious settlement in England led him to assert the antiquity and authority of the common law, as well as defend the sovereignty of the prince. His long-standing preoccupation with the limitation of discretionary authority and due process is observable in his critique of the ecclesiastical courts and their workings, both prior to the break from Rome and after. From this framework of Protestant resistance we

58 Gray, *Writ of Prohibition*, 4:96–102; *Porter and Rochester's Case* (1608), 13 Coke Report 4, 77 ER 1416.

59 'Propositions grounded upon this . . .', Inner Temple, MS 511/16, 140; Knafla, *Law and Politics*, 284.

60 Edward Coke, *Second Part of the Institutes of the Laws of England* (Union, NJ: Lawbook Exchange, 2002, repr. 2009), 55.

can begin to trace the development of his peculiar constitutionalism with its emphasis on the superiority of the common law in a pluralist legal system.

But Coke's religious thought, drawing as it did on the logic of corruption, was dynamic and as events developed, unpredictable. Arguments informed by his faith might be directed at supporting the royal supremacy against popish usurpation, but they could also be aimed against the Church of England as a critique of its practices. The unifying themes were a search for stability as well as justice, the bounding of the church courts within their jurisdiction and the recognition of the monarch's prerogative over the Church.

Coke understood himself as a participant in the confessional struggles of his time. These continued a centuries-old battle between the true and false churches. Among his possessions is a rare map by Jodocus Hondius (c. 1596) depicting the world along with allegorical figures. The Christian Knight stood in the centre of the drama, armed with his faith in Christ and tensed for the assault of the fiery darts of the Devil. Ephesians 6:17 glossed the scene: 'And take the helmet of salvation, and the sword of the Spirit, which is the word of God.'[61] Protestants read the passage's exhortation to embrace faith alone as a rejection of the teachings of the Catholic Church. Coke paraphrases the line in his account of the 'Foundation of His Faith'. There he writes to beseech God for '[a] saving Faith and Patience together with the Testimony of a good conscience to the End and in the End against the Tem[p]tations and Fiery darts of the Enemy'.[62] The religious drama in which Coke participated was both his personal struggle for spiritual salvation and the worldly contest for true religion. Against the Catholic and English churches Coke had insisted on the proper balance between temporal and spiritual things, and its reflection in law and political stability. As he had wanted to emulate Job bearing the burden of his principles, in restless moments he might also have felt like the Christian Knight, battling for stability in a chaotic world against the many fiery darts of his enemies.

[61] The map is bound into Holkham Hall, MS 677. [62] BL, Add. MS 22591, f. 289r.

Richard Hooker, illustration from *The Church of England: A History for the People* by H.D.M. Spence-Jones, (c. 1910), English School (19th century) / private collection / The Stapleton Collection / Bridgeman Images

6

Richard Hooker
Priest and Jurist

Norman Doe

Scholars generally classify Richard Hooker as a theologian, philosopher or political theorist rather than as a jurist. He does not appear in the studies of modern Anglican canon lawyers or in those of historians of English ecclesiastical law.[1] However, his contribution to Christian jurisprudence, namely the law created by the Church for itself, marks out the 'Judicious Hooker' unequivocally as a great jurist, more so as he had no formal legal education, qualification or practice. While the novelty of elements of his thought is debatable, its application to the Elizabethan Church is original, and its relevance today for ecclesiastical law should be more fully recognised. His *Laws of Ecclesiastical Polity* may be read as a theological, philosophical or political text – but it is first and foremost a law book. It provides a 'theology of law' *and* a practical statement of principles of English church law. As such, Richard Hooker *is* a jurist: he was a commentator on ecclesiastical law, lived out that law in his ministry and administered it as an ecclesiastical judge, presiding over the Court of the Sub-Dean at Salisbury in 1591.[2] This chapter seeks to rehabilitate Hooker squarely in the juristic canon, by re-packaging *The Laws* in categories familiar to modern church lawyers, and to reveal something of Hooker the man.

Descended from a Welsh family, Hooker was born in April 1554 at or near Exeter, and educated at Exeter Latin High School. His father, Roger Vowell *alias* Hooker, was descended from Iago, son of Gevaph Vowell of Pembroke, who married Alice Hooker from Hampshire. Hooker attended Corpus Christi

1 There is no mention of Hooker in the index of either the seminal study of J. H. Baker, *Monuments of Endlesse Labours: English Canonists and Their Work 1300–1900* (London: Hambledon Press with the Ecclesiastical Law Society, 1998) or that of R. H. Helmholz, *The Canon Law and English Ecclesiastical Jurisdiction from 597 to the 1640s* (Oxford: Oxford University Press, 2004), vol. 1 in the series *The Oxford History of the Laws of England*.

2 W. J. Torrance Kirby, *Richard Hooker: Reformer and Platonist* (Aldershot: Ashgate, 2005), 1.

College, Oxford, as disciple (1569), scholar (1577) and fellow (1579); John Jewel, Bishop of Salisbury, played a part in Hooker's admission to Corpus, where Jewel had been a fellow. In 1579, recommended by Robert Dudley, Earl of Leicester, Hooker became deputy professor of Hebrew and was ordained deacon by the Bishop of London, John Aylmer. With other fellows, Hooker was suspended from college in 1580 for opposing a move to oust the college president. On his father's death in 1582, Hooker was granted a pension by the corporation of Exeter, and in 1583 a bursary by the Canterbury Cathedral chapter. After serving in a Buckinghamshire parish, in 1585 he was appointed on the suggestion of Bishop Aylmer and the Archbishop of York, Edwin Sandys, whose son he had tutored at Oxford, as Master of the Temple in London. Here he engaged with the judges and lawyers, and it was also the scene for his celebrated exchanges with the Puritan Walter Travers, the afternoon lecturer at the Temple, stimulating the quip that 'the pulpit spoke pure Canterbury in the morning, and Geneva in the afternoon'. Edward Coke, whose chambers neighboured the Temple Church, regularly sat in the congregation during this time.[3]

Hooker married Jean Churchman, his 'well-beloved wife', in 1588; they had four daughters surviving him and two sons dying as infants. In 1591 he became sub-dean of Salisbury Cathedral, and in 1595 rector of Bishopsbourne, Kent, where he died on 2 November 1600 and was buried. A monument was erected there in his memory in 1635:[4] his statue outside Exeter Cathedral was unveiled in 1907.

The context for Hooker's writing of *The Laws* was the political and religious context of the Elizabethan Settlement 1559. Following the break with Rome and the unfolding establishment of the English Church under Henry VIII, shift towards Protestantism under Edward VI (d. 1553) and restoration of Rome under Mary, the reign of Elizabeth I fixed the legal terms of the settlement with the consolidation of royal supremacy (Act of Supremacy 1559), liturgical conformity in the Book of Common Prayer 1552 (Act of Uniformity 1559), doctrinal unity in the Thirty-Nine Articles of Religion (1562) and statutes against various matters including papal bulls (1571, following Elizabeth's excommunication in 1570), reconciliation with Rome (1581), Jesuits (1585) and recusants (1593). Elizabeth had sent military aid to Protestants in Scotland, France and the Netherlands, and the Spanish Armada threatened in 1588. Hooker therefore wrote *The Laws* for a variety of Christians living under the settlement: supporters; Puritans (such as Thomas Cartwright)

3 See Chapter 5 on Coke in this volume.

4 P. B. Secor, *Richard Hooker: Prophet of Anglicanism* (Tunbridge Wells: Burns & Oates, 1999), 1. See also A. S. McGrade, 'Hooker, Richard (1554–1600)', in *Oxford Dictionary of National Biography* (Oxford, 2004).

looking to Geneva and urging further reform on Presbyterian lines; and Catholics looking to Rome. He published in English, not in the Latin of international discourse. However, he conceded that some might find his work 'perhaps tedious, perhaps obscure, dark, and intricate' (book I) and that he upheld the establishment to profit from it.[5]

The Laws consists of eight books. Books I–IV were published in 1593 (under licence of the Archbishop of Canterbury and in time for Hooker to send to Lord Burghley to support a bill against Puritan separatists and Catholic recusants).[6] Book V followed in 1597, with books VI and VIII in 1648–51 and book VII in 1662.[7] Broadly, books I–IV refute Puritan objections to the governance and worship of the English Church, and books V–VIII address particular issues about jurisdiction. *The Laws*' preface describes the origins and development of Elizabethan Puritanism (against 'popish' ceremonies and for Presbyterian 'discipline' to replace episcopal governance), and it sets out his aim: 'Nor is my own intent any other in these several books of discourse, than to make it appear unto you, that for the ecclesiastical laws of this land, we are led by great reason to observe them, and ye by no necessity bound to oppugn them' (ch. 7).

Hooker provides the first ever systematic statement, explanation and evaluation of the contemporary ecclesiastical law of the Church of England: '[O]ur whole question concerns the quality of Ecclesiastical laws' (I.16.1) – their nature, sources, subject-matter and purposes.[8] He draws on an extraordinary range of sources: most are scriptural, patristic and theological, but many are juridical, including earlier civilian and canonical material which he adapts to the Elizabethan Church to elucidate its substantive law in the form of principles. In *The Laws*, as elsewhere, we learn much about Hooker the Christian – his faith, personality, motivation and concerns. These are vividly portrayed by Thomas Fuller in 1655 in a passage which depicts Hooker preaching:

> his voice was low, stature little, gesture none at all, standing stone-still in the Pulpit, as if the posture of his body were the emblem of his mind,

5 A. S. McGrade (ed.), *Richard Hooker: Of the Laws of Ecclesiastical Polity: A Critical Edition with Modern Spelling*, 3 vols. (Oxford: Oxford University Press, 2013) 1:xxv–xxix, xcix [hereafter *Laws*].

6 *Laws*, Preface; ch. 8 was hard-line and suitable for the bill which became 35 Eliz. I, cc. 1–2.

7 There is some debate about whether Hooker finished books VI–VIII and if they are genuinely his work.

8 Henry Swinburne (d. 1624) was the first writer on canon law in English, with a treatise on wills (1590/1) and another on marriage contracts (published 1686): see Baker, *Monuments of Endlesse Labours*, 60. Francis Clarke's *Praxis in curiis ecclesiasticis* (1590s) (see Helmholz, *Canon Law and English Ecclesiastical Jurisdiction*, 255) was narrower in scope than *The Laws*.

unmoveable in his opinions. Where his eye was left fixed at the beginning, it was found fixed at the end of his Sermon. In a word, the doctrine he delivered had nothing but itself to garnish it.'[9]

THE CHURCH AND ECCLESIASTICAL LAW

There is a hint of ecumenical sensitivity in Hooker's treatment of the Church and church law. He distinguishes the Church universal and a church. The Church, a supernatural society (I.15.2), 'the people of God' (V.19.2), professes one Lord, faith and baptism; in turn: 'the Catholic Church is ... divided into a number of distinct societies, every of which is termed a Church within itself ... a society, that is, a number of men belonging to some Christian fellowship, the place and limits whereof are certain'.[10] Yet, ecumenically, he proposes 'mutual fellowship' between different churches (III.1.11–14); the 'urgent necessity of mutual communion for preservation of our unity in these things, as also for order in some other things convenient to be everywhere uniformly kept, makes it requisite that the Church of God here on earth have her laws of spiritual commerce between Christian nations' (I.10.14).

The Church of England is a 'reformed' church (IV.13.10) of a 'moderate kind' (IV.14.6). In England, the Church and commonwealth are identical (VIII.1.5). It is a system in which 'our laws made concerning religion do take originally their essence from the power of the whole Realm and Church of England than which nothing can be more consonant to the law of nature and the will of our Lord Jesus Christ' (VIII.6.11). Indeed, every church has a polity: 'Church-polity ... contains both government and also whatsoever besides belongs to the ordering of the Church', 'a form of ordering the public spiritual affairs of the Church of God' (III.1.11–14), which do not need to be the same in all churches (III.2.1). In England: 'the present form of Church government which the laws of this land have established, is such, as no law of God, nor reason of man has hitherto been alleged for sufficient to prove they do ill' (preface, 1). The 'Ecclesiastical law' is that 'whereby we are governed' (II.Introduction), and '[t]he laws of the Church' those whereby 'we have been guided in the exercise of Christian religion, and the service of the true God', dealing with 'our rites, customs, and order of Ecclesiastical government' (I.1.3). These 'laws of the Church of England' (V.81.5) treat 'the exercise of Christian duty' (V.4.2) i.e. '[s]olemn duties of public service to be done to God

9 Thomas Fuller, *The Church History of Britain from the Birth of Jesus Christ until the Year 1648*, 6 vols. (Oxford: Oxford University Press, 1845; repr. Westmead: Gregg, 1970), Book 9, 216.

10 See also the uncited Articles of Religion (1562, confirmed 1571), art. XIX.

[which] must have their places set and prepared in such sort, as beseems action of that regard' (V.11.1), for religion is 'the root of all true virtues and . . . stay of all well-ordered commonwealths' (V.76).

THE COSMIC LEGAL ORDER

Hooker develops his concept of ecclesiastical law within a wide cosmological perspective: eternal law, natural law, divine law in Scripture and human law. This not only indicates Hooker's respect for traditional categories concerning the legal order (drawn in part from Aquinas). His taxonomy is also intended to show that regulating Church affairs is more complicated than the Puritans suggested in their emphasis on the supremacy of Scripture; it is wise for men 'to learn how many laws their actions in this life are subject to' (I.16; 16.8).

The eternal law is 'that order which God, before all ages, has set down with Himself to do all things by'; it is an order which God has placed 'upon himself [as] his own free and voluntary act' (I.2.6) and expresses God's wisdom and reason (I.2.5). Hooker advises against excessive speculation on the eternal law as God's greatness is 'above our capacity and reach' (I.2.2). Natural law is the application of eternal law to human beings (I.3.1). It gives knowledge of ethics (I.8.9), as 'nature teaches laws and statutes to live by' (I.10.1), but it is darkened by sin (I.12.1). As natural law is that which human reason considers binding, it may be called 'the law of reason' (I.8.4 and 9), 'which binds reasonable creatures . . . and with which by reason they may most plainly perceive themselves bound' to 'obey' (I.3.1–2).

Scripture contains 'divine laws written' (I.10.14 and 13.1), revealed by God (I.16.1), and 'the principal intent of scripture is to deliver the laws of duties supernatural' (I.14.1). As the word of God (III.8.14), it contains all things necessary to salvation,[11] is perfect as to the actions it directs towards this 'natural' end for which God intends it (I.11–15), and some of what it teaches is such 'as could not by the light of nature easily have been known' (I.12.3). Reason should be used to interpret it (V.8.2); many 'natural or rational' laws are set out in Scripture (I.12), and it is not the sole source of practical wisdom for every human action (I.14; II.1.4). Moreover, it contains 'positive law' which, when made for circumstances no longer existing, may be changed (I.15). However, the need to find a scriptural basis for every action would make Scripture 'a torment to weak consciences' (II.8.6). Importantly, not all divine commandments found in Scripture are immutable: it depends on the reasons

[11] This is an unattributed representation of the Articles of Religion, art. VI.

for which God issues them; changed circumstances may remove these divine reasons (VII.5.7).

As God empowers humans to create laws for themselves, human laws derive from 'an order expressly or secretly agreed upon, touching the manner of this union in living together'. This order is 'the law of a common weal, the very soul of a politic body, the parts whereof are by law animated, held together, and set on work in such actions as the common good requires'. Humans create laws because they are obstinate, rebellious and averse to obedience to natural law. In turn, those to whom authority to legislate is given must exercise it for 'the peace, tranquillity, and happy estate of the rest'. Consent is critical: 'Without which consent there were no reason than one man should take upon him to be lord or judge over another' (I.10).[12] Therefore, government by many is the ideal (VIII.3.2–3). Moreover: 'laws human must be made according to the general laws of nature, and without contradiction to any positive law in scripture. Otherwise they are ill made' (III.9.2) – but not, interestingly, void.[13]

THE DEFINITION OF 'LAW'

Hooker's teleological definition of 'law' embraces continental ideas of *lex* (positive) and *ius* (implying justice).[14] Law consists of 'rules of action' (I.16.7) and serves an end: 'That which does assign to each thing the kind, that which does moderate the force and power, that which appoints the form and measure of working, the same we term a Law'; thus, 'no certain end could ever be attained, unless the actions whereby it is attained were regular, that is to say, made suitable fit and correspondent to their end, by some canon, rule or law' (I.2.1); e.g. church law is directed to 'the outward conduct or government of the Church' (III.11.10). As a law is 'a directive rule to goodness of operation', so reason is 'to define in particular actions what is good' (I.8.4). Further, '[l]aws do not only teach what is good but they enjoin it, they have … a certain constraining force'; but 'to constrain men to anything inconvenient does seem unreasonable'. The making of laws, therefore, should be exercised by the wise (I.10.7).

12 There are echoes here of Thomas Smith (1513–77), John Fortescue (c. 1394–c. 1476), the French jurist Jean Bodin (c. 1526–1596) and the Calvinist jurist Johannes Althusius (c. 1563–1638).

13 For earlier ideas, see N. Doe, *Fundamental Authority in Late Medieval English Law* (Cambridge: Cambridge University Press, 1990).

14 C. J. Friedrich, *The Philosophy of Law in Historical Perspective*, 2d ed. (Chicago: Chicago University Press, 1963), 70.

Hooker links the legal orders: 'human laws are defined to be ordinances, which such as have lawful authority given them for that purpose, do probably draw from the laws of nature and God, by discourse of reason, aided with the influence of divine grace'; and 'for that cause ... Ecclesiastical canons ... by instinct of the holy Ghost ... have been made, and consecrated by the reverent acceptation of all the world' (III.8.17, citing *Gratian's Decretum*). Similarly, positive laws, '[l]aws being imposed', are not only those 'made and invented of men'; eternal law, natural law, divine-scriptural law may all contain 'positive laws' (I.15.1; also III.9.1); e.g. '[l]aws that concern supernatural duties, are all positive, and either concern men supernaturally as men, or else as parts of a supernatural society ... the Church' (I.15.2).

These ideas pave the way for Hooker to connect law and reason: 'the laws of well-doing are the dictates of right reason' (I.7.4). So he develops the category 'the law of reason': 'a law is properly that which reason in such sort defines to be good that it must be done'; 'the law of reason or human nature is that which men by discourse of natural reason have rightly found out themselves to be all for ever bound to in their actions' (I.8.8); laws of reason are 'investigable by reason without the help of revelation supernatural and divine'; and 'knowledge of them is general, the world has always been acquainted with them' (I.8.9). Consequently, 'mixed' laws are human laws which the law of reason prescribes; and 'merely' human laws are those which 'make that a duty which before was none' (I.10.10).[15]

FORMAL HUMAN SOURCES OF CHURCH LAW

Hooker is Catholic in his use of external and native sources for his principles of ecclesiastical law: the canons of the early councils; classical canon law; (Roman) civil law (and medieval civilians); English common law; and, though more rarely, Jewish law and Byzantine law.

Hooker draws heavily on the 'authorities of Councils' (VI.6.10), to substantiate or challenge a wide range of norms, on e.g. excommunication, Nicaea, Canons 11–13 (VI.5.8); reading Scripture, Laodicea, Canon 59 (V.20.1); keeping Sunday, Apostolic Canons, Canon 55 (V.72.10); and barring bishops from uninvited ministry outside their diocese, Antioch, Canon 9 and First Council of Constantinople, Canon 2 (VII.8.3). He also makes frequent use of the canon law of the Roman Church, medieval and post-Reformation.[16]

15 For the general orthodoxy of these definitions, see R. W. Carlyle and A. J. Carlyle, *A History of Medieval Political Theory in the West*, 6 vols. (Edinburgh: Blackwood, 1903–36), 6:354.

16 As to the former, he may do so under the Submission of the Clergy Act 1533, but he does not cite it.

Taking centre stage is, in Hooker's own words, 'Gratian, the founder of the Canon Law' (VI.4.6). He cites Gratian's *Decretum* on many issues, including the examination of candidates before ordination (VII.14.6), the quality of penance (VI.4.6), signing with the cross in baptism (V.65.14), the nature of judgment (VI.4.7), episcopal titles (VII.16.9), the election of a bishop (VIII.7.2) and church property (VII.22.6). He also cites a host of other canonists of and before his generation.[17]

Hooker modestly admits he has 'not much been conversant' in the study of civil law, but it should be consulted for its 'singular treasures of wisdom' and 'the great use we have thereof both in decision of certain kinds of causes arising daily within ourselves, and especially for commerce with Nations abroad' (preface, 8.4). Thus, he often invokes the 'imperial laws' (VII.24.22), 'the Laws and Customs of Rome' (VII.8.7), the Law of the Twelve Tables (V.79.14), Justinian's Code (VII.8.2), the Digest (VIII.5.2), and the New Laws (VII.8.10) and 'Laws concerning Religion' of Theodosius and Valentinian (VII.18.2).

Hooker rarely cites English law expressly, but he recognises 'the practice of the Common law among us' (preface, 1.13), the value of the 'books of the Common law' (preface, 8.4) and the need 'to rely and build upon the judgement of such as are famous for their skill in the laws of this land' (II.7.2). The few specific statutes cited are on episcopal appointments, 25 Edward III, c. 3 and 25 Henry VIII, c. 20 (VIII.7.3); church courts, 1 Elizabeth, c. 1 (VIII.8.4); and appeals, 25 Henry VIII, c. 19 (VIII.8.5). As to the nature of statutes, he cites Sir William Staunford: 'our statutes sometimes are only the affirmation or ratification of that which by common law was held before' (I.10.10).[18] He also cites Bracton (VIII.3.1 and 8.9).

Custom is treated as law (I.10.8), and it is based on tacit consent (IV.14.5). Customs include 'the assembling of the people of God together by the sound of a bell, the presenting of infants at the holy font by . . . Godfathers, or any other like received custom' (II.7.2) and receiving Communion at a wedding (V.73.7). Hooker also discusses 'apostolic customs' (V.62.6), 'ancient practice . . . the Church has continued time out of mind' (V.10.1) and 'unreasonable custom' against 'right reason', such as polygamy (I.10.10, citing Justinian's New Laws).

He is well known in using tradition as a normative source: 'we mean by traditions ordinances made in the prime of Christian religion, established with

[17] R. H. Helmholz, 'Richard Hooker and the European *ius commune*', *Ecclesiastical Law Journal* 6 (2001): 4.

[18] W. Staunford, *Pleas of the Crown* (London: Richard Tottell, 1557; facsimile ed. London: Professional Books, 1971); Staunford (1509–58) was a judge of the Court of Common Pleas.

that authority which Christ left to his Church for matters indifferent, and in that consideration requisite to be observed till like authority see just and reasonable cause to alter them'; they are not 'rudely and in gross to be shaken off' because they are humanly made (V.65.2); e.g. signing with the cross at baptism is a reasonable tradition to aid Christians not to be ashamed of Christ (V.65.6–7).[19] However, Hooker does not expressly cite norms from the contemporary English Canons or case law.[20]

THE STRUCTURE, EFFECTS AND PURPOSES OF ECCLESIASTICAL LAW

Hooker's treatment of ecclesiastical law matters reveals him to be a highly competent legal technician. Like lawyers before and since, Hooker recognises the value of 'first principles', 'axioms' and 'maxims'. Nothing 'can be thoroughly understood, or soundly judged of till the very first causes and principles from which originally it springs be made manifest'; the cosmic legal orders, indeed, 'all concur as principles' (I.16.1); again, 'there is and ever will be great use of human laws and ordinances deducted by way of discourse as conclusions from the former divine and natural, serving for principles thereto' (VIII.6.4). For instance, 'axioms' include the proposition that 'a small thing in the eye of Law is nothing' (V.7.3);[21] and it is a 'maxim' that '[l]east of all may those things be changed which have always had a fixed interpretation' (V.59.3). Needless to say, 'general axioms' may be 'subject to just exceptions' (V.5.1).[22]

Hooker is knowledgeable about technical juridical categories which he deploys extensively. As to prohibitions: 'When prohibited things are done, they do not hold. In prohibitions concerning favourable matters, however, the contrary obtains' (V.62.13, citing Gratian's *Decretum*). So, '[w]e may not from Laws that prohibit anything with restraint conclude absolute and unlimited prohibitions', but 'even things lawful are well prohibited, when there is fear lest they make the way to unlawful more easy' (V.62.3, citing the Institutes). On duties: 'A law be it civil or Ecclesiastical is as a public obligation' by which

19 See also Articles of Religion, art. XXXIV: traditions of the Church need not 'be in all places one, and utterly alike'.

20 For these, see G. Bray (ed.), *The Anglican Canons: 1529–1947* (Woodbridge: Boydell Press, 1998).

21 He cites André Tiraqueau (c. 1480–1558), a French jurist who followed Bartolus.

22 Many axioms that he cites are from civil and canon law: see N. Doe and S. Pulleyn, 'The Durability of Maxims in Canon Law: From *regulae iuris* to Canonical Principles', in T. L. Harris, ed., *Studies in Canon Law and Common Law in Honor of R. H. Helmholz* (Berkeley: Robbins Collection, 2015), 303–36.

'the whole stands charged' (VIII.6.7); the 'public exercise of duties' includes instruction, Holy Communion and prayers (III.1.14). He links 'rights' with 'interests' (VI.1.2): 'Peace and justice are maintained by preserving to every order their rights and by keeping all estates ... in an even balance' (VIII.6.7). There are also natural rights, e.g. 'the right that naturally belongs to a Commonwealth' to make laws (VIII.6.5); citing Gratian's *Decretum* again, a 'natural right' is 'the right which extracts those general duties', namely, those 'that concern men naturally even as they are men' (I. 12.1).

Hooker contrasts 'privileges' with 'common right' (familiar in common law as *common droit*). As a 'peculiar right', a privilege is said to be 'that for favour of certain persons comes forth against common right; things prohibited are dispensed with because things permitted are dispatched by common right, but things forbidden require dispensation' (V.81.3). Hooker also discusses 'words of obligation' in relation to contracts, relying on 'stipulations' in the Digest and Institutes: 'A stipulation is a form of words by which he who is questioned replies that he will give or will do what the question requires' (V.64.4).

Popular consent gives law its coercive force: 'Laws are not made ... which public approbation hath not made so' (I.10.8); Hooker cites Roman law and Gratian's *Decretum* for the principle *Quod omnes tangit ab omnibus tractari et approbari debet* – what touches all ought to be treated and approved by all (VIII.6). Consent is also justified so that 'all men might see their duties beforehand, and know the penalties of transgressing them' (I.10.5); and in Parliament, 'although we be not personally ourselves present, notwithstanding our assent is by reason of others agents there in our behalf. And what we do by others, no reason but that it should stand as our deed, no less effectually to bind us than if ourselves had done it in person' (I.10.8).

The laws of the Church deal primarily with external, visible order:

> No man doubts that for matters of action and practice in the affairs of God, for the manner of divine service, for the order in Ecclesiastical proceedings about the regiment of the Church there may be oftentimes cause very urgent to have laws made. But the reason is not so plain wherefore human laws should appoint men what to believe.

Thus: (1) 'in matter of opinion the law does not make that to be truth which before was not ... but it manifests only and gives men notice of that to be truth, the contrary whereto they ought not before to have believed'; and (2) 'as opinions do cleave to the understanding and are in heart assented to it is not in the power of any human law to command them, because to prescribe what men think belongs only to God' (citing Romans 10.10). Nevertheless, '[a]s opinions are either fit or inconvenient to be professed, so man's law has to determine of them' and require assent to, or prohibit contradiction to, specific articles of doctrine (VIII.6.4). Laws should also promote 'the universal or common good' (VIII.3.4), ascertained by reason (I.7.7), equality (I.8.7, citing the Code and Digest) and liberty, the natural inclination of man (I.7.6) and mark of a healthy community (VIII.3.3); but freedom has limits (I.6, title; V.71.4) and 'the present liberty of law' may be 'turned to great abuse' (V.81.15). Hooker warns about the seriousness of judging Church law (VII.15.14).

THE MUTABILITY AND RELATIVITY OF CHURCH LAW

For Hooker the realist, laws change and differ according to circumstances: 'experience of time may breed both Civil and Ecclesiastical change' (VII.14.7). Therefore, 'Canons, Constitutions, and Laws which have been at one time meet, do not prove that the Church should always be bound to follow them' (VII.15.14, citing the Code). We should presume that legislators have reasons for their laws, but it may be difficult to find them (VII.15.14), or 'troublesome' to alter a law which 'continual practice' approves (IV.14.1). Nevertheless, if the reason for a law no longer pertains, it should be changed rationally not by 'private fancy' (VII.15.13–14). In sum, '[p]ositive laws are either permanent or else changeable, according to the matter itself is concerning which they were first made. Whether God or man be the maker of them, alteration they so far admit, as the matter does exact' (I.15.1; and II.10.1).

Therefore, Hooker asks, if 'the end for which [a] law was ordained is now fulfilled past and gone: how should it be but cease any longer to be, which has no longer any cause of being in force as before?' He cites Gratian (III.10.2). For example, if 'received laws' of the Church of England (i.e. Roman 'orders rites and ceremonies') are a 'hindrance to piety and Religious service of God', they should be abrogated; after all, '[l]aws, as all other things human, are many times full of imperfections', and 'the number of needless laws unabolished does weaken the force of them that are necessary'. However, desuetude too may abrogate law: 'laws as have been made upon special occasions, which occasions ceasing, laws of that kind do abrogate themselves' (IV.14.1). But positive laws 'perhaps cannot be abrogated saving only by whom they were made: because the intent of them being known to none but the author, he alone can judge how long it is requisite they should endure' (III.10.1).

In turn, Hooker proposes the relativity of law: 'Laws positive are not framed without regard had to the place and persons for ... which they are made' (III.11.6). Therefore, the laws of different churches differ: 'Moral laws are the rules of politic, those politic which are made to order the whole Church of

God rules to all particular Churches, and the laws of every particular Church rules to every particular man within the body of the same Church' (V.81.4).

RELAXATION OF LAW: EQUITY AND CONSCIENCE

Hooker develops his ideas on the relationship between Church law and morals in his treatment of the limits of law and its liberal relaxation, and the associated ideas of justice and equity.[23] Once more, here he is firmly in the tradition of the civil law, canon law and common law.

As 'the ordinary course of common affairs is disposed of by general laws, so likewise men's rarer incident necessities and utilities should be with special equity considered' (V.9.3). So the Church is to avoid 'a rigorous observation of Spiritual ordinances, without relaxation or exception' when 'equity, permitting in cases of necessity that, which otherwise it disallows and forbids' (V.9.1, citing Panormitanus). Hooker also recognises 'the Law of Equity' (VII.13.5), and he deploys equity in many contexts, e.g. to relax 'justice' and 'common right' (V.81.4); in the administration of rites (V.58.4, citing the Digest), e.g. baptism 'according to the rules of natural equity' (V.60.5); and by equity 'everyone ought to enjoy his own; that what is ours no other can alienate ... but with our own deliberate consent; [and] that no man having passed his consent or deed may change it to the prejudice of any other' (V.79.11).

In similar vein, Hooker often uses conscience to explain or justify Church laws. For instance, private administration of Holy Communion to the sick is justified for spiritual comfort and ease of conscience (V.68.12); the 'unconscionable absence' of clergy from their cures is not lawful but may be justified by 'reasons and maxims of common right' (V.81.1); people 'are in conscience bound to attend the work of their heavenly calling'; and 'conscience is against ignorance in them that have charge and cure of souls' (V.81.2). In turn, Hooker offers maxims of conscience; e.g. 'Conscience is the proper court of God' and 'Men are not able to make any law that shall command the heart' (VIII.6.9). He also discusses conscientious objection to the law and limits on it, citing the French jurist Jean Bodin (VIII.6.9).

CHURCH GOVERNANCE AND THE RULE OF LAW

For Hooker, 'the Church ... and the Commonwealth are two corporations independently each subsisting by itself'; yet there 'is not any man of the

[23] Echoes of this in more recent times can be found in the judgments and extra-judicial statements of Lord Denning, who is the subject of Chapter 15 in this volume.

Church of England but the same man is also a member of the commonwealth; nor any man a member of the commonwealth which is not also of the Church of England' (VIII.1.2); '[f]or if the Commonwealth be Christian, if the people ... do publicly embrace the true religion, this very thing does make it the Church' (VIII.6); and religion is the 'highest of all cares appertaining to public regiment' (V.1.2).[24]

In England, the 'power in Ecclesiastical causes is by the laws of this Realm annexed to the Crown' (VIII.1.2),[25] by 'the general consent of all' (VIII.6.11). Under this 'supremacy' or 'dominion', the monarch may convene church assemblies, make ecclesiastical law, appoint church governors and 'keep all Ecclesiastical persons within ... their duties and constrain them to observe the Canons of the Church to follow the rules of ancient discipline'.[26] Each function is exempt from clerical censure but cannot involve sacramental acts or preaching. Rather, the monarch is directed 'to what affairs by the said law their supreme authority and power reaches' – 'so is the power ... over all and in all limited [so] that to all its proceedings the law itself is a rule': thus, 'in regard of Ecclesiastical laws' the monarch has authority 'to exercise in Ecclesiastical causes but according to the laws of the Church' (VIII.3).[27]

Moreover, '[t]he Parliament of England, together with the Convocation annexed thereunto, is that whereupon the very essence of all government within this kingdom does depend'. As 'the body of the whole Realm', it consists of the monarch and of all in the realm subject to him 'for they all are there present either in person, or by such as they voluntarily have derived their very personal right to'. Therefore, laws 'take originally their essence from the power of the whole Realm and Church of England'; and the monarch's role in 'making laws ... rests principally in the strength of a negative voice, which not to give them were to deny them that, without which they were but Kings by mere title and not in exercise of dominion' (VIII.6.11).

In turn,

> [s]ome things ... the King alone has no power to do without the consent of the Lords and Commons assembled in parliament. The King of himself cannot change the nature of pleas nor courts, no not so much as restore

24 See also VII.18.2 for the benefit of religion to society, citing Justinian, Code, 1.3.34 and 1.4.34; and Institutes, book 1, title 14.4 (V.80.6). He also cites Digest, 1.2.11, for government by one (VIII.3.4).

25 This is an unattributed re-presentation of e.g. the Articles of Religion (1562), Declaration.

26 Citing Choppin, *On Sacred Public Policy*, Preface (VIII.3.3); René Choppin (1537–1606) was a French jurist. Hooker, on royal authority, also uses Boethius Epo, a sixteenth-century professor of canon law at Douai (VIII.6.8).

27 He does not here discuss the Articles of Religion, art. XXXVII, but anticipates Canons Ecclesiastical 1603, canons 1–2.

> blood, because the law is a bar to him, not any law divine or natural, but the positive laws of the realm have abridged therein and restrained the King's power. (VIII.3.3)

Hooker asserts, therefore, that 'we should count any Statute a law which the high Court of Parliament has established about the matter of Church regiment' – and he refutes the claim 'that the Parliament being a mere temporal Court can neither by the law of nature, nor of God have competent power to define of such matters' (VIII.6.10).

In sum, then, the 'spiritual jurisdiction' of the Church of England is the power of 'ruling'.[28] Its purpose is 'to provide for the health and safety of men's souls, by bringing them to see and repent their grievous offences committed against God, and also to reform all injuries'; this 'spiritual authority' is 'a power, which Christ has given to be used over them ... according to his own most sacred laws, and the wholesome constitutions of his Church' (VI.2).

MAKING ECCLESIASTICAL LAW

Not only is Hooker a unionist, he is also a populist. The Church has authority to create laws for itself (III.10.2, citing Gratian's *Decretum*), which exact faithful obedience (V.8.4); indeed, '[t]he Church ... being a Politic Society or Body, cannot possibly want the power of providing for itself' (VII.14.3). Moreover, 'the true original subject of power ... to make church laws is the whole entire body of that church for which they are made' (VIII.6.1–2); the 'general consent of all ... gives them the form and vigour of laws' (VIII.6.11). This includes innovation (V.8.1); it is 'absurd to imagine the Church ... abridged of this liberty', so that 'no law, constitution, or canon, can be further made' (VI.2.2). It 'has the same authority still, and may abrogate old laws, or make new, as need shall require' (VII.14.3) at 'the instinct of the Holy Spirit' and as 'by the ... acceptation of all' (III.8.18, citing Gratian). While making Church 'laws with other like actions ... are still termed the deeds of the King' (VIII.1.1),[29] 'to define of our own Church's regiment, the Parliament of England has [a] competent authority' (VIII.6.11); also, the English Church may 'receive orders rites or customs from the Church of Rome' (IV.5.1).

As this power is to be used to attain divine and natural ends (III.10.2), it is not the case that the law gives 'the Church a liberty which has no limits or bounds'. Rather, law-making power extends 'to sundry things of Ecclesiastical jurisdiction and such other matters'; and in this, 'we have nowhere altered the laws of

28 He distinguishes 'Ecclesiastical order' and 'Ecclesiastical jurisdiction' (VI.2; 3.5).

29 See also VIII.6.11, citing the Institutes, 1.2.6: 'What pleases the Prince has the force of law, since ... the people have conceded to him their ... authority to command'.

Christ further than in such particularities only as have the nature of things changeable according to the difference of times, places, persons, and other like circumstances'. However: 'Christ has commanded prayers to be made, sacraments to be ministered, and his Church to be carefully taught and guided'; these 'must be kept till the world's end' – but the Church may add to these if no law of Christ forbids this (III.11.13). There are also doctrinal limits:

> The Church has authority to establish that for an order at one time, which at another time it may abolish, and in both do well. But that which in doctrine the Church does now deliver rightly as a truth, no man will say that it may hereafter recall and as rightly avouch the contrary. Laws touching matter of order are changeable, by the power of the Church; articles concerning doctrine not so. (V.8)[30]

Hooker states that

> till it be proved that some special law of Christ has for ever annexed to the Clergy alone the power to make Ecclesiastical laws, we are to hold it a thing most consonant with equity and reason that no Ecclesiastical law be made in a Christian Commonwealth without consent as well of the laity as of the Clergy but least of all without the consent of the highest power.

Thus, the king may be present at law-making touching the laity. Also, '[a]s the laity should not hinder the Clergy's jurisdiction, so neither is it reason that the laity's right should be abridged by the Clergy' (VIII.6.7). The laity participates when ecclesiastical law is made by the Sovereign in Parliament in the form of statutes. However, the clergy in Convocations may create canons with royal assent if they are not repugnant to statute, custom and royal prerogative (Submission of the Clergy Act 1533, uncited). Therefore, for Hooker, with canons, the monarch assents on behalf of the laity: it is *not* the case that 'any Canon devised by the Clergy alone in their Synods whether provincial, national or general has by mere force of their agreement taken place as a law making all men constrainable to be obedient thereto without any approbation from the King before or afterwards required in their behalf' (VIII.6.8);[31] the monarch confers with clergy here 'partly for information of their own consciences' (VII.18.9).[32] For Hooker, then, canons bind the

30 The basic thrust of these limitations repeats the Articles of Religion, art. XX: 'it is not lawful for the Church to ordain any thing which is contrary to God's Word written'.

31 'A law be it civil or Ecclesiastical is as a public obligation wherein seeing that the whole stands charged, no reason it should pass without his privity and will whom principally the whole does depend upon' (VIII.6.7).

32 Hooker argues that the Council of Jerusalem did not set a precedent against lay participation (III.11.13).

laity,[33] but '[w]ith those duties which the Law of God, and the Ecclesiastical Canons require in the Clergy, lay Governors are neither for the most part well acquainted, nor so deeply and nearly touched' (VII.18.6).

ENFORCEMENT OF CHURCH LAW

Hooker is a pragmatist: 'The due execution of Laws spiritual depends most upon the vigilant care of the [chief] spiritual Governors, whose charge is to see that such Laws be kept by the Clergy and people' (VII.18.6); the monarch has a particular responsibility for the execution of law (VIII.8.9). Hooker deals with the erection, standards, jurisdiction, process, judges and supervision of the courts of the Church of England. In treating these matters, again, he uses a mix of continental Roman civil law and (uncharacteristically, named) English law.[34]

He writes, '[J]udgment Ecclesiastical ... is necessary for decision of Controversies rising between man and man and for correction of faults committed in the affairs of God, to the due execution whereof there are three things necessary: Law, Judges and a Supreme Governor of judgements' (VIII.8.3); so, 'let there be careful provision that justice may be administered, and in this shall our God be glorified more than by such contentious Disputes' (VII.14.13). The jurisdiction of courts is fixed by law and exercised in applying law (VIII.8.3, citing the Institutes). Ecclesiastical judges are appointed 'under the King's commission' (VIII.3.3), 'to convert, judge and punish' (VI.4.11). In Church law there are 'Ordinary or Commissary' judges – the former are spiritual persons; thus, '[i]n spiritual causes a lay person may be no Ordinary'; but for 'a Commissary Judge there is no let but that he may be [lay]' (VIII.8.3). In exercising 'judicial wisdom' (I.1), ecclesiastical judges must practise godliness (V.1.2).[35]

As courts are 'erected for the maintenance of good Order', so they should not be 'disordered' (VII.24.7); in them 'nothing but singular integrity and Justice should prevail'; if corruption is found (VII.24.10), or they act 'otherwise ... than according to the law of reason and of God; we must ... endeavour to have them reformed' (VIII.8.3). He criticises abuses for 'want

33 See R. H. Helmholz, 'The Canons of 1603: The Contemporary Understanding', in N. Doe, M. Hill and R. Ombres, eds., *English Canon Law* (Cardiff: University of Wales Press, 1998): 31.

34 For the church courts, see Helmholz, *Canon Law and English Ecclesiastical Jurisdiction*, 282–309.

35 For chancellors, commissaries and officials, see e.g. the Canons of 1571, canon 4.

either of care or of conscience' (II, introduction). Hooker also deals with royal visitation of courts to uphold their jurisdictions (VIII.8.4, citing 1 Elizabeth, c. 1), and appeals when individuals are wronged by 'inferior judges' (VIII.8.5, citing 25 Henry VIII, c. 19). Moreover, the law forbids 'a spiritual Court to entertain those causes which by law are civil, nor yet if the matter be indeed spiritual, a mere civil Court to give judgement of it' (VIII.8.8).[36] Importantly, the king cannot intervene in court decision-making (VIII.3.3) or assume their functions (VIII.8.1, 7).[37] But, no 'Ecclesiastical Judges should have authority to call their ... Sovereign to appear before them' to examine, judge, or excommunicate the monarch (VIII.9.6).

THE LAW OF PUBLIC MINISTRY

Ordained ministry is instituted by God but exercised within the ecclesiastical jurisdiction, and 'ministerial power is a mark of separation'. Ordained persons are 'Christ's ambassadors and his labourers'. The power (or jurisdiction) of orders is to preach, administer sacraments and declare absolution (V.77.1–8); and 'there are at this day in the Church of England no other than the same degrees of ecclesiastical order, namely, Bishops, Presbyters, and Deacons, which had their beginning from Christ and his blessed Apostles themselves' (V.78.10).[38]

A bishop is 'a Minister of God, to whom ... there is given' the power to administer Word and sacraments, ordain, govern 'Presbyters as well as Laymen' and be 'a Pastor even to Pastors themselves'; bishops are 'principal pastors' (VII.2.3). Episcopacy itself is instituted of God (VII.5.10), but it has developed from 'the custom of the Church' and so may be changeable (VII.5.8). Bishops exist for the benefit of the Church (VII.1.4; VII.14.11). On choice of bishops, 'the laws have annexed it to the Crown' (VIII.7.3), but (citing Gratian's *Decretum*) the monarch cannot choose candidates 'whom desert of most holy life and the gift of divine wisdom did not commend' (VIII.7.7). He cites several Roman canonists to support royal appointment but refutes the ideas of 'some base Canonists' who do not. A cathedral dean and chapter may elect as bishop the person named by the king (citing 25 Edward III, c. 3 and 25 Henry VIII, c. 20), and lay people are involved in episcopal selection (VIII.7.1–3, citing Gratian).

36 He cites e.g. 'the statutes of Edward I and Edward II and *The New Nature of Briefs*', i.e. Anthony Fitzherbert, *Natura Brevium* (London: Richard Tottell, 1576).

37 He cites here Staunford, *Pleas of the Crown*, book 2, c. 3.

38 He might here have cited the Articles of Religion, art. XXXVI.

It is 'necessary' that there is 'an inequality among Bishops' (VII.8.8), namely, diocesan bishops (equal in the exercise of diocesan ministry), and archbishops (who as metropolitans enjoy a precedence in exercise of provincial ministry); the former must respect the latter, and the latter must confirm the election of the former (VII.8.9). The functions of metropolitans are to convoke episcopal assemblies in the province, grant bishops leave of absence from the diocese, hear causes against a bishop and receive appeals of inferior clergy 'in case they found themselves overborne by the Bishop their immediate Judge' (VII.8.12).[39]

A diocesan bishop may ordain without 'the people's consent', excommunicate, imprison, bear civil office (VII.14.1),[40] and make visitations for the 'observation of Church Laws, the correction of faults in the service of God and manners of men' (VII.24.9).[41] In discussing a wide range of norms from the early Councils, Roman law and Gratian, for Hooker bishops must engage in 'mutual consultation' (VII.24.3); exercise power within territorial limits, with presbyters and with other bishops (VII.5–8); and, as to office, 'acknowledge that the Church has power by universal consent upon urgent cause to take' away their authority (VII.5); also, bishops must not 'be led by human affection, in bestowing the things of God' (VII.24.8).[42]

As to clergy, distinguishing 'the nature of the ministry from the exercise thereof', for Hooker '[a]ll ecclesiastical laws and canons' deal with the ordination of a cleric, 'charge or portion of the Church allotted ... for exercise of his office', 'performance of his duty' and 'maintenance which in that respect he receives' (V.80). Ordination is administered by bishops with the laying on of hands (V.77.12); it is indelible but 'the exercise of power' by ministers may be suspended or terminated (V.77.3). It is against conscience to ordain the ignorant (V.81.2), and 'maxims of common right' render 'ordinations of ministers unable to preach, tolerations of absence from their cures, and multiplications of their spiritual livings' unlawful, but not 'universally and without exception' (V.81.17). Clergy are not by ordination consecrated to places but to functions (V.80), including the '[p]ower to exercise the duty itself and some charge of people whereon to exercise the same; the former of these is received at the hands of the whole visible Catholic Church'. Thus, ministry may not be

[39] He cites, by way of example, New Laws, Council of Antioch, canons 4, 16, 23, and the Apostolic Canons, canon 34.

[40] On the power of bishops, at VII.8.7, he cites Justinian, Digest [1.16.4]; Code, 1.27.1.

[41] This is an unattributed re-representation of e.g. the Canons of 1584, canon 7.

[42] For episcopal functions, see e.g. the Canons of 1571, canon 1.1–4. See also Articles of Religion, art. XXXVI.

exercised against the will of its beneficiaries; and, no cleric is 'possessed with Pastoral charge over any Parish, but the people in effect do choose him thereto' through a patron acting on behalf of the people (VII.14.10–12). As to non-residence of clergy, it is not 'justice to punish [one] whom superior authority pleases to call . . . elsewhere',[43] if equity allows this and clerics also recall their 'duty to the Church and in conscience towards God'; but seeking preferment for personal gain offends the 'conscience of the public good' (V.81). Hooker also set out norms on the office of 'parish minister' (V.30.4), equality of parishes (VIII.8.5), rights of patrons and how some offices may be 'executed by the laity', e.g. catechists, exorcists and readers (V.78.10). Needless to say, each of these principles may be induced from the norms of the English canons.[44]

DOCTRINE, WORSHIP AND RITUAL

Hooker presents the basics of law on doctrine and worship, faith and ceremonies: 'matters of faith, and in general matters necessary to salvation are of different nature from ceremonies, order, and the kind of Church government; that the one are necessary to be expressly contained in the word of God, or else manifestly collected out of the same, the other not so' – ceremonies are lawful if not forbidden by Scripture (III.2.2).[45] As such, ceremonies may differ between churches: 'it a just and reasonable cause for any Church, the state whereof is free and independent, if in these things [of ceremonies] it differs from other Churches' (IV.13.3; see also II.7).[46] However, the Church must proclaim the gospel: 'The Church as a witness preaches his mere revealed truth by reading publicly the sacred scripture' (V.19.1).[47]

As seen already, whereas law on polity is changeable, doctrine is not (V.8.1), and doctrinal definitions of the Church Fathers are preferable to private judgments (V.20.10); but some matters may be indifferent (*adiaphora*) (V.65.2). As clergy must subscribe publicly to the Articles of Religion, e.g. on admission to a benefice, so the Church exercises doctrinal discipline for

43 He relies here on Digest 48.5.61.1.

44 For: titles and benefices see e.g. Canons of 1575, canon 7; qualifications for ordination, e.g. Canons of 1571, canon 1.6; plurality, e.g. Canons of 1584, canon 5; non-residence, Canons of 1556, canon 3; 1571, canon 7; patrons, e.g. Canons of 1571, canon 10; churchwardens, e.g. Canons of 1571, canon 5.

45 See Articles of Religion, art. VI: 'whatsoever is not read [in Scripture], nor may be proved thereby, is not to be required of any man, that it should be believed as an article of the Faith'.

46 He also cites in his discussion of ceremonies the Digest, 50.17.183.

47 For preaching, see e.g. the Canons of 1556, canon 4; Canons of 1571, canon 6; and Canons of 1575, canons 8–9.

'correcting or silencing them that trouble and disturb the Church with doctrines which tend to innovation, it being better that the Church should want altogether the benefit of men's labours than endure the mischief of their inconformity to good laws' (V.81.11).[48] So, apostasy is 'direct denial, utter rejection of the whole Christian faith' and 'cuts off clean from the visible Church of Christ'; schism involves those who 'divide themselves from their brethren'; and heresy is failure on 'points of doctrine' (yet heretics are still within the visible Church but not its fellowship) (V.68.6). Church courts

> shall not adjudge for heresy anything but that which heretofore has been so adjudged by the authority of the Canonical scriptures, or by the first four general Councils or by some other general Council wherein the same has been declared heresy by the express words of the said Canonical scriptures or such as hereafter shall be termed heresy by the high Court of Parliament of this Realm with the assent of the Clergy in Convocation. (VIII.3.3, citing the statute 'Year 1 of Queen Elizabeth')

No action is more important than public worship (V.6.1), its aim to edify the faithful (IV.1.3). In common prayer, 'the people of God join themselves in this action, as with him that stands and speaks in the presence of God for them' (V.25.3). Various criteria may be used to judge liturgical practice: fitness to promote godliness (V.6.2), tradition (V.7.4), the judgment of the Church (V.8.5), and 'custom' approved by 'public authority' (V.43.4). Liturgical norms may be relaxed by equity (V.9.5), e.g. if there is a shortage of clergy (V.81),[49] as may norms on labour on Sunday (V.71.8, citing several civilians and canonists). Places of worship, which should reflect the beauty of heaven (V.6.2), are used for 'mutual conference and as it were commerce to be had between God and us' (V.18.1). The custom of consecrating churches is lawful (V.12.1, citing Durand and Gratian) and, through its right to property (VII.22.6, citing Gratian's *Decretum*), it is proper 'to preserve ... all rights which now ... belong to the ... Church' so that 'her patrimony should remain entire and uninjured for all time': (VII.24.22, citing the Code and Institutes). Thus, making donations is 'a duty which all men are bound to and a very part of the worship of God', a 'natural duty' (V. 79.1, discussing the Digest and Twelve Tables).

Hooker also discusses the sacraments and other rites. For example, baptism is a sacrament divinely instituted and covenantal (V.64.4). Its valid administration depends neither on the worthiness of its minister (V.58.2),[50] nor on the

48 As to subscription, this re-presents the Canons of 1575, canon 1; and, later, the Canons 1603, canons 36–8.

49 For the basic norm in liturgical practice, see e.g. the Canons of 1571, canon 5.

50 He cites J. P. Lancelotti, *Institutes of Canon Law*, and could have cited the Articles of Religion, art. XXVII.

signing of the cross (V.65.14, citing Gratian). Christian parents have a 'right' to their child's baptism (III.1.12),[51] 'equity requires' that children be admitted to baptism (V.64.4), and, indeed, God gives children 'right by special privilege of birth' to baptism (V.62.15). While baptism should normally be public (V.59–60), private baptism may be permitted on the basis of equity (V.58.4); and women may validly baptise (V.62).[52] Similarly, administering Holy Communion is a public duty (III.1.14), and there is a right to it (VI.4.13).[53] Ordinarily administered publicly, it may be administered privately in a 'case of necessity' (V.68.11); Roman Catholics must receive Holy Communion in the Church of England despite their objection in 'conscience' (V.68.8), and a person may be excluded from it (and he lists the grounds) but excommunication takes a person outside the fellowship of the Church though not the embrace of the Church universal ((VI.4.15; III.1.13). Lastly, the 'duty of Christian burial' is 'a duty which the Church does owe to the faithful departed', 'to show that love towards [them] which nature requires', to do 'honour' and 'to testify the care which the Church has to comfort the living, and the hope which we all have concerning the resurrection of the dead' (V.75.1–4). In all of these norms, Hooker offers a representation of the contemporary principles of English ecclesiastical law.[54]

CONCLUSION

Hooker has been described as, variously, 'the apologist of the Elizabethan Settlement',[55] representing 'the beginning of the English Enlightenment',[56] and writing 'much more than a museum piece . . . on how to run churches', but 'a classic of doctrinal reflection'.[57] However, there is debate today whether he was the first systematic defender of an Anglican *via media*

[51] Hooker criticises Calvin for advising Reformed ministers not to baptise the children of Catholic parents.

[52] In discussing baptism, he cites e.g. the Digest (V.59.3) and the Theodosian Code (V.62.10).

[53] He does not cite here the Sacrament Act 1547, which contains this right as correlative to a clerical duty.

[54] He also discusses the law on voluntary confession (VI.1.15–16); for confirmation see e.g. V.66.3; for marriage, see e.g. V.73.7, VII.15.12; and for the churching of women after childbirth, V.74.1 (citing Gratian).

[55] F. L. Cross and E. A. Livingstone, eds., *The Oxford Dictionary of the Christian Church* (Oxford: Oxford University Press, 2005), 793.

[56] F. C. Beiser, *The Sovereignty of Reason* (Princeton: Princeton University Press, 1996), 46.

[57] R. Williams, 'Richard Hooker: *The Laws of Ecclesiastical Polity* Revisited', 8 *Ecclesiastical Law Journal* 8 (2006): 382–91.

between Rome and Geneva.[58] For some, he was a thoroughly Reformed theologian.[59] His prose style is 'perhaps the most perfect in English'.[60] While Puritans challenged *The Laws*, Pope Clement XII suggested its translation into Latin (as did Grotius). James I expressed his admiration, Charles I recommended it to his children and James II enigmatically attributed his conversion to Rome to it.

Hooker's impact in political theory was spectacular, particularly in the work of John Locke, William Warburton and in Samuel Taylor Coleridge's *Constitution of Church and State* (1830).[61] However, his use as a *legal* authority was more muted: while echoing his concern to reduce complex legal materials to principles of law, Hooker is not prominent in the works on Church law of Edmund Gibson, Richard Grey and Richard Burn. Robert Phillimore has more references to turnips than to Hooker,[62] and Mark Hill makes no mention of him at all.[63]

Today, Anglicans see Hooker as 'inventing' Anglicanism,[64] 'the prophet of Anglicanism',[65] and as shaping the doctrine of churches of the worldwide Anglican Communion.[66] He has also figured in recent debate on the Anglican Communion Covenant,[67] and his legal method is echoed in the project on canonical principles common to Anglican churches globally.[68] But modern

58 N. Atkinson, *Richard Hooker and the Authority of Scripture, Tradition and Reason* (Carlisle: Paternoster Press, 1997).

59 N. Voak, *Richard Hooker and Reformed Theology: A Study of Reason, Will and Grace* (Oxford: Oxford University Press, 2003). For greater caution, and the need to compare Hooker with e.g. Vermigli (d. 1562), see W. B. Littlejohn, 'The Search for a Reformed Hooker: Some Modest Proposals', *Reformation and Renaissance Review* 16 (2014): 68.

60 C. S. Lewis, *Poetry and Prose in the Sixteenth Century* (Oxford: Clarendon Press, 1990), 462.

61 M. Brydon, *The Evolving Reputation of Richard Hooker: An Examination of Responses 1600–1714* (Oxford: Oxford University Press, 2006). Hooker is also cited by J. Finnis, *Natural Law and Natural Rights* (Oxford: Clarendon Press, 1980) 281–2, 412.

62 R. Phillimore, *Ecclesiastical Law*, 2d ed. (London: Sweet and Maxwell, 1895), 531; for turnips (and tithes), see 1150 and 1159.

63 M. Hill, *Ecclesiastical Law*, 3d ed. (Oxford: Oxford University Press, 2007).

64 P. Collinson, 'Hooker and the Elizabethan Establishment', in A. S. McGrade, ed., *Richard Hooker and the Construction of Christian Community* (Tempe, AZ: Medieval & Renaissance Texts & Studies, 1997), 151.

65 P. B. Secor, *Richard Hooker: Prophet of Anglicanism* (Tonbridge Wells: Burns & Oates; Toronto: Anglican Book Centre, 1999).

66 I. S. Markham, J. Barney Hawkins, J. Terry and L. N. Steffensen, eds., *The Wiley-Blackwell Companion to the Anglican Communion* (Chichester: John Wiley and Sons, 2013), 205, 418, 557, 608.

67 See e.g. B. M. Guyer, 'The Litany of Law: Richard Hooker and the Anglican Covenant', in B. M. Guyer, ed., *Pro Communione: Theological Essays on the Anglican Covenant* (Eugene, OR: Pickwick Publications, 2012), 67.

68 *The Principles of Canon Law Common to the Churches of the Anglican Communion* (London: Anglican Communion Office, 2008); for background, see N. Doe, 'The Contribution of Common Principles of Canon Law to Ecclesial Communion in Anglicanism', in ibid., 97.

English ecclesiastical lawyers use him little: the Archbishops' Commission on Canon Law 1947 invoked Hooker very sparingly,[69] Halsbury has one reference, and he is occasionally cited by church courts.[70] The various different editions produced over the years, the literary complexity of *The Laws*, and resultant inaccessibility, may have contributed to this.[71]

Be that as it may, Hooker in *The Laws* offers the first systematic treatment of the substantive law of the Church of England. He describes, explains and evaluates it in a wide theoretical framework, and provides modern English ecclesiastical lawyers with historical antecedents capable of practical use today as legal authority. Hooker also teaches us important lessons about juridical method: to be critical of legal arrangements; circumspect over change for its own sake; clear on the reasons for propositions; alert to theological dimensions of church law and polity; and bold in adaptation of the legal wisdom of other juridical traditions. He also recognises the value of articulating complex legal materials as general principles for the digestion and legitimisation of law. Doubtless, there are still issues to address: his reasons for turning to Roman civil law and canon law in preference to named English statutes and canons; the degree to which the norms he presents were (and still are) rules of English ecclesiastical law; and the extent to which his work was used (if at all) in the church courts of the seventeenth century and beyond. It will also prove instructive to establish – beyond conjecture and his obvious industry, technical prowess and learning – that he was at heart a rationalist, a populist and a pragmatic liberal. Further research may reveal whether these traits were born of his unquestionably deep Christian faith. These questions may stimulate future work on how *The Laws* is what it says on the cover: a law book which may also be read theologically, politically and philosophically. It is fitting that Hooker, of Welsh forebears, was the greatest ecclesiastical lawyer of the Tudor dynasty – and his lasting inspiration to Christians is summed up in the Collect which the Church of England uses for his feast day each year on 3 November: 'after the example to us of your servant Richard Hooker, give grace to us your servants ever to rejoice in the true inheritance of your adopted children and to show forth your praises now and ever'.[72]

69 *The Canon Law of the Church of England* (London: SPCK, 1947), 3, citing *Laws*, III.8, and 4, citing III.1.

70 *In re St Alkmund, Duffield* [2013] Fam 148; *R v. Dowds* [2012] 1 WLR 2576 (privilege); see also *Grant v. Grant* (1869) LR 2 P&D 8; and *Bishop of St Albans v. Fillingham* [1906] P 163.

71 J. Keble, ed., *The Works of Mr Richard Hooker*, 7th ed., rev. R. W. Church and F. Paget (Oxford: Clarendon, 1888); W.S. Hill, ed., *The Folger Library Edition of the Works of Richard Hooker*, 7 vols. (Cambridge, MA: Belknap Press (vols. 6 and 7 Binghamton, NY: Medieval & Renaissance Texts & Studies), 1977–98); McGrade, *Richard Hooker: Of the Laws of Ecclesiastical Polity*.

72 See the Collects for Lesser Festivals, November 3: Richard Hooker.

John Selden (1584–1654) from *The Gallery of Portraits*, (1833) (19th century) / private collection / Ken Welsh / Bridgeman Images

7

The Integrative Christian Jurisprudence of John Selden

Harold J. Berman and John Witte, Jr.

John Selden (1584–1654) was a legal historian of the first rank and master of the Society of Antiquaries, the leading English historical society of his day. He was an accomplished natural law philosopher who drew classical, biblical, Jewish, Christian and other sources into an arresting account of the nature of law and its roots in divine and human commands. And he was an ardent defender of constitutional law-making by the king in Parliament, but with legislation always limited by the enumerated rights and liberties of all Englishmen. 'Liberty Above All Things' was the motto that graced the title pages of his books – albeit usually written in Greek, *peri pantos ten eleutherian*. John Milton called Selden 'the chief of learned men reputed in this Land'.[1] Lord Clarendon regarded him as a scholar of 'stupendous Learning in all Kinds, and in all Languages'.[2]

Selden is better known today for the famous Selden Society of legal history than for his own legal writings. Indeed, the society's first president, F. W. Maitland,[3] thought Selden's 'cumbrous' writings might disqualify him from such recognition.[4] Selden's three-volume *Opera omnia*[5] is an intimidating

This chapter incorporates several edited paragraphs from Harold J. Berman, 'The Origins of Historical Jurisprudence: Coke, Selden, Hale', *Yale Law Journal* 103 (1994): 1651, and draws on conversations the two authors shared during their twenty-five years of association. Most of the writing is new but aims to reflect both authors' views about Selden. Berman died in 2007; Witte is his literary executor.

[1] John Milton, *Areopagitica*, ed. John W. Hales (Oxford: Clarendon Press, 1886), 16.

[2] Edward Hyde, Earl of Clarendon, *The Life of Edward, Earl of Clarendon* (Oxford: Clarendon Press, 1759), 16.

[3] See Chapter 14 on Maitland in this volume.

[4] See discussion in Sir John Baker, 'John Selden and English Legal History', in id., *Collected Papers on English Legal History*, 3 vols. (Cambridge: Cambridge University Press, 2013), 2:755, 755–8.

[5] John Selden, *Opera omnia*, 3 vols., ed. David Wilkins (London: T. Wood, 1726) [hereafter Opera].

mass of forty-four titles, several of them written in a ponderous and pedantic Latin style, with pages stuffed full of Hebrew, Greek, Arabic and other foreign passages, and with endless citations, parentheticals and digressions interrupting his arguments and narratives. Early English translations saved some of his works from obscurity. Selden's legendary erudition made even his most difficult Latin texts a must-read for later jurists who came upon legal problems that he had addressed. But Selden was in desperate need of a good editor. Happily, his elegant, witty and sardonic *Table Talk*, oft reprinted, kept his distinguished name alive. But, unlike other great Christian jurists collected in this volume, only a few studies had been devoted to Selden's legal work, before the very recent publication of a brilliant two-volume study by Gerald Toomer.[6]

BIOGRAPHICAL AND BIBLIOGRAPHICAL

Selden was born in 1584 into a Christian family in Salvington, Sussex, and baptised on 30 December 1584. His father was a part-time musician in Chichester Cathedral, and young John was educated at the local grammar school attached to the cathedral. In 1600, he enrolled at Oxford but left before graduation in 1602 to commence legal studies at Clifford's Inn. In 1604, he joined Inner Temple and in 1612 was called to the bar. He counted among his early friends the distinguished historians William Camden and Sir Robert Bruce Cotton, whose massive law library proved invaluable to Selden. While he kept a modest legal practice, and served with ample profit as steward to the family of Earl Henry Grey, Selden's main passion in this early period was historical writing. In the 1610s, he wrote his first major tracts: a history of trial by combat,[7] three histories of early England and its common law,[8] annotations on a poetic book on geography[9] and on the works of John Fortescue and Ralph de Hengham,[10] and a history of false gods in the Bible.[11] His major early works were two

6 G. J. Toomer, *John Selden: A Life in Scholarship*, 2 vols. (Oxford: Oxford University Press, 2009) [hereafter Toomer].

7 John Selden, *The Duello or Single Combat* (1610), in Opera, III.1:51–84.

8 John Selden, *Analecta Anglobritannica* (1608; pub. 1615), in Opera, II.2:861–960; id., *Janus Anglorum facies altera*, in Opera, II.2:961–1032; id., *England's Epinomis* (1610), in Opera, III.1:4–46; see further Nathaniel Bacon, *Historicall Discourse on the Uniformity of the Government of England … Collected from Some Manuscript Notes of John Selden* (London: Matthew Walbanke, 1647).

9 John Selden, *Illustrations to Poly-Olbion*, in Opera, III.2:1728–1878.

10 Opera III.2:1881–1928.

11 John Selden, *De diis Syris* (1617; 2d ed. 1629), in Opera, II.1:202–407.

massive tomes, one on the history of *Titles of Honor* (1614)[12] the second on *The History of Tythes* (1617).[13]

The History of Tythes

The History of Tythes proved controversial because it questioned 'whether by God's immediate moral law' a churchman has a 'right to tythes in equal degree as a layman' has a right to property, or whether tithing is part and product only of 'human positive law'.[14] Surveying the topic from the earliest biblical sources on, Selden concluded that tithe-paying was ultimately voluntary not obligatory, customary not natural, and legislatively prescribed not divinely ordained. To the extent the law of tithes came from the Church's own canon law, he deemed it self-serving. To the extent it came from the state, it could be repealed, for 'the practiced common law hath never given way herein to the canons' of the Church.[15] This argument was deeply troubling to Church officials, for Selden was questioning a longstanding and valuable source of revenue for the Church and its clergy, already bereft of a good deal of its property seized during the Tudor Reformation. It was also troubling to state officials, since critics wondered what other traditional divine rights claims he would attack – perhaps even the divine right of the king? Selden's book was censored, and he was summoned to appear before various lords in the High Commission and Privy Council, and ultimately before King James I himself to answer for his book. Protesting that it was simply the historical record that led to these inconvenient truths about tithes, not his own bias or brief, he ultimately issued a public apology for publishing the book, but he retracted none of its contents.

This early brush with the authorities pulled Selden away from his writing desk into politics.[16] He took part in the escalating clash between King James and Parliament about the freedom of speech in the making of laws. Traditions going back to the thirteenth century gave members of Parliament license to speak freely, frankly and forcefully within the confidence of their chambers in

12 1st ed. (1614) excerpts in Opera, III.1:927–1058, 2d ed. (1631) in ibid. III.1:85–926; 3d ed. separately printed as *Titles of Honor By the Late Famous and Learned Antiquary John Selden* (London: E. Tyler and R. Holt, 1682; facsimile ed., Clark, NJ: The Lawbook Exchange, 2006). See also his *Privilege of the Baronage*, written in 1621 but not published until 1642, in Opera III.2:1472–1586. See also Toomer, 1:126–68.

13 In Opera III.2:1065–1344; see also John Selden, *The Historie of Tithes*, facsimile ed. (New York/ Amsterdam: Da Capo Press, 1969). See Toomer, 1:257–310.

14 Selden, *Historie of Tythes*, I.6–7. 15 Ibid., I.9.

16 Paul Christianson, *Discourse on History, Law, and Governance in the Public Career of John Selden, 1610–1635* (Toronto: University of Toronto Press, 1996), 87–196.

order to offer their best counsel to the Crown and to craft the best legislation. Thus when the king suspended Parliament for a time and then tried to shut off debate when Parliament was called, the members rose up in indignant protest. The Commons sought Selden's help in defending their rights, the Lords in defending their privileges.[17] In 1621, Sir Edward Coke[18] and other parliamentarians called upon Selden to dig out the medieval sources that supported their famous Protestation of 1621. Here they declared 'that the liberties, franchises, privileges, and jurisdictions of parliament are the ancient and undoubted birthright and inheritance of the subjects of England; and ... every member of the house hath, and of right ought to have, freedom of speech to propound, treat, reason, and bring to conclusion'.[19] This document and Coke's epic speech in the Commons against the king, landed Coke, Selden and others in the Tower. After Selden was released, Sir Francis Bacon sought his counsel on the privileges of the Lords, and he obliged him, drawing on his *Title of Honors*.

Political Controversies

In 1623 and again in 1626, Selden was elected to Parliament. But he achieved greater fame for his role as counsel in the famous *Five Knights' Case* in 1627. Denied revenue by Parliament, Charles I had resorted to compulsory loans imposed on those who would normally be taxed. Those few who refused to 'loan' the money were imprisoned. Representing one of the imprisoned knights, Selden argued that to imprison a person without giving a specific reason violated chapter 29 of Magna Carta, which Selden rendered as: 'No freeman shall be imprisoned without due process of law.' The Magna Carta actually referred to '... by law of the land' (*per legem terrae*), but Selden adduced various medieval authorities that had read chapter 29 as a guarantee of 'due process of law'.[20] Selden rebutted the attorney-general's contention that 'law of the land' meant 'the law of the state' which now required the loans and ordered the arrest. Selden retorted: 'We read of no law of state' in Magna Carta or in its later interpretations. The 'law of the land' means 'the common law, the principal and general law', which enjoys 'a way of excellency' that is, supremacy. '[T]hough each of the other laws which are admitted into this

17 Timothy Brook, *Mr. Selden's Map of China* (New York: Bloomsbury Press, 2013), 33.

18 See Chapter 5 on Coke in this volume.

19 In Sir Edward Nicholas, *Proceedings and Debates in the House of Commons, 1620–1621*, 2 vols. (Oxford: Clarendon Press, 1766), 2:359–60.

20 On the evolution of Magna Carta's rights and liberties, see Robin Griffith-Jones and Mark Hill, eds., *Magna Carta, Religion, and the Rule of Law* (Cambridge: Cambridge University Press, 2015).

kingdom by custom or act of parliament may justly be called "a law of the land", yet none of them can have the pre-eminence to be styled "the law of the land".'[21] And the 'constant and settled common laws of this kingdom' make clear that the King or his delegates simply cannot force a man to make a loan or imprison him without a stated just cause. The law of the day must accord with the traditional common law of the land.[22]

Selden lost the case, but it underscored his evolving understanding of the binding quality of the common law tradition. It also impressed on him the importance of enumerating the rights and liberties of all subjects of the realm, not just those of the parliamentarians who represented those subjects, and not just through general clauses such as 'due process of law'. Selden thus joined Coke and others again in 1628 in crafting the famous Petition of Right, which gathered 'the diverse rights and liberties' of Englishmen in and beyond Magna Carta, and assembled them as a clear check against illegitimate exercises of authority, including those of the king himself. Parliament pressed this document on a very reluctant King Charles in exchange for their consent to new taxes to support his unpopular wars. The petition called for no taxation without 'the good will' and 'common consent' of the Parliament; no forced loans from the people; no taking of a man's life or liberty 'but by the lawful judgment of his peers, or by the law of the land'; no taking of a man's land, no imprisonment and no disinheritance without 'due process of law'; no suspension of the writ of habeas corpus; no forced quartering of soldiers or mariners in private homes; no criminal prosecution or punishment without a clear statute; and no use of martial law save in true emergencies.[23] The Petition of Right would eventually become an important step in enumerating 'the rights and liberties of Englishmen' based on natural law and the common law, as well as in developing the doctrine of 'judicial review'.[24] But it got nowhere in its day, despite Coke and Selden's strenuous arguments in support of it. In response, the king suspended Parliament and had Selden, Coke and seven others consigned to the Tower. This time Selden served for two years, part of the time without his books, which for him was the graver penalty.

21 Robert C. Johnson et al., eds., *Commons Debates 1628*, 4 vols. (New Haven: Yale University Press, 1977), 2:530.

22 *The Five Knights' Case*, in Thomas B. Howell et al., eds., *A Complete Collection of State Trials and Proceedings for High Treason and Other Crimes and Misdemeanors*, 34 vols. (London: T. Hansard, 1809–28), 3:17.

23 In Carl B. Stephenson and Frederick G. Marcham, *Sources of English Constitutional History* (New York: Harper and Bros., 1937), 450–3.

24 See R. H. Helmholz, 'Bonham's Case, Judicial Review, and the Law of Nature', *Journal of Legal Analysis* 1 (2009): 325–54; John Witte, Jr., 'Towards a New Magna Carta for Early Modern England', in Griffith-Jones and Hill, eds., *Magna Carta*, 109–35.

Selden's deep involvement in politics in the 1620s slowed his pen, but he produced two short works on the history of intestacy and testamentary jurisdiction,[25] an annotated work on early medieval English courts,[26] and another on an ancient art collection.[27] His most important work in this period was his *Mare clausum* (literally 'The Closed Sea').[28] He had started this work in 1618, but he published an expanded edition at the king's insistence in 1635, probably in exchange for Selden's conditional release from the Tower in 1631 and the final lifting of bail four years later. This ample tome was Selden's answer to Dutch jurist Hugo Grotius' erudite tract on *Mare liberum* (literally 'The Open Sea'). It aimed to prove the King of England's claim to dominion over the seas surrounding England and their resources, not least over the abundant fish that the Dutch were netting within sight of the English shore but without royal taxation. The book created a clash of great legal minds, with both Grotius and Selden mining deeply the conflicting Greek and Roman law precedents and their interpretations by medieval and early modern jurists. This was Selden's most serious study of ancient Roman law, before his later-life *Notes on Fleta* that traced Roman law influences on the common law.[29] In *Mare clausum*, Selden proved himself equal to Grotius in his command of Roman law and civilian jurisprudence. Though he respected Grotius deeply, he thought the weight of ancient authority favoured private and public property claims over the land and the surrounding sea, including claims by the king. He showed how several ancient peoples, and a good many historical Englishmen, had claimed dominion over the surrounding seas. He also pressed biblical arguments well beyond those of Grotius, interpreting a score of Old Testament texts about property, which he read with close attention to their interpretation by the Talmudic scholars.[30]

Jewish Law and Ecclesiastical Law

This was not Selden's first venture into Jewish law, but in the later 1630s until his death in 1654, the topic became a central preoccupation. Selden saw

[25] Opera, III.2:1663–85. [26] Ibid., II.2:1588–1685. [27] Ibid., II.2:1439–1586.

[28] Ibid., II.2:1179–1414, later translated as *Of the Dominion or Ownership of the Sea*, trans. Marchamont Nedham (London: William Du-Gard, 1652; facsimile ed., New York: Arno, 1972). See also Toomer 1:388–437.

[29] Opera II.2:1034–1120; reprinted with facing translation as *Ioannis Seldeni Ad Fletam dissertatio*, trans. and ed. David Ogg (Holmes Beach, FL: Wm. W. Gaunt and Sons, Inc., 1986).

[30] Opera, II.2:1195–1203, 1250–8, interpreting Genesis 1:29, 10:19; Numbers 34; Deuteronomy 34:2; Job 38:10–11; Psalms 72:8, 89:25, 95:4–5, 115:16; Proverbs 8:29; Ezekiel 26:16, 27:9,34, 28:2, Isaiah 23:4; I Esdras 4:2; II Esdras 7:3–4. See further Jonathan Ziskind, 'International Law and Ancient Sources: Grotius and Selden', *Review of Politics* 35 (1973): 537–59; Brook, *Mr. Selden's Map*, 19–44.

Jewish law as a sophisticated but neglected legal resource, ultimately on the scale and authority of Roman law and even the English common law. Jewish law had the added advantage of being rooted in divine legislation recorded in the Bible, and promulgated for a people who were the ancient ancestors of modern-day Christians. It could and should be studied with profit in an established Christian commonwealth, Selden thought. He thus published works on Jewish inheritance law and priestly inheritance,[31] a lengthy work on the Jewish calendar,[32] plus three massive volumes: one *On Natural Law and on the Law of Nations According to the Teachings of the Jews* (1640),[33] a second *On the Hebrew Wife* (1646)[34] and a three-volume work *On The Sanhedrins and the Juridical Offices of the Hebrews* (1650–5).[35] In all these works he drew on the Pentateuch and Mishnah in Hebrew and the Talmuds in Aramaic, but relied most heavily on the medieval Jewish sage, Moses Maimonides. In his later works, Selden also drew in Karaite and Kabbalist sources and cited parallel provisions in Muslim law and various Arabic and Oriental sources.[36] No English jurist to date had worked so hard to incorporate Jewish law into his jurisprudence, and Selden was probably the most learned Hebraist of the land. Indeed, Jason Rosenblatt recently dubbed this learned Gentile: 'Renaissance England's Chief Rabbi'.[37]

In striking contrast to his appreciative treatment of the Jewish legal tradition, alongside the common law and civil law traditions, Selden was dismissive of the Catholic canon law tradition, especially the medieval canon law. Selden was not anti-Catholic; he was one of the few parliamentarians to argue for the legal toleration of Catholics, which would be withheld until the Catholic Emancipation Act of 1829.[38] Moreover, Selden appreciated the learning of the medieval scholastics and the medieval canonists' adaptations and extensions of Roman law, and he recognised the authority of the canons when they were reflected in secular legislation or when they were issued by Church councils convened by the Crown. His real concern, typical of early Protestants, was with 'papal usurpation' of secular jurisdiction, which he called 'an intolerable wrong'.[39] He inveighed against the medieval papacy's

[31] Opera II.1:i–xviii, 1–200; I.1:x–xiv.

[32] John Selden, *De anno civili* (1644), in Opera I.1:1–63.

[33] John Selden, *De jure naturali & gentium, iuxta disciplinam Ebraeorum* (1640), in Opera I.1:64–757.

[34] Opera II.1:529–860; translated as *John Selden on Jewish Marriage Law: The Uxor Hebraica*, trans. and comm. Jonathan Ziskind (Leiden: E. J. Brill, 1991).

[35] Opera I.2:758–1892.

[36] See Toomer, 2:595–691.

[37] Jason P. Rosenblatt, *Renaissance England's Chief Rabbi John Selden* (Oxford: Oxford University Press, 2006).

[38] See sources in Toomer, 2:574–5.

[39] Opera, III.2:1861.

'pretence' of 'universal authority' in Western Christendom, which he regarded as an affront to the prerogatives and freedoms of Crown, Church, Commonwealth, commoner and conscience alike.[40] The king can legislate for the Church, but the Church cannot legislate for the king, the commonwealth or even itself, he said. 'There is no such thing as spiritual jurisdiction.' 'A bishop as a bishop, had never any ecclesiastical jurisdiction.' '[A]ll jurisdiction is temporal, and in no church.'[41]

Selden's insistence that even spiritual or ecclesiastical laws had to be issued or authorised by the king in Parliament also made him dismissive of Presbyterianism. The topic came to dominate discussions during the Interregnum in the 1640s and 1650s. Selden had reluctantly accepted election to the Long Parliament, and even more reluctantly agreed to participate as a parliamentary delegate to the Westminster Assembly of Divines that met intermittently from 1643 to 1652 to debate reforms in liturgy, discipline and Church government. Selden argued strenuously but fruitlessly against the effort to abolish the royally appointed Anglican episcopacy in favour of a democratically elected Presbyterian system of Church government. Part of his concern was that it was bishops, not presbyters, who were prescribed for the New Testament church and had served continuously in the history of the Church until then. The Westminster Assemblymen's attempts to justify this new form of Presbyterian government using the Bible and the '*jus divinum*', Selden argued, was 'a satire' akin to a penniless drunk 'fumbling in his pockets' to pay his bar tab. Moreover, without royal appointment or even parliamentary approval or supervision, '[p]resbyters have the greatest power of any clergy in the world, and gall the laity most' for once appointed 'they govern as they please'.[42]

Selden was called 'an Erastian' in Church-state relations. He was, at least insofar as he wanted the state to control the polity, property and personnel of the Church, and he opposed the appointment of bishops in the House of Lords. 'Clerics let loose to govern by laws are a menace to public order', he wrote. They serve the public better if 'they tend to their appointed offices of word and sacrament'. And again in answering the question 'whether is the church or the Scripture judge of religion?' he answered: 'In truth, neither, but the state.'[43]

40 Ibid. See further David Sandler Berkowitz, *John Selden's Formative Years: Politics and Society in Early Seventeenth-Century England* (Washington, DC: Folger Books, 1988), 73.

41 John Selden, *Table Talk 1689*, ed. Edward Arber (London: Alex Murray and Son, 1868; repr. ed. Philadelphia: Albert Saifer, 1972) [hereafter TT], 'Bishops before Parliament' and 'Bishops in the Parliament'.

42 Ibid., 'Presbytery'; see also Toomer, 2:569–75.

43 TT, 'Religion'. See also Sir Eric Fletcher, *John Selden 1584–1654* (London: Bernard Quaritch, 1969), 12–15; Reid Barbour, *John Selden: Measures of the Holy Commonwealth in Seventeenth-Century England* (Toronto: University of Toronto Press, 2003), 3–22, 243–94.

Selden and Theology

Unlike other great seventeenth-century Christian legal and political thinkers, from Hugo Grotius to John Locke, Selden left no commentaries or sermons on the Bible or formal tracts on Christian theology. He did pepper his writings with all manner of biblical citations and discussions, particularly from the Hebrew Bible and Apocrypha. He also quoted freely from the major patristic and scholastic sources, and sundry Catholics and Protestants of his day. But he was largely content to work at the edges of theology – 'treading unexplored soil and drinking from new springs', as he put it, most notably Jewish law.[44] His longest theological work was a rather sterile history of all the false gods mentioned in the Old Testament, which got no better in a second edition.[45] On the order of James I, in 1618, he offered a short speculation on how the Bible came to use '666' as the mark of the Beast[46] and a short squib praising Genevan reformer John Calvin both for his theology and legal humanism.[47] And he offered the king a long and rather tedious essay on how 25 December came to be treated as *The Birth-Day of Our Savior*.[48] Though Selden regularly used the Bible and historical theological texts as sources for his legal and historical studies, formal theology and conventional biblical commentary were not for him.

Selden was a man of simple and steady Christian piety, even though he was contemptuous of pretentious churchmen and impatient with theological disputes. 'Religion is like the fashion', he wrote:

> one man wears his doublet slash'd, another lac'd, another plain; but every man has a doublet. So every man his religion. We differ about the trimming. Men say they are of the same religion for quietness sake; but if the matter were well examin'd, you would scarce find three any where of the same religion in all points.[49]

And about the vaunted doctrine of the Trinity he wrote sarcastically: 'The second person is made of a piece of bread by the Papist, the third person is made of his own frenzy, malice, ignorance, and folly by the Roundhead. One the baker makes, the other the cobbler; and betwixt those two, I think the First Person is sufficiently abused.'[50] His *Table Talk* is filled with such jibes against theological niceties and fruitless dogmas as he saw them.

Nonetheless, Matthew Hale[51] called Selden 'a resolved serious Christian' who counted Archbishops Laud and Ussher and John Donne among his

44 *De jure naturali*, title page. 45 *De diis Syris* (see n. 12). 46 Opera, III.2:1403–4.
47 Ibid. 48 Ibid., III.2:1405–50. 49 TT, 'Religion'. 50 TT, 'Trinity'.
51 See Chapter 8 on Hale in this volume.

friends. He was by all accounts faithful and upright, disciplined and punctual, pious and earnest, generous to friends, often reserved in private, but eloquent and forceful when given the floor.[52] He was a life-long bachelor, though he evidently did wander sexually, and spent so much time with the widow of his client Earl Henry Grey that tongues began to wag about a private marriage.[53] But Selden said rather little about his interior domestic, moral or spiritual life. He was a life-long Anglican, finding this a comfortable via media between Catholicism 'whose many ordinances and opinions appeared contrary to divine authority', and various Protestants who 'rashly explained the holy Scriptures by the sole efforts of their own understanding [and] are occasionally found to disturb the peace of Christendom by ridiculous and impious innovations'.[54] Selden liked the settled doctrine, liturgy and traditions of the Church of England and the settled Anglican episcopacy and polity under royal control. On his deathbed, Selden confessed to Archbishop Ussher

> that he had his Study full of Books and Papers of most subjects in the world; yet at that time he could not recollect any passage out of the infinite Books and Manuscripts he was the Master of, wherein he could Rest his Soul, save out of the Holy Scripture, wherein the most remarkable passage that lay most upon his spirit was Titus 2:11–14: 'For the grace of God has appeared that offers salvation to all people. It teaches us to say "No" to ungodliness and worldly passions, and to live self-controlled, upright and godly lives in this present age, while we wait for the blessed hope – the appearing of the glory of our great God and Savior, Jesus Christ, who gave himself for us to redeem us from all wickedness and to purify for himself a people that are his very own, eager to do what is good.'[55]

SELDEN'S INTEGRATIVE HISTORICAL JURISPRUDENCE

Sir John Baker, quoting F. W. Maitland, reminds us:

> [T]he guiding logic of the lawyer is different from that of the historian. What the lawyer wants is authority, and the newer the better; what the historian

[52] Richard Baxter, *Additional Notes on the Life and Death of Sir Matthew Hale* (London: Richard Janeway, 1682), 40.

[53] Selden would likely have kept this quiet. As he wrote in his *Table Talk*: 'Of all actions of a man's life, his marriage does least concern other people, yet of all actions of our life, 'tis most meddled with by other people. Marriage is nothing but a civil contract, 'tis true 'tis an ordinance of God: so is every other contract, God commands me to keep it when I have made it.' TT, 'Marriage'.

[54] Quoted by John Aikin, *The Lives of John Selden, Esq. and Archbishop Usher* (London: Mathews and Leigh, 1812), 166; see further on his religion, ibid., 161–70; Barbour, *John Selden*, 54–8.

[55] In TT, preface, p. 8.

> wants is evidence, and the older the better ... Selden was both a lawyer and a historian. But he differed from most of his contemporaries in not confusing the two logics.[56]

What held these two logics together in Selden's mind was his deep appreciation for both 'nomos and narrative',[57] both canon and interpretation, both the *ur*-texts of antiquity and the traditions of interpretation and application they inspired. His method of legal history, in effect, combined the *sola Scriptura* method of Protestant theology with the legal humanism of continental jurists. First one must go 'back to the sources' and only after discerning the original text and its original meaning, can one responsibly assess the layers of interpretation that time and tradition have attached to that text or one's imagination, or inspiration might impute to it, especially as a judge or an advocate.[58]

The Task of Legal History

Selden the legal historian thus insisted on a return to authentic legal sources, ideally unprinted manuscripts in their original languages and forms – the older the better. 'My thirst compelled me always to seek the fountains, and by that, if means grant it, judge the river's nature.'[59] Particularly for ancient texts, authentication was critical, Selden insisted, and it was the historian's task to put the sources to 'a kind of trial'.[60] Find 'the authorities of best choice', he wrote, by comparing various ancient manuscripts, sifting through them for transcription and printing errors, and various 'confusions of time and action'. Sniff out forgeries and self-serving interpolations. Look for later sources to corroborate earlier texts. Learn ancient languages so you can read the texts in and on their own terms. Parse etymology so you can be sensitive to shifting meanings in terms. Be careful not to impose contemporary meanings on identical earlier terms. Understand the context of the text, too, and study the politics, religion, science, poetry, art, coinage and architecture of the day to help illuminate its original meaning. Only through this empirical scientific method can the legal historian gradually come to an 'historical deduction of our ancient laws'.[61]

[56] Baker, *Collected Papers*, 2:761, 763, citing F. W. Maitland, *Why the History of English Law Is Not Written* (Cambridge: Cambridge University Press, 1888).

[57] Robert M. Cover, *Narrative, Violence, and the Law: The Essays of Robert Cover*, ed. Martha Minow et al. (Ann Arbor: University of Michigan Press, 1992), 95–172.

[58] TT, 'Bible/Scripture'; see also Berkowitz, *Selden's Formative Years*, 42, 72–3.

[59] Opera III.2:1751–86.

[60] Ibid., III.2:1359.

[61] Ibid., III.2:1729–31; see also Harold D. Hazeltine, 'Selden as Legal Historian: A Comment in Criticism and Appreciation', *Harvard Law Review* 24 (1910): 105, 114–18; Berkowitz, *Selden's Formative Years*, 44–6.

Here was one reason for Selden's 'cumbrous' habit of piling on all manner of ancient authorities and citations in support of his every proposition, and for looking at these old texts through all kinds of different lenses and sources. Selden sought to tell the historical truth.[62] The legal historian's task, he wrote, is 'to know and to tell those things which are true'.[63] It is 'to relate, not to discuss opinions [or] to give a verdict of what he relates'.[64] But that was only the first step. Selden also warned against idle antiquarianism: 'the too studious affectation of bare and sterile antiquity, which is nothing else but to be exceeding[ly] busy about nothing'.[65] The real job of the legal historian, he insisted, is to harvest 'the fruitful and precious' and 'useful part' of this history 'which gives necessary light to the present, in matter of state, law, history and understanding of good authors'; 'Light to the practice and doubts of the present'; 'Light, that is clear and necessary'.[66] Indeed, for both the historian and the lawyer, 'there is nothing [that] more conduces to right judgment than the careful examination of the constitutions and customs, their received interpretations, and their force, in the state and age of which any civil disquisition is raised. For they are the very compass to direct all judicial proceedings; and of singular use also in whatsoever is deliberative.'[67]

The 'fruitful and precious and useful part of history' includes earlier laws and legal writings that have now been replaced, Selden insisted.

> For though, on account of their antiquity and many subsequent legal changes, these writings have not an inherent authority such as would suffice by itself in judicial decisions or opinions of counsel, they yet contain many things either still valid or not completely abrogated, especially in questions of tenure, felony, inheritance, contract, conveyancing, and other everyday matters. They may contain many things which reveal ancient laws and customs prior to these changes. Clearly therefore, in both abstract and recent cases, they provide not only a literary embellishment, but a confirmation on which the interpretation of the law may depend ... Even an abrogated law, not to mention an altered or revived one, provides the new law with its fullest authority and best interpretation if the reason for the abrogation, change, or renewal be carefully considered. Without such preliminary survey, the lawyer cannot form an accurate judgment.[68]

62 See Christianson, *Discourse*, 197–211.

63 From Selden, *Uxor Hebraica*, using translation in Hazeltine, 'Selden', 111.

64 Opera, III.2:1362. See further ibid., III.1:572; III.2:1372, 1455; John Selden, *The English Janus*, in R. Wescot, ed., *Tracts Written by John Selden* (London, 1683; repr. ed. Clark, NJ: The Lawbook Exchange, 2006), a2.

65 Opera III.1:105; see also TT, 'Learning'.

66 Opera, III.1:105–6.

67 Selden, *Titles of Honor*, b3v–b4r.

68 Selden, *Ad Fletam dissertatio*, 5–9.

Every law has a spirit, end or purpose for which it was enacted or has come into being, Selden argued, and understanding earlier laws helps to discern and apply that law to new law. To illustrate this point, Selden showed how the earlier *Theodosian Code* aided the interpretation of Justinian's *Corpus Iuris Civilis*, how reading Burchard and Ivo and other early canonists helped in understanding the *Decretum* and *Decretales*, and how ancient Roman law helped illuminate the shape and substance of the Continental *ius commune* as well as the English common law.[69] These earlier laws were all part of a tradition, of an ongoing and developing legal system, Selden argued. The legal historian's task is to discover and narrate this development, however circuitous and digressive it might need to be, from the earliest sources to the present day.

The Common Law Tradition

Selden had a strong sense of legal tradition, and he stressed the development, growth, adaptation and perpetual reformation of each legal tradition. He focused especially on the English common law tradition, with its basic constitutional institutions and principles, such as government by assemblies of notables and judicial responsibility to law, as well as its basic private law doctrines of marriage, tort, contract and property. Much like churches and their doctrines, he said, states and their laws gradually change over time, usually doctrine by doctrine, case by case, statute by statute, but sometimes also by momentous new legal documents like Magna Carta or momentous political events like the Roman invasion, the Norman Conquest or the Tudor Reformation of England.[70] These produced decisive breaks in the evolution of English law, 'watersheds in the river' of the common law tradition, as Selden called them. He recognised, for example, that the Norman Conquest introduced new feudal laws and the establishment of separate church courts into England, and that the twelfth-century revival of Roman law and Greek philosophy had a profound effect on all learning. Indeed, in this high medieval period, he wrote, 'physics, moral philosophy, logic, medicine, and mathematics began almost simultaneously to shine out like stars that had long been obscured, and so likewise canon law and theology'.[71]

Selden saw in this living history of a legal tradition – especially that of England – a long-range process of gradual improvement, even gesturing towards the 'providential view of history' that had become fashionable

[69] Ibid. [70] Opera III.2:1751. [71] Selden, *Ad Fletam dissertatio*, 95.

among some English churchmen of his day.[72] Moreover, he attached to the historical development of English law a normative significance. For example, he traced a development of the Germanic *wapentakes* described by Tacitus into the *witans* of the Anglo-Saxons, which in the thirteenth century became the parliaments of England. And he found in that development principles applicable to parliamentary government in his own time. He treated the Ancient Briton, Saxon and Norman periods of English history as three distinct phases of a single historical development, whose common elements were successively refined. Although most of the ancient laws were superseded, their fundamental structure not only survived but underwent improvement.[73]

Historical Jurisprudence

Selden's historical jurisprudence was more than a philosophy of English law alone, however. All sophisticated legal systems, he wrote, are to be understood as historical and developmental in character. In a remarkable passage, he set forth his historical theory of law in the following terms:

> [A]ll laws in general are originally equally ancient. All were grounded upon nature . . . and nature being the same in all [nations], the beginning of all laws must be the same . . . [T]his beginning of laws . . . remained always [what] they were at first, saving that additions and interpretations in succeeding ages increased, and somewhat altered them, by making a *determinatio juris naturalis* [a specification of natural law], which is nothing but the civil law of any nation. For although the law of nature be truly said [to be] immutable, yet it is as true that it is limitable, and limited law of nature is the law now used in every state. All the same may be affirmed of our *British* laws, or *English*, or other whatsoever. But the diverse opinions of interpreters proceeding from the weakness of man's reason, and the several conveniences of diverse states, have made those limitations, which the law of nature hath suffered, very different. And hence is it that those customs which have come all out of one fountain, *nature*, thus vary from and cross one another in several commonwealths . . . Diverse nations, as diverse men, have their diverse collections and inferences; and so make their diverse laws to grow to what they are, out of one and the same root. Infinite laws we have now that were not thought on a thousand years since. Then were many [laws] that a thousand

72 See sources in Harold J. Berman, *Faith and Order: The Reconciliation of Law and Religion* (Grand Rapids, MI: Wm. B. Eerdmans, 1993), 105–9.

73 Paul Christianson, 'John Selden and the Ancient Constitution, ca. 1610–18', *Proceedings of the American Philosophical Society* 128 (1984): 271, 276. See further Martha A. Ziskind, 'John Selden: Criticism and Affirmation of the Common Law Tradition', *American Journal of Legal History* 19 (1975): 30–3.

> years before had no being, and less time forward always produced diverse new [laws]; the beginning of all here being in the first peopling of the land, when men by nature being civil creatures grew to plant a common society. This rationally considered, might end that obvious question of those which would say something against the laws of *England* if they could. 'Tis their trivial demand. *When and how began your common laws?* Questionless it is fittest answered by affirming, when and in like kind as the laws of all other States, that is, *When there was first a state in that land which the common law now governs:* Then were natural laws limited for the convenience of civil society here, and those limitations have been from thence, increased, altered, interpreted, and brought to what now they are; although . . . now, in regard of their first being, they are not otherwise than the ship that by often mending had no piece of the first materials, or as the house that's so often repaired *ut nihil ex pristina materia supersit* [that nothing remains of the original material], which yet, by the civil law, is to be accounted the same still . . . Little then follows in point of honor or excellency specially to be attributed to the laws of a nation in general, by an argument thus drawn from difference of antiquity, which in substance is alike in all. Neither are laws thus to be compared. Those which best fit the state wherein they are, clearly deserve the name of the best laws.[74]

Here Selden laid the foundation of an integrative historical jurisprudence that also drew in natural law theory and legal positivism. He postulated as an immutable law of nature that men are civil creatures, who, when they first people a land, 'plant a common society'. In succeeding ages, however, they add to, interpret and 'limit' by statute the natural law according to 'the several conveniences', that is, the particular wants and needs, 'of diverse States'. The relative quality of the positive law of a people, therefore, including the common law of England, must be judged not by its superior antiquity, but by the extent to which it 'best fits' the wants and needs of the particular people. At the same time, the diverse customs of diverse peoples, which are the source of their respective systems of civil law, though rooted in a common human nature, are subject to a continuous organic process of change, by which natural law is specified and altered. Thus the relative quality of the law of a people must be judged also by the extent to which it remains faithful to its past.

Selden used the famous analogy of a ship that leaves the harbour on a trip around the world, and returns many years later with none of its original parts or original crew. It is still the same ship, so long as all the new parts work and so long as the ship still serves its ultimate end, namely sailing safely. So, too,

74 John Selden, *Notes on Fortescue*, in Opera, III.1:1891–2.

Selden believed, a nation's or people's legal tradition that has adapted and changed over centuries of legal development so that it has none of its original laws are in force, is still the same legal tradition – so long as the new laws have been properly promulgated and implemented and so long as they, like the laws that they replaced, serve the ultimate legal ends of justice, order and peace.

NATURAL LAW THEORY AND LEGAL POSITIVISM

As the foregoing lengthy quotation reveals, Selden traced the ultimate source of all human, positive or 'civil law' back to a 'natural law'. In his earlier writings, Selden left the 'natural law' rather vaguely defined, often running together the terms 'divine, morall, or natural Law'[75] the 'law of God',[76] 'the holy law', the 'universal law', the 'primitive law' and what St Paul had called 'the law written on hearts of all men'.[77] But in his 1640 title, *On Natural Law*, and in his later writings on Jewish law, Selden set out his theory of law more systematically and in way that effectively integrated the teachings of natural law and legal positivism.[78]

A Command Theory of Natural Law

In a nutshell, Selden argued that the ultimate source of all law lies in God's commandments which God has 'posited' or set down for the entire human race. In turn, the legitimate authorities of each nation and people, acting as God's vice-regents, posit civil laws for their subjects. These civil laws adopt the ultimate principles of natural law, adapt them to the needs and circumstances of their time, and adjust them in a process of perpetual reformation and replenishment that are the hallmarks of every legal tradition. Over time, each of these human civil or positive law traditions becomes and expresses its own 'limited form of natural law'.

Selden described this 'command theory' of natural law in various ways. In his *Table Talk*, he wrote:

> I cannot fancy to myself what the law of nature means, but the law of God. How should I know, I ought not to steal, I ought not to commit adultery,

75 Selden, *Historie of Tithes*, VII.6.

76 John Selden, *Mare clausum: seu de dominio maris, libri duo* (London: William Stanesby for Richard Meighen, 1635), I.6.

77 Ibid., I.7.

78 While Selden may have been disparaging of the arbitrary use sometimes made of natural law, he did not question its existence: see R. H. Helmholz, *Natural Law in Court: A History of Legal Theory in Practice* (Cambridge, MA: Harvard University Press, 2015), 100.

> unless someone has told me so? Surely, 'tis because I have been told so. 'Tis not because I think I ought not to do them, nor because you think I ought not; if so, our minds might change; whence then comes the restraint? From a higher power; nothing else can bind: I cannot bind myself, for I may untie myself again; nor an equal cannot bind me, for we may untie one another: It must be a superior power, even God almighty.[79]

In *On Natural Law*, he wrote that 'the Author and Most Holy Name, who created nature at the time the human race was created, established the notion that the human race must be instructed, administered, and ordered'.[80] And in *The Hebrew Wife*, he wrote, 'What we call natural law is simply what the Author of nature himself by his most sacred will ordained and impressed at creation upon the human heart and has been a law that has been regularly and continuously observed as immutable by all posterity.'[81] Selden believed that ancient Greeks and Romans, Jews and Christians 'Pagans, Mahometans, and others of that sort, as well modern as ancient' were all subject to this divinely commanded natural law, and that rationally attuned and 'morally better' people could ultimately discern its contents.[82] But he resisted the view of his day that the common law of nations (the *ius gentium*) was tantamount to the natural law (*ius naturale*) itself – given the variant applications of reason to a wide range of legal circumstances.[83]

Natural Law and Positive Law

All other laws, Selden called 'civil laws', 'human laws' or 'positive laws'. He included in this category the Mosaic laws of the Bible and the later royal legislation and rabbinic interpretations of the Jews and their applications by the Sanhedrin; he called all these 'the civil law of the ancient Hebrews'.[84] 'God at the first gave laws to all mankind, but afterwards he gave peculiar laws to the Jews, which they were only to observe', he wrote. 'Just as we have the common law of England', which only we observe, so they had their Jewish law, which only they observed.[85]

Compared to all other positive legal systems, however, the Jewish legal tradition was unique in that the 613 civil laws of the Torah were directly commanded by God for his chosen people. Moreover, the record of the promulgation of these civil laws was set out in the same opening books of

79 TT, 'Law of Nature'.
80 Using translation in Jonathan R. Ziskind, 'Introduction' to Selden, *Uxor Hebraica*, 11.
81 Selden, *Uxor Hebraica*, 1–2.
82 Selden, *Mare clausum*, I.7.
83 Selden, *De jure naturali*, I.7.
84 On title page of Selden, *Uxor Hebraica*.
85 TT, 'Jews'.

the Bible that also recorded God's commandments of the natural law to all humanity. That makes these biblical laws and the biblical narratives surrounding their promulgation eminently 'useful for ascertaining the content and meaning of the natural law'.[86] But, Selden hastened to say, this does not mean that these Mosaic or rabbinical laws bind modern-day Christians, as some theologians and bishops insist when they 'run to the [biblical] text for something done amongst the Jews that nothing concerns England'.[87] 'Laws belonging to the land of Israel . . . are those which are received by the Jews, touch the observance of the sabbatical year, oblations of fruits, the Levitical custom of tithing and others of that kind. For by the law of God, they will not yield those things should be observed out of the Israelitish dominions.'[88] Selden largely eschewed the conventional Christian division of Mosaic laws into 'ceremonial laws' that were binding only on Jews, 'juridical laws' that were useful prototypes for all peoples and 'moral laws' that were universally binding. In his view, all Jewish law set out in the Mosaic law was just that – Jewish law, not Christian law and not English law.

Noahide Law and Its Discernment

There was a fine line, however, between the 'natural law' that God commanded for all people, and the 'civil law' that God commanded only for his chosen people of Israel. Selden drew that line between the natural laws that God gave to Adam, Noah and their descendants, and the civil laws that God gave to Moses at Sinai, which later Jewish judges, kings, priests and rabbis expanded and expounded. Following Maimonides, Selden called this pre-Mosaic natural law, the 'Noahide law', which he distilled into the same seven major natural law principles that Maimonides had used to structure his *Mishneh Torah*. The first six principles, Selden said, 'were enjoined upon Adam, the first parent, and were perennial obligations' of the whole human race that God's covenant with Noah after the Flood later confirmed.[89] These principles were (1) not to commit idolatry, (2) not to blaspheme God's name, (3) to establish courts of justice, (4) not to kill unjustly, (5) not to have illicit sex and (6) not to steal. All these can be seen in the Book of Genesis, which describes the interactions between God and various ancient patriarchs, said Selden, and these biblical stories had parallels in other ancient literature about the origins of law and humanity. To this Selden added (7) not to eat

[86] Ziskind, 'Introduction', 13. [87] TT, 'Bishops in the Parliament'.
[88] Selden, *Mare clausum*, I.6.
[89] Selden, *De jure naturali*, I.8, using translation in J. P. Sommerville, 'John Selden, The Law of Nature, and the Origins of Government', *Historical Journal* 27 (1984): 437–47, at 439.

flesh from a living animal, which was a prohibition that came from God's covenant with Noah that was explicitly extended to 'every living creature'.[90] This last prohibition, too, he said, had echoes in other ancient literature. These were the seven universal natural laws that governed all human beings, said Selden; they stood as the font of all human laws that flowed from them.[91]

In Selden's view, these universal natural laws were

> given to the human race at its very creation, and every rational soul was then naturally endowed with a faculty by which those things that had been ordained, and which were always to be observed, were revealed and made manifest, like principles or theorems in demonstrative matters, to every man whose mind was not depraved, who was not corrupted, and who intuited rightly and diligently enough.[92]

For Selden, these natural laws were 'self-evident' to anyone with the capacity to see and understand them.

> Just as when the light is clear and is shining in the opposite direction, objects which are suitably placed are perceptible by an eye which is not diseased or badly positioned ... so illuminated by the aid of the *intellectus agens*, a human mind or intellect which is not depraved and which intuits diligently is informed of these commands which are to be observed by decree of the father of nature, and indeed of other objects of the intellect (that is to say, of truth and falsehood, as well as good and evil).[93]

Selden believed that this '*intellectus agens*' was either God himself, whose image each person bears, or an 'ultimate intelligence' that serves as the 'agent' (*agens*) of God – perhaps an angel or the Holy Spirit. Medieval and early modern philosophers debated fiercely whether this faculty *intellectus agens* was part of the human soul, human reason or another human faculty. Selden thought this ultimately a sterile debate. His main point was this: what gave natural law binding authority for humans was that it was commanded or posited by God for the governance of all persons and peoples.[94]

For Selden, natural law could not be reduced to the dictates of right reason, the promptings of conscience, the vagaries of equity or the inclinations of

90 Genesis 9:4,10. 91 Selden, *De jure naturali*, I.5–9; see also Toomer, 2:493–505.

92 Selden, *De jure naturali*, I.9.

93 Ibid., with discussion in Sommerville, 'John Selden', 440–1.

94 Selden, *De jure naturali*, I.9; Toomer, 2:502–4; Johann P. Somerville, 'Selden, Grotius, and the Seventeenth-Century Intellectual Revolution in Moral and Political Theory', in Victoria Kahn and Lorna Hutson, eds., *Rhetoric and Law in Early Modern Europe* (New Haven: Yale University Press, 2001), 318–44.

common sense alone.[95] Nor could it be equated with the natural patterns and practices of animals, or even the common practices of human civilisations. And it certainly could not be imagined if one accepted Grotius' 'impious hypothesis' that the law of nature would exist 'even if we should concede that which cannot be conceded without the utmost wickedness, that there is no God, or that the affairs of men are of no concern to him'.[96] For Selden, natural law was impossible without God the law-giver. It was God's commands that brought natural law into being. And just and proper human law-making, in turn, was impossible without these prior natural law commands, for the just human legislator's commands were ultimately echoes of these prior divine commands.[97] As St Paul had written: 'For there is no power but of God. The powers that be are ordained by God.' The Psalmist put it even more strikingly: 'God standeth in the congregation of the mighty; he judgeth among the gods.' And he says to kings, though they are mortal: 'Ye are gods' on the earth, who command and rule on God's behalf, in imitation and implementation of God's commands.[98]

Selden's Theory in Comparative Perspective

Selden's theory of natural law was neither typical of other Christian theories of his day nor prototypical of the theories of later Enlightenment liberalism. In particular, Selden departed from most Protestants of his day who saw the Ten Commandments as the most important source and summary of natural law and of the natural rights and duties that attached thereto. The First Table of the Decalogue, many Protestants argued, governed the relations between God and humanity – setting out duties not to worship false gods or idols or to take God's name in vain and to observe the Sabbath Day and keep it holy. The Second Table of the Decalogue governed the relations among people – requiring them to honour their parents, not to kill, not to commit adultery, not to steal, not to bear false witness and not to covet. Some Protestants, such as Christopher Goodman and Theodore Beza, had further translated these Two Tables of religious and civil duties towards God and neighbour into reciprocal religious and civil rights. Others, such as Johann Oldendorp and Johannes Althusius, had used the Ten Commandments as a framework for creating new systematic

95 Selden, *De jure naturali*, I.3–4; TT, 'Equity' and 'Conscience'.

96 See Hugo Grotius, *De jure belli ac pacis libri tres*, trans. F. W. Kelsey (Oxford: Clarendon Press, 1925), Prol. 11.

97 Selden, *De jure naturali*, I.5–8; see also Toomer, 2:497–501; Sommerville, 'John Selden', 447.

98 Selden, *De jure naturali*, I.8; see also Barbour, *John Selden*, 217–36.

accounts of secular law in place of the seven sacraments used to systematise the canon law.[99]

Selden saw the Ten Commandments as just another *ur*-text of Jewish civil law, which was built on natural law, but not a restatement of natural law itself. The Ten Commandments embodied the principles of natural law for the ancient Jews, much in the same way that the Twelve Tables did for the Romans, or the Magna Carta did for medieval Englishmen. None of these ancient sources could or should be viewed as tantamount to the natural law itself. Obviously, five of the Noahide principles that Selden lifted up – prohibiting idolatry, blasphemy, homicide, theft and illicit sex – had parallels in the Ten Commandments. But the Noahide law went further, in Selden's view, in commanding the establishment of courts of justice to implement the laws that God and his vice-regents had commanded for the people. And it went further in protecting animals and nature. Moreover, the Noahide law said nothing at all about the Decalogue's five commandments about observing the Sabbath, honouring one's parents, bearing false witness or coveting one's neighbour and his household. In particular, Selden's idea that Sabbath day observance was not a natural right and duty rankled the establishment of his day to no end.

Not only did Selden's natural law theory start with the seven pre-Mosaic principles given to Adam and Noah, rather than the Ten Commandments given to Moses, but Selden also interpreted and elaborated these natural law principles quite differently from standard jurisprudence, catechesis or moral instruction in his day. The conventional Protestant method of interpreting, say, the commandment against adultery started with further biblical teachings and examples from both Testaments (not least the parallel commandments to honour one's parents and not covet the neighbour's wife, maidservant or household). It would then consult the early Church Fathers and Christianised Roman law, then the medieval *ius commune*, then the laws and customs of one's day before making a final judgment of what specifically was prohibited and permitted by this natural law command. And the accumulation of this interpretation into various rules would eventually form a Christian jurisprudence of sex, marriage and family life.[100]

99 See John Witte, Jr., *Law and Protestantism: The Legal Teachings of the Lutheran Reformation* (Cambridge: Cambridge University Press, 2002), 121–68; id., *The Reformation of Rights: Law, Religion, and Human Rights in Early Modern Calvinism* (Cambridge: Cambridge University Press, 2007), 102–33, 156–81.

100 See e.g. John Witte, Jr. and Robert M. Kingdon, *Sex, Marriage, and Family Life in John Calvin's Geneva*, 2 vols. (Grand Rapids, MI: Wm. B. Eerdmans, 2006, 2018).

The prohibition against illicit sex was one of Selden's Noahide natural law principles, too. But in discerning its meaning, Selden looked first and foremost to all the conflicting rabbinic interpretations of this principle, since this ancient people had access not only to God-given natural law, but also God-given civil law. He also sometimes looked for interesting parallels and divergences in sundry other classical, Christian, Muslim, Oriental, 'pagan' and any other relevant sources. In his *On Natural Law*, he devoted separate chapters to exegeting each of the seven natural law principles in this way. In his *The Hebrew Wife*, he did the same thing on the natural principles of sexuality alone. This method led Selden to postulate all manner of natural law teachings about sex, marriage and family life, some of them quite congenial to the establishment of his day, some of them scandalous, such as permissive polygamy, divorce and remarriage, cross-dressing and bisexuality, among many other topics.[101] Unlike other natural law theorists, however, Selden did not take it upon himself to 'prove' the exact content of each of his seven natural law principles by close reasoning or to 'demonstrate' it by comparative examples. He was instead largely content to describe the precepts, procedures and practices that the long Jewish tradition offered, with occasional comparative examples thrown in.[102]

Later Enlightenment philosophers such as Samuel von Pufendorf frowned on this method. 'Selden does not deduce natural law from any principle or hypothesis for which the evidence is acknowledged by all nations, or which they could be brought to acknowledge by arguments drawn from the light of reason', Pufendorf complained. 'He only expounds what Hebrew scholars thought; he does not sufficiently examine whether their opinion accords with sound reason.'[103] But Selden was operating primarily as an historian, not as a philosopher or advocate in describing the principles of this Jewish 'natural law' in action. He was laying out what he thought was a valuable but understudied Jewish law on various legal topics that fellow jurists could read alongside the more familiar legal sources of the Western tradition. But whether a person or people might find in this Jewish jurisprudence more biblical, rational or useful teachings was not for him to decide or prescribe. Their veracity or utility would become self-evident to any person or people who followed their own *intellectus agens*.

[101] See Selden, *De jure naturali*, book V and expanded in *Uxor Hebracia*, with discussion in Rosenblatt, *Chief Rabbi*, 54–73; see also Toomer 2:534–44.

[102] Sommerville, 'Selden, Grotius', 336–8.

[103] Quoted in ibid., 336.

CONCLUSIONS

John Selden integrated the three classic schools of jurisprudence – natural law theory, legal positivism and historical jurisprudence.[104] He defined natural law as a set of fundamental legal principles commanded by God for the creation of a just legal order. He defined positive laws as those rules and procedures created by a just legislature in accordance with both the principles of natural law and the needs of the particular community. And he defined legal history as the account of each community's legal tradition, which gives expression to natural law and provides limitations on the laws of any given sovereign, even the king himself. While fellow English jurists such as Edward Coke had parallel theories of historical jurisprudence, and others including Matthew Hale had parallel theories of natural law, it was Selden who held all three of these schools in an interesting and original balance.

Selden did not create an expansive Christian jurisprudence, but he did build on a robust theology of God – God the creator, who set nature in order and motion in accordance with natural laws; God the law-giver who commands all human creatures to follow the principles of natural law and natural rights; God the judge who called his people to 'establish courts of justice' for the protection of justice and mercy in each community; God the covenant-keeper who called his chosen people of Israel to follow the particular commands of the Torah; and God the *intellectus agens* who guides each good person to self-evident truths, and guides each great legal tradition, most notably the common law, to ever greater approximation of divine justice.

104 See Harold J. Berman, 'Toward an Integrative Jurisprudence', *California Law Review* 76 (1988): 779, and discussion in Howard O. Hunter, ed., *The Integrative Jurisprudence of Harold J. Berman* (Boulder, CO: Westview Press, 1996).

Portrait of Sir Matthew Hale Kt (1609–76), Chief Justice of the King's Bench, Wright, John Michael (1617–94) / © Guildhall Art Gallery, City of London / Bridgeman Images

8

Matthew Hale as Theologian and Natural Law Theorist

David S. Sytsma

INTRODUCTION

Sir Matthew Hale (1609–76) is one of the most celebrated jurists of English common law. When reading modern literature on Hale, one frequently encounters the superlatives of praise. One historian refers to Hale as 'one of the greatest jurists of the modern common law',[1] while another observes, 'Hale has continuously enjoyed the reverence of lawyers as the greatest Stuart jurist after Coke, and treatments of his place in legal history have virtually always been tinged with piety.'[2] The greater part of this well-deserved reputation rests upon the impact of his posthumous publications. Among these, Hale's *Historia placitorum coronae* (1736) became an authority for criminal law, while his *History of the Common Law of England* (1713) was, in the words of William Searle Holdsworth, 'the ablest introductory sketch of a history of English law that appeared till the publication of Pollock and Maitland's volumes in 1895'.[3] Likewise, Hale's *Analysis of the Law* (1713) served as an important model for Sir William Blackstone, who drew upon Hale for his own *Analysis of the Laws of England* (1756).[4]

Although Hale has long been justly revered for his contributions to common law, he was also a great polymath. Indeed, his interests ranged across a wide spectrum of theological and philosophical topics. Traditional biographies long

1 Thomas Garden Barnes, *Shaping the Common Law: From Glanvill to Hale, 1188–1688*, ed. Allen D. Boyer (Stanford: Stanford University Press, 2008), 222. For a discussion of Blackstone as a great Christian jurist, see Chapter 10 in this volume.

2 Alan Cromartie, 'Hale, Sir Matthew', in *Oxford Dictionary of National Biography*, 60 vols. (Oxford: Oxford University Press, 2004), 24:539.

3 William Searle Holdsworth, A *History of English Law*, 17 vols. (London: Methuen, 1922–72), 6:586.

4 William Blackstone, *An Analysis of the Laws of England* (Oxford: Clarendon Press, 1756), vii. See also David Lieberman, *The Province of Legislation Determined: Legal Theory in Eighteenth-Century Britain* (Cambridge: Cambridge University Press, 1989), 35.

neglected Hale's theological manuscripts,[5] but after Alan Cromartie brought them to our attention, the formative importance of Hale's religious views on his life and thought is now apparent.[6] Furthermore, a case can easily be made that Hale's theological writings rival professional clergy of his day in terms of mastery of scholastic theology, so that he deserves to be ranked along with Sir Henry Finch (d. 1625) as among the great English lawyer-theologians of the seventeenth century.[7] At the end of Hale's life, his close friend, the famous Puritan Richard Baxter, expressed to Hale his own hope that 'many that highly valued your secular wisdome will be induced to thinke the better of spirituall wisdome when they see what it is that you have highlyest valued'.[8] In the spirit of Baxter's wish, the present chapter will introduce readers to the importance of Hale's Christian faith for his life in general, as well as his legal thought. In what follows, we will first highlight the importance of Hale's Christian faith in his life before turning to a survey of his theological writings. We will then demonstrate the importance of Hale's theology for his vocation as judge. We will conclude with an examination of his theory of natural law, which was foundational to his legal thought. Hale's natural law theory, which forms a crucial bridge linking his theological beliefs to his legal thought, merits far more attention than the sparse treatments it has received to date.[9]

HALE'S LIFE AND RELIGIOUS DEVELOPMENT

Hale was born in Alderley, Gloucester, on 1 November 1609 into a family of strong religious conviction.[10] His father, Robert, matriculated at Broadgates Hall, Oxford, in 1580 and was later called to the bar at Lincoln's Inn in 1594.

5 E.g. Edmund Heward, *Matthew Hale* (London: Robert Hale, 1972), 173. This otherwise good biography of Hale's legal career suffers from complete neglect of Hale's Lambeth manuscripts, discussed later in this chapter.

6 See Alan Cromartie, *Sir Matthew Hale, 1609–1676: Law, Religion and Natural Philosophy* (Cambridge: Cambridge University Press, 1995), which remains the best overall introduction to Hale's thought.

7 Finch's major theological works include *The Sacred Doctrine of Divinitie* (1589, 1613), *The Summe of Sacred Divinitie* (c. 1620) and *An Exposition of the Song of Solomon* (1615). *The Summe*, previously attributed to John Downame (d. 1652), is now recognised as the work of Finch. See Randall J. Pederson, *Unity in Diversity: English Puritans and the Puritan Reformation, 1603–1689* (Leiden: Brill, 2014), 123–7.

8 Baxter to Hale, 2 May 1676, in 'An Unpublished Letter of the Reverend Richard Baxter to the Chief Justice Sir Matthew Hale', *Bulletin of the John Rylands Library* 24 (1940): 173.

9 See David S. Sytsma, 'General Introduction', in Matthew Hale, *Of the Law of Nature*, ed. David S. Sytsma (Grand Rapids, MI: CLP Academic, 2015), ix–lv.

10 The facts of Hale's biography are generally taken from Gilbert Burnet, *The Life and Death of Sir Matthew Hale, Kt. sometime Lord Chief Justice of His Majesties Court of Kings Bench* (London: William Shrowsbery, 1681); Heward, *Hale*; Cromartie, *Hale*, 1–7.

Robert later married Matthew's mother, Joan Poyntz of Alderley, in 1599. According to Hale, his father was a serious student of theology and the Scriptures.[11] Sadly, Hale's parents died while he was still a small child. Joan died when Hale was just two and one-half years old (13 April 1612), and Robert died in 1614 before Hale turned five. Hale's guardianship fell to the nearest kin on his father's side, Anthony Kingscot (d. 1654), who oversaw Hale's education. A man of strong Puritan convictions, Kingscot wished Hale to pursue a career in divinity, and accordingly sent him at the age of sixteen (1626) to Magdalen Hall, Oxford, where his tutor was Obadiah Sedgwick (d. 1658), later to become a well-known Puritan divine. By this time, Magdalen Hall had become a 'stronghold of the Puritans in Oxford',[12] and during his time there, Hale became familiar not only with Puritan divinity but also – as was typical of Oxford education at the time – with the works of Thomas Aquinas, John Duns Scotus and Francisco Suárez, along with other unnamed scholastics.[13]

A series of unplanned circumstances led to Hale's entrance into the legal profession. During his Oxford years, Hale became attracted to the military and thought of becoming a soldier rather than a pastor. Neither path of divinity nor military materialised, however, for Hale had to leave Oxford for London to deal with a lawsuit claiming part of his estate. While in London he consulted a barrister, John Glanville (1586–1661), who, recognising Hale's potential as a lawyer, persuaded Hale to forsake his plan to be a soldier and instead study law. On 8 November 1628, at the age of nineteen, Hale entered Lincoln's Inn as a student. He was called to the bar on 17 May 1636.

If his biographer Burnet is to be believed, soon after beginning his studies at Lincoln's Inn, Hale had a conversion experience which appears to have reinvigorated the strict Puritanism of his earlier youth. Up until this time, Hale had been increasingly taken with fine clothes, wine and company. But one day while out on the town, a friend got so drunk that he fell over as if dead. According to Burnet, Hale was so overcome by this event that he went to another room and prayed to God for his friend's life and also for forgiveness for himself. He vowed to God not to drink or keep bad company again, and from this point onwards took his religious duties and studies seriously.[14] Although this second-hand (seventeenth-century) account remains the only mention of an evangelical-style conversion experience, Hale did recount that from the age

11 Cromartie, *Hale*, 2, citing Hale's biographical note on his father (Lambeth MS 3516, f. 2).

12 Sidney Graves Hamilton, *Hertford College* (London: F. E. Robinson & Co., 1903), 108.

13 Matthew Hale, *A Discourse of the Knowledge of God, and of Our Selves* (London: William Shrewsbery, 1688), sig. A3v. On Oxford's scholastic education, compare Charles B. Schmitt, *John Case and Aristotelianism in Renaissance England* (Kingston: McGill-Queen's University Press, 1983), 64–7.

14 Burnet, *Life*, 13–15.

of twenty-five or twenty-six (1635–6) he began to grow in obedience, faith and dependence on God.[15]

By the time Hale was called to the bar, he had begun to take his religious practice seriously. His life, as evidenced by his scheme for daily living from his diary, manifested characteristics consistent with Puritan introspective Christianity: prayer, watchfulness over one's passions, the daily mingling of 'spiritual employments' with one's ordinary calling, suspicion towards recreations (and specifically games) and attention to the 'evidences' of one's salvation.[16] Following standard Puritan practice, Hale dedicated Sunday (the 'Lord's Day') strictly to religious observance for the rest of his life (the only permissible activity being works of piety, charity and necessity), regularly quizzing his family on Sunday sermons and then spending two to three hours in theological meditation, and advising his children and grandchildren to do the same.[17] At the same time, Hale remained a loyal member of the Church of England and did not follow the Puritans in denouncing the church holiday of Christmas.[18] He favoured the *Book of Common Prayer* over the *Directory for the Public Worship of God* (1644), which he construed narrowly as belonging to 'some of the presbyterian judgement'. He also supported the right of the magistrate to determine indifferent things (*adiaphora*), although he wished accommodation to scrupulous Puritans for the sake of unity. His Puritanism was of the more conformist variety along the lines of what Baxter referred to as 'moderate episcopal men'.[19]

Hale's strict morality affected his early work as a barrister. If he judged a person or case to be clearly immoral, he refused to provide counsel. (This

15 Lambeth MS 3500, f. 240r. See also Cromartie, *Hale*, 2.

16 See the scheme printed in Burnet, *Life*, 16–19; and Heward, *Hale*, 21–2. This evidence renders problematic the interpretation of Cromartie, *Hale*, 141: '[Hale] differed from most puritans in taking no great interest in himself, either as chief of sinners, or as a rescued saint.' On Puritan introspection, see Theodore Dwight Bozeman, *The Precisianist Strain: Disciplinary Religion and Antinomian Backlash in Puritanism to 1638* (Chapel Hill: University of North Carolina Press, 2004), 84–144.

17 Burnet, *Life*, 76; Richard Baxter, *Additional Notes on the Life and Death of Sir Matthew Hale, the Late Universally Honoured and Loved Lord Chief Justice of the Kings Bench* (London: Richard Janeway, 1682), 23–4; Matthew Hale, *The Works, Moral and Religious*, ed. T. Thirwall, 2 vols. (London: H.D. Symonds, 1805), 1:194–204; Matthew Hale, 'Concerning the Observation of the Lord's Day or the Christian Sabbath', in *A Letter of Advice to His Grand-children, Mary, Gabriel, Anne, Mary and Frances Hale* (London: Taylor and Hessey, 1816), 72–8.

18 Robert C. Evans, Stephen Paul Bray and Christina M. Garner, 'The "Christmas Poems" of Sir Matthew Hale: Brief Preface and Annotated Texts', *Ben Jonson Journal* 20:1 (2013): 95–125; Burnet, *Life*, 112–15; Chris Durston, 'Lords of Misrule: The Puritan War on Christmas 1642–60', *History Today* 35 (December 1985): 7–14.

19 Cromartie, *Hale*, 178, 181–3. See also Richard Baxter, *Reliquiae Baxterianae* (London: T. Parkhurst et al., 1696), part II, 229.

position stands at odds with what is today known as the cab-rank rule.) He also refused to accept full profits for his practice. In ordinary cases, he returned one-half of the fee to clients, and in easy cases he accepted a set fee of 10 shillings. When he acted as arbitrator in a case, he refused payment altogether on the grounds that arbitrators are in essence judges.[20] Politically, Hale was a royalist.[21] He served as council to Archbishop Laud (1643–4), the Duke of Hamilton (1649) and the royalist Christopher Love (1651). He also married into the royalist family of Anne Moore (c. 1642).[22]

While at Lincoln's Inn, Hale became good friends with John Selden, who was one of the most important influences on his life. Baxter said of Hale late in life, 'I know you are acquainted [with] how greatly he valued Mr Selden, being one of his Executors; his Books and Picture being still near him'. According to Burnet, Selden's relationship set Hale on 'a more enlarged pursuit of Learning', consisting of the study of Roman law, mathematics, philosophy, medicine, anatomy, history and chronology.

> But above all these he seemed to have made the study of *Divinity* the cheif of all others, to which he not only directed everything else, but also arrived at that pitch in it, that those who have read, what he has Written on these Subjects, will think, they must have had most of his time and thoughts.[23]

This judgment is certainly justified by Hale's extensive corpus of theological manuscripts (discussed later in this chapter). When Selden died in 1654, Hale was among the executors of his will. In his *Of the Law of Nature*, Hale later paid Selden the distinct honour of citing his *De jure naturali & gentium* (1640) on six occasions – more than any other work besides the Bible.

Throughout the 1650s and 1660s Hale's public reputation increased. In 1652 he chaired the famous Hale Commission, which proposed reforms of judicial administration, the mitigation of penalties in criminal law and the correction of miscellaneous abuses. These proposals, which mostly did not come to fruition at the time, nonetheless anticipated reforms carried out centuries later. In 1653 he began his judicial career as Judge of the Common Pleas and served there until the death of Cromwell in 1658, during which time he also served as MP for Gloucestershire (1654–5). At the Restoration Hale was made Chief Baron of the Exchequer (1660–71) before being appointed Chief Justice of the King's Bench (1671–6). He mourned the divisions created over matters of ceremony by the Act of Uniformity (1662) and whenever possible came to the assistance of nonconformists.[24]

20 Heward, *Hale*, 25–7. 21 Cromartie, *Hale*, 3, 42–57. 22 Heward, *Hale*, 33.

23 Baxter, *Additional Notes*, 40; Burnet, *Life*, 23–8. On Selden, see Chapter 7 in this volume.

24 Heward, *Hale*, 36–47, 65, 68.

After moving to Acton in 1667, Hale became good friends with Richard Baxter. The two attended St Mary's church and soon struck up a friendship which lasted until Hale's death in 1676. By Baxter's own account, he and Hale carried on lively conversations about the nature and immortality of the soul until Baxter moved to Totteridge in 1669. These conversations Baxter found 'so edifying, that [Hale's] very Questions and Objections did help me to more light than other mens solutions'.[25] After Baxter's move, he and Hale continued to prod each other's thinking forwards regarding pressing philosophical questions through exchange of manuscripts and correspondence. In his own culminating systematic theology, *Methodus Theologiae Christianae* (1681), Baxter credited Hale with pressing him to expand his doctrine of creation to include an enlarged discussion of physics, so Baxter's *Methodus* would not exist in its present form without the intervention of Hale.[26] Baxter, himself one of the most learned Puritans of the seventeenth century, clearly saw in Hale a uniquely gifted theological mind. 'I cannot easily praise [him] above his worth', Baxter wrote. 'And I scarce ever conversed so profitably with any other person in my Life.'[27]

Hale's life after the Restoration was also characterised by a transition towards Arminian ideas on salvation that approximated the theology of post-Restoration Latitudinarians. According to his editor, in later years Hale 'somewhat altered his opinion touching some Points in Controversie, especially between the Remonstrants and Contra-Remonstrants'.[28] In the late 1650s, Hale still affirmed the traditionally Calvinist belief that the light of nature is insufficient for salvation, but after the Restoration he came to affirm the belief, associated with Arminianism and Latitudinarianism, that virtuous pagans could be saved through obedience to the natural law.[29] Yet Hale was not a party man. Unlike the Latitudinarians who were generally favourable to Cartesian philosophy, he along with Baxter 'greatly disliked' the mechanical philosophy of René Descartes (1596–1650) and the Neo-Epicureanism of Pierre Gassendi (1592–1655).[30] His discussion of natural law especially retained a good part of his views from his early Puritan or Calvinist pre-Restoration phase.

25 Ibid., 94–100; Baxter, *Reliquiae Baxterianae*, part III, 47.

26 Richard Baxter, *Methodus Theologiae Christianae* (London: M. White & T. Snowden, 1681), 'Praefatio', sig. [A6r].

27 Baxter, *Additional Notes*, 6.

28 Hale, *Discourse*, sig. A1v. The editor was probably Edward Stephens. On Hale's Latitudinarianism, see Cromartie, *Hale*, 156–72. Remonstrants and Contra-Remonstrants refer respectively to the Arminian party and their traditional Reformed opponents in the Netherlands.

29 Cromartie, *Hale*, 164, n. 43; Sytsma, 'General Introduction', lii–lv.

30 Baxter, *Additional Notes*, 6. See also Sytsma, 'General Introduction', xxi–xxiii.

The end of Hale's life was marked by grief and apparent personal theological doubts. Six of his ten children from his first marriage to Anne Moore (d. c. 1658) had survived to adulthood. Hale remarried in 1667 to Anne Bishop (d. 1694), likely his servant, but in the intervening years prior to his own death, half of his adult children died. Hale's first son, Robert, and his wife, Frances, both died in 1670, leaving Hale to look after five grandchildren. Hale's second son, Matthew, died in 1675, leaving another grandson in Hale's care. His third son, Thomas, died about half a year after his marriage in 1676. Hale himself became suddenly sick in October 1675, which forced his retirement in early 1676. Despite his sickness, Hale continued with his theological studies right up until his death at Christmas 1676.[31] Baxter had sent him his recently published *Catholick Theologie*, which attempted to reconcile controversies over predestination, grace and free will. Hale personally told Baxter, 'I am more beholden to you than you are aware of', and particularly thanked him for his *Catholick Theologie*. Yet Baxter judged Hale's late fascination with controversies over predestination and free will as unhealthy for a man preparing to die, and on one occasion told him 'more practical Writings were most suitable to his case, who was going from this contentious world'.[32] In retrospect, Hale's late theological interest in Baxter's *Catholick Theologie* was probably indicative of his personal theological struggles brought on by his post-Restoration transition to more Arminian theological ideas.

THEOLOGICAL WRITINGS

Modern readers of Hale's works have long been familiar with his short theological essays and meditations first published as *Contemplations Moral and Divine* (three volumes; 1677, 1679, 1700) and later brought together in *Works, Moral and Religious* (two volumes; 1805). These published writings are only a fraction of Hale's theological manuscripts, still largely unpublished, which are mainly located in the Fairhurst Papers of the Lambeth Palace Library. These manuscripts comprise thousands of pages spread across dozens of volumes.[33] There

31 Heward, *Hale*, 112–14, 116–19.

32 Baxter, *Additional Notes*, 30, 33–4. Baxter claimed that his *Catholick Theologie* helped to resolve Hale's uncertainties. See Baxter, 'Preface', in Matthew Hale, *The Judgment of the Late Chief Justice Sir Matthew Hale, of the Nature of True Religion, the Causes of Its Corruption, and the Churches Calamity, by Mens Additions and Violences: With the Desired Cure* (London: B. Simmons, 1684), sig. A3.

33 Hale's theological writings are in Lambeth MSS 3480–3509 of the Fairhurst Papers (MSS 3470–3533). For contents, see Cromartie, *Hale*, 241–2; the online catalogue of the Lambeth Palace Library (http://archives.lambethpalacelibrary.org.uk/CalmView) includes detailed descriptions based on the typescript Catalogue of the Fairhurst Papers (1990) by Geoffrey Bill.

are also three manuscript copies of Hale's treatise on the law of nature, also a heavily theological work, housed at the British Library.[34] To date Cromartie has examined the Lambeth manuscripts in greatest detail, and I have worked on a critical edition of Hale's treatise on natural law. Yet these studies only scratch the surface and much work remains before a complete picture of Hale's theological mind can be drawn. Here I will set about the modest task of introducing readers to the main contours of Hale's large theological corpus in order to show that this aspect of his thought was far from marginal. Instead, Burnet's observation that Hale early in his legal career 'seemed to have made the study of *Divinity* the chief of all others' ought to be taken quite seriously.

Most of Hale's theological writings originated, appropriately enough, from his rigorous observation of the Lord's Day as a time set aside specially to God. In addition to his weekly duties of public and household worship, he set aside time on Sunday afternoons, between the evening sermon and supper, for personal theological meditation.[35] He was in the habit of writing his thoughts down, he tells us, for a threefold end:

> 1 To keepe my thoughts fixed
> 2 To keepe them from beinge wholly lost
> 3 That I might in after tyme when perchance my understandinge were better informed see ~~and corre~~ my former mistakes and judge of ~~my~~ the improvement of my own knowledge in the intervall ~~of~~ <between> the wrightinge & second readinge of it[36]

These remarks of Hale applied both to his large multi-volume theological works and to shorter exegetical studies on Scripture. An eyewitness to Hale's practice of writing, most likely his son-in-law Edward Stephens, recorded the following observations regarding Hale's methodical and spontaneous manner of writing:

> His usual Manner of writing these things was this: When he had resolved on the Subject, the first thing he usually did, was with his pen upon some loose piece of paper, and sometimes upon a corner or the margin of the Paper he wrote on, to draw a Scheme of his whole Discourse, or of so much of it as he designed at that time to consider. This done he tap'd his thoughts and let them run, as he expressed it to me himself; and they usually ran as fast as his

34 In chronological order: Add. MS 18235, ff. 41–147 (1693); Harley MS 7159, ff. 1–266 (1696); Hargrave MS 485 (late eighteenth century). The autograph is not extant. See my textual introduction in Hale, *Law of Nature*, lvii–lxvi.

35 Hale, *Discourse*, sig. A3v; Baxter, *Additional Notes*, 31.

36 Lambeth MS 3493, f. ii. Cf. Lambeth MS 3509, f. 70; [Edward Stephens], 'Preface', in Matthew Hale, *Contemplations Moral and Divine* (London: William Godbid, 1676), sig. A2r; Hale, *Discourse*, sig. A4r; Cromartie, *Hale*, 6, 156.

> hand (though a very ready one) could trace them; insomuch that in that space, as he hath told me, he often wrote two sheets, and at other times between one and two; and I have my self known him write according to that proportion, when I have been reading in the same room with him, for divers hours together. So that these writings are plainly a kind of extempore Meditations, only they came from a Head and Heart well fraught with a rich Treasure of Humane and Divine Knowledge, which the famous Legislator Justinian makes the necessary qualifications of a compleat Lawyer. And here it is farther to be observed, that all his larger Tracts, such as this [*Discourse of the Knowledge of God, and of our Selves*], which could not be finished at one time, were written upon *great intervals of time*, and such wherein much business of a quite different Nature had interposed, which usually interrupt the thread of a Mans thoughts.[37]

Besides his stated intention of writing to 'fix' his own thoughts, Hale may have intended such manuscripts for a wider audience, whether through future publication or limited circulation. He himself at the end of his life revised one of these earlier manuscripts, which was published as *Primitive Origination of Mankind* (1677), while circulating other manuscripts to friends, including John Wilkins and John Tillotson.[38] Although in his will Hale forbade the posthumous publication of his manuscripts, his son-in-law Edward Stephens claimed that Hale changed his mind, and in his codicil of November 1666 Hale provided directions for how proceeds from his future publications should be spent. Burnet understood Hale's original prohibition to be the result of a licensing law, which would have resulted in deletions and alterations of Hale's texts.[39]

The theological manuscripts cover a variety of genres typical of the seventeenth century. They can be classed into the following broad categories: exegetical and chronological studies of Scripture, theoretical doctrinal works, works on theological ethics and natural law, polemical works, devotional works and correspondence.[40]

Exegetical Works

There are at least two Old Testament exegetical studies. One on Proverbs is described as 'som observations upon the proverbs of Solaman the wise speeches

37 Hale, *Discourse*, sig. A4. Whereas Cromartie, *Hale*, 6, 141–2, assumed this preface to be written by Baxter, in fact the author of the preface, in a page later inserted into it, refers to himself as 'Mr. S.' and took responsibility for publishing Hale's *Contemplations* (1676), which we know was edited by Edward Stephens. See Hale, *Discourse*, sigs. *3r, *4r.

38 See Cromartie, *Hale*, 157.

39 Hale, *Discourse*, sig. A5v; Burnet, *Life*, 185; Heward, *Hale*, 121–2.

40 Unless otherwise noted, manuscripts refer to the Lambeth Palace Library.

of the wisest of men' (21 November 1669; MS 3509, ff. 70–95). Another consists of a commentary on the book of Job (MS 3488, ff. 106v–185v). Like his contemporaries, Hale was also interested in biblical chronology. There are more than two volumes of notes on chronology (MSS 3486; 3487; 3488, ff. 3–103).

Doctrinal Works

The doctrinal works constitute the bulk of Hale's manuscripts. To Hale's early Puritan period belongs 'Of the knowledge of God and of ourselves 1. by the light of Nature 2. by the S. Scriptures' (c. 1639–41; MS 3505, ff. 1–195v), later published as A *Discourse of the Knowledge of God, and of Our Selves* (1688).[41] The discussion of God, humanity and salvation in this book is representative of Reformed orthodoxy and in continuity with the teachings of the Westminster Confession of Faith published shortly thereafter. A treatise on the divine origin and purpose of the creation of man (30 January 1651; MSS 3481), along with a continuation as part 2 on the existence of God in two separate attempts (MSS 3483, ff. 117–120v; 3484), also dates from this early period. A short eschatological work 'Of judgment' (1 January 1654; MS 3509, ff. 1–13), which addresses Christ's role in the final judgment, likewise belongs to Hale's early period.

Burnet relates that Hale was at work over the course of seven years on a multi-part project against atheism.[42] According to Burnet, the first part was the *Primitive Origination of Mankind* (1677), of which an apparently early draft exists (Sept. 1659; MS 3482). Related to this work are two volumes 'Concerninge the secondary origination of mankind by naturall propagation' (MSS 3489 [book 1]; 3490 [book 2]) which concludes with a discussion of spiritual regeneration (MS 3490, ff. 75–79v). Following Burnet's scheme, part 2 of Hale's project addressed the nature and immortality of the soul, of which there are at least seven partial or complete treatises (MSS 3498, ff. 21–78; 3499; 3500; 3504; 3509, ff. 18–52).

According to Burnet, the third part of Hale's anti-atheist project dealt with the doctrine of God's attributes and the related doctrines of providence and morality, while the fourth part addressed the truth and authority of the Scriptures. These third and fourth parts of Burnet's scheme correspond to a massive ten-part manuscript 'De Deo' (1662–7) spread out over five volumes and, according to Cromartie, consisting of nearly a million words (MSS 3491–5).[43]

In addition to his massive 'De Deo' manuscript, there exist a number of short manuscripts covering a variety of theological topics. Hale was greatly

[41] For dates, see preface to Hale, *Discourse*, sig. A2r; Cromartie, *Hale*, 141.

[42] Burnet, *Life*, 81–2. [43] Cromartie, *Hale*, 156–7.

concerned with matters of theological prolegomena, and among his manuscripts are short works on reason and faith, religion and revelation. On the relation of reason and faith, Hale wrote: 'That reason not a sufficient in guide in matters of fayth' (MS 3506, ff. 101–8);[44] 'Concerninge humane reason and learninge in matters of Religion' (MS 3509, ff. 122–5); 'The confession and reason of my fayth' (MS 3488, ff. 3–103); and 'A breife disquisition touchinge the rule of fayth in relation to devine truthes accordinge to the ordinary evidences of reason' [December 1665] (MS 3497, ff. 71–117).

On the nature of religion and revelation, Hale wrote a number of works. These include 'Of religion and the contests concerninge religion' (1661; MS 3497, ff. 1–64v); 'Concerning Religion, the Superstructions upon it and Animosities about them' (MS 3485, ff. 105–12v), published in *Works* 1:318–30; 'Religion the ends and uses of it and the errors of men touchinge it' (MS 3485, ff. 115–26v), published in *Works* 1:288–307; 'Concerninge prophesyes and predictions of future events' (MS 3507, ff. 51–54v); 'Evidences touchinge the truth and devine authority of the holy scriptures' (MS 3509, ff. 107–111v); and 'The evidence of the truth of the gospell' (MS 3485, ff. 1–102).

A handful of other manuscripts discuss the Church and ceremonies, as well as other miscellaneous topics. Those discussing ecclesiology and ceremonies include 'Of the Church' (MS 3507, ff. 117–122v); 'Touchinge church government' (MS 3507, ff. 143–73); 'Touchinge ceremonyes' (MS 3506, ff. 99–100); 'That a preachinge ministry of the Gospell must bee kept up' (MS 3506, ff. 125–128v); 'Concerninge the commemoration of the birth of Christ 2 thinges considerable. 1 Whither it bee to bee observed. 2 How it is to bee observed' (MS 3507, ff. 59–73); 'Church musiqe' (MS 3507, ff. 115–16); and 'A contemplation touchinge the variety of men and sects' (MS 3509, ff. 57–60v). Other short miscellaneous doctrinal manuscripts include 'Concerninge the state of immortallity' (MS 3506, ff. 109–10); 'The world' (MS 3509, ff. 61–2); 'Observations touchinge the feast of Pentecost' (MS 3509, ff. 55–56v); theological speculations on the magnet (MS 3499, ff. 226–41); and 'Concerninge the greate mercy of God in preservinge us from the power and malice of evill angells' (16 March 1662; MS 3506, ff. 111–14), printed in *A Collection of Modern Relations of Matters of Fact, Concerning Witches and Witchcraft* (London: John Harris, 1693), 1–8.

Theological Ethics and Natural Law

Hale's greatest work of theological ethics is certainly his unpublished treatise *Of the Law of Nature*. This work has rightly been referred to as belonging to

[44] Cromartie dates this to the early 1660s (ibid., 164).

a 'hybrid' genre, 'being partly legal and partly religious'.[45] A number of occasional works overlap with subject matter in *Of the Law of Nature* and address ethics or law from a theological standpoint. Two parts of 'De Deo' (already discussed) include books on ethics and conscience (MS 3492). Other occasional ethical writings include 'Concerninge the innate light of conscience' (MS 3507, ff. 1–12v), 'Certain difficultyes occurringe in the treatises of liberty of conscience' (MS 3498, ff. 268–276v), 'Concerninge thinges indifferent' (MS 3507, ff. 14–36v), 'Concerninge the punishment of offences and the proportion between the offences and punishments with theyr mitigations' (MS 3507, ff. 139–140v) and 'The use of the law' (MS 3506, ff. 121–122v).

Hale wrote many occasional pieces on Christian virtues and practice. Included in his *Works* are essays on the virtues of humility, modesty, contentedness, self-denial, moderation and patience. They also include essays on the redemption of time, stewardship, happiness, the golden rule and provision for the poor. Among the unpublished manuscripts are various short works: 'Of Moderation' (MS 3497, ff. 121–135v); 'Of contentment or contentation' (MS 3498, f. 195); 'Of contentation' [on Philippians 4:11] (MS 3498, ff. 196–199v); 'Concerninge the procuringe causes of evils and afflictions' (MS 3498, ff. 218–22), a reflection on Proverbs 1:30–31; and 'The feare of the Lord is the beginninge of wisdome' (MS 3505, ff. 207–229v). With respect to his own practice as a judge, Hale discusses the obligations and difficulties of his vocation in light of his theological beliefs in a diary entry dated 1668.

Polemical Works

For most seventeenth-century Protestants, the Church of Rome and Socinianism constituted two of the greatest threats to theological orthodoxy. Hale was no exception. He has a treatise on Roman Catholicism titled 'Touchinge policy and the use therof in matters of religion' (MSS 3496; 3498, ff. 279–305). He also has a few pages of reflections on the adoration and veneration of saints (MS 3507, ff. 125–126v). He has one work that addresses Socinianism: 'Touchinge punishments, the relaxation, remission and translation of them in order to the disputes between us and the socinians' (MS 3498, ff. 309–333v).

Devotional Works

Since Hale's theological writing often took place on Sunday afternoons much of it arose in a devotional context. Indeed various manuscripts can be

45 Heward, *Hale*, 132.

described as specifically directed to devotional subjects. Hale composed prayers, the most significant of which is that composed at the end of his life to thank God for the completion of his theological writings (3 August 1673; MS 3500, ff. 240–4). Hale also composed poems regularly on Christmas Day to celebrate the birth of Jesus.[46] He reflected on the duty of thanksgiving to God on more than one occasion (MS 3509, f. 99; ff. 101–3). He wrote about the nature of true wisdom: 'Concerninge true wisdome, the knowledge of and conformity unto the cheif end of our beinge' (MS 3509, ff. 116–17) and 'A great pt. of wisdome to know the tymes' (MS 3509, ff. 120–1). And he reflected on 'The state of this lyfe' (MS 3509, ff. 118–19) and 'Observations concerninge the present providences' (1660; MS 3507, f. 137).

Correspondence

Most of Hale's correspondence consists of advice to his children. He wrote to his children about the principles of religion (MS 3840, ff. i–iv), affliction (MS 3506, ff. 97–8), the 'Infermityes of youth' (MS 3508, ff. 37 v–49v) and 'Directions touching the keeping of the Lord's Day' (MS 3508, ff. 13v–21).[47] An important correspondence between Hale and Richard Baxter is also extant (MS 3499, ff. 63–115). Sometime in 1672, Baxter had sent Hale a draft of his 'Of the Nature and Immortality of Humane Soules'.[48] Hale replied with an undated introductory letter (MS 3499, ff. 65–77), followed by annotations on Baxter's entire treatise dated '1 January 1672' [1673 NS] (ff. 83–115r). Baxter replied with a short letter thanking Hale on 20 September 1673 (f. 81v), along with his own notes in reply to Hale's annotations.

THEOLOGICAL REFLECTIONS ON THE OFFICE OF JUDGE

The impact of Hale's theological exercises was not limited to the speculations of theological treatises or private meditations, but extended to his practical self-reflection on his own vocation as a judge. Shortly after becoming Lord Chief Baron in 1660, Hale wrote down a series of rules for himself, 'Things Necessary to be Continually had in Remembrance'. These rules express reliance on God and emphasise the need for self-denial, impartiality and compassion:

> I. That in the administration of Justice, I am intrusted for God, the King and Country; and therefore,

46 Evans et al., '"Christmas Poems" of Sir Matthew Hale', 95–125.
47 A partial printing of the last (ff. 13v–14v) is in Hale, *Works*, 1:194–6.
48 Dr Williams's Library, London, Baxter Treatises MS 19.351.

II. That it be done, 1. Uprightly, 2. Deliberately, 3. Resolutely.
III. That I rest not upon my own Understanding or Strength, but Implore and rest upon the Direction and Strength of God.
IV. That in the Execution of Justice, I carefully lay aside my own Passions, and not give way to them, however provoked.
V. That I be wholly intent upon the Business I am about, remitting all other Cares and Thoughts, as unseasonable and Interruptions.
VI. That I suffer not my self to be prepossessed with any Judgment at all, till the whole Business and both Parties be heard.
VII. That I never engage my self in the beginning of any Cause, but reserve my self unprejudiced till the whole be heard.
VIII. That in Business Capital, though my Nature prompt me to Pity; yet to consider, that there is also a Pity due to the Country.
IX. That I be not too Riged in matters purely Conscientious, where all the harm is Diversity of Judgment.
X. That I be not biassed with Compassion to the Poor, or favour to the Rich, in point of Justice.
XI. That Popular, or Court Applause, or Distaste, have no Influence into anything I do in point of Distribution of Justice.
XII. Not to be sollicitous what Men will say or think, so long as I keep my self exactly according to the Rule of Justice.
XIII. If in Criminals it be a measuring Cast, to incline to Mercy and Acquittal.
XIV. In Criminals that consist merely in words, when no more harm ensues, Moderation is no Injustice.
XV. In Criminals of Blood, if the Fact be Evident, Severity is Justice.
XVI. To abhor all private Sollicitations, of what kind soever, and by whom soever, in matters Depending.
XVII. To charge my Servants, 1. Not to interpose in any Business whatsoever, 2. Not to take more than their known Fees, 3. Not to give any undue precedence to Causes, 4. Not to recommend Councill.
XVIII. To be short and sparing at Meals, that I may be the fitter for Business.[49]

It seems that these rules reflect a genuine intention on Hale's part actually to live in conformity to them. Edmund Heward observes various examples from Hale's life that are consistent with rules XI, XVI and XVII.[50] Two of the rules are overtly theological (I and III), so there is no question that Hale's theological perspective played a general role in his self-understanding as judge.

But a further and more specific argument can be sustained that the remainder of his rules regarding the conduct of his profession are largely taken from

[49] Burnet, *Life*, 57–60. Burnet claims to have copied these from Hale's own hand.
[50] Heward, *Hale*, 67–9.

theological considerations. In the autumn of 1668, while on circuit, Hale wrote down reflections in his diary on the office of judge. (This was the same diary and time in which he drafted an outline for his treatise on natural law discussed in the next section.)[51] This diary entry begins with biblical citations from the Old Testament, largely from the Mosaic law, on the topic of judging. Hale reproduces the following verses in sequence: Exodus 23:2–3, 6–8; Deuteronomy 16: 18–20; 2 Chronicles 19:5–7, 9, 11; Exodus 18: 21–22; Leviticus 19:15; and Deuteronomy 13:14 (ff. 2r–3r). He then reflects on the difficulties and qualifications of the office (ff. 3r–13v). His reflections not only mirror the content of the rules, they are also interspersed with theological explanation.

When Hale's diary entry is placed side by side with the rules, it is easy to perceive an underlying theological motivation for a number of those rules. First and most obviously, rule III (not to rest 'on my own Understanding or Strength' but on God) is in all likelihood an allusion to Proverbs 3:5, 'lean not unto thine own understanding' (KJV). This rule also has parallels in the diary, first to the office of judge which 'requires a mind constantly awed with the fear of almighty God and sense of His presence' (f. 3v) and, second to Hale's recitation of the admonition of Jehoshaphat to judges (2 Chron. 19:6) that 'they judge not for man but for God' (f. 4v).

Rules VI and VII deal with hearing the entire case before forming a judgment. This corresponds to Hale's diary reflections on avoiding hasty judgments, where Hale writes that the judge must 'pause and consider, turn every stone, weigh every question, every answer, every circumstance, follow the wise direction of Moses in a case of importance to inquire, ask, diligently inquire, behold if it be true and the thing be certain' (f. 6r). The example of Moses here mentioned is that of Deuteronomy 13:14, which Hale had cited at the beginning of his diary entry: 'Then shalt thou inquire and make search and ask and behold if it be truth and the thing be certain, that such abomination is wrought among you' (f. 3r). Thus, the example of Moses provides a theological rationale for rules VI and VII.

Rules X, XI and XII relate to the problem of bias engendered by various groups: rich and poor (rule X), popular or court praise (rule XI) and common

[51] Matthew Hale, 'Notes on circuitus autumnalis' [1668], ff. 2r–14r, the James Marshall and Marie-Louise Osborn Collection, Beinecke Rare Book and Manuscript Library, Yale University, New Haven, CT. Digital copy at http://brbl-dl.library.yale.edu/vufind/Record/3882610; printed in Maija Jansson, 'Matthew Hale on Judges and Judging', *Journal of Legal History* 9:2 (1988): 201–13. The last three pages (ff. 15r–16r) contain Hale's outline for a 'treatise on natural law' (*De lege naturali tractatus*). This work is also discussed in David Saunders, 'The Judicial *Persona* in Historical Context: The Case of Matthew Hale', in *The Philosopher in Early Modern Europe: The Nature of a Contested Identity*, ed. Conal Condren, Stephen Gaukroger and Ian Hunter (Cambridge: Cambridge University Press, 2006), 140–59.

opinion (rule XII). These rules have obvious parallels in Hale's diary citations of Exodus 23:2–3, 6 and Leviticus 19:15. The former, in Hale's citation, reads, 'Thou shalt not follow a multitude to do evil; neither shalt thou speak in a cause to decline after many to wrest judgment. Neither shalt thou countenance a poor man in his cause. Thou shalt not wrest the judgment of the poor in his cause' (f. 2r). The latter reads, 'Ye shall do no unrighteousness in judgment, thou shalt not respect the person of the poor nor honor the person of the mighty, but in righteousness shalt thou judge thy neighbor' (f. 2v). These verses chosen by Hale forbid bias towards or against the poor, and towards the mighty and the multitude. These groups are precisely Hale's concern in rules X–XII.

Rule XIII states that in criminal cases difficult to judge ('measuring Cast') the judge ought to incline towards mercy and acquittal. In his diary, Hale provides a theological justification for this position. He says that 'though to condemn the innocent and to acquit the guilty are both abomination to God', still it is much worse to condemn even one innocent person to death than ten guilty ones. The reason given is that 'the hand of divine justice in the way of His providence may reach in after time a guilty person, or of evidence to convict him, he may hereafter repent and amend; but the loss of the life of an innocent is irreco[n]ver[t]able in this world' (f. 6v). Hale's reason here seems to derive in part from his citation of Exodus 23:7, 'Keep thee far from a false matter; the innocent and righteous slay thou not, for I will not justify the wicked' (f. 2r). Hale also argues that the Jewish law requiring at least two witnesses for a death sentence reflected the expectation of 'full evidence' for conviction in order to exclude the conviction of the innocent (f. 7r). Thus the presumption of innocence found in rule XIII is laden with theological import, both from the example of Mosaic law and Hale's understanding of God's providence.

Hale balances the mercy of rule XIII with severity in rule XV. In cases of murder ('blood') where crime is evident, he says, 'Severity is Justice'. In his diary, Hale explains that although the example of capital punishment acts as a deterrent for similar offences, the primary reason is 'because the everlasting edict of almighty God is of perpetual obligation that the shedders of human blood should be punished with death' (f. 9v). This 'everlasting edict' is almost certainly a reference to Genesis 9:6, 'Whoso sheddeth man's blood, by man shall his blood be shed: for in the image of God made he man' (KJV). In his *History of the Pleas of the Crown*, Hale interpreted Genesis 9:6 as indicating an exception to the general rule that the degrees and applications of penalties are a matter of positive and not natural law. According to Hale, 'Only in the case of *murder* there seems to be a justice of retaliation, if not *ex lege naturali* [from the law of nature], yet at least by a general divine law given to all mankind, *Gen.* ix.6.' Exceptions to capital punishment in the case of murder may be permitted, says Hale, citing the example of God remitting Cain's punishment. But they 'ought to be very rare, and upon great occasions'.[52]

Rule XVI states that the judge should 'abhor all private Sollicitations'. In his diary, Hale explains that solicitations are an instance of temptation which corrupts judgment: 'That a man avoid all such temptations as may be an occasion of perverting his judgment, as solicitations, prepossessions, gifts, kindnesses, addresses for or against any cause or person' (f. 6r). This rule clearly corresponds to Hale's diary citation of Exodus 23:8 and Deuteronomy 16:19. The former reads, 'And thou shalt take no gift, for the gift blindeth the wise and perverteth the words of the righteous.' The latter reads, 'Thou shalt not wrest judgment, thou shalt not respect persons neither take a gift, for a gift doth blind the eyes of the wise and perverteth the words of the righteous' (f. 2r).

This brief comparison of Hale's rules on judging with his diary reflections on the same topic reveals the practical impact of Hale's theological views on his own vocation as a judge. Many rules that Hale formulated to guide his general conduct first as Chief Baron of the Exchequer (1660–71) and then as Chief Justice of the King's Bench (1671–6) are rooted in theological considerations. These theological considerations also demonstrate that Hale understood the Mosaic law to embody universal principles of justice or natural law which could be applied to his own situation. In this respect Hale reflected the widespread contemporary belief that the judicial laws of the Old Testament contained eternally valid precepts of general equity.[53]

NATURAL LAW THEORY

Of the Law of Nature is the title given by Burnet in his *Life of Hale* (1681) to Hale's treatise on the natural law, which is often cited by the title of its late-eighteenth-century copy, *Treatise of the Nature of Lawes in Generall and Touching the Law of Nature*. The original manuscript *Of the Law of Nature* is no longer extant, but several copies remain, including a seventeenth-century copy of the original. Hale originally composed his treatise sometime between late 1668 and 1671 after drawing up an initial outline for a 'treatise on natural law' (*De lege naturali tractatus*) in autumn of 1668.[54] The mature *Law of Nature* consists of thirteen chapters, of which the initial cover the nature, effect and kinds of laws in general (chapters 1–3), while the remainder discuss natural law

[52] Matthew Hale, *Historia placitorum coronae: The History of the Pleas of the Crown*, 2 vols. (Savoy [London]: E. and R. Nutt, and R. Gosling, 1736), 1:13–14.

[53] See also Richard J. Ross, 'Distinguishing Eternal from Transient Law: Natural Law and the Judicial Laws of Moses', *Past and Present* 217 (November 2012): 79–115.

[54] See my textual introduction in Hale, *Law of Nature*, lvii–lviii.

(chapters 4–13). The initial outline from 1668 organised the description of natural law into Aristotle's four causes, and Hale's *Law of Nature* generally follows an Aristotelian causal framework regarding the material (chapters 4–6), formal (chapters 7–11) and final (chapter 13) causes of natural law. The most substantial description of the content of the natural law is contained in chapter 5, while the obligation of the natural law is addressed in chapter 7 and the promulgation of the natural law, both naturally in the soul and through supernatural revelation, is discussed in chapters 8–11. Connections to positive law are most clearly set forth in chapter 12, 'Concerning human Law's and their use in relation to the Law of Nature', although these connections are also touched on throughout the work. The treatise concludes with an argument, reflective of Hale's later Arminian theology, that virtuous pagans could be saved by obedience to natural law (chapter 13).

Given the quantity and importance of Hale's theological output, it is remarkable that the theological dimension to his treatise on natural law has received so little attention.[55] Yet Hale's treatise bristles with Scriptural references and theological distinctions. He defines natural law as 'the Law of Almighty God given by him to Man with his Nature discovering the morall good and moral evill of Moral Actions, commanding the former, and forbidding the latter by the secret voice or dictate of his implanted nature, his reason, and his concience'.[56] He also cites the apostle Paul (Rom. 1–2) as an authority, and his identification of the law written on the heart (Rom. 2:15) with Stoic common notions reflects traditional Protestant exegesis of that *locus classicus*.[57]

I have elsewhere discussed the theological import of Hale's *Law of Nature* at length. Briefly, although Hale is often presented as closely following John Selden, Hale's views on natural law, despite his Arminian argument for the possible salvation of non-Christians, in other respects show strong continuity with his earlier Puritanism and the natural law theories of Francisco Suárez (1548–1617) and Hugo Grotius (1583–1645). Disregarding Selden's objections to deriving the content of the natural law from reason and the more civilised nations (*gentes moratiores*) as unreliable guides, Hale follows Grotius rather than his mentor. Moreover, Hale's account of the principles and conclusions of the natural law (the order and extent of knowledge) is itself an expansion of Suárez's account, while Hale's views on the nature of formal reason (*ratio formalis*) of the natural law follow Suárez's resolution to the scholastic question whether natural law is properly indicative (*lex indicativa*; the intellectualist position) or prescriptive (*lex praeceptiva*; the voluntarist position). Hale,

55 Sytsma, 'General Introduction', xiii. 56 Hale, *Law of Nature*, 41.
57 Ibid., 41–42, 150–51 with explanatory note on 42.

following Suárez, argues that the natural law is both indicative and prescriptive, according to which the divine wisdom is the foundation of the intrinsic goodness of the natural law, while the divine will is the foundation for the formal reason or obligation of the natural law. Selden's views on Noachic precepts and the importance of the precept 'faith must be kept' (*fides est servanda*) are incorporated into this larger framework. With respect to the publication of the natural law first in the human mind through common notions, inclinations and conscience, and next through its republication in special revelation in the Decalogue and Christ's Sermon on the Mount, Hale recapitulates at greater length the Reformed Puritanism of his youth as expressed in his treatise *Discourse of the Knowledge of God, and of Our Selves*. There is no sense of a novel moral epistemology or secularisation of the natural law which historians commonly associate with the natural law theory of Samuel Pufendorf (1632–94) and Christian Thomasius (1655–1728). In fact, Hale was overtly critical of the reduction of natural law to self-preservation, an opinion commonly associated with the natural law theory of Thomas Hobbes (1588–1679).[58]

With these considerations regarding the sources and content of Hale's natural law theory in mind, we now turn to the relation of natural to positive law, since this topic is of direct relevance for how Hale understood natural law to apply to his wider legal thought. Hale is sometimes presented as following Selden down a path of legal positivism, according to which the obligatory force of law originates in explicit or implicit consent as is expressed in the command of a sovereign.[59] While this judgment contains a partial truth inasmuch as Hale emphasises the necessity of the will of the sovereign for obligation, it is problematic for two reasons. First, whether or not Selden fits the mould of a legal positivist, a careful reading of *Law of Nature* reveals that Hale was not a strict disciple of Selden. Second, although for Hale divine and human will create obligation, the contents of the natural law are rooted in their prior conformity to right reason. As the title of chapter 6 from *Law of Nature* states, 'these Natural Laws have in their Matter an intrinsick Moral goodness & Congruity to Right reason and Conveniency to the Condition of Mankind Antecedent to, and Abstractive from any Law injoining Them'.[60] The natural law is an expression of God's wisdom, and the moral validity of human law depends on its conformity to this natural law. For Hale, it is

58 Sytsma, 'General Introduction', xxxiii–lv. On Selden's natural law theory, see the contribution of John Witte, Jr. in this volume.

59 Michael Lobban, *A History of the Philosophy of Law in the Common Law World, 1600–1900* (Dordrecht: Springer, 2007), 61–4.

60 Hale, *Law of Nature*, 107.

possible to evaluate the will of a human sovereign against a higher standard; and even God's prescriptive will conforms to God's wisdom.

Hale most clearly sets forth his understanding of the relation between natural and positive law in chapter 12 of *Law of Nature*, 'Concerning human Law's and their use in relation to the Law of Nature'. A good part of this chapter consists of Hale's exposition of the concept of permissive law (*lex permissiva*), a category distinct from both natural and human law, which by the seventeenth century had already been well established in natural law theory. Permissive law, says Hale, is properly of divine institution: 'it is that Law of Almighty God whereby things not determined by the Law of Nature are left to the determination of human Law's'.[61] Just as he had analysed the natural law according to its matter and formal reason, Hale analyses the permissive law according to its matter and formality. There is here more than a parallelism of language. For both natural and permissive law, the formality corresponds to will, whether divine or human, that provides obligatory force, while the matter refers to content with characteristics considered antecedently to obligation arising from will.

The matter of permissive law, according to Hale, consists of 'those moral actions that are left indifferent and unprohibited or uncommanded by the Law of Nature'.[62] Hale enumerates three kinds of moral actions that fall under the material content of permissive law:

1. Indifferent moral actions that 'in themselves fall neither under the Command or prohibition of the Natural Law'.
2. Things that do fall under the 'precipient part' of natural law, but their circumstances (time, place, manner, etc.) are not determined by natural law.
3. The exact determination of external punishments for things prohibited by the natural law.[63]

Under the description of natural law, Hale adds that permissive law entails that 'No human Law can derogate from the Law of Nature, it cannot forbid what the Law of Nature injoins, nor Command what the Law of Nature prohibits.' Likewise, it also entails that when human laws command or forbid what the natural law also forbids, this is only 'a Further manifestation' of an 'Original Obligation' of natural law.[64] Thus, with his explanation of the matter of

[61] Ibid., 194. On permissive law, see Brian Tierney, 'Permissive Natural Law and Property: Gratian to Kant', *Journal of the History of Ideas* 62:3 (2001): 381–99; and Brian Tierney, *Liberty and Law: The Idea of Permissive Natural Law, 1100–1800* (Washington, DC: Catholic University of America Press, 2014).

[62] Hale, *Law of Nature*, 194. [63] Ibid., 192–4. [64] Ibid., 194.

permissive law, Hale affirms both that human law is an expansion of natural law and that it ought not contradict natural law.

The formality of permissive law corresponds to God's will. Hale says this formality consists in 'three Acts of the Divine will manifested in the Law of Nature':

1. 'In the Leaving of some things out of the Command or prohibition of any Law of God whither Natural or positive';
2. 'In subjecting those things thus left undetermin'd to the power of the Civil Magistrate to determine & specificate';
3. 'In obliging of the Subjects of such Magistrates to the Obedience to those Laws by the very law of Nature'.

This third point regarding obligation to the civil magistrate arises from two heads of natural law (*Capita Legis Naturalis*): first, the Noachic law concerning the establishment of judges which is confirmed by Deut. 16:18 and Deut. 17:12; and, second, the obligation to keep faith (*fidem servare*), by which our consciences are obligated to obey authority either by express or tacit consent.[65] These last two heads of natural law, of course, are taken from Selden.[66]

In setting forth his understanding of permissive law, Hale thus incorporated Selden's insight that human government arises from a contract with the duty 'faith must be kept' (*fides est servanda*). At the same time, he limited this Seldenian influence to the formality of permissive law. In his discussion of the material content of permissive law, Hale perpetuated an important aspect of early modern natural law theory, which viewed positive law as built on the natural law and sought to harmonise their contents.[67] Moreover, with his statement that human law 'cannot forbid what the Law of Nature injoins, nor Command what the Law of Nature prohibits',[68] Hale opened up the theoretical possibility to declare a human law 'void' and no longer obligating.

It is interesting to observe that in Hale's concept of permissive law are contained all the elements – natural law theory, historical jurisprudence and the theory of sovereignty – which Harold Berman labelled Hale's 'integrative jurisprudence'.[69] The permissive law's material content, which allows for

65 Ibid., 195.

66 See also ibid., 87, 103–6, 180–1. For a discussion of Selden as a great Christian jurist, see Chapter 7 in this volume.

67 See also H. Richard Helmholz, 'Bonham's Case, Judicial Review, and the Law of Nature', *Journal of Legal Analysis* 1:1 (2009): 333–5.

68 Hale, *Law of Nature*, 194.

69 See Harold J. Berman, 'The Origins of Historical Jurisprudence: Coke, Selden, Hale', *Yale Law Journal* 103:7 (1994): 1708–9; also Chapter 7 on Selden in this volume. Unfortunately Berman may not have been aware of Hale's *Of the Law of Nature*.

innumerable indifferent matters and determinations beyond the natural law, provides the context for a historical jurisprudence, according to which the historical evolution of customary laws (or common law) takes on moral authority as the accumulated wisdom of generations. The permissive law's formal obligation arises from the will of the sovereign (God or magistrate). And behind the material and formal aspects stands the natural law, which provides an evaluative moral framework for historical development and sovereign authority.

If, according to Hale, the material content of human law derives its moral legitimacy from its conformity to, or at least its non-contradiction of, the natural law, what about cases of conflict between natural and human law? Hale clearly recognises the possibility. He writes:

> But in case of human Laws, this Obligation of an active obedience in the Subject to the Laws of his Soveraign is under this limitation so far as the same is not repugnant to the Law of God: For it is an Eternall Truth in the contradiction of human Laws to the Law of God, it is better to obey God than Man [Acts 5:29] thô the decission of such a contradiction requires great Judgment and integrity in the Subject, for if he err in his Judgment his disobedience is at his perill.[70]

Hale elsewhere elaborates that 'since the duty we owe to God as the Supream Lord of all things is greater and prior to the duty we owe, or can owe to human Government', there is tacitly implied in all relations between rulers and subjects the condition that this obedience does not violate the allegiance owed to God. Thus, 'a Man is not bound to offend God by the active obeying of the Comands or Laws of Men'.[71]

Having recognised the necessity of disobeying unjust human laws, Hale proceeds to outline a theory of passive resistance. Hale reasons that even when a human law contradicts a natural law, this does not negate that other natural law that faith must be kept *(fides est servanda)*, which is the basis of human society and government. Therefore even while refusing to obey an unjust law, subjects ought to yield to any suffering that results. In essence, Hale argues that while a conflict between human and natural law nullifies the obligation to obey such a law, it does not nullify the authority of the sovereign to punish.[72]

Hale's discussion of the relation of natural law to positive law in *Law of Nature* is not only of interest in itself. It is also important as a framework for understanding his historically influential published works. When one reads *Law of Nature* beside Hale's famous treatise of criminal law, *Historia placitorum coronae* (1736), one is impressed by conceptual parallels to such an extent that it is difficult not to conclude that *Historia* presumes concepts more fully elaborated in *Law of Nature*. For example, the opening page of *Historia* states that,

[70] Hale, *Law of Nature*, 31. [71] Ibid., 105. [72] Ibid., 105–6.

while offences are prohibited by the law of nature, particular punishments are determined by positive laws.[73] The difference between natural and positive law thus stated presumes the framework of permissive law from *Law of Nature* discussed earlier. Again, in the *Historia* the theory of exemptions to general punishments (e.g. infancy, dementia) is based on a theory of the capacities of intellect and will as necessary for moral culpability. The nature of these faculties in relation to moral action is explained at greater length in *Law of Nature*.[74] In the *Historia*, Hale also appeals to an understanding of natural law when he permits killing in self-defence but regards suicide as prohibited by natural law on the basis that human dominion is not absolute but derived from God. Both self-defence and the nature of dominion are discussed in *Law of Nature*.[75] As these examples from Hale's *Historia* illustrate, *Law of Nature* forms an important context for understanding his larger legal corpus.

CONCLUSION

Sir Matthew Hale is famous as a jurist. Yet he also deserves recognition as a theologian in his own right who earned the respect of famous contemporary theologians – notably Richard Baxter and Gilbert Burnet – for his theological and philosophical acumen. Hale's early Puritan education strongly shaped his writing for the first fifty years of his life, after which he altered his theology in a more Latitudinarian and Arminian direction on soteriological points. But even during this later period when he rose to the highest ranks of the English judiciary, he never completely abandoned the habits of life and mind from his early Puritanism. The abundance of Hale's theological manuscripts exhibits a fertile theological mind intent not only on private theological meditation, but also on the integration of Christian faith with his vocation as a judge and with his speculation as a natural law theorist. His treatise *Of the Law of Nature*, drafted just prior to Samuel Pufendorf's *De jure naturae et gentium* (1672), is a testament to the importance of natural law to English common lawyers. Not too long ago many historians of common law assumed, as Roscoe Pound remarked, that 'English lawyers have never had much concern with philosophy and natural law found little place in their books'.[76] The very existence of Hale's *Law of Nature* constitutes a vivid illustration to the contrary.

73 Hale, *Historia*, 1:1. 74 Ibid., 1:14–15. See also Hale, *Law of Nature*, 9–12.

75 Ibid., 1:51, 411–12. See also Hale, *Law of Nature*, 14, 77, 88, 93.

76 Roscoe Pound, *The Development of Constitutional Guarantees of Liberty* (New Haven: Yale University Press, 1957), 74, as cited and refuted in Richard H. Helmholz, 'Natural Law and Human Rights in English Law: From Bracton to Blackstone', *Ave Maria Law Review* 3:1 (2005): 3. See also Richard H. Helmholz, *Natural Law in Court: A History of Legal Theory in Practice* (Cambridge, MA: Harvard University Press, 2015).

Portrait of William Murray (1705–93), 1st Earl of Mansfield, Copley, John Singleton (1738–1815) / National Portrait Gallery, London, UK / Bridgeman Images

9

Lord Mansfield
The Reasonableness of Religion

Norman S. Poser

INTRODUCTION

Although Lord Mansfield, who was Chief Justice of the Court of King's Bench from 1756 to 1788, is not known particularly for his religious beliefs, there is evidence that he was a deeply religious man. Mansfield's faith is reflected in decisions supporting religious toleration and establishing that morality was a fundamental element of the common law, as well as in the conscientious conduct of his own life. His greatest contribution to the development of English law was in the field of commerce, where, entirely through judicial decisions, he constructed a system of principles and rules that has survived to the present day.

BIOGRAPHICAL SKETCH

Mansfield's life spanned almost the entire eighteenth century (1705–93). He was born William Murray, a younger son of a Scottish nobleman. At the age of thirteen, having demonstrated his scholarly aptitude at the Perth Grammar School, Murray travelled alone riding a pony the 400 miles to London, where through family connections he gained admittance to Westminster School, then the principal training ground of the elite. His education continued at Christ Church, Oxford University, and he learned the law at Lincoln's Inn, one of the Inns of Court where barristers were trained. In truth, he was largely self-educated, since Lincoln's Inn required little of him except that he eat a certain number of dinners there before being admitted to the bar.

Unlike many of his fellow law students, Murray was extraordinarily diligent, making it his business to study not only the English common law but also the laws of Ancient Rome and continental Europe, as well as the works of the great legal philosophers, particularly the seventeenth-century English philosopher John Locke. As we will see, Locke had an important influence on Mansfield's thinking on politics, economics, law and religion – an influence that has been largely overlooked by earlier commentators on his life and work.

Within ten years after the start of his professional career, Murray had become England's most highly esteemed lawyer. He also had made many friends among the nobility, higher clergy and the politicians who were to become Britain's leaders of the next generation. Most important to his future career, he came to the notice of the Duke of Newcastle, the leading politician of the day. Under Newcastle's patronage, Murray was appointed solicitor general of England and elected to Parliament at the age of thirty-seven. When the attorney-general, Sir Dudley Ryder, was named chief justice of the Court of King's Bench, Murray replaced him as attorney-general. For fourteen years as a law officer of the Crown, Murray was also a leading spokesman for the ruling Whig ministry in the House of Commons. Murray's advocacy, both in court and in Parliament, was incomparable. A contemporary of his wrote: 'Murray was all grace, ease, suavity, and mellifluence; his bare narrative was worth any man's argument; this arose from the perfection of his logic, the excellence of his arrangement, and his thorough mastery of the subject in hand.'[1]

At the age of thirty-three, Mansfield married Lady Elizabeth Finch, a member of one of the richest and most powerful families in England. It was a family of lawyers. Her grandfather, Heneage Finch, Earl of Nottingham, was Lord Chancellor during the Restoration. Their marriage, which lasted forty-six years until her death in 1784, was happy and companionable, though they remained childless. Contemporary accounts, as well as her own letters, show Lady Mansfield to have been a warm, friendly and unpretentious person. Doubtless, Mansfield's connection to the Finch family helped his career and enabled him to gain acceptance from the small circle of grandees who ruled Britain; but his diligence, brilliance and ability to acquire influential friends played an even greater role in his success.

When Chief Justice Ryder died in 1756, nobody challenged Murray's claim to succeed him. His eminence as a lawyer was supported by the tradition of the office of solicitor general being the first step to becoming chief justice or lord chancellor. Murray's predecessors on this well-worn path included, in

1 Abraham Hayward, *Lord Chesterfield and George Selwyn* (London: Longman, 1854), 37.

addition to Ryder, Edward Coke, who became chief justice; Heneage Finch, who became lord chancellor; and Philip Yorke, Earl of Hardwicke, who occupied both offices – first chief justice and then lord chancellor.

Before he would agree to take the office of chief justice, Murray insisted on being made a peer, but King George II, of whom it has been said that 'peerages were proverbially as difficult to extract ... as banknotes',[2] was reluctant to make a nobleman of a mere lawyer. A man of focused ambition, he rejected both blandishments and bribes, insisting that he would not take the chief justiceship without the peerage. Eventually the king gave way and William Murray became Baron Mansfield. Twenty years later, George III gave him an earldom. Mansfield continued to sit in Parliament, but now in the House of Lords, which was then an important part of the government. It was not only the upper house of the legislature, whose assent was required for the passage of legislation, but also the final court of appeal for cases coming from the English and Welsh and the Scottish courts. As a Law Lord (a judicial member of the House of Lords, to whom the other members tended to defer on legal questions), Mansfield occasionally sat on appeals from his own court.

So, at the age of fifty-one, Mansfield took his seat in the Court of King's Bench, England's principal trial *and* appellate court, where he would preside for an unprecedented thirty-two years. As chief justice, he dominated the court; during the first twenty years of his tenure, there were only two dissents by fellow judges,[3] and during his entire time on the bench only six decisions of his court were reversed on appeal by the House of Lords.

Although one of the reforms of the Glorious Revolution of 1688 was to make the common-law judges independent of both the king and Parliament, there remained other examples of institutionalised conflicts of interest in Mansfield's time. Mansfield had life tenure on the court unless found guilty of misconduct or removed by both Houses of Parliament, yet he remained an active politician while sitting as a judge, and he served as a member of the Cabinet for many of these years. Even after he left the Cabinet, he remained an unofficial but influential adviser to King George III and Prime Minister Lord North. Before and during the American Revolution, Mansfield was a strenuous supporter of the unyielding and

[2] Norman S. Poser, *Lord Mansfield: Justice in the Age of Reason* (Montreal and Kingston: McGill-Queens University Press, 2013), 116.

[3] The dissents were in *Millar v. Taylor*, 98 Eng. Rep. 201 (1769), a copyright case; and *Perrin v. Blake*, 98 Eng. Rep. 355 (1770), which involved the construction of a will. Professor James Oldham informs me that there was one additional dissent, in an unreported case.

ultimately unsuccessful policy that led to the loss of Britain's North American colonies.

Mansfield was a man of contrasts and complexity. Although he was extraordinarily innovative and forward-looking as a judge, many of his contemporaries considered him irresolute and even duplicitous as a politician. Contemporaries accused him of timidity, but he could also display an unpleasing arrogance. A twentieth-century American judge summarised:

> As a judge [Mansfield] was brilliant, valiant, daring and resourceful. He possessed not only great intellectual courage, but real moral courage as well. He sounded a note vibrant and clear for ethical values in the law. He had a fine sense of justice, a keen insight into the future trend of the law ... In the political arena he was most unhappy. On the Bench he was completely at home; there he was sure of himself; there he was fearless.[4]

Lord Mansfield left an imprint on virtually every branch of the law. It is no exaggeration to say that he invented modern commercial law, bringing it into conformity with commercial practices. He had a decisive influence on the law of negotiable instruments, insurance and contracts. On the issue of slavery, his famous decision in *Somerset v. Stewart*[5] did not end slavery or the slave trade, but modern historians of slavery agree that it started Britain on the path to abolition.[6] Many of Mansfield's rulings show an extraordinary prescience. He ruled that a wager on the outcome of an election was void as contrary to public policy because it gave an individual an economic incentive to spend money to affect the election.[7] He established that individuals have a right to privacy, a right that was only recognised in the United States in the 1960s.[8] He was the

4 Bernard I. Shientag, 'Lord Mansfield Revisited: A Modern Assessment', *Fordham Law Review* 10 (1941): 345.

5 98 Eng. Rep. 499 (1772).

6 Seymour Drescher, *Abolition: A History of Slavery and Antislavery* (Cambridge: Cambridge University Press, 2009), 101–3; David Brion Davis, *The Problem of Slavery in the Age of Revolution 1770–1823* (New York and Oxford: Oxford University Press, 1999), 377.

7 *Daily Universal Register*, 25 November 1785, Arthur T. Vanderbilt (1888–1957) Political, Professional, and Judicial Papers in the Collection on Legal Change at the Olin Library at Wesleyan University, Middletown, Connecticut [hereafter Vanderbilt Collection], Box 316.

8 In *Da Costa v. Jones*, 98 Eng. Rep. 1331 (1778), the issue was the enforceability of a wager on whether a certain individual was a man or a woman. Mansfield held that the wager could not be enforced because 'it materially affects the interest of a third person'. Mansfield explained the court's ruling: 'Suppose two person were to lay a wager upon a mark or defect in a woman's body. Will the Court say they would suffer her chambermaid to be called, to give evidence upon such a question ... [T]he present case is indecent in itself, and manifestly a gross injury to a third person.' 98 Eng. Rep. at 1335. For a key U.S. decision on the right of privacy, *see* *Griswold v. Connecticut*, 381 U.S. 479 (1965).

first to hold that an unsuccessful attempt to commit a crime was itself a crime,[9] the first to admit the testimony of expert witnesses,[10] and the first to define the limits of the attorney/client privilege.[11]

The decisions of no judge of the eighteenth – or perhaps even the twentieth – century have so often been referred to when seeking an answer to a question of law. The United States Supreme Court has cited Lord Mansfield's decisions more than 330 times, most recently in a case decided in December 2014, reaffirming Mansfield's rule that a statement made during jury deliberations is inadmissible to invalidate the jury's verdict.[12] Ten years earlier, the Supreme Court cited Mansfield as authority when it ruled that the writ of habeas corpus is available to a prisoner at Guantanamo Bay, a location under the control of the government but outside the sovereignty of the United States.[13]

In Britain, Mansfield's jurisprudence remains equally relevant. In the year 2011 alone, judges cited Mansfield's decisions to support their rulings in at least ten reported cases. Mansfield continues to be a source of legal wisdom for courts in countries or jurisdictions that have adopted, to a greater or lesser degree, the English common law, including Australia, Hong Kong, India, Israel, New Zealand and South Africa.[14]

The key to Mansfield's enduring influence lies in his method of deciding cases, as well as in the fundamental values on which he based his decisions. He believed that, while it was important that the common law provide precedents that judges and lawyers could use for guidance, a precedent is valuable only if it is based on a principle. Thus, when he followed, modified or established a precedent, he distilled from it a principle that clarified the law and could be applied to a variety of basically similar, although perhaps superficially different, situations. Many, possibly most, of these principles, expressed in clear English and standing like guideposts, have stood the test of time. Even as social and economic conditions have changed, Mansfield's principles are sufficiently general to be relevant in many different circumstances and sufficiently specific to be of practical value to lawyers and judges.

9 *Rex v. Scofield*, Cald. 397 (1784). 10 *Folkes v. Chadd*, 99 Eng. Rep. 589 (1782).

11 Mansfield defined the limits of the attorney/client privilege not in his courtroom but in the House of Lords in the bigamy trial of the Duchess of Kingston. *The Trial of Elizabeth Duchess Dowager of Kingston for Bigamy* (London: Charles Bathurst, 1776), 146.

12 *Warger v. Shauers*, 135 S.Ct. 521, 526 (2014), citing *Vaise v. Delaval*, 99 Eng. Rep. 944 (1785). The rule is codified in U.S. Federal Rule of Evidence 606(b).

13 *Resul v. Bush*, 542 U.S. 466 (2004), citing *King v. Cowle*, 97 Eng. Rep. 587 (1759).

14 Poser, *Lord Mansfield*, 401.

Based as they were on Mansfield's deep and broad understanding of the law and of practical affairs, the lasting principles he established were realistic and full of common sense. He combined an astute understanding of human nature with a vigorous aspiration to achieve justice. As discussed later in this chapter, to Mansfield morals were an essential element of law, and he declared his court to be the custodian of the morals of the people.

Mansfield's political views defy easy categorisation. In the eighteenth-century meaning of the word, he was a liberal: that is, he supported religious freedom and opposed almost any government regulation of commerce. For example, in the *Somerset* case, although he criticised the institution of slavery as 'odious', he went out of his way to assure the West Indian planters and merchants that his decision to set free a recaptured slave would not affect the slavery law of the colonies.[15] Other Mansfield decisions showed an authoritarian bias: he stifled press criticism of the government through his rigorous enforcement of the seditious-libel laws; he instructed juries that labour organisers were criminal conspirators;[16] he was implacable in imposing capital punishment or other harsh penalties for many crimes, including theft and forgery; and he tried unsuccessfully to give authors perpetual copyright protection, despite a statute that limited such protection to twenty-eight years. To one of Mansfield's most prominent twentieth-century admirers, 'Mansfield's difficulty was his fear of the people.'[17] To say that Mansfield was a man of his era is true, but it is an incomplete response to criticism of his less admirable decisions, since he was deeply unpopular in his own times for some of his views and decisions.

Throughout his life, Mansfield was unwilling to challenge the authority of the government. Near the end of his career, one observer wrote of this trait: 'This conduct will leave a stain upon his character which time cannot obliterate. The great man's errors universally admitted to be such ought to serve as a beacon to minor judges.'[18] Mansfield's family background provides a possible explanation for his servility. In 1715, when Mansfield was ten years of age living in the Scottish city of Perth, Jacobite supporters of the exiled Stuart monarchs staged a rebellion against the British government. Mansfield's father, two of his older brothers and a brother-in-law supported the Jacobite uprising. After the government crushed the rebellion, Mansfield's father and one brother served a year in prison, while the other

15 Ibid., 295. 16 See e.g. *Rex v. Eccles*, 168 Eng. Rep. 240 (1783).
17 Arthur T. Vanderbilt to Thomas O'Brien, 17 September 1943, Vanderbilt Collection, Box 316.
18 *General Advertiser*, 24 October 1785, Vanderbilt Collection, Box 322.

brother and the brother-in-law went into permanent exile as courtiers of the Jacobite king in France and Italy. For the rest of his life, Mansfield's political enemies liked to remind him of his treasonous family and to insinuate that he was a secret Jacobite.

There is strong evidence that Mansfield himself entertained Jacobite sympathies in his youth: at the age of twenty while on holiday in France, he wrote two letters to his exiled brother-in-law pledging his loyalty to the Jacobite king.[19] The two letters never came to light during Mansfield's life, and there is no reason to believe he was disloyal to the government during his long career as a lawyer and judge. Nevertheless, his knowledge that the letters existed – and might lead to blackmail or exposure – could hardly have added to his peace of mind and may well have contributed to his deferential attitude towards the government.[20] This fear is likely to have played a part in Mansfield's desire to seek the security of the bench rather than high political office and to have accounted for the timidity and moral cowardice with which he was sometimes charged. It has been observed that Mansfield was unbelievably secretive about himself and at the same time intensely social by nature. The apparent inconsistency in Mansfield's character might be explained by the existence of the two secret letters.[21]

From his boyhood, Mansfield displayed great acuity. James Boswell, who was a lawyer as well as the biographer of Samuel Johnson, wrote in his journal that a conversation with Mansfield was like being cut with a very, very cold instrument. Mansfield's rise to the top was also due to his exceptional diligence, enormous ambition and an ability to make friends who could be useful to him. Soon after his appointment, when he sent a draft of an argument to a fellow judge from his home, he wrote: 'While the company is at cards, I play my rubbers at this work, not the pleasantest in the world; but what must be done I love to do, and have it over.'[22] Though hardworking, Mansfield was intensely sociable. His wide circle of friends included, in addition to numerous members of the nobility, bishops, lawyers, politicians and judges, the actor David Garrick, the painter Joshua Reynolds, the playwright Oliver Goldsmith and the colonial administrator Warren Hastings.

19 A reviewer of my biography of Lord Mansfield suggests that Mansfield's secret approach to the Jacobites may have been a shrewd career move, for in 1725 there was still a possibility that the Jacobites would be successful in restoring the Stuart kings to the British throne. Sir Stephen Sedley, 'I Have No Books to Consult', *London Review of Books*, 22 January 2015: 20.

20 Poser, *Lord Mansfield*, 33–5, 100–11.

21 Arthur T. Vanderbilt to LeRoy Kimball, 10 April 1946, Vanderbilt Collection, Box 316.

22 Mansfield to Justice Wilmot, 29 December 1757. Add. MSS. 9828, f. 33, Vanderbilt Collection, Box 324.

Mansfield was, above all, a man of reason. The following anecdote published shortly after his death, if genuine, provides a fine example of his rationality, hatred of prejudice, wisdom and sense of humour. Mansfield was travelling on circuit outside London when he was called on to try a woman accused of witchcraft. Several witnesses testified that they had seen the defendant walk upside down in the air. When he came to address the jury, Mansfield saw that it would be fruitless to challenge their testimony, so he approached the case from a different angle. This is what he said:

> I do not doubt that this woman has walked in the air with her feet upwards, since you have all seen it; but she has the honour to be born in England as well as you and I, and consequently cannot be judged but by the laws of the country, nor punished but in proportion as she has violated them. Now I know not one law that forbids walking in the air with the feet upwards. We have all a right to do it with impunity. I see no reason therefore for this prosecution, and this woman may return home when she pleases.[23]

Mansfield retired from the bench in 1788. He died in 1793 at the age of eighty-eight and was buried in Westminster Abbey, where a huge monument honours his memory.

JOHN LOCKE AND NATURAL LAW

Intellectually and politically, Lord Mansfield was a child of the Glorious Revolution of 1688. When the British ruling class forced King James II to abdicate and brought in William and Mary as joint monarchs, they changed Britain into a constitutional monarchy. The new political system increased the power of Parliament, fostered growth of industry and commerce, promoted a religiously tolerant society and guaranteed the independence of the judiciary. Its intellectual father was John Locke, who believed in political freedom, religious toleration and economic individualism. In view of Locke's apparent influence on Mansfield's thinking, on religion as well as on other matters, it is necessary to devote a few words to this greatest of English philosophers.

Locke was born in 1632 and educated at Westminster School and Christ Church, Oxford, as Mansfield was seven decades later. Again like Mansfield, Locke was a lover of the classics, believing that Latin was 'absolutely necessary to a gentleman . . . and a man can have no place amongst the learned, in

23 John Adams, *Elegant Anecdotes, and Bon-mots*, 3d ed. (London: C. and G. Kearsley, 1794), 19–20.

this part of the world, who is a stranger' to either Greek or Latin.[24] Like Mansfield, he believed in the need for proficiency in the English language and, like Mansfield, he placed a great value on civility, believing that this quality was not only the greatest ornament of life but also a Christian duty.[25] According to a biographer, Locke was 'a temperate apostle of reason, sceptical of enthusiasm, but of a passionate heart, of a fine grace and temper in thought, conduct and religion'.[26] He may well have appealed to Mansfield for his personal qualities as well as for his political, economic and religious philosophy.

Locke expounded his theory of law and politics in *Two Treatises of Government*, published in 1690. Here he provided the theoretical underpinning for the Glorious Revolution by rejecting the theory that kings ruled by divine right and replacing it with a theory of government based on a social contract. He hypothesised that before the existence of any government, men were free to do what they liked with their selves and their property. They were governed only by natural law, laid down by God, which dictated that no one ought to harm another in his life, health, liberty or property. Because there were transgressors who might deprive people of their God-given rights, members of the community entered into a social contract to give up to the government their individual right to punish transgressors in exchange for protection against them. But the positive laws established by the government should, to the extent possible, be guided and inspired by natural law, which is based on morality and reason.[27]

The theory of natural law predated Locke by two millennia. According to Roscoe Pound, the ancient Greeks

> had the notion of an ideal form of the social status quo – a form that expresses its nature, a perfect form of the social organization of a given civilization – as that which the legal order is to further and maintain. They are to measure all situations by an idealized form of the social order of the time and place and are so to shape the law as to make it maintain and further this ideal of the social status quo.[28]

24 David G. James, *The Life of Reason: Hobbes, Locke, Bolingbroke* (Freeport, NY: Books for Libraries Press, 1972), 82–3 (quoting John Locke, *Thoughts on Education*, 152).

25 For an example of the importance Mansfield attached to civility, see Poser, *Lord Mansfield*, 58.

26 James, *Life of Reason*, 86.

27 John Locke, *Two Treatises of Government* (New York: E. P. Dutton and Co., Inc. Everyman's Library, 1943), 118–20, 181; Roy Porter, *The Creation of the Modern World* (New York & London: W. W. Norton & Company, 2000), 185–6.

28 Roscoe Pound, *An Introduction to the Philosophy of Law*, rev. ed. (New Haven: Yale University Press, 1959), 12.

Plato promoted the idea that an ideal state 'being . . . constituted according to nature, will be wise'.[29] The notion that there was a determinable law of nature can be traced from the ancient Greeks to the Romans. Cicero believed that all law was based on general principles that were grounded in the universality of human reason. Natural law doctrine was passed on from the classical writers to medieval scholars. St Thomas Aquinas wrote in the thirteenth century that 'every law framed by man bears the character of a law exactly to the extent to which it is derived from the law of nature. But if on any point it is in conflict with the law of nature, it at once ceases to be a law; it is a mere perversion of the law.'[30] And several great English jurists who preceded Mansfield, including Richard Hooker and John Selden, were adherents of natural law, as detailed in Chapters 6 and 7 in this book.

Mansfield wrote no books or articles describing his views on the nature of law or the role of law and the courts in society. It is possible that a speech or article of this kind was among the papers that were destroyed in the Gordon Riots of 1780; if so, it is irretrievably lost. What we know of his religious philosophy must therefore be gleaned from his judicial decisions and from his letters.

Mansfield believed in natural law: namely, that the particular laws of a country, however different in their particulars, are based on 'an eternal and immutable moral code'.[31] A letter he wrote in 1775 to his long-time friend Warren Hastings, the governor general of Bengal, gives us a valuable window into his thinking. Hastings was facing the task of creating a legal system for Britain's newly acquired colony of India. Instead of imposing British laws on the Indians, Hastings decided to leave existing Indian laws in place (subject, of course, to British supervision). He sent a translation of these laws for Mansfield for his comment.

Mansfield began his reply by praising Hastings for not trying to change the laws of a foreign country with a culture radically different from that of England: 'No measure could be more barbarous . . . than to change the laws of any people, except by slow degrees and in consequence of long experience.' Mansfield continued, expounding his belief that while the laws of each society reflect its particular culture, customs and traditions, all legal systems have a common root in reason and morality:

> As to right and wrong, human reason is much the same at all time and in all places. Greeks, Romans, Arabians, [Hindus], and Christians draw the same

[29] Plato, *Republic*, trans. Benjamin Jowett (New York: Barnes & Noble Classics, 2004), 127.
[30] Bertrand Russell, *The History of Western Philosophy* (New York: Simon & Schuster, 1945), 623.
[31] Pound, *Introduction to the Philosophy of Law*, 62.

conclusions from principles of natural justice and equity, but every people and age have to have them vouched by the authority of their own doctors.[32]

THE REASONABLENESS OF RELIGION

Social historians have emphasised that it is a common error to regard eighteenth-century Britain as irreligious.[33] An ethical code based on Christian doctrine remained a rule of life to a large portion of the community, just as it had in earlier ages. But religious thought was undergoing a profound change at the time that Mansfield was appointed chief justice in 1756. The increasingly scientific spirit of the age demanded that the reasonableness of Christianity be proved and emphasised. Philosophers and scientists of the previous century, notably Francis Bacon and Isaac Newton, had introduced rational, empirical modes of thought, based on inquiry, observation and experiment. Faith no longer could be simple and unquestioned; it had to be tested by the standard of reason. Even as traditional a thinker as Dr Johnson found it necessary to establish his religious life on a rational basis.

Although Locke was the founder of the philosophy of empiricism, which maintains that all knowledge (with the possible exception of logic and mathematics) is derived from experience,[34] he was profoundly religious. In his essay on *The Reasonableness of Christianity*,[35] published in 1695, Locke tried to reconcile revealed religion with empiricism and reason. He wrote that some things are unknowable and cannot be disproved and that, furthermore, revealed religion is consistent with reason and common sense. Locke was not a lawyer, but if he had written in legal jargon he might have said that those who sought to *disprove* supernatural Christian faith had the burden of proof, a burden they were unable to meet.

MANSFIELD'S FAITH

It appears likely that Mansfield had studied Locke's writings with diligence and deep understanding before he went to the bench. As a young solicitor general, he explicitly cited Locke's economic theories in arguing to the Board

32 Mansfield to Hastings, 3 March 1775, British Library, Add. MSS. 39871, f. 2.

33 See e.g. Porter, *Creation of the Modern World*, 96–129; G. M. Trevelyan, *English Social History: A Survey of Six Centuries: Chaucer to Queen Victoria* (London: Longmans, Green and Co., 1942), 353.

34 Russell, *History of Western Philosophy*, 609.

35 John Locke, *The Reasonableness of Christianity as Delivered in the Scriptures*, ed. George W. Ewing (Washington, DC: Regnery Publishing, Inc., 1965).

of Trade that a usury law adopted by a West Indian colony should be revoked on the grounds that money, like any other commodity, should be traded freely, and that regulation of it was futile since people would find ways of getting around the usury laws. And on matters involving religious freedom, Mansfield's views were consistent with Locke's teachings to an extent that strongly suggests that Locke had an important influence on his thinking.

Whether or not Mansfield shared Locke's belief in revealed religion is unknowable. All his life, Mansfield was a member of the established Church of England and attended church services. His last will and testament, executed at the age of seventy-seven, begins with the words, 'When it shall please God, to call me to another State, to which, of all I now enjoy, I can only carry the Satisfaction of my own Conscience, & my firm Reliance upon his Goodness, through Jesus Christ.' It is possible, of course, that this statement was less a declaration of a personal belief in God and the divinity of Christ than a conventionally religious way of referring to the end of his life.

Mansfield did not talk or write about his faith, even with those closest to him. Reticence about personal matters was deep-rooted in his character, but it also stemmed from his ambitious nature. As a rising lawyer and politician, he had every reason to avoid expressing his views on the controversial subject of religion, which could only earn him enemies. From habit and preference, he remained tight-lipped even after he was seated securely on the bench. The Duke of Newcastle, Mansfield's friend and closest political ally, once remarked, 'I wish I knew a little more of My Ld Mansfield's *thoughts* than I do.'[36]

Nor do we learn anything about Mansfield's religious beliefs from examining the list of his personal friends, a list that spanned the spectrum of religious belief. It comprised high-ranking clerics of the Anglican Church, including William Warburton, Bishop of Gloucester, a strenuous, hot-tempered advocate of the literal truth of the Bible, and Richard Hurd, Bishop of Worcester, a less vehement but equally orthodox clergyman, a scholarly type whom Dr Johnson described as an old maid in breeches. His friends also included the poet Alexander Pope, whose Roman Catholicism placed him under severe legal disabilities, and the politician and philosopher Henry St John, Viscount Bolingbroke, a deist who denied the divinity of Christ and a literal interpretation of the Bible. On one occasion shortly before Pope's death in 1744, Pope, Warburton and Mansfield dined together. Warburton, hoping to detach Pope

[36] Newcastle to the Marquess of Rockingham, 3 June 1768, British Library Add. MSS. 32990, f. 153.

from his Catholicism and also from his friendship with Bolingbroke, vehemently tried to persuade Pope that Bolingbroke did not believe in the moral attributes of God. A shocked Pope told Warburton he must be mistaken. A heated discussion followed, in which, so far as is known, Mansfield characteristically remained silent.[37]

Mansfield demonstrated his Christian virtues, which have been defined as those 'showing the qualities associated with Christ's teachings', not so much in professing his faith as in his conduct, both on and off the bench.[38] While he was famously severe in sentencing criminals, including gang leaders and forgers, there are numerous reports of his helping the weak and vulnerable. When a fourteen-year-old orphaned girl, whose brother had tried to force her into prostitution, was brought into Mansfield's court without an attorney or friend to speak for her, Mansfield gently coaxed her unhappy story from her and acted 'as counsel, attorney and sole friend of a helpless orphan girl'.[39] On another occasion, the overseers of a parish had caused a man to be indicted for converting his house into a hospital for unmarried women to give birth. Expressing surprise that such an indictment could be found, Mansfield asked: 'By what law is it criminal to deliver a woman when she is with child?' The indictment was dismissed.[40]

In his personal life, Mansfield habitually acted in a decent and charitable manner, distributing large sums to the poor of the neighbourhoods in which he lived, in London and at Kenwood in Hampstead.[41] Mansfield's acceptance of his great-niece Dido Elizabeth Belle, the daughter of his naval captain nephew and a West Indian slave, into his home at Kenwood, to live for many years as a virtual member of his family, suggests strongly that he harboured little or no racial prejudice.

MANSFIELD'S RELIGIOUS TOLERATION

Whatever his personal faith, Mansfield was a staunch supporter of religious freedom for adherents of religions other than the Established Church. His toleration may, at least in part, have been a reaction against his own family's involvement in religious bigotry. The brutal Scottish civil strife between Episcopalians and Presbyterians, known as Covenanters, had ended less

37 Brean S. Hammond, *Pope and Bolingbroke: A Study of Friendship and Influence* (Columbia: University of Missouri Press, 1984), 107–8.

38 *The Oxford American Dictionary and Thesaurus* (New York and Oxford: Oxford University Press, 2003).

39 *General Evening Post*, 22 April 1777.

40 *Rex v. Felix MacDonald*, 97 Eng. Rep. 1026 (1765).

41 Poser, *Lord Mansfield*, 210–11.

than twenty years before Mansfield's birth. A collateral ancestor, Sir Robert Grierson of Lag, a leader of the Episcopalians, had been zealous in suppressing the Covenanter movement. In 1685, he ordered the hanging of two men without a trial. He also was responsible for the notorious execution of the Wigtown martyrs: two Presbyterian women who refused to renounce their religion were tied to stakes in Solway Firth and sang hymns until the tide came in and drowned them.[42] One can speculate that shared remembrance of these events contributed to Mansfield's hatred of religious intolerance.

Here too Mansfield was likely influenced by Locke, whose support for religious toleration was an integral part of his theory of a social contract. In *A Letter Concerning Toleration*, published in 1689, Locke argued that since temporal security was the only reason for people to enter into society, the social contract did not affect their freedom to worship as their conscience dictated. Moreover, he argued, the civil authorities had no special competence to guide men and women on their path to salvation. Locke declared: '[T]he care of souls is not committed to the civil magistrate any more than to other men ... [because] his power consists only in outward force; but true and saving religion consists in the inward persuasion of the mind, without which nothing can be acceptable to God.'[43] Locke also pointed out that it is not the diversity of religious opinions, but rather the refusal of toleration to those of different opinions, that has produced all the religious wars in history.[44]

Mansfield's belief in the separation of Church and state, a fundamental tenet of Locke's thinking, is illustrated by his decision in an action for reinstatement against Dr Warren, the rector of the parish of Hampstead, by his clerk. The clerk had stood father for a bride and gave her in marriage. Warren fired him because, as soon as the ceremony was over, the clerk kissed the bride, without any objection from her. The clerk's lawyer argued that Warren probably fired the clerk because he was angry that he didn't get a kiss. Mansfield ruled for the clerk, but on a different ground that emphasised the separation of Church and state. He said the clerk, a servant of the parish, could not be dismissed at the pleasure of the rector because the clerkship was a civil, not an ecclesiastical position.[45]

42 Ian B. Cowan, *The Scottish Covenanters 1660–1688* (London: Victor Gollancz Ltd, 1976), 125–7.

43 John Locke, *A Letter Concerning Toleration* (New York: Macmillan Publishing Company; London: Collier Macmillan Publishers, 1950), 18.

44 Ibid., 57. 45 *Gazetteer*, 24 January 1776.

As a practising lawyer, Mansfield shared Locke's respect for a person's religious beliefs, whatever they might be. In *Omychund v. Barker*,[46] Mansfield represented the plaintiff in the Court of Chancery in a dispute over the sale of goods in India.[47] The question before the court was whether the testimony of witnesses who refused to swear a Christian oath could be admitted in evidence in an English trial. Commissioners had been sent to India to take written evidence, and the witnesses had sworn an oath in the manner of their Hindu religion, which was to touch the foot of a Brahmin priest with their hand.

Mansfield's argument for admitting the testimony was both practical and moral, as well as consistent with Locke's teachings on religious toleration. Echoing Locke's reasoning in *A Letter Concerning Toleration*, he argued that a solemn oath is a security for a person's speaking the truth; it is an appeal to God for the truth. It would be self-defeating to compel a man to swear by a God in whom he does not believe. The Chancellor agreed and the testimony was admitted.

On at least two occasions, Mansfield spoke publicly about his belief in religious toleration. When, as solicitor general, he defended himself before the Cabinet against an accusation that he had drunk toasts to the exiled Jacobite Pretender as a young man, he emphasised both his loyalty to the Church of England and his belief that everyone should be free to practice his or her own religion: 'Tyranny in the State and persecution in the Church are equally bad; and I would, upon principles of Christianity and sound policy, support the Toleration in its full extent, with the same warmth, and the same zeal, as I would the Established Church.'[48] Many years later, after the anti-Catholic Gordon Rioters had destroyed his home and his possessions, addressing the House of Lords he pointed with pride to his long record of religious toleration:

> My desire to disturb no man for conscience's sake is pretty well known … I have no leaning to Roman Catholics … I have shown equal favour to Dissenters from the established Church of all denominations; and … I have always reprobated attempts to molest them in the celebration of their religious worship as unworthy of the apostolical Protestantism which we profess.[49]

46 26 Eng. Rep. 15 (1744).

47 Although Mansfield was solicitor general at the time, law officers of the Crown were permitted to represent private clients, attracting lucrative business.

48 William Murray's speech on 23 February 1753, The Council Examination of the Jacobite Charges, British Library, Add. MSS. 33050, ff. 200–368.

49 John Campbell, *The Lives of the Chief Justices of England*, 3 vols. (London: John Murray, 1849–57), 2:529–30.

Mansfield's belief in religious toleration was widely shared in mid-eighteenth-century England, at least in the upper ranks of society, where prejudice against Catholics and Protestant Dissenters had largely died out. Religious toleration was also in the air in continental Europe.[50] Philosophers of the Enlightenment who supported toleration included Voltaire and Jean-Jacques Rousseau in France and Gotthold Ephraim Lessing and Moses Mendelssohn in Germany. In his play *Nathan the Wise* (1779), Lessing, like Locke, argued eloquently for religious toleration and maintained that faith could be supported by reason. Even some European rulers supported toleration: Frederick the Great of Prussia believed that 'everyone must be allowed to go to heaven in his own way', although he also saw political and economic benefits in toleration.[51]

At first glance, Mansfield's support of religious toleration may seem inconsistent with his political conservatism, including his heavy-handed suppression of press freedom and labour movements. This inconsistency disappears, however, when seen in the context of British politics of the time. While religious toleration was gaining ground with the elite, a large part of the population still harboured prejudice against Catholics, Protestant Dissenters and Jews. According to the historian Neil Bunker, 'the bulk of the population lagged far behind the cabinet in its toleration of Roman Catholics'.[52]

Anti-Catholic feeling, both in Britain and the American colonies, was exacerbated by the passage in 1774 of the Quebec Act, a measure sponsored by Mansfield, which gave freedom of worship to the French-speaking Catholic population of Britain's newly acquired possessions in Canada and the Ohio Valley. While Mansfield and other British leaders saw the act as a move to support religious toleration and to solidify the support of Britain's new subjects, the American colonists and their supporters in Britain saw it as a nefarious plot to bring Catholicism into America and to prevent westward expansion by the colonists. John Wilkes, the populist leader whom Mansfield's court had sentenced to prison for a purportedly libellous attack on the government, was a zealous anti-Catholic as well as an advocate of political freedom. According to Bunker, the Wilkesite protest against the Quebec Act 'owed as much to sectarian hatred [against Catholics] as it did to love of freedom'.[53] In mid-eighteenth-century

50 Neil Bunker, *An Empire on the Edge* (New York: Alfred A. Knopf, 2014), 275.

51 Robert Zaretsky, *Boswell's Enlightenment* (Cambridge, MA, and London: Harvard University Press, 2015), 132, 145.

52 Bunker, *Empire on the Edge*, 276.

53 Ibid., 276.

politics, authoritarian government could play the role of protecting the religious freedom of its subjects. Thus, Mansfield's belief in religious toleration is reconcilable with his authoritarian political views.

MANSFIELD'S TOLERATION OF ROMAN CATHOLICS

England in the mid-eighteenth century was predominantly Anglican. Out of a population of about six million, there were only about 100,000 Roman Catholics, who were in England under many onerous restrictions, which Parliament had enacted during the Restoration period a hundred years earlier. Although Mansfield himself worshipped in the Anglican Church, he was well aware of the anti-Catholic laws. His close friendship with the poet Alexander Pope, whose life these laws restricted in many ways, most certainly provided Mansfield with a keen awareness of this. Mansfield may have felt a kinship with Pope because both were in a sense outsiders in Protestant England: Pope was a Roman Catholic while Mansfield was a Scot, a nationality that many Englishmen despised.

Catholics were prohibited from gathering together to practice their religion; holding government employment; inheriting, purchasing or owning land; sending a child out of the country to be educated; possessing most types of weapons; coming within ten miles of London; and bringing a legal action. A priest who held a Catholic Mass could be imprisoned for life, and an informer who achieved a conviction in such cases was entitled to a bounty of £100. Although these laws were not always enforced, they effectively made Catholics second-class citizens.

Interestingly, Locke's support of toleration did not extend to Catholics. In an implicit reference to Catholic France, he wrote that a Church that requires all those who enter into it to deliver themselves up to the protection of a foreign prince has no right to be tolerated. Locke clearly believed that English Catholics were loyal to Louis XIV, in much the same way that during the cold war many in the West believed that local communists were loyal to the Soviet Union.

In his judicial decisions interpreting the anti-Catholic laws, Mansfield stayed consistent with Locke's underlying views while rejecting Locke's conclusion. These decisions tell us much about Mansfield's way of thinking on religious freedom, but also about his own jurisprudence and his view of the role of the courts in society and the nature of law itself.

In *Foone v. Blount*,[54] a man who owned real estate left a sum of money to Foone, a Catholic, with instructions to his executor to sell the land and to pay

54 98 Eng. Rep. 1188 (1776).

the legacy out of the proceeds of the sale. Foone sued the executor for the money in Mansfield's court. The executor argued that Foone could not take the legacy because the law excluded a Catholic from any interest or profit arising out of land.

In deciding in favour of Foone, Mansfield could have simply interpreted the law as having no application to the case because Foone's legacy was for money, not land. But he went much further, coming close to challenging the validity of an act of Parliament because he believed it had outlived its usefulness. The Catholic laws, he said, were passed because they were thought to be necessary to the safety of the state, and they could be defended only on that ground. 'From the nature of these laws, they are not to be carried by inference, beyond what the political reasons, which gave rise to them, require.' Finally, he declared that he was unwilling to deny Foote the legacy 'only because he happens to be of a different way of thinking from the established mode of religion'.

In *Rex v. Webb*,[55] Mansfield went even further in limiting the impact of the anti-Catholic laws. A carpenter named Payne accused James Webb of celebrating a Catholic Mass. Payne was a professional informer who made a career out of bringing criminal proceedings against Catholics in order to earn bounties. When Payne testified, Mansfield asked him, 'You are *sure* that this man is a Popish priest; and that he said Mass?' Payne answered, 'Yes.' Mansfield then asked, 'You know then what a Mass is?' Payne remained silent. This is how Mansfield addressed the jury:

> A Popish priest convicted of exercising his functions is subject to fine and perpetual imprisonment. But, first, he is to be proved a priest, for unless he is a priest, he cannot be touched for the enormity of saying mass; and then, unless he is proved to have said mass, the crime of being a priest will escape with impunity. Now the only witness to the mass is Payne – a very illiterate man, who knows nothing of Latin, the language in which it is said: and, moreover, he, as informer, is witness in his own cause; for, upon conviction, he is entitled to £100 reward.
>
> ... You must not infer that he is a priest because he said mass, and that he said mass because he is a priest.
>
> At the Reformation, they thought it in some measure necessary to pass these penal laws; for then the Pope had great power ... Now the Pope has

[55] Although there is no contemporary report of the case, it is described in detail in James Oldham, *The Mansfield Manuscripts and the Growth of English Law in the Eighteenth Century*, 2 vols. (Chapel Hill, NC, and London: University of North Carolina Press, 1992), 2:877–9; John Holliday, *The Life of William Late Earl of Mansfield* (London: P. Elmsly, et al., 1797), 176–9; and Campbell, *Lives of the Chief Justices*, 2:514–16.

> little power, and it seems to grow less every day . . . These penal laws were not meant to be enforced except . . . when there is a necessity for it; or, more properly speaking, they were not meant to be enforced at all, but were merely made in terrorem. . . .
>
> Take notice, if you bring him in guilty the punishment is very severe; a dreadful punishment indeed! Nothing less than perpetual imprisonment![56]

The jury acquitted Webb. In an extraordinary rejection of a legislative act, Mansfield interpreted the anti-Catholic law so strictly that afterwards it was practically impossible to get a conviction against a priest for saying Mass. Lord Mansfield, informed by a spirit of religious toleration, used the tools of a lawyer to make public policy.

Beyond the issue of religious toleration, Mansfield was expressing his belief that law was not a static system of knowledge and rules, but a living and growing body of legal principles that existed to serve society. Mansfield believed that the law must adapt itself to the various situations of mankind. The threat to England from Catholicism had disappeared since Locke's time, so the anti-Catholic laws must be interpreted as narrowly as possible and even expunged, if not by an act of Parliament, then by judicial decree. Mansfield had little patience with a legal precedent that was no longer relevant. In one case, he wrote, 'The law would be a strange science if we must go to the time of Richard I to see what is the law.'[57] In the cases involving the disabilities imposed on Roman Catholics, he went even further, showing himself willing virtually to read out of the statute book laws whose reason for enactment no longer existed.

English Catholics were the beneficiaries of the coming-together of two important strains in Mansfield's thinking: his deep conviction, based on Locke's philosophy, that civil government has no jurisdiction over an individual's religious beliefs and manner of worshipping, and his belief that the law should change when necessary to meet the needs of society.

Mansfield's toleration of Catholics eventually caused him great grief. The week-long Gordon Riots of 1780, the worst mob violence in London's history, were, at least initially, aimed at the legislative repeal of a statute that relieved Catholics of some of their disabilities, but the riots quickly turned into a frenzy of destruction of any symbols of authority the rioters could find. They quickly targeted Mansfield, breaking into his home in Bloomsbury

56 Campbell, *Lives of the Chief Justices*, 2:514–16.

57 *Jones v. Randall*, 98 Eng. Rep. 706 (1774).

Square and destroying his belongings and papers, and burning the house to the ground.

MANSFIELD'S TOLERATION OF PROTESTANT DISSENTERS

The seventeenth and eighteenth centuries saw the emergence of a plethora of Protestant sects, with differing beliefs and observances of Christianity. There were about 300,000 members of these sects, which included Presbyterians, Methodists, Quakers, Arminians, Socinians, Unitarians, Moravians and Swedenborgians, among others. In addition, deism, an approach to religion that rejected belief in revelation and miracles, life after death, and rewards and punishments, gained popularity. Deists believed that God was a First Cause, who then stood aside from his work and allowed the world to run its course. The deist Tory politician Viscount Bolingbroke saw God as a kind of constitutional monarch, 'limited by the rule which infinite wisdom prescribes to infinite power'.[58] By the middle of the eighteenth century, there was general toleration of Dissenters and deists, at least among the upper classes. The variety of religious beliefs led Voltaire to remark, 'If there were only one religion in England, there would be danger of tyranny; if there were two, they would cut each other's throats; but there are thirty, and they live happily in peace.'[59]

Protestant Dissenters from the established Anglican Church were not under the same prohibitions as Catholics. Many of the entrepreneurs, merchants and inventors, such as Josiah Wedgwood, the pottery maker, and James Watt, inventor of the steam engine, who were transforming England into a great commercial and industrial nation, were Dissenters. Mansfield, who throughout his career as lawyer and judge was deeply sympathetic to the interests of commerce, was naturally inclined to support toleration of Dissenters.

The Toleration Act of 1689 granted Dissenters religious freedom but not full political equality. They could vote if they met the applicable property qualifications, worshipped in their own churches, bore arms and could be elected to Parliament. But they were not permitted to hold any public office unless willing to conform to Anglican worship.

Mansfield consistently supported the rights of Dissenters. He allowed a Quaker witness, who refused to *swear* an oath, to *affirm* that he would tell the truth, and he upheld the right of a Dissenter to serve as a town clerk

58 Jeffrey Hart, *Viscount Bolingbroke: Tory Humanist* (London: Routledge & Kegan Paul; Toronto: University of Toronto Press, 1965), 113.

59 Voltaire, 'On the Presbyterians', in Fred R. Shapiro, ed., *The Yale Book of Quotations* (New Haven and London: Yale University Press, 2006), 791.

without taking the sacrament of the Anglican Church. In one case, he said, 'Methodists have a right to the protection of this Court, if interrupted in their decent and quiet devotion.'[60]

Mansfield's most memorable effort to prevent the persecution of Dissenters occurred not in his courtroom but in the House of Lords. Under the Corporations Act of 1661, no person was allowed to serve in the government of any municipality unless he had received the sacrament of the Church of England during the previous year. But a Dissenter could not in good conscience receive the sacrament. Although the purpose of the act was to prevent Dissenters from becoming public officials, the city of London used the act to raise money, some of which was used to build Mansion House, the lord mayor's official home. In 1748, the city adopted a bylaw imposing substantial fines on anyone who, having been nominated by the mayor for election as sheriff, declined to run for the office, or who, being elected, refused to serve. Several Dissenters were elected sheriff and paid the fines because their religious beliefs prevented them from receiving the sacrament. The city sued those who refused to pay.

The case of Albert Evans, a Dissenter who had been elected and had refused either to serve or to pay the fine, reached the House of Lords in 1767. As one of the Law Lords to whom the other peers looked for advice on questions of law, Mansfield focused on the injustice that the city was attempting to visit on Evans. In a speech that has been described as a 'noble vindication of the rights of conscience',[61] he pointed out that the purpose of the Corporations Act was to bar Dissenters from office and that, as a Dissenter, Evans would be breaking the law if he agreed to serve. Evans could not be prosecuted for refusing to take the Anglican sacrament because the Toleration Act freed him from that obligation. So the city had placed Evans and other Dissenters in an impossible dilemma:

> If they accept, punish them; if they refuse, punish them; if they say, yes, punish them, if they say, no, punish them ... It is my firm persuasion that he was chosen because he was incapable. If he had not been incapable, he had not been chosen; for they did not want him to serve the office.[62]

Mansfield moved to acquit Evans and the House of Lords voted its agreement.

Here again, two strains of Mansfield's thinking intersected. Beyond being an example of Mansfield's espousal of religious toleration, the *Evans* case tells us something else that is fundamental about his jurisprudence. Instead of

60 *Rex v. Wroughton*, 97 Eng. Rep. 1045 (1765).

61 Robert Aubrey Noakes, 'Lord Mansfield and Toleration', *The Month* (August 1940), 85, 89.

62 Speech of Mansfield in House of Lords, 4 February 1767, British Library. See Charles F. Mullett, 'The Corporations Act and Election of English Protestant Dissenters to Corporation Offices', *Virginia Law Review* 21 (1935): 660–4.

viewing a legal dispute in a formalistic way, Mansfield focused on ascertaining the intention of the person who had drafted a bylaw or statute. His humanist focus on the intent of the individual, whether in making a contract, writing a will or some other action, resonates with us today.

MANSFIELD'S TOLERATION OF JEWS

The population of England comprised about 8,000 Jews, including a few who were wealthy and some who were quite poor. In 1758, a group of financiers, headed by the immensely rich stockbroker Samson Gideon, underwrote an £8 million loan to the government to finance the war against France. Mansfield seems to have shared the mild anti-Semitic prejudice of the British upper classes, whose toleration of Jews was tempered by a condescending attitude towards them. Nevertheless, he did not let any personal bias affect his judicial attitude of toleration.

In his *Letter Concerning Toleration*, Locke wrote that Jews and Muslims should not be deprived of their civil rights because of their religion. There is every reason to believe that Mansfield agreed. In 1753, when Mansfield was solicitor general and a prominent member of Parliament, the government sponsored a Jewish Naturalisation Bill, which authorised Parliament to naturalise individual Jews by private bills without requiring them to take the Anglican sacrament. Henry Pelham, the prime minister, spoke at length in favour of the bill in the House of Commons, emphasising the economic benefits that wealthy Jews would bring to the nation. Although Mansfield did not speak in favour of the bill, it is likely that, as an important member of the government and a proponent of business interests and economic growth, he supported it.

The so-called Jew Bill was enacted without much dissent, but its passage was immediately greeted with anti-Semitic riots throughout the country.[63] The fury of the public demonstrations, which occurred shortly before a national election, persuaded the ministry to have the law repealed the following year. The easy passage of the bill and the public reaction that followed underscore the wide gap that existed between the spirit of religious toleration shown by the elite and the bigotry of a substantial section of the public.

A number of Jews, some of whom were practically penniless, tried to make a living by writing bail bonds for defendants in the courts. Some testified

63 For a discussion of the civil unrest and vicious anti-Semitism at the time, see M. Malik, 'Magna Carta, Rule of Law and Religious Diversity', in R. Griffith-Jones and M. Hill, eds., *Magna Carta, Religion and the Rule of Law* (Cambridge: Cambridge University Press, 2015), 248–63.

falsely that they had sufficient funds to be able to post the requested bail, and some were imprisoned for perjury. When Jewish bail bondsmen appeared before Mansfield, he seems to have displayed a mixture of disdain and toleration typical of the British upper classes.

On one occasion, a Jew named Mordecai Israel tried to justify writing a bail bond for £1,800. When asked if he was worth that amount after all his debts were paid, Israel admitted that he was not worth half that amount, but that the defendant's attorney had given him £20 to induce him to write the bail bond. Mansfield said, 'You are an honest Jew and I would advise you by all means to keep it.' According to a newspaper report, as Mansfield was leaving the court, Israel bowed to him and said, 'I humbly thank you, my lord: your lordship is the first that ever called me an *honest* man.'[64]

MANSFIELD'S TOLERATION OF ATHEISTS

Mansfield's belief in freedom of worship did not extend to attacks on all organised religion or on Christianity. When the Lord Chancellor sought advice from Mansfield, then solicitor general, about whether the author of a blasphemous pamphlet attack should be prosecuted, Mansfield replied in the affirmative, describing the pamphlet as the 'most impudent libel upon Christianity that ever was printed'. And when the philosopher David Hume asked Chief Justice Mansfield whether he could expect to be prosecuted if he published two treatises attacking organised religion and attempting to prove that there was no such thing as an immortal soul, he advised Hume not to publish.[65] In his lack of toleration for atheists, Mansfield's view was consistent with, and very possibly influenced by, Locke's teachings. Locke wrote that atheists are not to be tolerated, since 'promises, covenants, and oaths, which are the bonds of human society, can have no hold upon an atheist'.[66]

LAW AND MORALS

In his decisions, Mansfield asserted that morals were an essential element of the law. Again, the likely influence of Locke shines through. Although the separation of Church and state was a bedrock of Locke's political philosophy, he believed that both the Church and the state could properly regulate morality. Locke wrote:

> A good life, in which consists not the least part of religion and true piety, concerns also the civil government; and in it lies the safety both of men's souls and of the commonwealth. Moral actions belong therefore to the jurisdiction

64 *London Evening Post*, 2–4 February 1779. 65 Poser, *Lord Mansfield*, 246–7.
66 Locke, *Letter Concerning Toleration*, 52.

> both of the outward and inward court, both of the civil and domestic governor; I mean both of the magistrate and conscience.[67]

Mansfield expressed his belief that morals are part of the law most clearly in *Rex v. Delaval.*[68] A music teacher had turned a talented fifteen-year-old girl singer over to the socially prominent rake, Sir Francis Delaval, ostensibly to continue her music lessons with him, but in fact to be his mistress. For this, the music teacher received £200 from the baronet. Mansfield had no trouble in seeing through the deception. 'The girl goes and lives with Sir Francis, notoriously, as a kept mistress . . . No man can avoid seeing all this; let him wink ever so much.'

The key question was whether the court had jurisdiction over an immoral transaction in the absence of a specific statute prohibiting it. Mansfield ruled that, with the exception of certain cases which fell under the jurisdiction of the ecclesiastical courts, 'this Court is the custos morum [guardian of the morals] of the people, and has the superintendency of offences contra bonos mores [against good morals]'.[69] Thus, Mansfield made clear that morality was an essential part of the English common law. Following the tenets of John Locke, Mansfield believed that the manner in which a person worships is a private matter between that person's conscience and God, but how a person treats his or her fellow human beings may also be a public matter for the courts to decide. This was not the least of Mansfield's lasting contributions to Anglo-American law and culture.

Under the bifurcated English legal system, the common law courts considered only legal rights, while the courts of equity could also take morality into consideration. Mansfield was accused by his more traditional legal colleagues of importing some of the principles of equity into the more rigid common law. Mansfield believed that it would make the life of litigants easier if law and equity were fused into a single system, and he himself reportedly said that he 'never liked the law so much as when it was most like equity'.[70] Although the separation survived his tenure, Mansfield was able to introduce some of the principles of equity into the common law.[71]

CONCLUSION

Lord Mansfield's greatest accomplishment was to reform the Anglo-American common law and adapt it to the changing needs and circumstances of society.

67 Ibid., 46. 68 97 Eng. Rep. 913 (1763). 69 Ibid. at 915.

70 Poser, *Lord Mansfield*, 218.

71 For example, Mansfield ruled that a person who was unjustly in possession of another's property might not keep the property, even though he made no promise to return it. A promise would be implied in law. *Moses v. MacFerlan*, 97 Eng. Rep. 679 (1760); *Longchamp v. Kenny*, 99 Eng. Rep. 91 (1779). Hence, Mansfield contributed to the development of the common-law right of action for unjust enrichment or, as some say, quasi-contract.

His abiding influence on virtually every area of the law continues to the present day. Though a churchgoer, he demonstrated his faith less by religious observance than by his conduct both on and off the bench. As a man of the Enlightenment, he furthered the idea of the separation of Church and state, insisted that all law is ultimately based on morals and reason, and made his court the custodian of public morals. Mansfield's steadfast support of toleration of all faiths, whether Roman Catholic or dissenting Protestant, was Christian in the truest sense.

Mr Justice Blackstone, engraved by Hall; Gainsborough, Thomas (1727–88) / private collection / Bridgeman Images

10

William Blackstone's Anglicanism

Wilfrid Prest

I hope I shall never be ashamed in this House to own myself a Christian. When I see all religion made a mockery and jest of, it behoves me to vindicate my God and my King.

William Blackstone MP[1]

INTRODUCTION

Sir William Blackstone's character, life story and personality have long been overshadowed by his *Commentaries on the Laws of England*. Based on lectures delivered over thirteen years at Oxford University from 1753, and first published in four volumes between 1765 and 1769, the *Commentaries* proved an instant bestseller. Tapping the long-felt need for a coherent, comprehensive and authoritative overview of English law and government, Blackstone also catered with great success to the Enlightenment craving for encyclopaedic treatment of bodies of knowledge. He did so in a manner that not only appealed to a large non-professional readership, but was also widely characterised as a literary triumph. By the time book IV of the *Commentaries* had appeared in 1769, book I was already in its third edition. When Dr Blackstone became a judge (and a knight) the following year, he sold the copyright for a handsome sum, but continued to add amendments and corrections to successive editions until his death in February 1780. Thereafter the *Commentaries* have remained continuously in print down to the present day. There are now nearly 200 recorded English, Irish and American editions, with many more abridgments, compilations, extracts, translations (into French, German, Italian, Polish, Russian, Chinese and Japanese) and other works derived from this uniquely influential text.[2] The book's major impact has been

[1] Debate on the expulsion of John Wilkes, 3 February 1769, British Library, MS Egerton 213, f. 130.

[2] See A. J. Laeuchli, A *Bibliographical Catalog of William Blackstone* (New Haven: Yale Law Library, 2015).

two-fold: as a general authority on the common law and the parliamentary system of government, and as an introduction to legal studies throughout the Anglophone diaspora.

Shortly after Blackstone's death in 1780, William 'Oriental' Jones, a former student and admirer, characterised him as a 'guarded man'.[3] He certainly showed some reluctance, at least after his teenage years, to wear his heart, or mind, on his sleeve. While some personal correspondence survives, it is mostly businesslike and formal; letters to his wife and close relatives are relatively few and far between. There is no archive of family or personal papers, no autobiography, diaries, journals or memoirs, apart from the preface, written by his brother-in-law and former colleague James Clitherow, to his posthumously published law reports. As an 'Account of the Life of this great Man', purportedly based on 'a short Abstract of every Circumstance of Consequence … written by himself with his accustomed Accuracy', this is essentially an authorised biography, an official brief life approved by its subject. Clitherow appended to that document what he terms

> the Outlines at least of, his Character. A hard Task indeed for the Pen of a Friend! to do Justice to the Merit of such a Character, without incurring the Imputation of Flattery, is as difficult as to touch on its Imperfections (and such the most perfect human Characters have) with Truth and Delicacy.[4]

Yet after a notably uncritical paragraph on 'his publick Line of Life', Clitherow provided an equally positive assessment of his subject's 'Religion':

> He was a Believer in the great Truths of Christianity from a thorough Investigation of its Evidence; attached to the Church of *England* from Conviction of its Excellence, his Principles were those of its genuine Members, enlarged and Tolerant. His Religion was pure and unaffected, and his Attendance on its public Duties regular, and those Duties always performed with Seriousness and Devotion.[5]

This chapter might be regarded as a commentary or gloss on that delineation of one defining characteristic of the Commentator.

3 G. Cannon, ed., *The Letters of Sir William Jones*, 2 vols. (Oxford: Clarendon Press, 1970), 1:609.

4 James Clitherow, 'Preface', in *Reports of Cases Determined in the Several Courts of Westminster Hall, from 1746 to 1779, Taken and Compiled by the Honourable Sir William Blackstone, Knt.*, 2 vols. (London, 1781), 1:ii, xxiv.

5 Ibid., 1:xxv.

INFANCY AND CHILDHOOD[6]

The third-born but posthumous son of a seemingly prosperous but in fact heavily indebted silk merchant trading on London's Cheapside, William Blackstone also lost his mother before he was twelve years old. Although not such an unusual experience in early eighteenth-century England, the orphaned William and his two elder brothers were peculiarly fortunate in the care taken of their upbringing and education by their maternal uncles. The Reverend Henry Bigg had been fellow and warden of New College, Oxford, before taking up the more lucrative headship of its sister institution, Winchester College, where the young Charles and Henry Blackstone were sent to school. But Thomas Bigg, a surgeon at St Bartholomew's Hospital in London, was much closer to hand and may well have helped ensure that, instead of following his elder brothers to Winchester, William was enrolled at London's Charterhouse – although the crucial determinant was probably a kinship connection which resulted in Prime Minister Walpole's exercise of his patronage prerogative as one of the school's governors, nominating the infant William to a scholarship place. Like his deceased father Charles, William Blackstone was later identified with the Tory opponents of Walpole and his political successors; but his mother's family seems to have had Whiggish connections, underlined by her choice of her third son's baptismal name. This mixed political inheritance may help explain a certain residual ambiguity, or independence of conventional party-political loyalties, in his own political stance.

A relatively recent foundation, richly endowed by the huge bequest of the Jacobean tycoon Thomas Sutton, Charterhouse offered its pupils, drawn mainly from metropolitan mercantile and professional families, the opportunity of acquiring a first-rate classical education. However, school life outside the classroom remained largely unregulated by adult authority and bullying was rife, institutionalised by the hierarchical fagging system. John Wesley, who attended the school twenty years before Blackstone, recalled that he was largely a vegetarian in his first two years because the older boys simply purloined all meat from their juniors. James Hotchkis, headmaster for most of Blackstone's time at the school, seems to have experienced serious problems of discipline, provoking his complaint to the school's governors that the 'gownboys' (or scholar boarders), instead of being in bed by 10 PM each night, 'walk about the House at all hours ... notwithstanding his positive orders to the contrary'.[7] William Blackstone was almost certainly not among

[6] Biographical references not otherwise identified are taken from Wilfrid Prest, *William Blackstone: Law and Letters in the Eighteenth Century* (Oxford: Oxford University Press, 2008, 2012).

[7] London Metropolitan Archives, PS/18/2, n.d.

these errant Carthusians; on the contrary, his stellar academic performance 'rendered him the Favourite of his Masters' – if perhaps less so of his schoolboy peers. It would not be entirely surprising if the diffidence, self-consciousness and public inarticulacy characteristic of Blackstone in later life were in part at least a legacy of his earliest years at Charterhouse, which he entered as a seven-year-old day-boy in 1730 (he did not actually take up his scholarship until his second-last year at the school).

Charterhouse School was not only housed in a former Carthusian priory, but itself constituted a quasi-religious foundation. The masters were clergymen, the day's studies began and ended with Latin prayers and collects, the school maintained both a chapel and a preacher, while each boy in the upper form was provided with a Greek New Testament 'for their Use in the Chapel', and required on Sundays to 'set up in the Great Hall four Greek and four Latin verses a-piece, upon any part of the Second Lesson appointed for that Day'.[8] The reader or preacher at the Charterhouse for twenty years from 1733 was William Salisbury BD, fellow of St John's College, Cambridge, and Rector of Newton, Buckinghamshire. Salisbury presented young Blackstone in 1736 with a copy of Rev Edward Young's verse satire, *Love of Fame, the Universal Passion*, a gift doubtless intended to reward and further encourage the talented schoolboy's own early poetical efforts.

We are fortunate to have the printed text of the sermon which Salisbury preached the following year at the annual 'Commemoration of the Founder', the last such sermon he delivered before Blackstone left the school. Salisbury took as his text Deuteronomy viii.10: 'Thou shalt bless the Lord thy God for the good Land which he hath given thee.' As Moses charged the Israelites to show due gratitude to the Lord for leading them out of the wilderness to a land of milk and honey, so Salisbury's hearers were urged to a proper appreciation of the very substantial material benefits which Thomas Sutton's endowment had given them, by 'a diligent Adherence to Virtue, Learning and Good Manners', paying 'due Regard and Honour to your Instructors', whose efforts they would better appreciate 'when the Seeds of Virtue and Learning, which you have received here, shall have sprouted into goodly Fruit, and raised you to the Preferments and Emoluments of the World'. Salisbury's prime concern was not with matters of doctrine or faith, or with the state of his hearers' souls, but rather with their worldly well-being, that they should be 'ever after happy in your selves and serviceable to Mankind'. Freely selecting and adapting from the text of Proverbs chapters 1–4 ('Wisdom is the principal Thing; therefore get Wisdom, and with

8 *Rules and Orders Relating to Charterhouse. And to the Good Government Thereof* (London, n.d. [1748]), 20–1.

all thy gettings [*sic*: recte "getting"] get Understanding' and 'Exalt her and she shall promote you'), he pointed to the beneficial effects of good learning, which 'many of those, who have gone before you in this School, have happily experienced; some of whom are now an Ornament to the Bench, the Senate, and the Court'. His hearers were accordingly exhorted to 'industrious Application in the Pursuit of Virtue and Learning. So may you heap Honours on your selves, be useful to your Country, and do Credit to the Place of your Education'.[9] Even after making some allowance for the nature of the occasion and his audience, this does sound very much like the sort of thing which has earned the Hanoverian Church of England a reputation for spiritual somnolence and smug accommodation to the powers that be. In passing, Blackstone and Salisbury did not entirely lose touch after the former had left school. For in the late 1770s, after Salisbury's translation of the French historian Jean-Baptiste Bullet's hostile response to Edward Gibbon's *Decline and Fall* had appeared, Blackstone evidently supplied Salisbury with information about the provenance and condition of the classical marble statuary he himself had played some part in acquiring for the University of Oxford a quarter-century before.

Quite another perspective on the religious culture of Charterhouse during William Blackstone's schooldays is provided by the text of a school play. This *Dramatic Piece: By the Charter-House Scholars: In Memory of the Powder-Plot. Perform'd At the Charter-House, November 6th 1732* rehearsed a series of standard contemporary political and sectarian stereotypes, involving an unholy alliance of devil, pope, Jesuits and Jacobite followers of the exiled Stuart Pretender to the British throne, also known as 'the soft sham Monarch here we keep at Rome'. A series of heavenly revelations check their evil plans, which in any case would have had small chance of success so far as 'Albion' was concerned, since

> Firm on her Throne in circling Glories Reign,
> The Greatest Monarch and the Brightest Queen
> Scatt'ring angelic, with a lavish hand
> Blessings and Glories through their Wide Command . . .
> The Scourge of Tyrants and of Rome the Flail.

The attractions of George II's Britain are indeed sufficient to persuade one Jesuit to abjure

> This wretched Church! – The Villanies of Rome!
> O ALBION, to thy blissful Seats I come.

9 W. Salisbury, *A Sermon Preached in Charter-House Chapel, On Monday Dec. 12, 1737. Being the Day appointed for the Commemoration of the Founder* (London, 1738), 23–7.

> I seek for Reason, Truth, and Liberty,
> Pearls from the Skies, they say, abound in Thee.

Blackstone would have been only about nine years old when this play was performed; there is no direct evidence that he even saw it, let alone what impact that performance may have had upon him. Yet at very least we can see that his schooldays were hardly isolated from the popular anti-Catholic prejudices which continued to exercise enormous power throughout the eighteenth century, albeit increasingly repudiated in elite circles. The same clearly applies to the simple binary contrast between villainous Rome and blessed Albion, land of 'Reason, Truth, and Liberty'. Continuities and parallels between these themes and Blackstone's later writings are not hard to find.

OXFORD

One reason for dwelling on such admittedly sparse indicators of the religious environment within which the young Blackstone grew up is the lack of more substantial evidence about his family circumstances, where and with whom he lived, let alone his emotional, psychological and spiritual development. It is clear that his maternal uncles were closely involved with their orphaned nephews, doubtless to a greater extent after their sister Mary's death in 1735. The extended Bigg family, with its Wither and Bethell branches, seems to have been entirely orthodox, its adherence to the Church of England reinforced by a strong clerical tradition: Walter, another of Mary's siblings, served as rector of Worting, Hampshire, for forty years, after his elder brother Henry resigned the living on being elected warden of Winchester College. Thomas, the surgeon uncle most closely concerned with William's upbringing, evidently had a taste for theological writings, subscribing in 1729 to William Webster's *History of Arianism* and in 1742 to a volume of sermons by Richard Mason.[10] That his young ward inherited similar bibliographical interests is among the little we know about the everyday pattern of Blackstone's undergraduate years at Pembroke College, or indeed about his long bachelor existence as a fellow of All Souls from 1743 to 1761. The first book he appears to have acquired at Oxford was the large folio of Bishop George Smalridge's *Sixty Sermons Preached on Several Occasions* (Oxford, 1724), now in the Balliol College Library, which bears his bookplate and holograph ownership inscription,

[10] Data from 'U.K. and U.S. directories, 1680–1830', available at http://ancestry.com. Thomas' will, made some six years before his death in 1761, includes what had become by that time the uncommon bequest of his 'Soul to Almighty God relying on the Merits of the Blood of my blessed Saviour and Redeemer Jesus Christ for the Pardon of all my Sins': The National Archives (TNA), PROB/11/864/118.

together with an added 'Donum Dr Bethell'; although this person has not been positively identified, he was possibly Thomas Bethell, husband of Mary Blackstone's younger sister Dorothy. But while still at Pembroke William bought on his own behalf Joseph Trapps's *Popery Truly Stated and Briefly Confuted* (1727), Charles Leslie's *A Short and Easie Method with the Deists: Wherein the Certainty of the Christian Religion Is Demonstrated by Infallible Proof* (1712), Laurence Fogg's *Theologiae Speculativae Schema ... Sacrarum Scripturarum autoritate confirmatum, nec non Ecclesiae Anglicanae Articulis maxime consonum* (1712), John Conybeare's *Defence of Reveal'd Religion against the Exceptions of a Late Writer* (Oxford, 1732), directed against the free-thinker Matthew Tindal, Peter Browne's *The Procedure, Extent and Limits of Human Understanding* (2nd edition, 1729), Robert Sanderson's *De Obligation Conscientiae* (1682) and James Ussher's *Historia Dogmatica Controversiae ... De Scripturis et Sacris Vernaculis* (1690). Although most of these volumes were by no means recent imprints, Blackstone also subscribed to a copy of Thomas Bisse's sermons on the Lord's Prayer, published at Oxford in 1740. While his book purchases and library reading were not confined to religion and theology, there is now no way of telling how far these topics preoccupied the undergraduate Blackstone. But they were plainly of considerable importance, at least until early adulthood.

It is also worth noting that Blackstone did not confine himself to authors of what might loosely be termed High Church sympathies. Although such works were represented in his personal library, its shelves also evidently housed the writings of a surprisingly heterogeneous assortment of late-seventeenth- and early-eighteenth-century divines. Besides Bishops Sanderson and Ussher, there was Cambridge's Isaac Barrow, the Calvinist John Edwards, William King, Archbishop of Dublin and the ultra-orthodox Daniel Waterland, author of *Scripture Vindicated* (1731), another refutation of Matthew Tindal. Other works which Blackstone is known to have owned or read at Oxford include Hugo Grotius' *De Veritate Religionis Christianae* (1731), a volume of Port Royal or Jansenist tracts, and a Greek psalter. Finally, while antiquarian, historical and legal material predominated among the printed books and manuscripts which Blackstone called up in the Bodleian Library between the 1740s and 1760s, he appears also to have consulted John Eachard's *Grounds and Occasions of the Contempt of the Clergy and Religion Enquired Into* (1670), as well as numerous works by the ecclesiastical historian and orientalist Humphrey Prideaux (1648–1724).

Of course we all know that books owned cannot be equated automatically with books read – and Blackstone was undoubtedly a bibliophile with a passion for old books. Among his proudest possessions in later life was a collection of more than 120 works by William 'Marginal' Prynne, whose achievements as a 'painful and judicious antiquarian' in the 1660s and 1670s possibly outweighed his religious heterodoxy and political opposition stance in the 1620s and 1630s, so far as Blackstone was concerned. But overall the bibliographical evidence suggests that the young Blackstone took a serious interest in religion and theological issues, while seemingly favouring orthodox Anglican divines as distinct from High Churchmen, non-Jurors, avowed Latitudinarians, free-thinkers or anti-Trinitarians. This impression is reinforced by the evidence of Blackstone's own writings.

His earliest known collected work, a seventy-seven-page compilation of 'Select Poems and Translations Between Ye Years 1736 and 1744', was last seen at the law library of the University of California at Berkeley in the early 1950s; since then both the original manuscript itself and all microfilm copies have mysteriously disappeared. Fortunately an auction catalogue from 1932 included a partial list of contents. This establishes that Blackstone's poetic juvenilia addressed religious themes, including paraphrases of Psalms 29 and 95 and a treatment of the Lamentation of Job, alongside more numerous occasional verses ('To Miss *****' and on 'Being ask'd to describe Miss A***'), together with translations of some of Anacreon's odes and the idylls of Theocritus.[11] Blackstone's brother-in-law biographer James Clitherow makes no mention of their subject matter in alluding to 'a small Collection of juvenile Pieces, both Originals and Translations, which do him no Discredit'. Clitherow does refer to an architectural treatise which Blackstone composed 'at the early Age of Twenty ... intended for his own Use only, and not for Publication'. But he preserves total silence on the subject of Blackstone's first published work, which (as its preface states) was 'written at the University, towards the Close of the Year 1743'. Since the fact of his authorship was evidently well known to the All Souls common room, this omission can only be because Blackstone himself was unwilling to acknowledge responsibility for *The Pantheon: A Vision*. Even in 1747, when the work was issued by the printer-publisher Richard Dodsley without his name on the title page, Blackstone was ready to disown it. Thus he claimed on presenting a copy to an All Souls' colleague that it had been 'written when I was under the Age of 21, in a state of legal Infancy; ever since which time I have absolutely bid adieu to such amusements, finding myself as unfit for them as they are for the Profession I have engaged in'.[12] These sentiments plainly strengthened with the passing years, and his growing eminence as professor, Head of House, MP, Crown law officer and judge.

11 Maggs Bros. Catalogue 576 (Autumn 1932), item 843.

12 W. R. Prest, ed., *The Letters of Sir William Blackstone 1744–1780*, Selden Society Supplementary Series 14 (London: Selden Society, 2006), 7.

But in 1747 the author's unsigned 'Advertisement' or preface explained that *The Pantheon*

> take[s] a *Poetical* View of the several Religions, that have prevailed in the World; which are represented by different *Genii* residing in their different Temples, with the proper Symbols of their respective Faiths. These are reduced to Four principal Heads; *Paganism, Mohammedanism, Judaism,* and *Christianity*. The latter is subdivided into Three, viz. *Popery, Sectarism,* and *true Religion*; by which last the Author would be understood to mean THE CHURCH OF ENGLAND; a Church, he believes, both in its Doctrine and Constitution, the most pure and Apostolical upon Earth.

This 460-line verse essay in comparative religion presents in turn the 'Pagan dome', 'stately mosque' and Solomon's temple ('a glorious pile, / Of workmanship divine'), all superficially impressive, but variously flawed. Similarly, both 'the gay Corinthian mode, Rich with luxuriant art and wanton pride' of 'Rome's grey genius' and 'the adverse structure', with its 'clumsy Tuscan dress, unhewn and rude' are depicted in largely negative terms. Yet popish 'Tyranny', 'Persecution', 'Ignorance' and 'Superstition' are summarily dismissed in well under half the space devoted to displaying 'the four Parents of the motley rout' who symbolise non-Anglican protestantism: 'wild Anarchy', who 'Tramples on crowns, high waving in her hand, / A martyr'd Sov'reign's head'; ' Enthusiast Zeal', 'Schism' and 'Hypocrisy':

> On these the jarring crew, in all besides
> Dissentient, all on these infix their eyes,
> Thence draw new life, and in firm phalanx join'd
> Support with stubborn league the good old cause.

Various stock figures appear: the 'precisely sour' elder who 'harmonious hymns / Enraptur'd nonsense, and with holy leer, / Gloats on the saintly dames who grace his flock'; the mad fanatic ('Loudly he raves, with uncouth roar'); and even a 'secret band' of Jesuit conspirators, who 'garb transformed, in sable cloaks and puritan disguise . . . fire the crowd'.

In stark contrast to this disorderly turmoil, the Church of England is represented by a 'beauteous dome, whose marble portal, deck'd / With chaste Ionic ornaments, disclos'd / A female form, the guardian of the fane'. Attending on this figure, 'Her aspect grave, yet chearful and divine', are 'mitred Moderation', 'Gay Liberty, Britannia's darling saint', 'Sweet Piety' and 'Science beyond, her leaden shackles broke', supported by 'two gentle maids, / Fair Cam, and Isis crown'd with learn'd tow'rs'.

As the narrator's guide (who turns out to be his 'guardian Seraph') leaves him to pursue 'Thy steps to pure RELIGION', the other structures 'From their firm bases nod; then headlong fall / In universal wrack', leaving only 'Our sacred structure' to grow 'larger, and yet larger'. Into this expanded space, 'torrent-like in numbers numberless, / In rush'd, obedient to the clarion's call, / A mighty host, the pride of ev'ry clime'. Among this 'zealous throng', the narrator prostrates himself in prayer:

> Accept, great Parent, source of Truth, accept,
> These tributary vows, this slender All,
> The last, the meanest of thy sons can pay!
> O may'st thou stand till time itself shall fail,
> Rocklike, tho' papal storms around thee roar
> Or hollow faction's undermining guile
> In secret plot thy fall! Long may'st thou reign
> Restor'd to all thy rights, and, greatly just,
> Reform, with due severity, mankind;
> Bid from the dust her head pale Virtue rear,
> From recreant Prelates strip the sullied lawn,
> And teach the Atheist not to scorn his God;
> Then, fill'd with deathless glory, from the world
> Triumphant rise, and fix in heav'n thy throne!

Opinion may differ as to the literary merits of this whole composition, as also the theoretical possibility that it reflects the power of the poet's creative imagination, insofar as this may be distinguished from his own deeply held convictions. Yet *The Pantheon* clearly expresses something of a quite different emotional and intellectual order from mere outward commitment to the forms and ceremonies of the Anglican Church.

Even so, it was the work of a very young man. That point is reinforced by Blackstone's earliest surviving letter, written to Seymour Richmond, yet another uncle and a fellow Oxford graduate, in August 1744, hence at least eight months after *The Pantheon* was composed. Following various pieces of family news, he turns to university matters:

> We were last Friday entertained at St Mary's by a curious Sermon from Wesley the Methodist. Among other equally modest Particulars, he informed us 1st That there was not one Christian among all the Heads of Houses; 2dly that Pride, Gluttony, Avarice, Luxury, Sensuality, & Drunkenness were the general Characteristicks of all Fellows of Colleges, who were useless to a proverbial Uselessness. Lastly, that the younger Part of the University were a Generation of Triflers, all of them perjured & not one of them of any Religion at all. His Notes were demanded by the

> Vice-Chancellor, but on mature Deliberation it has been thought proper to punish him by a mortifying Neglect.[13]

While hardly a fair or even accurate report of the contents of John Wesley's last university sermon, the cool detachment of this account strikes a very different note to that of *The Pantheon*. Wesley's hyperbole is represented as sufficiently discrediting the would-be reformer out of his own mouth, with no need for explicit condemnation of such patently absurd propositions from such an obvious outsider. Blackstone here has clearly assumed the lofty persona of a fellow of All Souls, a role which he would continue to relish for many years to come, even at the cost of establishing a practice at the London bar.

For although admitted as a student to the Middle Temple in 1741, after changing his Oxford undergraduate enrolment from Arts to Law, he delayed departing to London until January 1746. Having graduated BCL six months before, it seems clear that he had not previously undertaken any serious study of the common law, until he then and there embarked on his first reading of Littleton's *Tenures*, as reported in another letter to Seymour Richmond. Yet having acquired from his earlier admission the requisite standing in the house to qualify for call to the bar, he was actually called in November of that year. This was only possible because, as he would later explain in his first public lecture as foundation Vinerian Professor in the Laws of England, at the eighteenth-century Inns of Court 'all sorts of regimen and academical superintendence, either with regard to morals or studies, are found impracticable, and therefore entirely neglected'.[14]

Blackstone's initial venture into legal practice coincided with the nadir in what seems to have been a long-term decline in the volume of litigation going through the courts of Westminster Hall. Apart from the bad timing, Oxford distractions in the form of college administration and university politics evidently trumped the practical demands of building a professional career. So after seven years he abandoned the London bar in favour of mounting a private fee-paying course of lectures on English law and government, first delivered in the hall of All Souls College during Michaelmas Term 1753. These lectures were not part of the university's official curriculum (which still covered only Roman or civil law), and Blackstone clearly planned them in part as a money-making venture, to supplement his modest fellowship stipend. But he also relished the challenge of presenting an accessible, comprehensive and well-organised overview of English law and government. What was for the

13 Ibid., 1–2.

14 William Blackstone, *Commentaries on the Laws of England*, 4 vols. (Oxford: Clarendon Press, 1765–9; Oxford University Press, 2016), 1:24.

time a daring pedagogical experiment proved remarkably popular with its target audience, for Blackstone was not merely catering to a small minority of aspirant lawyers, but the much larger group of Oxford undergraduates who could appreciate the potential value of learning about their country's political constitution and legal system, the better to equip themselves for later life as proprietors of landed estates, justices of the peace and members of Parliament.

Notes taken by students attending these lectures reveal that Dr Blackstone's antipathy towards non-Anglicans had not diminished in the decade since *The Pantheon* was written. A junior All Souls colleague recorded Blackstone, in the fourth or Trinity (summer) term segment of the initial lecture course of 1753–4, expatiating on 'Offenses against Divine Law and the Law of Nations' in what would eventually become the fourth chapter of the fourth and final book of the *Commentaries*. Roman Catholics and Protestant non-conformists were both schismatics from the established Church of England, but

> with this difference, That the Papists divide upon Material [tho' Erroneous: interlined] Reasons, & the Dissenters upon no reason at all; however the Laws against the Papists are much more severe than those against the Dissenters, but yet it may be questioned whether one deserve more indulgence than the other or which are the greater Enemies to the Church; This much is certain, that within a Century past, the Dissenters have once totally effected the Ruin of the Constitution both of Church and State, whereas the Papists with their utmost efforts have never been able to compass it.[15]

Such sentiments, reproduced with little change in the first edition of the published *Commentaries*, would later provoke fierce protests.

LONDON AND WALLINGFORD

By the time the first book of the *Commentaries* appeared in November 1765, Blackstone had become successively a professor, a husband, a father, a member of Parliament and a crown law officer, as solicitor general to George III's consort, Queen Charlotte. His 1758 election as the inaugural holder of Oxford University's Vinerian chair in the laws of England made him for successive generations of legal academics 'Blackstone noster, our Blackstone, the first ever professor of the common law'.[16] The success of his Oxford lectures not only encouraged his return to the London bar, but brought him into a larger world of patronage and power, symbolised by the honorarium of £200 forwarded as 'a present from the Prince of Wales' after he had

15 British Library, Add. MS 38838, f. 157.

16 P. Birks, 'Rights, Wrongs, and Remedies', *Oxford Journal of Legal Studies* 20:1 (2000): 1.

provided copies of his lectures to Lord Bute, the future king's tutor and first prime minister. It was also Bute who in 1761 supplied the necessary funds for Blackstone's election as a member for the pocket borough of Hindon in George III's first parliament, with the new king's 'Approbation' (if not indeed 'insistence'); while the day after his marriage to Sarah Clitherow, Blackstone was honoured with a royal patent of precedence (or pre-audience) at the bar, the functional equivalent to a king's counsel's silk gown. He brought his bride home to Priory Place, the house on the banks of the River Thames, downstream from Oxford at Wallingford, where Blackstone had served as recorder since 1749. Meanwhile his Oxford connections gradually ran down, while his professional life during the law terms increasingly centred on London, where he leased houses in the legal quarter of Holborn, first on Carey Street and then in Lincoln's Inn Fields.

Yet it was from Wallingford that he wrote a letter of condolence to his cousin Lovelace Bigg in July 1765, following the death of the latter's wife Rachel, Sarah Clitherow's sister. One of the very few items of intimate personal, or at least non-business, correspondence surviving from his pen, this document (now only known in incomplete edited form) expressed his firm conviction that

> there is nothing can afford us any solid relief in deep affliction, but the doctrines of Christianity, in which we have been so happily educated, and the sure expectations of a future state. I feel for you as a Friend, and a relation, and the more especially as a husband; but I write to you as a Man, and a Christian.[17]

The only other comparable letter known to exist was written ten years later to his wife. In response to her expressions of alarm at the news of the incapacitating illness suffered by a fellow judge, her husband sought to assure 'My dear Sally' that

> We are all, my dear Love, in the Hands of Providence, who will call Us at his appointed Time; & no Solicitude or Anxiety of Ours will hasten or retard the allwise Decrees of Him, who best knows what is fit for Us & whose goodness will choose what is best. Our principal Care should be that Our general Course of Life be such, that (with a merciful Allowance for human Infirmity) the Approach of Death may never be terrible, although it always is an awful Event. And, if it pleases God to bless Us with such an even Frame of Mind, we shall not imbitter our Lives with continual Apprehensions of Evils, that may possibly befall Ourselves or Our nearest Friends; but, when the Stroke comes, shall feel it for once, and no oftener: Whereas, to indulge a Habit of

[17] Prest, *Letters*, 108.

> Apprehension & Fear, is to suffer the Evil an hundred Times before it really happens. Do not think, my dearest, I say this by Way of chiding Your tender Anxiety, but only to fortify Your Mind lest they [sic. *cf. p. 217, line 1*] gain too great a Dominion over You.[18]

Outside the family circle Blackstone's faith found practical expression in his close association with the parish church of St Peter, whose grounds adjoined the garden of his Wallingford home. Here his administrative energies, financial expertise and practical experience in the supervision of construction projects at All Souls College came jointly to the fore. Having acquired the advowson or right of presentation to the rectory of St Peter's with the purchase of Priory Place, he became committed to the successful completion of a scheme to rebuild the church left derelict after the siege of Wallingford during the civil wars of the previous century. Although fundraising had begun in 1759, the project appears to have proceeded very slowly until 1767, when Blackstone persuaded the vestry to approach the architect Robert Taylor, with whom he was already involved in a major construction project on the city of Oxford's western approaches. After Taylor's plan for completing and fitting out the church building was accepted and Blackstone had been elected to the office of church warden, he began a renewed drive to raise money. In soliciting a subscription from the Bishop of Salisbury as ordinary of the parish, he outlined at some length a scheme 'to establish a resident Clergyman at Wallingford', whose four parishes were at this time served only by a cleric riding in from Oxford 'on Sundays to read Prayers in the Morning & Preach in the Afternoon & also to perform now & then some weekly Duty', remunerated from an annual subscription raised among the townsfolk.

Far from ideal, if scarcely atypical of the Hanoverian Church of England (around 1780, the year of Blackstone's death, it seems likely that fewer than half of all English parishes were served by a resident minister), this situation reflected the relative poverty of three of Wallingford's parochial livings.[19] The fourth was a sinecure, its church also demolished and the endowment impropriated by Oxford's Pembroke College (Blackstone's alma mater). His plan would have involved presenting the rectories of St Peter's and St Mary's ('a decent old Church, but the Endowment hardly £10 a year') to the same incumbent, who

[18] Ibid., 151.

[19] See Wilfrid Prest, *Albion Ascendant: English History, 1660–1815* (Oxford: Oxford University Press, 1998), 205–6; J. Hoppit, *A Land of Liberty? England 1689–1727* (Oxford: Clarendon Press, 2000), 212–13; P. Virgin, *The Church in an Age of Negligence* (Cambridge: James Clarke, 1989), 191.

> should serve both Churches on Sundays, one in the Morning, the other in the Afternoon; should read Prayers on Wednesdays, Fridays and Holydays in either; & should do the occasional Duty in the three parishes of St Mary's, St Peter's, & AllSaints. This would not be very laborious. And, when the Incomes of St Mary's & St Peters are united, with some Allowance which I think should be made from Pembroke College for doing the occasional Duty in the Parish of AllSaints; the Subscriptions, which I hope will in some measure continue; the Surplice Fees & perhaps the Queen's Bounty superadded – all these together might make it worth the temporary Acceptance of a resident Clergyman, especially of one who might wish to make occasional Visits to Oxford.[20]

Although the immediate fate of this proposal is uncertain, the rectory of St Peter's was held from 1768–87 by Samuel Viner (a namesake and possibly distant relative of the benefactor after whom Blackstone's Oxford chair was named), assisted initially by Thomas Wintle, who served also as minister of St Mary's church, and then by Richard Bethell, ordained as curate in 1775, who was Blackstone's brother-in-law, having married another sister of James Clitherow.[21] From 1769 Blackstone and his growing family occupied the front pew: 'No. 1 ... assigned to Mr Blackstone as Patron of the Church'. He was also empowered by the vestry to negotiate a further contract with Robert Taylor for erecting the remarkable neo-gothic steeple which still adorns St Peter's, and to furnish the church tower beneath with a clock and a bell. In 1778 he presented to the church 'a handsome Chalice, Paten & Plate of Silver double Gilt with proper Inscriptions thereon'. Following his death in London two years later at the age of 56, Blackstone's mortal remains now lie where he was, according to his will, 'privately Buried by day light in my vault in the parish church of St Peter Wallingford'.[22]

Blackstone's brother-in-law biographer identified one of his subject's most notable attributes as a zeal for what contemporaries commonly termed 'improvement', by promoting 'whatever he thought useful or advantageous to the Public in general, or to any ... Neighborhood he was connected with'.[23]

20 Prest, *Letters*, 134–5.

21 Bodleian Library, MS Arch. Pars. Berks d. 10; Wiltshire and Swindon History Centre, Bishop of Salisbury Administrative Records, D/1/20/1/2; D/1/14/1/14, 16; J. Foster, *Alumni Oxonienses ... 1715–1886*, 4 vols. (London: Parker & Co., 1887–8), 1:104; 4:1475, 1591 (where Wintle is mistakenly listed as rector of St Peter's 1767–74). I am grateful to David Pedgley for assistance with these details.

22 Berkshire Record Office, Wallingford Parochial Records, St Peter's Wallingford Church Wardens Book, D/P 139/5/2, 20 May 1769, 26 September 1775, 6 January 1777, 22 April 1778. TNA, PROB/11/1061, f. 101v.

23 Clitherow, 'Preface', xxv; P. Slack, *From Reformation to Improvement* (Oxford: Clarendon Press, 1999), 2, 80–1.

During the last decade of his life, while he served as puisne justice in the courts of King's Bench and Common Pleas, penal reform was the main general cause to which Blackstone committed his still formidable abilities. It seems likely that practical experience on the judicial bench sharpened disquiet already expressed in his lectures and the published *Commentaries* about the narrow range of penal options provided by England's criminal law, hence its excessive reliance on capital and corporal punishment. Of course such concerns were not unique to Blackstone. Indeed, it seems that his first attempt at drafting a parliamentary bill on the subject in 1776 followed directly upon what he later referred to, somewhat obliquely, as a 'Command which I could not decline' – from, in other words, no less a personage than King George himself.[24] With the American war of independence in full swing, the problem of what to do with convicted felons sentenced to transportation had suddenly become acute.

The distinctive element in Blackstone's thinking was the concept of what he termed 'experimental Houses of Hard Labour (call them, if You please, for Distinction's sake, Penitentiaries or Ergastuleries)', designed not merely to confine and punish, but actively to reform offenders. The most explicit statement of Blackstone's views and hopes, insofar as they were embodied in the statute passed by Parliament in 1779, now known as the 'Penitentiary Act', comes from a passage added for the first time to book IV, chapter 28 in the ninth (1783) edition of the *Commentaries*:

> But now, by statute 19 Geo. III. c. 74. all offenders liable to transportation may in lieu thereof at the discretion of the judges, be employed, if males (except in the case of petty larceny) in hard labour for the benefit of some public navigation; or, whether males or females, may in all cases be confined to hard labour in certain penitentiary houses, to be erected by virtue of the said act, for the several terms therein specified, but in no case exceeding seven years; with a power of subsequent mitigation, and even of reward, in case of their good behaviour ...
>
> In forming the plan of these penitentiary houses, the principal objects have been, by sobriety, cleanliness, and medical assistance, by a regular series of labour, by solitary confinement during the intervals of work, and by due religious instruction, to preserve and amend the health of the unhappy offenders, to inure them to habits of industry, to guard them from pernicious company, to accustom them to serious reflection, and to teach them both the principles and practice of every christian and moral duty. And if the whole of this plan be properly executed, and its defects be timely supplied, there is reason to hope that such a reformation may be effected in the lower classes of

[24] Prest, *Letters*, 183. See generally S. Devereaux, 'The Making of the Penitentiary Act, 1775–1779', *Historical Journal* 42 (1999): 405–33.

> mankind, and such a gradual scale of punishment be affixed to all gradations of guilt, as may in time supersede the necessity of capital punishment, except for very atrocious crimes.[25]

As enacted, the statute itself ran to seventy-four clauses, specifying in detail the internal arrangements of the two penitentiary houses, whereby

> solitary imprisonment, accompanied by well-regulated Labour, and religious Instruction . . . might be the Means, under Providence, not only of deterring others from the commission of the like Crimes, but also of reforming the Individuals, and inuring them to Habits of Industry.[26]

To that end both institutions were to include a chapel, staffed by a chaplain, with attendance at morning and evening prayers and twice-daily Sunday sermons compulsory for all inmates, and no provision made for those professing adherence to denominations other than the Established Church.[27] In the immediate event these elaborate regulations fell by the wayside, thanks largely to the inability of the commissioners appointed under the act to agree upon a site for the new prisons, a deadlock exacerbated by the sudden death of 'Sir W. Blackstone, the great promoter of the design'.[28] But for better and for worse, his idea of the penitentiary – with its strong religious connotations and overtones – would live on long after these initial setbacks had been forgotten.

CHRISTIANITY IN THE *COMMENTARIES*

From what we have seen so far, there can be little doubt that William Blackstone was no merely nominal member of the Church of England. Yet an important question remains: in what ways did his religious principles influence the form and content of his magnum opus? Would the *Commentaries on the Laws of England* have been a different book if it had not been written by a committed Christian?

The *Commentaries* are plainly written by a believer and enunciate the explicit principle that 'christianity is part of the laws of England'.[29] That this was not an uncontroversial proposition is suggested by a critical report of Blackstone's speech in a House of Commons debate on the expulsion of John

25 W. Blackstone, *Commentaries on the Laws of England*, ed. R. Burn, 9th ed., 4 vols. (London, 1783), 4:371–2. In his preliminary editorial 'Advertisement' to book I, Burn claimed that all 'alterations . . . since the publication of the last edition, were made by the author himself'.

26 Statute 19 Geo. III c. 74, clause v.

27 Ibid., clause xlii.

28 J. Aiken, A *View of the Character and Public Services of the Late John Howard Esq* (London, 1792), 107.

29 Blackstone, *Commentaries*, 4:39; quotations here and below are from the 2016 Oxford edition.

Wilkes, 'which was much ridiculed by Alderman Beckford. Blackstone said that opposing the Gospel was opposing the common law of this kingdom'.[30] Further, the entire system of jurisprudence outlined in the opening of book I rests upon supernatural foundations. Thus the second paragraph of the introductory section 'Of the Nature of Laws in General' begins '[W]hen the supreme being formed the universe', and the fifth paragraph notes that 'Man, considered as a creature, must necessarily be subject to the laws of his creator'. The law of nature is then introduced as God's will, which

> being co-eval with mankind and dictated by God himself, is of course superior in obligation to any other. It is binding over all the globe, in all countries, and at all times: no human laws are of any validity, if contrary to this.

However, the law of nature is itself subordinate to 'the revealed or divine law ... found only in the holy scriptures', since 'one is the law of nature expressly declared so to be by God himself; the other is only what, by the assistance of human reason, we imagine to be that law'.[31] Likewise Blackstone rejects as 'too wild to be seriously admitted' the notion of human society emerging from 'an actually existing unconnected state of nature' only when individuals first entered into an original contract: 'and besides it is plainly contradictory to the revealed accounts of the primitive origins of mankind, and their preservation two thousand years afterwards; both which were effected by the means of single families'.[32]

Yet while grounding his jurisprudence on God's ordinances, Blackstone is anxious to distinguish the sphere of municipal law ('that is, the rule by which particular districts, communities, or nations are governed') from that of divine law. Thus he maintained that human laws exist

> only to regulate the behaviour of mankind, as they are members of society, and stand in various relations to each other, they have consequently no business or concern with any but social or relative duties. Let a man be therefore ever so abandoned in his principles, or vitious in his practice, provided he keeps his wickedness to himself, and does not offend against the rules of public decency, he is out of the reach of human laws. But if he makes his vices public, though they be such as seem principally to affect himself (as drunkenness, or the like) they then become, by the bad example they set, of pernicious effects to society; and therefore it is then the business of human laws to correct them.[33]

30 'The diary of the Reverend Thomas Fry ... 1768–1772', ed. W. N. Hargeaves-Mawsley; typescript, Archives of St John's College, Oxford, Munim. LXXXVI.D.8., 37; the opening quotation to this chapter comes from a diarist's record of that speech.

31 Blackstone, *Commentaries*, 1:33–5. 32 Ibid., 1:38. 33 Ibid., 1:36, 84.

This vital distinction, reminiscent of the separation of the spheres of nature and of grace debated in the Council of the Army at Whitehall in 1648, meant that only 'offences which are directly or by consequence injurious to civil society' were liable to incur any sanction under the laws of England.[34] The point is made most forcefully in the opening pages to the fourth chapter of book IV, 'Of Offences against God and Religion':

> The vice of lying, which consists (abstractly taken) in a criminal violation of truth, and therefore in any shape is derogatory from sound morality, is not however taken notice of by our law, unless it carries with it some public inconvenience, as spreading false news; or some social injury, as slander and malicious prosecution, for which a private recompence is given. And yet drunkenness and lying are *in foro conscientiae* as thoroughly criminal when they are not, as when they are, attended with public inconvenience. The only difference is, that both public and private vices are subject to the vengeance of eternal justice; and public vices are besides liable to the temporal punishments of human tribunals.[35]

So actions against God or religion, 'affronts to christianity, or endeavours to deprecate its efficacy' are liable to be punished, but not at all because they offend God and his laws. The reason is simply that 'the preservation of christianity, as a national religion, is, abstracted from its own intrinsic truth, of the utmost consequence to the civil state'. For

> belief of a future state of rewards and punishments, the entertaining just ideas of the moral attributes of the supreme being, and a firm persuasion that he superintends and will finally compensate every action in human life (all which are clearly revealed in the doctrines, and forcibly inculcated by the precepts, of our saviour Christ), these are the grand foundation of all judicial oaths ....[36]

In other words, true religion must not be impugned or mocked, simply in order to defend and maintain the potency of the oaths sworn by judges, jurors and witnesses, on which the overall efficacy of the entire legal system depends. This rather modestly instrumental reason alone explains why '*blasphemy* against the Almighty, by denying his being or providence; or by contumelious reproaches of our Saviour Christ ... profane scoffing at the holy scripture, or exposing it to contempt and ridicule ... are offences punishable at common law...'.[37]

It is not easy to see Blackstone's faith distinctively at work in other aspects of the *Commentaries*. There are some scriptural references, overwhelmingly to the Old Testament and largely functioning as ethnographic evidence of customs and practices which illustrate the development of particular legal

[34] Ibid., 4:42. [35] Ibid., 27. [36] Ibid., 4:28. [37] Ibid., 4:39.

rules and doctrines, whether these contrast with or confirm current English practice. Thus, in discussing the development of property law over the very long term, Blackstone cites 'the book of Genesis (the most venerable monument of antiquity, considered merely with a view to history)' and its 'frequent instances of violent contentions concerning wells', even where no exclusive property rights in land had yet emerged, as with Abraham 'asserting his right to a well in the country of Abimelech …'. Similarly, the story of Abraham and Lot separating to Canaan and Jordan with their herds and households is recounted as another example of the 'savage state of vagrant liberty … which Tacitus informs us continued among the Germans until the decline of the Roman empire'.[38] Examples drawn from the Old Testament flank those from *The Modern Part of an Universal History* (1759–66) with no apparent sense of incongruity; thus, the establishment of district and local courts is said to be '[a]n institution that seems highly agreeable to the dictates of natural reason, as well as more enlightened policy; being equally familiar to that which prevailed in Mexico and Peru before they were discovered by the Spaniards; and that which was established in the Jewish republic by Moses'.[39]

Blackstone's attitude to Church–state relations as expressed in the *Commentaries* is unashamedly Erastian. If 'genuine and pure' religious principles make better citizens, when 'perverted and erroneous' they tend to subvert civil government, as 'both the cloak and the instrument of every pernicious design that can be harboured in the heart of man'; indeed,

> civil and ecclesiastical tyranny are mutually productive of each other. And it is the glory of the church of England as well as a strong presumptive argument in favor of the purity of her faith, that she hath been (as her prelates on a trying occasion once expressed it) in her principles and practice ever most unquestionably loyal.[40]

The following characterisation of the Anglican clergy of his day as 'holy in their doctrines and unblemished in their lives and conversation … also moderate in their ambition' could well be one of those passages evoked in an annotation to a later edition, 'wherein the constitution of our laws and government are represented as nearly approaching to perfection; without descending to the invidious task of pointing out such deviations and corruptions, as length of time and a loose state of national morals have too great a tendency to produce'.[41]

38 Ibid., 2:3–4. 39 Ibid., 3:20.

40 Ibid., 4:68. The reference is to the Seven Bishops' petition to James II, 18 May 1688: see J. P. Kenyon, ed., *The Stuart Constitution 1603–1688: Documents and Commentary* (Cambridge: Cambridge University Press, 1966), 442.

41 Blackstone, *Commentaries*, 4:103; 1:338. Blackstone's characterisation also reflects the cooling of High Church aspirations since the heady days of Queen Anne.

In keeping with convention, book I's account of 'The People' treats the clerical estate in a separate chapter, before those on the civil and military and maritime states. This 'venerable body of men' is said to be 'separate and set apart from the rest of the people, in order to attend the more closely to the service of almighty God'. But the 'large privileges allowed them by our municipal laws' turn out to comprise only various personal exemptions and immunities retained from before the Reformation; and 'as they have their privileges, so also they have their disabilities, on account of their spiritual avocations'.[42] The church courts, or courts Christian, are dealt with in summary fashion in a brief chapter ('Of Courts Ecclesiastical, Military, and Maritime') of book III, where Blackstone makes clear that in his view the ecclesiastical courts were a 'fatal encroachment' at the time of the Norman conquest upon the 'moderate and rational' arrangements 'of our Saxon ancestors', which made no distinction between lay and ecclesiastical jurisdiction: 'whether actuated by principles of bigotry, or by those of a more refined policy, in order to discountenance the laws of king Edward abounding with the spirit of Saxon liberty, is not altogether certain'.[43]

CONCLUSION

James Clitherow's appraisal of his brother-in-law's religious beliefs and principles[44] seems to hold up well, in all but one particular. Notwithstanding his insistence that the state must be the dominant partner in the Church–State alliance, Blackstone was both an informed believer and a committed churchman.[45] Yet, on the face of it we can hardly credit as a man of 'enlarged and Tolerant' principles the author of *The Pantheon* and the chapter 'Of Offences against God and Religion' in book IV of the *Commentaries*. That was not only the view of the Nonconformist ministers Joseph Priestley and Philip Furneaux, who in 1769 both published spirited refutations of what they took to be Blackstone's bigoted slurs on the integrity, loyalty and law-abiding character of their co-religionists. A review of book IV by the barrister Owen Ruffhead also expressed regret that in chapter 4 and elsewhere

> our Author shows a narrow and somewhat illiberal turn of mind ... and of course a strong attachment to what are called High Church principles ... we

[42] Ibid., 1:242, ch. 11 *passim*. [43] Ibid., 3:41–5.

[44] Cited in the introduction to this chapter.

[45] I have suggested elsewhere that his Anglicanism was a good deal more than merely conventional, or lacking in emotional attachment: W. Prest, 'The Religion of a Lawyer? William Blackstone's Anglicanism', *Parergon* 21:2 (2004): 153–68.

> are really concerned to see so able and judicious a Writer betray a littleness and peevishness of spirit, which he might easily have concealed without any injustice to his subject.[46]

A few years later, Jeremy Bentham would label Blackstone 'the professed champion of religious intolerance', a judgment echoed in our own times by the historians Jonathan Clark and Robert Willman.[47] Even the late Tom Barnes, while discerning that 'Blackstone belonged more to the Age of Faith than the Age of Reason', maintained that his 'religious intolerance was a genuine measure of his devotion to the Church by Law Established'.[48]

Yet Clitherow's assessment dates from 1781, not 1769. This is an important distinction, for in that same year which saw the publication of the final volume of the *Commentaries*, Blackstone publicly acknowledged the justice of many of the criticisms levelled at his text by Priestley; in subsequent editions he also made numerous changes, eliminating or at least modifying most of the objectionable content, which, as he pointed out, had been 'written above fifteen Years ago'.[49] Furneaux commended these 'very considerable alterations in the most obnoxious passages' as 'a noble sacrifice to truth'.[50] There is further (albeit fragmentary) evidence of a mellowing, or maturing, in Blackstone's attitudes to non-Anglicans during the last decade of his life, including his cordial reaction from the bench when Priestley appeared as a witness in a *nisi prius* case tried before him, and his role in advising the Archbishop of Canterbury on a bill successfully enacted in 1779 for the relief of protestant ministers and teachers from their previous obligation to subscribe to the Thirty-nine Articles of the Church of England.[51] This last episode gains added significance when coupled with the fact that Blackstone did not join his former political ally and friend Sir Roger Newdigate, or another ex-Oxford friend Thomas Winchester, in opposing the relaxation of religious tests at Oxford and Cambridge.[52] Nor should we overlook his successful efforts at

46 *The Monthly Review* 41 (October 1769): 292–304.

47 J. Bentham, *A Fragment on Government*, ed. J. H. Burns and H. L. A. Hart (Cambridge: Cambridge University Press, 1988), 16; J. C. D. Clark, *English Society 1688–1832* (Cambridge: Cambridge University Press, 2000), 245–7.

48 T. G. Barnes, 'Introduction', in W. Blackstone, *Commentaries on the Laws of England, Book the Third* (Birmingham, AL: Legal Classics Library, Gryphon Editions, 1983), 16, 21.

49 [W. Blackstone], *A Reply to Dr. Priestley's Remarks on the Fourth Volume of the Commentaries on the Laws of England* (London, 1769), 5, 9–11. See also Prest, 'Religion of a Lawyer', 154–5, 164–8; all authorial variations in editions two to nine of the *Commentaries* are identified in the Oxford University Press edition (Oxford, 2016).

50 P. Furneaux, *Letters to the Honourable Mr. Justice Blackstone*, 2d ed. (London, 1771), iv.

51 Prest, 'Religion of a Lawyer', 156–7, 165–6.

52 Prest, *William Blackstone*, 277–8; I. Doolittle, 'William Blackstone, Edward Gibbon and Thomas Winchester: The Case for an Oxford Enlightenment', unpublished paper, 2015, 4, 12.

negotiating with prominent Dissenters, including the prison reformer John Howard and the Quaker physician John Fothergill, following the passage of the Penitentiary Act.

So Blackstone's published denial, in response to Priestley, that he was 'a bigotted High-Church-Man, and of a persecuting Spirit in Matters of Religious Differences' deserves more credence than it has sometimes been given.[53] But then, as he himself recognised, this was

> not an Age in which a Man who thinks for himself, and endeavours to think with Moderation, can expect to meet with Quarter from any Side, amid the Rage of contending Parties. If, in a Matter of mere History and Speculation, he condemns the Conduct of the elder Charles [i.e. King Charles I], but disapproves of the tragical Extremes to which his Opponents proceeded, he is a Friend to Popery and arbitrary Power ... If he argues for Toleration and Indulgence to Dissenters of all Denominations, but censures with some Warmth all indecent Attacks upon the Establishment, he commences a Bigot and a Persecutor. In this Temper of the Times, I am sensible that all Apologies are idle, and all Vindications useless.[54]

53 Blackstone, *A Reply*, 6. 54 Ibid., 26–7.

Lord Kenyon, engraved by William Holl (1807–71) from *National Portrait Gallery*, volume III, (*c.* 1835), Shee, Martin Archer (1796–1850) / private collection / Ken Welsh / Bridgeman Images

11

Lord Kenyon
Preaching from the Bench

James Oldham

On 8 June 1788, Sir Lloyd Kenyon succeeded Lord Mansfield[1] as Chief Justice of the Court of King's Bench, taking a peerage as the first Baron Kenyon. He had previously held judicial office as Chief Justice of Chester and as the Master of the Rolls in Chancery. His legal career began when he was admitted to the Middle Temple in November 1750. He was admitted to the bar in February 1756. He practised for more than twenty-five years and, according to Douglas Hay, Kenyon 'much preferred office work', writing 'opinions on stated cases [that] were prompt, practical and succinct'.[2] His opinion writing became lucrative, and he achieved substantial wealth by the time he became a crown lawyer and member of Parliament in 1774.

Apart from Douglas Hay's fine biographical summary in the *Oxford Dictionary of National Biography*, other biographical efforts date from the nineteenth century. The first of note was William Townsend's ninety-five pages (two chapters) in his *The Lives of Twelve Eminent Judges*, published in 1846.[3] This was followed in 1857 by a biography of comparable length as the first entry in volume 3 of Lord Campbell's *Lives of the Chief Justices of England*.[4] A book-length biography was published in 1873 by Lord Kenyon's great-grandson, George T. Kenyon. In the preface, the author explains that he undertook the biography after reading Lord Campbell's treatment and determining that, in the interest of the family name, corrective action was called for, quoting the *Law Magazine*'s swipe

1 For a discussion of Lord Mansfield, see Chapter 9 in this volume.

2 Douglas Hay, 'Kenyon, Lloyd, First Baron Kenyon', in *Oxford Dictionary of National Biography* (Oxford: Oxford University Press, 2004).

3 William C. Townsend, *The Lives of Twelve Eminent Judges*, 2 vols (London: Longman, 1846), chs. 2 and 3.

4 John Lord Campbell, *The Lives of the Chief Justices of England*, 2d ed., 3 vols. (London: John Murray, 1857).

that Lord Campbell's political virus 'oozes out in sly general remarks and bantering innuendoes'.[5]

All accounts of Lord Kenyon stress his strict moral code and his integrity. An editorial in *The Times* that appeared four days after Kenyon took office stated that Kenyon claimed no merit as a statesman and 'scarcely ever ventured to say anything material during his very short period in the House of Commons', yet notwithstanding, the office of chief justice was given 'to a man whose sole claim was great abilities, and proven integrity'.[6]

In personal demeanour, Lord Kenyon was often blunt and irascible. He was not a polished speaker and was often vexed by the habits of lawyers appearing before him. Even Kenyon's great-grandson in his biography acknowledged these and other faults, quoting the following passage from Nathaniel Wraxall's memoirs:

> Little conversant with the manners of polite life, he retained, even when Lord Chief Justice of the King's Bench, to which high station he afterwards rose, all the original coarse homeliness of his early habits. Irascible in his temper, destitute of all refinement, parsimonious even in a degree approaching to avarice, he nevertheless more than balanced these defects of deportment and character by strict morality, probity, and integrity.[7]

In 1832, the retired barrister Isaac Espinasse published notes on a number of contemporaries, including extensive comments on Lord Kenyon.[8] Espinasse had practised in the Court of King's Bench for the entire time that Lord Kenyon was chief justice. Despite a favourable first impression, Espinasse was ultimately disenchanted. He acknowledged Kenyon's 'great legal knowledge', also that 'his morals were pure, and his religion unaffected'.[9] Yet in Espinasse's opinion – and evidently that of others at the bar – Kenyon sullied the dignity of his court by an obsessive 'love of money', evidenced by his threadbare dress and oft-soled shoes. Espinasse said that 'the threadbare remains of what might once have been appropriate costume' were the 'daily subject of jokes or comment at the Bar'. Espinasse recollected a conversation he had with Thomas Erskine when Lord Kenyon had just arrived in court, prompting Espinasse 'involuntarily' to quote Alexander Pope's lines in the *Dunciad* on the poet Elkanah Settle, viz:

5 George Kenyon, *The Life of Lloyd, First Lord Kenyon, Lord Chief Justice of England* (London: Longmans, Green and Co., 1873), vi.

6 *The Times*, 12 June 1788, 2.

7 Kenyon, *The Life of Lloyd, First Lord Kenyon*, 87, quoting Wraxall's memoirs, first series, 165.

8 I. Espinasse, 'My Contemporaries: From the Note-Book of a Retired Barrister', *Fraser's Magazine for Town and Country* 6 (1832): 220–30, 314–24, 417–31 (Espinasse's notes were published in three monthly instalments – September, October and November 1832).

9 Ibid., 417.

> Known by the band and suit which Settle wore –
> His only suit for twice three years before.

Laughing, Erskine scoffed at the period of six years, saying, 'I remember the green coat which he now has on for at least a dozen years'; Espinasse in his recollections, added that '[i]t must have been originally black; but time had mellowed it down to the appearance of a sober green, which is what Erskine meant by his allusion to its colour'.[10]

Penurious dress was, according to Espinasse, but one of many aggravating habits exhibited by Lord Kenyon. Among others were said to be 'a kind of phosphoric temper', belittling condescension to barrister Edward Law (who later became Lord Ellenborough, Kenyon's successor as Chief Justice of King's Bench), treating the opinions of brother judges in a manner that 'bordered on contempt' and habitually garnishing legal principles with 'intrusive scraps' of bad Latin.[11]

These shortcomings notwithstanding, Espinasse recalled that Lord Kenyon 'possessed a singular quickness of apprehension, a most retentive memory, and an unparalleled promptness of decision'.[12] His extensive knowledge of both law and equity equipped him with sound principles that he applied 'with unerring judgment' in his decisions – rulings 'which, though pronounced without premeditation, have stood the revision of all succeeding judges, and received their approbation and adoption'.[13]

Espinasse thought that Lord Kenyon's 'ideas of rectitude' were 'visionary and extravagant' – notions that were frankly unattainable by others.[14] The high ground that Kenyon occupied on public morals was nevertheless in significant measure due to his deeply held Christian beliefs. He wore these beliefs on his sleeve, as was very often exhibited in his instructions to juries at Westminster Hall, the Guildhall and on assize. It is no exaggeration to describe Lord Kenyon as frequently 'preaching from the bench'. Numerous examples are given in this chapter, but preliminarily it is worth considering how, at the remove of the twenty-first century, we can know what Kenyon said to his juries.

When Kenyon succeeded Lord Mansfield as Chief Justice of the Court of King's Bench in 1788, no regular reporting of trials at *nisi prius* existed and, even after Peake and Espinasse began that practice in the 1790s, the number of published reports of jury trial cases was but a small percentage of the number of trials actually conducted.[15] Moreover, even when printed reports of jury

10 Ibid., 418. 11 Ibid., 419–21. 12 Ibid., 420. 13 Ibid., 424. 14 Ibid., 422–3.

15 See J. Oldham, 'Law-Making at Nisi Prius in the Early 1800s', *Journal of Legal History* 25 (2004), 221–47. Table 5 (p. 233) shows that, across the years 1802–18, the percentage of *nisi*

trials were produced in the nominate reports, jury instructions were rarely found to be of reportable value and did not appear.

Journalists, however, were a different breed. The English press, especially in London, experienced robust growth in the second half of the eighteenth century, and the public appetite for news stories from the law courts – both as newspaper readers and as auditors at coffee houses and public houses – was large and growing. Criminal trials had been printed in the Old Bailey Sessions Papers for decades and, although the facts brought out in trials at *nisi prius* did not compare to the deviant drama of the criminal trial, there was still much of interest in the trials taking place in the principal common law court, the Court of King's Bench.

Law reporting in the newspapers had increased steadily during Lord Mansfield's thirty-two years as Chief Justice of the Court of King's Bench;[16] in 1785, near the end of Lord Mansfield's active years as a sitting trial judge, *The Times* was founded. Throughout most of the eighteenth century, the longevity of a new newspaper venture was uncertain, but *The Times* quickly became a leader, continuing daily from its founding to the present. When Lord Kenyon took over King's Bench jury trials, *The Times* was well established.

Additional aspects of *nisi prius* trials attracted the journalists. Many of the newspaper readers and auditors had participated in the trials as jurors.[17] Also, jury trials were often live theatre, featuring brilliant forensic displays, especially by a select group of talented barristers. William Garrow, who was famous for his electric cross-examinations at the Old Bailey, also appeared frequently in the central common law courts. Even more prominent was Thomas Erskine, sometimes Garrow's co-counsel but more often his opposing counsel. Erskine was well known to Lord Kenyon from Kenyon's years at the bar, and Kenyon's respect and admiration for Erskine were palpable in their courtroom exchanges during Kenyon's entire fifteen years as chief justice.

In consequence of these and other contributing factors, a great many of Lord Kenyon's verbal interactions with counsel and his speeches to his juries

prius cases tried by Lord Ellenborough that appeared in the printed reports ranged from a low of 3.2% (1805) to a high of 15.9% (1815).

16 See J. Oldham, 'Law Reporting in the London Newspapers 1756–1786', *American Journal of Legal History* 31 (1987), 177–206.

17 In a widely publicised adultery case tried in February 1794, *Howard v. Bingham*, counsel for the plaintiff (James Mingay), while addressing the jury, observed that many of them, he believed, 'had been witnesses to the very pathetic, earnest, oral addresses, that had fallen from the noble and learned Judge who presided at these questions with infinite concern, during the time his Lordship had with such satisfaction and benefit of the public, and with so much honour to himself, administered the justice of the country'. *The Times*, 6 March 1794, 2. (See also text at nn. 32–3, in this chapter.)

were printed in the *Times* and other newspapers and remain accessible today. In addition, several of Lord Kenyon's best-known opinions were preserved in verbatim reports of notorious trials that were published in *State Trials* from shorthand reporters' notes. One in particular is a striking exhibit of Lord Kenyon's deeply held Christian views. The case was the libel and blasphemy trial of Thomas Williams for having published part II of Thomas Paine's *Age of Reason*, fully reported in *State Trials* in 1797.[18] The presence of Lord Kenyon's religious beliefs is unsurprising, given the theological content of the publication (subtitled, 'An Investigation of True and Fabulous Theology'). The prosecution was preferred by the Society for Carrying into Effect His Majesty's Proclamation against Vice and Immorality. Prior to seeking an indictment, the Society had obtained a legal opinion from barrister John Bayley, who endorsed the prosecution, stating in his introduction to his lengthy opinion 'that blasphemy was not only an offence to God and religion, but a crime against the laws, state, and government; and therefore, punishable by indictment: for to say religion is a cheat, is to dissolve all those obligations whereby civil societies are preserved; and to reproach the Christian religion is to speak in subversion of the law'.[19]

Bayley appeared for the prosecution at the trial, but he was overshadowed by his co-counsel – William Garrow and Thomas Erskine. With his widely admired eloquence in full bloom, Erskine read aloud selected passages from Thomas Paine's work and exclaimed, 'How any man can rationally vindicate the publication of such a book, in a country where the Christian religion is the very foundation of the law of the land, I am totally at a loss to conceive.'[20] He described the publication as 'a public attack *upon all revealed religion*'.[21]

The defendant's counsel was Stewart Kyd. His lengthy opening statement has a special resonance to the religious temperament of the twenty-first century – as, for example:

> A Christian might call a Turk blasphemous, impious and profane, for maintaining the divine mission of Mohammed, and ascribing his actions to the immediate influence of God. The Turk would speak of the Christian in the same terms, for denying that mission, disputing the divine authority of the Koran, and ridiculing and reviling its doctrines.[22]

Kyd also proposed to read to the jury passages from the Bible that, even from his youth, he regarded as describing obscenities or voluptuous debaucheries, but on reconsideration, he decided only to list these, itemising chapter and verse for approximately twenty Old Testament stories from the Bible. He next

18 26 S.T. 653 (1797). 19 26 S.T. at 654. 20 Ibid. at 665.
21 Ibid. at 668 (emphasis in the original). 22 Ibid. at 674.

turned to biblical descriptions of what he considered to be cruel and tortuous executions, but again, after being interrupted by Lord Kenyon, he merely cited nine examples. Kyd then entered upon a lengthy discussion of the passages in Paine's *Age of Reason* dealing with whether the Bible tells the truth. Again Lord Kenyon interrupted, stating, 'I cannot sit at this place, and hear this kind of discussion', but despite his protest, Kenyon allowed Kyd to continue.

In summing up the case for the jury in *Rex v. Williams*, Lord Kenyon said, before reaching the merits, 'Gentlemen . . . I was extremely hurt, when the learned counsel for the defendant thought fit to state to you, with very considerable emphasis, and a very determined tone of voice, that this was a scandalous prosecution.' Kenyon explained that the prosecution was not oppressive – that it had proceeded by way of indictment instead of by information, so that a grand jury had been part of the process. He then continued as follows:

> Gentlemen, we sit here in a Christian assembly, to administer the laws of the land, and I am to take my knowledge of what the law is, from that which has been sanctioned by a great variety of legal decisions. I am bound to state to you what my predecessors in Mr. Woolston's case (2 Strange, 834) stated, half a century ago in this court, of which I am a humble member, namely, that the Christian religion is part of the law of the land . . . I am fully impressed with the great truths of religion, which, thank God, I was taught in my early years to believe, and which the hour of reflection and inquiry, instead of producing any doubt, has fully confirmed me in.[23]

Occasionally less notorious cases involving issues directly connected to religion came before Lord Kenyon. In *Middleton qui tam v. Blake*, for example, the defendant was the vicar of the parish of St. Leonard, Shoreditch, who had held his position for nineteen years but who resided on his estate of South Malton, in Devonshire, 'and never came up to London to visit his Parish but to retrieve their Easter offerings'.[24] In remarks to the jury, Lord Kenyon said the following:

> In every well-constituted Government, there must be attention to the service of God. Religion must always be in strict alliance to the State, otherwise it is impossible, humanly considering things, anything can go on prosperously. At the time the Government was not well conducted, before the Revolution, it was among the crying offences of the kingdom, that those to whom the celebration of religious services was committed, received their emolument

23 Ibid. at 704–5. Kenyon added that he had seen people taking notes in the courtroom, but the publication 'is so shocking that I hope nobody will publish this'.

24 *The Times*, 10 May 1799, 3.

> without any attention to the duties of their office. We all know that many of the richest Bishoprics in the kingdom were committed to foreigners, and among the first fruits of the Reformation was the Act requiring residence, and lately the wisdom of those who passed it, cannot be doubted. Our first duty is to God.

A much less serious dispute, almost trivial, was tried before Lord Kenyon and a special jury in *Bethell v. Grainger* in 1790.[25] In that case, the plaintiff's servant was carrying a basket of pineapples one Sunday during the time of divine service when the servant was imprisoned by the defendants 'under the idea that this servant had broken the Lord's Day', thus offending a statute of Charles II preventing people from keeping open shops on Sunday. Lord Kenyon asked counsel for the defendants whether he could defend his case, and the counsel answered that he could not. Lord Kenyon then observed, '[I]t was of vast importance to tend to the observation of the Sabbath, which was set apart for divine worship, and was the only means of keeping alive among us, what remained of religion.' He did, however, add that large damages would be 'abominable'. The jury returned a verdict for £2 and 9s, the price of the fruit.

One more case directly invoking religion deserves mention – another libel prosecution, *Rex v. Eaton*, tried before Lord Kenyon and a special jury of merchants in 1796.[26] This time, the defendant was accused of having published a book 'with an intent to scandalize and defame, and to bring into hatred and contempt, the King, and the established Government, Religion, and Laws of the Land, as well as the Clergy of the Church of England, and the Army'. The title of the publication was *A Summary of the Duties of Citizenship, Written Expressly for the Members of the London Corresponding Society, Including Observations on the Mysterious Neglect of the Secretary of State, with Regard to Their Late Address to the King*. Prosecuting counsel was the Attorney General John Scott (later Lord Eldon). The defence was that Mr Eaton's name had been put into the book as one of the publishers without his knowledge or consent, and that he had refused to sell the book. The defendant was, nevertheless, found guilty. Among Lord Kenyon's comments to the jury were the following:

> It is for the jury to say whether a book, which so scandalized the Ministers of the Gospel, and treated with so much contempt the Holy Religion which we profess, ought to be permitted to be circulated through the country. His Lordship said, he was a Christian, and he took it for granted, he was addressing the Jury as Christians, for they could not otherwise have got into the situation in which they then were, having been sworn on the Evangelists.

[25] *The Times*, 5 July 1790, 3. [26] *The Times*, 7 July 1796, 3.

As the examples that have been given demonstrate, Lord Kenyon's speeches to his juries were rarely technical or legalistic, but they were often studded with admonitory pleas to the jurors to help preserve some degree of moral decency and respect for religion. This was especially true in cases involving criminal conversation (adultery), customarily abbreviated 'crim. con.'. In these cases, in the view of many observers, Lord Kenyon could not restrain himself. As the author of one sketch of Lord Kenyon stated, 'The scandal monger – the gambler – the seducer – the adulterer – received no mercy at his hands: indeed, his anxiety to punish immorality, more than once hurried him beyond his province.'[27] The author went farther, stating that '[e]very sacrifice of the essential principles of justice to obtain an immediate good of whatever extent, is in truth a blot in the judicial character. But a hatred of vice was constitutional with Kenyon.'[28] Lord Campbell in his biography of Lord Kenyon agreed, declaring that '[i]n actions for criminal conversation his ardent love of morality blinded his judgment, preventing him from distinguishing the merits of each particular case, and led him to confound the principles of civil and criminal justice'.[29]

Many crim. con. cases presided over by Lord Kenyon could be cited. In *The Times* alone, at least forty such cases appear. Douglas Hay states that jury awards of more than £2,000 'increased fourfold while he was chief justice, and the increase in litigation that he encouraged merely reinforced his conviction that sexual misconduct was undermining social order'.[30]

An early example revealing Kenyon's crim. con. jury instructions on damages was *Parslow v. Sykes*, reported in *The Times* on 10 December 1789. There, the plaintiff sought damages of £10,000 and, after hearing the evidence, Kenyon said that the jury should not run wild in assessing damages; nevertheless, '[l]arge, very large and exemplary damages were proper in this case, and the jury would fall short of that justice which they owed to the country if large damages were not given'. The jury co-operated, returning a verdict for the plaintiff for £10,000.

The crim. con. cases bedevilled Lord Kenyon throughout his career. In *Sheridan v. Newman*,[31] Kenyon said the following to the jury:

> I am extremely sorry to say, that although this is only the third day I have unworthily filled this place, this is the second cause of this kind that has come before me. To you, juries, the guardianship and protection of families is committed; – it is your duty to teach men who thus transgress the laws of God

[27] [A. Polson], *Law and Lawyers; or, Sketches and Illustrations of Legal History and Biography*, 2 vols. (London: Longman, Orme, Brown, Green and Longmans, 1840), 1:230.

[28] Ibid., 1:230–1. [29] Campbell, *Lives of the Chief Justices*, 3:67.

[30] Hay, 'Kenyon, Lloyd, first Baron Kenyon'. [31] *The Times*, 28 June 1788, 3.

> and of society, that it is their interest as well as their duty, to restrain their passions, and regulate them according to the rules of morality and decency; and that if they will break into the domestic peace of families, they shall not do so with impunity.

In 1794, a notorious crim. con. action filled the news: *Howard v. Bingham*.[32] The plaintiff was said in *The Times* to be 'the presumptive heir to the dukedom of Norfolk' and the defendant the son and heir to another member of the nobility. Damages were laid at £10,000. In addressing the jury, counsel for the plaintiff, James Mingay, said that they 'lived in an era in which the most important questions were decided by the newspapers' and that the case before them had become notorious by false accounts of the affair in some of the daily prints. Erskine, for the defendant, said that Mr Howard's marriage to Mrs Howard was a misery to her from the start – she said that 'she would rather go to Newgate than to the embraces of her husband; and that day after day, and night after night, she spent her time in tears'. Erskine then expostulated on the sorry state to which the nobility of the country had descended. In a typically flamboyant speech, he said that 'these were the most extraordinary times that were ever recorded in history, when the whole habitable earth seemed to be in a state of change and fluctuation'. He recognised that 'rank and station must always exist, in some shape or other', but '[w]ould to God the Nobles of the land would imitate a little more closely the examples of their illustrious ancestors, and instead of going from the Opera to the Play, and from the Play to Ranelagh or to a Masquerade . . . let them set an example to others of genuine morals'.

Lord Kenyon then began his address to the jury with the following remarkable declaration: 'I had not been long on the Seat of Justice before I felt I should best discharge my duty to the public by making the law of the land subservient to the laws of morality and religion.' Thus, he said:

> [I]n various cases that have come before me, when I saw a considerable degree of guilt, I have pressed the judgment of Juries to go along with me in enforcing the sanctions of religion and morality, by the heavy penalties of the law; and I have found Juries co-operate with me, in trying how far the immorality of a libertine age would be corrected, by letting all parties know that they best consulted their own interest by discharging those duties they owed to God and society.[33]

By the second half of the 1790s, however, the crim. con. cases were growing tedious to Lord Kenyon. In *Houlditch v. Goodhew*,[34] counsel Thomas Erskine

[32] *The Times*, 6 March 1794, 2. [33] The jury returned a verdict for the plaintiff of £1,000.
[34] *The Times*, 7 December 1795, 3.

apologised to the jury, saying that he had represented plaintiffs in criminal conversation actions 'so very, very often' that he feared he had 'said the same things over and over again'. This prompted Lord Kenyon to remark that even though

> the learned Gentleman [Erskine] who opened this cause for the plaintiff, has reason to complain that . . . he has drudged through so many causes of this kind, there is a very obvious reason why I, who am a man of plain understanding, should feel myself much more oppressed; and I almost nauseate my own voice in repeating the same observations over and over again to Juries.

In *Webster v. Lord Holland*,[35] Lord Kenyon stated that, though he was 'now at a time of life that was very far advanced' and consequently 'he had been concerned in more causes of this kind than had fallen to the lot of any other man', 'it was a horrible picture of the depravity of the times'. He said 'It shewed that all the efforts that had been made by Courts and Juries to stem the torrent of vice as far as they could, had hitherto proved ineffectual.' Yet they (he and the jury) must persevere because '[s]ometimes perseverance had got the better of long habits of vice'. Thus:

> To the Gentlemen of the Jury was committed the Guardianship of the Morals of the Times; and if the principle of Virtue which ought to be included in the early person of youth were not sufficient to bridle the passions of men, and to prevent excesses, they must be taught.

As he said in *Howard v. Bingham*, Lord Kenyon was gratified by the co-operation he received from his juries in the crim. con. cases. There were, however, occasional outbursts of protest. On 26 March 1798, *The Times* published a letter from 'a Juror' to 'The Right Hon. Lord Kenyon'. The author explained:

> It was my lot, My Lord, to sit as a Juror on a late cause . . . where, after hearing the accusation and defence, with all the evidence which was adduced, and retaining as much of it as men of plain understanding are capable of, we were informed by your Lordship that the 'Defendant was hacknied in the ways of vice – that his house was a brothel, kept solely for the seduction of tradesmen's daughters, and virtuous wives', and with these denunciations, your Lordship dismissed us.

The juror then confessed:

> With a degree of zealous, and, I will add, laudable indignation against such offenders as the one described to us by your Lordship, I went to the

[35] *The Times*, 22 February 1797, 3.

> consideration of a cause whose issue rested on presumptive evidence, where the criminality was constructive – where a verdict was to be given, not grounded on the incontestable proof of facts, but on the fallibility of human discretion; and amidst my doubts, I need not blush to own that I thought the well-known sagacity, the unimpeached integrity of your Lordship, a safer guide than the imbecility of my own judgment.

Thus the juror 'concurred in returning a verdict which I thought would make a deserved inroad on the Defendant's fortune, and exhibit him to the world with just ignominy'. On returning to his 'rank as a private citizen', however, the juror was shocked 'to meet with expostulations upon what men have deemed a preposterous verdict!' This was heightened by the realisation that he had approved exemplary damages.

The juror's letter surely became known to Lord Kenyon, but even assuming so, it had no impact whatever, as is shown in a crim. con. case tried a year later, *Henderson v. Tempest*.[36] Lord Kenyon observed to the jury 'that the scene of profligacy and debauchery that had been described that day, exhibited a dreadful picture of the times in which we lived'. He said that 'he had tried many causes of that kind, and he had felt greatly, and had endeavoured to speak up to his feelings'. He acknowledged that '[h]e had pressed Juries, as far as money could be any compensation to injured husbands, to make that compensation, and also, in order to make some recompence to the injured Laws of their Country, to give large damages' and '[t]hey had followed his wishes, and had done it'. Kenyon also admitted that 'too much prudery had been objected to [in] him', but he had been doing his duty and 'could bear reprehension'. To those who said that 'too moral a judge is a bad thing', his maxim was that *leges, sine moribus vanæ*,[37] and '[h]e thought no Judge could do better than make the laws and their administration subservient to the purposes of religion and morality'. His advice was 'to imitate the example of the Patriarch of old, who said, "As for me and my house, we will serve the Lord."'

During his last two years in office, Lord Kenyon's voice in the crim. con. cases grew even wearier, and he was increasingly aware of the extent to which he was thought by many to be old school, out of touch with changing times. In a brief report of a crim. con. case from the Maidstone assizes in August 1800, Lord Kenyon said that his abhorrence of the crime of adultery remained unchanged, even though 'he understood that he had been considered as a man secluded from society, and not merely unhackneyed, but totally inexperienced in the ways of the world'. He said 'he must plead guilty to the

36 *The Times*, 21 June 1798, 3.

37 Laws without morals are valueless.

charge; but he trusted that society was not so degenerate as to make immorality a necessary consequence of mixing with the world'. And besides,

> he knew a little of the character of the persons who had taken upon them to censure his conduct in the administration of justice; they were persons of the highest rank and elevation in society; but high and elevated as they were, he thought it right to say that during the short interval that he might continue in the administration of justice, he never wished to have any intercourse or acquaintance with them, moral, religious, or social.

Finally, perhaps the best known example of the extent to which Lord Kenyon's religious beliefs infiltrated his courtroom was the case of *Taylor v. Birdwood*, described by an editorial insert at the outset of the case report as a case 'full of calamity on both sides'.[38] The plaintiff was an 'eminent attorney' who had married his wife when he was twenty-one and she was twenty-two. Living in the neighbourhood was the Rev Mr Birdwood, a young man of twenty-three years of age, the son of a physician. Lord Kenyon began his remarks to the jury by complimenting counsel who had conducted the case 'with that decency and attention to the cause of religion and morality, which were to be expected of Christian advocates in a Christian Court of Justice'. But he said that the times required corrective action: 'the public mind, if it has gone wrong, should get right again, by reverting to the principles on which all our moral and religious duties are founded'. He declared that '[t]he generality of men believe that the laws of morality and religion ought to have some effect on their conduct; but if it is rendered doubtful, whether the laws of God have been promulgated or not, what will be the consequence?' He said, '[I]n this country no impudence had ever gone so far as to declare in any assembly that the laws of God have not been promulgated to mankind', asserting that this 'is language fit for the French Assembly, and the next step is, that there is no God – no religion – and that death is a perpetual sleep'. He told the gentlemen of the jury:

> [S]omebody or other, at least some publications, tell us, that the Judges (whether the observation extends to Juries, I know not) are legal Monks – that they know nothing of the world – that they are shut out from the world, and bring along with them crude opinions of their own, by which they are guided in Courts of Justice.

But then he asked, 'What is the world?' – is knowledge of the world 'to be got by sauntering like young men of fashion about Bond Street' or is it 'to be obtained at gaming tables; or on the course at Newmarket' or 'in private brothels'? If so,

38 *The Times*, 2 June 1800, 3.

he disavowed being acquainted with it. Lord Kenyon's concluding remarks to the jury were these:

> My consolations in this life, and my expectations in what is to come, are grounded on the revealed word of God. There I anchor: and it holds this to be an offence of high magnitude. It becomes the Legislature of the Country, and I hope they will give the sanction of penalties in support of Religion and Morality. This is at all times to be expected from them. – Gentlemen, with you this case is, and I am sure you will be glad, if by enforcing the principles of justice, you are able at the same time to enforce the laws of Morality and Religion.

Near the end of his life, Lord Kenyon confessed how discouraged he had become by his failure to achieve discernible success in combatting criminal conversation. In the last of his several opinions in *Hoare v. Allen*, issued six months before he died,[39] Kenyon declared that, in these cases,

> what he had done was to meet what he thought was for the benefit of society, morality, and religion; and God knew all his endeavours had fallen much short of producing the effect that one might have expected from them; but he was afraid that as long as human nature was in its present defective state, all the sanctuary of Laws, both human and divine, would often not be perfectly adequate.

A month later, perhaps inspired by Lord Kenyon's morose reflections in the *Hoare* case, *The Times* published a 'Crim. Con.' editorial expressing what it called 'a strange species of consolation' in the fact that 'the manners of our Ancestors were altogether as depraved and vicious as our own'.[40] Nearly a century ago, 'we find the excellent Mr. ADDISON complaining of the profligacy of his times, and the prevailing *practice*, as he calls it, of conjugal infidelity'. Further,

> In the reign of CHARLES the FIRST . . . the *Company of Stationers*, who were Patentees for printing the Bible, made a very remarkable blunder in one of the editions; for instead of 'Thou shalt *not* commit adultery', they printed off several thousand copies with 'Thou *shalt* commit adultery.' For this gross negligence, Archbishop LAUD severely fined them in the *Star-Chamber*. But the books were eagerly bought up by the noble and wealthy families, who have ever since *observed the Commandment*, according to that faulty reading.

In bringing to a close this chapter on Lord Kenyon, I pose what may seem a surprising question: Was Lord Kenyon a judicial activist? A predictable

39 *The Times*, 10 September 1801, 4. 40 *The Times*, 15 October 1801, 2.

response might be 'of course not' – Lord Mansfield stood accused of this allegedly renegade judicial behaviour,[41] but surely not Kenyon. Lord Kenyon, after all, firmly believed that the line between law and equity ought to be strictly observed. Likewise he thought that long-established principles should not be dislodged by common law judges – for example, he heartily disapproved of Lord Mansfield's decisions that expanded the circumstances in which married women could receive credit in the marketplace.[42] In *Ringsted v. Lady Lanesborough*,[43] Lord Mansfield said that although [g] rules are adapted to the frequent and ordinary state of the subject matter to which they relate, at the time when they are made', yet 'in the process of time, through the succession of ages, new manners arise' that call for exceptions; otherwise, 'injustice and many absurdities must follow if the letter of the general law was to govern cases not within the reason'.[44] In what was clearly a direct response, Lord Kenyon in a 1794 decision, *Ellah v. Leigh*,[45] said, 'I do not think that the courts ought to change the law so as to adapt it to the fashion of the times; if an alteration in the law be necessary, recourse must be had to the Legislature for it.'[46] Yet Kenyon's declaration in *Howard v. Bingham*, discussed previously, bears repeating: 'I had not been long on the Seat of Justice before I felt I should best discharge my duty to the public by making the law of the land subservient to the laws of morality and religion.'[47]

That declaration, beyond dispute, represents judicial activism. On questions of religion, also on other basic issues of public morality, Lord Kenyon was fundamentally evangelical. As a common law judge, he naturally played no part in selecting the types of cases that came before him for trial, yet the flow of cases that involved central issues of religion and morality was unrelenting, especially the numerous crim. con. actions. In these cases, Lord Kenyon used his judicial office as a bully pulpit, successfully encouraging juries to return punitive verdicts in the hope, perhaps vain, that the verdicts would have

41 See James Oldham, 'Judicial Activism in Eighteenth-Century English Common Law in the Time of the Founders', *Green Bag* 2d ser. 8 (2005): 269–70.

42 See J. Oldham, 'Creditors and the Feme Covert', in M. Dyson and D. Ibbetson, eds., *Law and Legal Process: Substantive Law and Procedure in English Legal History* (Cambridge: Cambridge University Press, 2013), 227–33.

43 3 Doug. 197 (1783).

44 The quoted language is from a manuscript version of Lord Mansfield's opinion that is fuller than that given in Douglas's report. The manuscript version is at Scone Palace, Perth, Scotland, First Series, Box 68. See J. Oldham, *English Common Law in the Age of Mansfield* (Chapel Hill: University of North Carolina Press, 2004), 326.

45 5 T.R. 679 (1794). Six years later, in *Marshall v. Rutton*, 8 T.R. 546 (1800), Lord Kenyon and his brother King's Bench judges reversed the *Ringsted* line of cases. See Oldham, 'Creditors and the Feme Covert', 217–45.

46 5 T.R. at 682. 47 *Howard v. Bingham*, *The Times*, 6 March 1794, 2.

a deterrent effect beneficial to the public at large. In his opinion, the moral fibre of society in his time was in a state of alarming deterioration. Whether Kenyon's largely unproductive campaign to combat that deterioration was right or wrong, it clearly earned him a place in the present volume as one of England's great Christian jurists.

The Honorable Stephen Lushington, PC, DCL, 1873 engraving / private collection / Photo © Liszt Collection / Bridgeman Images

12

Stephen Lushington

A Civilian in the Last Years of Doctors' Commons

Stephen M. Waddams

INTRODUCTION

Dr Stephen Lushington belonged to the last generation of the English civil lawyers, attaining the presidency of Doctors' Commons (the office of Dean of the Arches) in the same year (1858) in which Doctors' Commons itself effectively ceased to function. Lushington practised ecclesiastical and admiralty law as an advocate, and later as a judge. He was a member of Parliament from 1806 to 1808, from 1820 to 1830 and from 1832 to 1841. He is principally known to historians of the nineteenth century as adviser to Lady Byron on her notorious separation from Lord Byron in 1816, as counsel to Queen Caroline at her trial for adultery in 1820 and as a leading figure in the anti-slavery movement. He was for thirty years judge of the London Consistory Court, and sat for twenty-nine years as judge of the High Court of Admiralty and as a member of the Judicial Committee of the Privy Council. His judicial decisions on a variety of ecclesiastical controversies are of interest to church historians, and his decisions in admiralty cases – and, to a lesser degree, in family law and testamentary cases – continue to engage the attention of modern lawyers.[1]

LUSHINGTON'S RELIGIOUS OPINIONS

The Church of England was influenced, in the nineteenth century, by several significant currents of theological opinion, which may be roughly identified as evangelical, Anglo-Catholic and liberal. These currents of opinion clashed with each other, causing acute controversy and copious litigation, much of which Lushington was called upon to adjudicate. His own religious views

[1] For a fuller account, and for further references, see S. Waddams, *Law, Politics and the Church of England: The Career of Stephen Lushington 1782–1873* (Cambridge: Cambridge University Press, 1992).

were formed in the eighteenth century and did not conform precisely to any of the three currents of opinion mentioned. It would be true to say of him, as one of Trollope's characters says of the Dean of Barchester, that he was 'of the old school, of course, as any clergyman over 70 years of age must necessarily be'.[2] These words were published in 1857, when Lushington was seventy-five.

Lushington worked closely with evangelicals, both those within the Church of England and Dissenters, in the anti-slavery movement, and he supported many of the Dissenters' grievances in Parliament. But he spoke disparagingly in the 1820s of 'that class of religious enthusiasts called Methodists' and of 'canters and Methodists', and he was not a strict sabbatarian. In a speech in Parliament in 1824, he indulged in some humour at the expense of an evangelical organisation called the Home Missionary Society:

> Some agent of the Society, who had been pursuing his labours through the county of Worcester, described it in terms: 'I shall here attempt a description of the very deplorable state in which I have found the people of this dark county ... I shall only touch upon the manner in which they profane the Holy Sabbath.' Here the learned doctor said, he feared the House would be lost in horror when they should hear of the enormities which were committed by the people of this 'dark' county. 'They play against each other at foot-ball, and at hurling in a field adjoining to the church. Some of them play at fives, some at ball, some with sticks upon the green, some go to the river with lines and nets, and the youth of both sexes' (Oh monstrous!) 'assemble together and spend the evening in social mirth. The zealous agent recommended that a march should be immediately commenced, they should go from house to house (and this was literally done) to collect subscriptions, the object of which was to spread the progress of dissent through the benighted county of Worcestershire.'

This was probably an injudicious indulgence and shortly afterwards Lushington rose again to beg 'most distinctly to disclaim every species of hostility to the Dissenters', but the speech is significant in showing that Lushington's instincts were by no means in accord with mainstream evangelical opinion. He was not puritanical in matters of church ceremony, writing of a visit to Canterbury Cathedral that 'fortunately too there was an anthem. The service was in my judgment beautifully performed.'[3] Shortly after his wife's death following a harrowing illness, he received a letter of consolation from 'Mr Marsh, the celebrated evangelical preacher'. Presumably, Marsh had urged Lushington to accept his wife's suffering and death with equanimity, but Lushington wrote to his sister-in-law, 'I cannot view all things in their light ... Humanly speaking

[2] A. Trollope, *Barchester Towers*, ch. 32.

[3] Lushington to Fanny Carr, 2 October 1837, Lushington Papers, Surrey History Centre, 7854/1/6/6a.

I cannot but think that a greater evil, a more entire destruction of this world's happiness, could not have occurred.'[4]

On the other hand, Lushington had no sympathy whatever with the Anglo-Catholic party (sometimes referred to as 'High Church', Tractarian, Oxford Movement or ritualist) and showed himself very hostile to the introduction of Catholic doctrine and ceremonial in every case on those subjects that came before him in his judicial capacity.

As for the liberal current of thought (sometimes referred to as 'broad church') Lushington was called upon, in 1862, to adjudicate an important dispute arising out of a book of essays by seven writers, six of whom were clergymen (*Essays and Reviews*, 1860). The book, following a liberal and rationalistic approach to theological truth, created a huge controversy. Two of the clerical contributors were prosecuted in the ecclesiastical courts, and Lushington, as Dean of the Arches, condemned them on certain points (notably, the necessity of belief in biblical inspiration and in eternal punishment). Lushington's decision was reversed in the Privy Council, prompting the facetious observation that Lord Westbury (in the Privy Council) had 'dismissed hell with costs'.

Lushington's decision in the *Essays and Reviews* case shows that, in 1862, he was not sympathetic with the then newly emerging liberal trends in theological thought, and this is hardly surprising considering his age (eighty). But there is evidence that he may later have modified his opinion in what must have been a decade of profound reappraisal, for thoughtful Christians, of the nature of biblical truth. The Dean of Westminster, A. P. Stanley, the most prominent proponent of the liberal or 'broad church' perspective, had himself been criticised for his liberal theological opinions and had welcomed the reversal of Lushington's judgment by the Privy Council. In 1872 Stanley was nominated as a select preacher for Oxford University, and his critics forced a vote on the matter – a very unusual procedure that constituted something of a test of the strength of liberal theology. All MAs of the university, resident and non-resident, were entitled to vote. Lushington, at the age of ninety, travelled from his home in Ockham in Surrey to Oxford in order to cast his vote in favour of Stanley (whose nomination was affirmed by 349 votes to 287). Returning to Ockham on the same day, Lushington fell ill, dying four weeks later, just after his ninety-first birthday.

A short account of Lushington's life published in 1894 suggested that he had died a martyr to the cause of religious toleration. It may seem extravagant to attribute the death of a man in his ninety-second year to martyrdom to any

[4] The same to the same, 4 October 1837, Lushington Papers, 7854/1/6/7.

cause. But the journey to and from Oxford does indicate a gesture, and it was so perceived at the time. The journey must have been long and strenuous, and it was all to cast a vote for an honorary post: Stanley's livelihood was not at stake. Stanley himself evidently perceived Lushington's acts as a gesture because he reciprocated by travelling to Ockham to officiate at Lushington's funeral on 24 January 1873; preaching in Cambridge shortly afterwards, Stanley paid tribute to Lushington, describing him as

> the venerable judge whose career, thus prolonged beyond the ordinary limits of human existence, was fired from first to last by generous sympathy with suffering, by noble indignation against wrong, by the firm persuasion of the indissoluble bond between what was highest in religion and what was greatest in morality.[5]

ANTI-SLAVERY

It is often difficult to judge the extent to which a person's professed religious views have actually influenced his actions, especially in the context of the Church of England, where zeal and enthusiasm have not generally, since the eighteenth century, been words of approbation. The article on Lushington in the *Dictionary of National Biography* describes him as 'an ardent reformer and a staunch churchman'. The writer (G. F. Russell Barker) would not have called him an ardent churchman and a staunch reformer. Actions speak louder than words, and in Lushington's case there is convincing evidence that his religious views did prompt action, particularly his extraordinary activity and influence in the anti-slavery movement. Stanley's words, just quoted, refer principally to this aspect of Lushington's life.

Lushington devoted thousands of hours over many years to the anti-slavery movement, though he derived no professional advantage from it, and though he had conflicting family interests, his sister-in-law having inherited a Jamaica plantation. Speaking on the bill to abolish the slave trade in 1807, he said:

> One of the nearest connections I have in the world has a great interest in this important question; yet whatever may be the concern which those I most love may have in it, when I read in the preamble of the bill that the Slave Trade is inconsistent with justice, humanity, and sound policy; admitting that to be a correct statement of the fact, I can have no option whether to preserve or abandon the trade; for, Sir, I have never been accustomed to balance the

5 A. P. Stanley, *Purity and Light: A Sermon Preached before the University of Cambridge*, 2 February 1873 (London: Macmillan, 1873), 7 (introduction, quoting from a sermon preached the previous week).

> social duties of justice and humanity against the commercial estimates of exports and imports ... Let us not continue a species of commerce inconsistent with every principle of justice and humanity.[6]

Lushington worked very closely with Thomas Fowell Buxton, the successor to Wilberforce as leader of the anti-slavery movement. Buxton's daughter wrote of Lushington:

> He is working most marvelously 15 & 16 hours a day *often* Mrs L told us & *yet* he has undertaken Jeremie's case [concerning Mauritius]. Of a man who *acts* in this way – what can be said? For that *mountain* of filthy papers in bad French & clothed in Jeremie's obscurity was enough to try the benevolence of most men. He *has done* it however, condensed the thing & says the Case is an excellent one.[7]

George Stephen, another prominent anti-slavery leader, wrote:

> Dr Lushington is one of those able and energetic friends of the cause who has never had full justice done to him by the scanty labours and ill-informed pens of our abolition historians ... his personal sacrifices have been large and generous, and ungracefully rewarded ... Dr Lushington knows exactly when and where to stop; most men are at a loss where to begin; and a certain ardour of temperament, which even age has scarcely suppressed, renders this prudential facility of self-arrest a quality as valuable as it is rare; it combined with his other excellences to give him much weight with his Anti-slavery colleagues, among whom he has from the first held most conspicuous rank.[8]

There are many indications in the Buxton Papers of the reliance that Buxton and others placed on Lushington's judgment. Buxton wrote to Macaulay, in 1832, that he was 'waiting for Lushington's plan'. In 1838 he wrote to Stephen, '[S]uch are my impressions; but before I can give any further opinion, I must, at least, have permission to consult Lushington'. Buxton's daughter said that 'difference of opinion with him [Lushington] is worse than anything to my father'. Buxton's son, Charles, in his account of his father's life, said that 'every idea, and every plan, was originated and arranged between them'.[9] Near the Houses of Parliament is a monument, erected by Charles Buxton in 1866, commemorating the emancipation of the slaves and in

6 Substance of the debates on the bill for abolishing the slave trade, London, 1808.

7 Priscilla Johnston to Sarah Buxton, 19 April 1835 (copy), Buxton Papers, Rhodes House Library, Oxford, 13; 442.

8 G. Stephen, *Anti-Slavery Recollections* (London, Thomas Hatchard, 1854), 66–8.

9 C. Buxton, *Memoirs of Sir Thomas Fowell Buxton*, Everyman's Library (London: J. M. Dent, c. 1925), 132–3.

memory of his father. Lushington's is one of the five names, in addition to Buxton's, inscribed there.[10]

Lushington was very active in the anti-slavery societies. He was a director of the African Institute, the oldest of the nineteenth-century societies. He was a vice-president of the Anti-Slavery Society founded in 1823 and was present at the committee that planned its first general meeting in 1824, at which he moved one of the official motions and spoke. He spoke at several general meetings and at the general anti-slavery convention in 1840, where he is shown in a painting of the scene standing next to Buxton on the platform. He was a vice-president of the Society from 1825 and played a leading role in establishing the British and Foreign Anti-Slavery Society. When he resigned in 1845, after Buxton's death, the minute book records a tribute to him second in warmth only to that adopted for Buxton. Meetings of the Society were, on several occasions, held at Lushington's house, and sometimes he took the chair. He was appointed to several subcommittees and was asked to advise on particular issues, and was formally asked to act on behalf of the Society in Parliament. He was a trustee of the Mico Charity, which promoted the education and welfare of black persons.

It is clear that anti-slavery must have occupied substantially all of Lushington's time, outside his professional duties and his other Parliamentary duties, between about 1822 and 1845. His wife's statement, mentioned earlier, that he was working '15 and 16 hours a day *often*' suggests that he allotted little time to leisure. In 1831 he said that anti-slavery was 'the principal object of my life'. He received no tangible reward for this activity. He opposed the pecuniary interests of his own relatives. He alienated himself from those in power in both political parties. He criticised the actions of the Church of England, to which he was personally and professionally attached. It is worth asking what combination of religious, political, social and legal perspectives led him into a path so little to be expected of a nineteenth-century ecclesiastical lawyer.

Lushington's speeches were forceful. He was accused of enthusiasm, but replied:

> [I will] advocate this truth ... regardless of the outcry that I am a wild enthusiast ... I hold him to be an enthusiast who, ignorant of the subject matter – without taking pains to investigate, imagines that he has come to the just conclusion; and, regardless of the ordinary process of arriving at the truth, professes himself at once the advocate of a cause without being able to explain the reasons of his opinion. But I hold, if a man has learned what is the truth by patient and deliberate inquiry, if he does know the system in all

[10] The others are Wilberforce, Clarkson, Macaulay and Brougham.

the atrocities of its villainy – to speak mildly, to utter sentiments (as they call them) of moderation on the subject, is to betray the truth – is to suppose that a man of feeling, honour and honesty, can behold these things, and yet talk of them as if they did not violate the laws of God and man, and outrage the feelings of every right-minded individual who justly appreciates them.[11]

Sometimes he was sarcastic ('we were taught to believe that there was nothing but merriment and joy in the West Indies; that the negroes danced in their chains'). Sometimes he aroused an emotional response. The report of a speech in 1832 records that 'Dr Lushington's statement of the case was given in language so forcible and affecting that many of the audience shed tears, and the ladies wept, many of them audibly.'[12]

Free persons who were black or of mixed race often suffered discrimination, and Lushington was a strong supporter of their claims to equal treatment. He was presented with a silver tray by the free black people of Trinidad, inscribed:

To Stephen Lushington LL.D. M.P. &c &c &c
The eloquent & intrepid advocate of the just rights of the human race
This tribute of gratitude for his eminent and successful services is
Presented by the free inhabitants of African Descent of the
Island of Trinidad, 16 July 1832

Lushington's views on racial equality were usually supported by references to God or Providence. Referring to the free coloured people of Jamaica, he said:

It is not in the nature of things that a large body, increasing in wealth and intelligence, should for ever submit in silence to restrictions so unjust and degrading founded upon no other principle, resting on no other basis, than the darkness of the colour with which the God of nature has distinguished their skin.[13]

In a speech to the anti-slavery convention of 1843, he said:

I am willing briefly to bear my testimony, as far as I have had an opportunity of forming an opinion by experience, that the coloured races as well as the pure black, possess, by the blessing of Providence, the same talents and the same capability of cultivating them as have been given to those of a different complexion . . . I wish that . . . all who cherish an absurd feeling of superiority, arising from the colour of their skin, may become ashamed of themselves;

[11] 'Speech of Dr Lushington delivered at a General Meeting of the Society for the Abolition of Slavery throughout the British Dominions, April 23, 1831', *Anti-Slavery Reporter* 4 (1831), 263, 267.

[12] Ibid. [13] HC Deb., 1825, vol. 13, col. 1174.

and that the old adage of 2,000 years' date may be felt to be a true one, 'Virtue constitutes the soul of man.'[14]

Lushington's anti-slavery speeches include many references to religion; for example: 'If there was any truth in philosophy; if they were to place confidence in the sacred Word of God himself – it was impossible to believe that such a system could continue to exist. It was never given by God to man to hold his fellow-man in slavery.'[15] Slavery was incompatible with Christianity, as slave-owners had recognised, asking, '[C]an you . . . use the words "dear brother" or "sister" to those you hold in bondage?' and drawing the conclusion that Christianity should not be taught. Lushington agreed with the premise but drew the opposite conclusion: 'Most true were the words they uttered . . . Make the slaves Christian – and (harder task yet!) make the owners of them Christians, and slavery must speedily cease.'[16] References to religious truth were usually closely linked to secular expressions of humanitarian values: 'happiness, justice, charity, and a regard for the Word of God',[17] 'mercy, humanity, religion and truth',[18] 'justice and humanity',[19] 'the eternal purposes of truth and justice',[20] and 'the laws of God and the inalienable rights of man'.[21]

Another theme, often closely linked with religious language, is that of national duty and national shame. Lushington expected a successful candidate for election to say, 'my soul sinks under that sin, and with the blessing of God, every effort shall be made by me to remove the load from my country and my conscience'.[22] He spoke of 'a time when the household fire of liberty was burning in every British bosom',[23] and of an oppressive colonial law as 'a law enacted within one year from the present hour by Christian men, boasting to be Englishmen, and followers of Christ'.[24] He asserted that the people of England were opposed to slavery and would make sacrifices for its abolition.[25]

Unlike many of the other leaders of the anti-slavery movement, Lushington was neither an evangelical nor a Dissenter. Nevertheless, he often praised the work of the Dissenters, comparing it, to its advantage, with that of the Church of England. Of the Dissenting missionaries he said:

> To them was the praise of the legislature and the country due. He cared not whether they were Methodists, or Baptists, or Anabaptists, or Presbyterians, or

[14] Speech at 1843 convention: J. F. Johnson, *Proceedings of the General Anti-Slavery Convention, 1843*. (London, 1843), 210, 212.

[15] *Anti-Slavery Reporter* (1825), 80. [16] 'Speech of Dr Lushington' (1831), 264.

[17] Ibid., 263. [18] Ibid. [19] *Substance of the Debates on the . . . Slave Trade* (1807), 80.

[20] *Anti-Slavery Reporter* (1825), 80. [21] Johnson, *Anti-Slavery Convention*, 1843, 156.

[22] 'Speech of Dr Lushington' (1831), 264. [23] *Anti-Slavery Reporter* 5 (1832), 154.

[24] Ibid., 156. [25] HC Deb., 7 May 1841, vol. 58, col. 88.

> by which of the numerous names distinguishing the religious sects of the country they were called. It was enough for him that they were Christians, and that they had nobly and fearlessly discharged their duty towards their fellow creatures.[26]

By contrast,

> The Church of England, he must say, had for a century and a half been grossly negligent in giving instruction to the slave population of our colonies. Whatever was done in that way (and much had been done for the dissemination of Christianity amongst the slaves) was done, not by the Church of England, but by the Moravians, Baptists, and Wesleyans. He was aware that he laid himself open to misrepresentation in this matter, but this was a time at which the truth ought not to be concealed.[27]

Special praise was due to the Wesleyan Methodists: 'To the Wesleyan Methodists is due all the amelioration which has yet been effected in the condition of the slaves, all the progress which has been made in their education, and all the success in their conversion.'[28]

In 1826, an attack occurred in Jamaica on the Methodist chapel and on the minister's house. The attack was said to have been encouraged by a sermon preached in the parish church (i.e. Church of England) by G. W. Bridges, chaplain to the Bishop of Jamaica, and a supporter of slavery. Lushington was scathing in his reference to Bridges: 'The Reverend Mr Bridge – no Wesleyan Methodist, thank God for that! But a clergyman of the Church of England, forgetful of the feelings of a man and disregarding the character of his cloth – ordered his female slave to be flogged for overroasting a turkey.'[29]

The economic and pragmatic argument, that free labour would in the long run be more profitable than slavery, played an important part in the emancipation movement. Where self-interest can be shown to point in the same direction as considerations of morality and high principle, the argument for reform is strengthened:

> There must be some motive to actuate man. You now actuate him by the fear of the lash, and alas! by the infliction of it. Make him a freeman, and reward him for his labour, and you hold out to him the very motive which God has designed to actuate mankind – the hope of benefiting himself and improving his condition.[30]

[26] HC Deb., 16 March 1824, vol. 10, col. 1174.
[27] *Anti-Slavery Reporter* 5 (1832), 161.
[28] *Mirror of Parliament*, 15 April 1831, 1468b.
[29] Ibid., 1468a.
[30] 'Speech of Dr Lushington' (1831), 264.

As a practical abolitionist, Lushington did not hesitate to appeal to the economic self-interest of slave-owners, nor to combine the appeal with considerations of religion and principle: 'According to all the principles which God has given to govern man, the free spirit of the individual working for his own benefit will infinitely surpass the greatest exertion which the slave can make.'[31] Referring to his relatives' interest in slavery, he said that 'for their sakes he hoped that the emancipation of the negroes would be undertaken by the legislature of this country and steadily pursued'.[32] He spoke of the 'happiness and prosperity' in which the West Indies could not share 'so long as slavery continued'.[33] He verged at times on the visionary looking forward to 'the vindication of the rights of humanity, the promotion of commerce, and the establishment of eternal liberty over the whole earth'.[34]

It will be seen that Lushington usually combined religious arguments with secular considerations. As an advocate (though unpaid in this cause), he naturally adduced all arguments that he thought likely to persuade his audience. Religious references are somewhat more frequent in the speeches to anti-slavery audiences than they are in Parliament, but there are no arguments that do not appear in both forums. In a phrase that well illustrates the relation, in Lushington's mind, of religion and politics he wrote to Buxton that 'Providence works not by miracles in these matters but by human action.'[35]

There has been some debate among historians as to whether the abolition of slavery in 1833 was primarily caused by moral and religious principle or, on the other hand, by economic self-interest. Lushington would scarcely have accepted such a rigid distinction. Religious truth was not the less real because it was *also* reflected in moral, legal, humanitarian, economic and social considerations. On the contrary, Divine Providence worked 'not by miracles ... but by human action', and not only through individuals but also through the action of human communities – hence Lushington's simultaneous attachment both to reform and to the established Church of England. Stanley's measured words, quoted earlier, while chosen, no doubt, to conform to liberal opinion in 1873 of the relation of morality and religion (which Lushington might not have shared fifty years earlier), are still an appropriate tribute to Lushington's motives in the anti-slavery campaign: 'the firm persuasion of the indissoluble bond between what was highest in religion and what was greatest in morality'.

[31] Speech, in Johnson, *Anti-Slavery Convention*, 1843, 156.
[32] HC Deb., 24 May 1832, vol. 13, col. 80. [33] HC Deb., 3 August 1832, vol. 14, col. 1135.
[34] HC Deb., 7 June 1833, vol. 18, col. 491.
[35] Lushington to Buxton, 9 May 1839, Buxton Papers, 18, 92n.

JUDICIAL DECISIONS

Consistory Court

The ecclesiastical courts were sometimes called the 'spiritual' courts, but by the nineteenth century much of their business was spiritual in name only. There is little reference in probate cases, for example, to religious considerations. As for matrimonial cases, Lushington said, outside the court, that he considered them to belong to the temporal rather than to the spiritual side of the court's jurisdiction, adding, however, 'except insofar as the due regulation of those causes would tend to the support of morality or to the suppression of immorality'.[36] He did not hesitate to assert the common purposes of law, religion, morality and social policy. His theology did not embrace the notion of marriage as a sacrament, strictly speaking. Marriage was indissoluble (except by Act of Parliament) not because the Church of England in the nineteenth century regarded it as a sacrament, but because the pre-Reformation Church had done so and the law had not been altered. But he considered that marriage was 'by the settled law of all these courts and impugned by no other … an obligation co-existent with the lives of the parties'.[37] He referred to marriage as part of 'the evident design of Divine Providence',[38]and his judgments include other references to the divine purpose: 'Under any other circumstances [than the need to protect the wife from injury] the Court cannot put asunder those whom God has joined … Marriage is in this country considered of … sacred and binding force.'[39] He spoke of adultery as able to 'sever the strongest ties by which God and man can consecrate the marriage union'.[40] The formal decrees of the court had a medieval flavour:

> In the Name of God, Amen. We, Stephen Lushington … having first called upon God, and having him alone before our eyes … do pronounce … that … the said Eleanor Cochrane … being altogether unmindful of her conjugal vow, and not having the fear of God before her eyes but being instigated and seduced by the Devil did … commit the crime of adultery.[41]

In many of his decisions, Lushington showed himself very sympathetic to the interests of women, particularly in the enforcement of alimony payments. He

36 Report of Select Committee of the House of Lords on the Privy Council (1844), q. 218.

37 *Dysart v. Dysart* (1844) 3 Notes of Cases 324, 366.

38 *D—e v. A—g* (1845) 1 Rob Ecc 279, 298. 39 *Neeld v. Neeld* (1831) 4 Hagg Ecc 263, 265–6.

40 *Davidson v. Davidson* (1856) Deane 132, 151.

41 From sentence in *Cochrane v. Cochrane* (1831), London Metropolitan Archives, DL/C AC 7377 53/1.

could not, however, be plausibly described as any kind of proto-feminist. He was strict in keeping divorce for cruelty within very narrow bounds, and there is no sign of political support of women's rights. He accepted the prevailing opinion of the time as to the status of women generally, but he was strong for enforcement of rights of individuals (male and female) under existing law, and he thought that if there were to be any distinction, it should be in favour of 'the wife, as the weaker party'. His views sprang rather from a lawyer's sense of balance and fair process than from a reformer's desire to effect social change.

Defamation cases, like the matrimonial cases, had ancient language in their forms. Almost all the defamation cases in Lushington's time were complaints by women of imputations of unchastity. The libel (statement of claim) recited that all persons who utter words to the reproach, hurt or diminution of the good name, fame and reputation of any other person 'contrary to good manners and the bond of Christian charity' ought to be compelled to retract, and continued with an assertion that the defendant:

> not having the fear of God before his eyes, did ... in an angry, reproachful, and invidious manner ... defame the said Ann Mills ... who was and is a person of good name, fame, and reputation, and charged the said Ann Mills with having committed the foul crime of adultery, fornication or incontinency, and speaking of and meaning and intending the said Ann Mills ... said, affirmed and published several times, or at least once, these or the like words, 'You, thou, or she are, art, or is a whore' or words to that or the like effect, or of the same import and meaning.[42]

Where the case was successful, the order of the court was that the defendant should perform penance, which, in the nineteenth century, involved a formal apology in the church vestry in the presence of the promoter and a few friends if she wished:

> The said Benjamin Hall shall, on Sunday, the 17th day of July, 1831, immediately after Divine service and sermon are ended in the forenoon, come into the vestry room in the presence of the minister and churchwardens of the said parish, and likewise in the presence of Mary Ann King ... and five or six of her friends, if they be there, otherwise in their absence, and shall with an audible voice confess and say as follows: – Whereas I, Benjamin Hall, have uttered and spoken certain scandalous and opprobrious words of and against Mary Ann King ... to the great offence of Almighty God, the scandal of the Christian religion, and the injury and reproach of my neighbour's credit and reputation by calling her a whore; I therefore before God and you humbly confess and acknowledge such my offence, am heartily sorry for the same,

[42] From H. C. Coote, *Practice of the Ecclesiastical Courts* (London: Butterworth, 1847), 272–3.

> and do ask her forgiveness, and promise hereafter never to offend her in like manner, God assisting me.[43]

Though there is religious language in the court forms, there was little reference to religion in the argument or in the judicial reasons in defamation cases. The jurisdiction was widely considered to be obsolete by Lushington's time and was objectionable because it did sometimes lead to imprisonment for failure to obey the citation (summons), to perform the penance or to pay costs. In one of Lushington's defamation cases, the defendant refused to perform the penance and petitioned for release after spending twenty weeks in prison, saying that he did not know that he was liable to be imprisoned for speaking the truth.[44] The petition is marked in pencil, perhaps by the Registrar: 'Judge can do nothing – the penance must be performed.'[45] The Ecclesiastical Courts Commission, of which Lushington was the most active member, recommended abolition of this jurisdiction in 1833, and Lushington said in Parliament, probably referring to the case just mentioned:

> I am rejoiced to find that one of the provisions of the Bill takes such offences as defamation out of the Ecclesiastical Courts. It was only in the month of May last, that I was compelled, in the discharge of my duty, to send an individual to gaol for defamation. I had no option, consistently with a due observance of my oath, but to act in the manner I have mentioned; although I know not by what law parties, so imprisoned, can be liberated.[46]

The Bill did not pass and the defamation jurisdiction was not abolished until 1855.[47]

The ecclesiastical courts had jurisdiction to punish 'brawling and smiting in church', not such uncommon occurrences as might be supposed, since 'brawling' included all angry speech and 'church' included the vestry room where meetings were often held on contentious local issues. Charles Dickens, in *Sketches by Boz*, presents a satirical account of a brawling case in which the defendant is proved to have used the words 'you be blowed', for which he is excommunicated for two weeks and condemned in costs. One writer has identified the source of this case as one of Lushington's decisions, of which a note in Dickens' hand survives. In that case the defendant had said 'you are

43 Ibid.

44 The question of truth as a defence is discussed in R. Helmholz, *Select Cases on Defamation to 1600* (London: Selden Society, 1985), xxx–xxxii, and in S. Waddams, *Sexual Slander in Nineteenth-Century England: Defamation in the Ecclesiastical Courts, 1815–1855* (Toronto: University of Toronto Press, 2000), 33–9.

45 *Roberts v. Cornell* (1834) Guidhall Library MS 12185/3.

46 *Mirror of Parliament*, 12 March 1835, 309b.

47 Ecclesiastical Courts Act, 18 & 19 Vic c. 61.

a liar' and called the complainant 'a drunken churchwarden'. Another of Lushington's cases, where the reality is closer to the fiction, is one where the defendant said 'you are a wretch'.[48] Probably Dickens drew material from various sources. In both cases the sentence was suspension from entering the church for two weeks (not, strictly speaking, excommunication) which, as Dickens wryly pointed out, was scarcely likely to be an effective deterrent (though costs might be). The jurisdiction was abolished in 1860.

Four cases of incest were brought during Lushington's time as a judge in the Consistory Court. These cases were commonly brought in order to annul a marriage, not infrequently of a man with his deceased wife's sister (incestuous by ecclesiastical law, though increasingly tolerated by public opinion). The order of the court, if the case succeeded, was to declare the marriage void, require the parties to live apart and order the defendant to perform penance. This took a more rigorous form than penance for defamation, for it was required to be performed in the church 'whilst the greater part of the congregation shall be then assembled to see and hear the same'. In a case in which such an order was made, the defendants applied for a remission of the penance, with a medical certificate to the effect that (in the case of the male defendant) 'very disastrous consequences might result from his performing the prescribed penance' and (in the case of the female defendant) that 'she would be exposed to dangerous risk if the penance be carried into effect'. Lushington recognised the obsolete nature of penance:

> Whatever may have been the reasons for the performance of penance in former days, certainly they do not apply with equal force at the present time. The facts stated in the certificate . . . render it the imperative duty of the Court not to enforce this part of its sentence, at least at the present time.[49]

He went on to remit the penance altogether, on the ground that suspending it for an indefinite period 'would be almost as detrimental as the actual performance of it'.

Church Rates

The church rate was a tax, primarily for the maintenance of the nave of the parish church, which all residents of the parish were obliged to pay. It had existed from the thirteenth century, and perhaps longer. It was said to have

[48] *North and Little v. Dickson* (1828) 1 Hagg Ecc 730.

[49] *Office of the Judge promoted by Chick v. Ramsdale and Chick, falsely called Ramsdale* (1835) 1 Curt 34, 37.

been described as early as 1370 as 'a custom from time immemorial'.[50] New trends in political and religious thought in the nineteenth century made a challenge inevitable; church rates were the principal grievance of the Dissenters in the forty-year period between the substantial repeal of the Test and Corporation Acts in 1828 and the ultimate abolition of compulsory rates in 1868.

Lushington was involved in the controversy both as a member of Parliament and as an ecclesiastical court judge. In Parliament, Lushington spoke against church rates on the ground that dissent should be unfettered: '[O]n all matters of religion a man must decide for himself.' To the argument that the abolition of the rate would weaken the Church of England, Lushington said that, on the contrary, the Church would be strengthened by the removal of just causes of complaint against it: 'unless the abuses of the Church were remedied it must be undermined and would fall'. If the Church were not reformed, it would be laid 'bare to the obloquy of the public'. He warned prophetically of the dangers of elitism:

> The Church of England ought to be a national Church, it ought to strive to gather around it the hearts and the respect of the people: the fact however was notorious that it had lived too long in the smiles of the rich and landed gentry, whilst it had been daily losing ground amongst the middle classes of society. Whilst it retained the nobility of the land in its ranks it was satisfied: let it take care that even these did not drop off from it by degrees ... The Church of England was like a besieged city; whilst its garrison was staunch and strong it might defy the enemy, but eventually, as the number of its assailants increased, and the courage and unanimity of its defenders began to flag, it must be subverted.[51]

In his last Parliamentary speech on the subject, Lushington said that the settlement of the question, 'so far from injuring, would benefit the church, in proportion as it tended to uphold it in the opinion, and affections, of the people'.[52] Whether the abolition of the rate was likely to strengthen the Church of England, or whether it did so in 1868, may be debatable, but the attraction of this line of thinking to a politically liberal member of the Church of England is clear: it enabled community interests, the interests of the Church of England and liberal political principles to coincide.

The opponents of the rate turned to civil disobedience by refusing to pay the rate or to recognise the authority of the ecclesiastical court. In 1838 John Thorogood was assessed for a small amount (5s. 6d.). Ordinarily enforcement

[50] See *Veley v. Burder* (1841) 12 Ad & Ecc. 265, 302.

[51] HC Deb., 14 March 1837, vol. 37, cols. 380–1. [52] HC Deb., 25 May 1841, vol. 68, col. 797.

of such a small claim would not have come before the Consistory Court, but Thorogood, in order to create a direct confrontation with the ecclesiastical court, certified that he intended to dispute the validity of the rate. He then refused to comply with the citation (summons to appear), thereby putting himself in contempt of court. Lushington, as judge of the Consistory Court, and still a member of Parliament at this date, certified that he was in contempt, and Thorogood was imprisoned until his contempt should be 'purged', that is until he should agree to recognise the authority of the court. But this was just what Thorogood refused to do, and he called on his friends not to pay the rate on his behalf, saying that he counted his life as nothing 'compared to the idolatry of paying to what I believe a most unchristian church'. This created an impasse because Lushington held that he had no power to release a person committed for contempt until the contempt was purged. Since Thorogood staunchly declared that he would never submit, it looked as though he might be imprisoned for life for failure to pay 5/6. Eventually, in August 1840, a special Act of Parliament was passed empowering the judge to release a person after six months' imprisonment even though his contempt had not been purged, and in November 1840, after Thorogood had spent nearly two years in prison, Lushington ordered his release pursuant to the statute.

It was in one sense ironic that it should have been Lushington, one of the principal opponents of church rates in the House of Commons, who was the instrument of Thorogood's imprisonment, though it might be said that, since these events contributed to the ultimate abolition of church rates, Lushington had played a part (though not one that he had chosen) in the political movement which he supported. He defended his conduct on the grounds that Thorogood had deliberately put himself in contempt and that Lushington was bound to uphold the authority of the court.

The opponents of the rate then turned to another line of attack by testing key legal questions in the courts. This led to two notorious cases (the *Braintree* cases) litigated in eight courts over a period of sixteen years. Rates were made at vestry meetings in each parish, and the question at issue in the *Braintree* cases was whether a valid rate could be made if the majority at a vestry meeting voted against it (an outcome that the opponents of the rate could now secure in several parishes). In the first case, Lushington held the rate valid on the ground that he was strictly bound to follow an obscure decision of the Arches Court in 1799, of which Lushington said that 'during the thirty years that I have been in this court I never heard the case adverted to, nor was I aware that such a case was in existence, till very lately'. He gave his decision immediately, without taking time for consideration, which suggests that he was not unhappy to find a reason for allowing the matter to be determined in a higher court: 'I think, that upon a question of such great importance, and which I suppose, from what fell in the course of argument, will be carried to another tribunal, it would be better that it should go there in no way affected by my judgment, in one way or the other.' The case then went to the Queen's Bench, which rejected the 1799 case and issued a prohibition, and then to the Court of Exchequer Chamber, which dismissed the appeal but suggested that the rate might have been valid if it had been made not by the wardens alone (as in the first case) but by the minority at a duly constituted vestry meeting.

This suggestion was tested in the second *Braintree* case. Lushington rejected it, pointing out in forceful terms the anomaly of summoning a meeting and then ignoring its decision:

> If this new doctrine be the law, it is a matter to me of extreme wonderment, that in the usage of centuries, when so many cases must have called for its application, when so many powerful minds have dedicated to the question their learning and ingenuity, it should first have been discovered in the year 1841.[53]

The case then went on appeal to the Arches Court, where Lushington's decision was reversed. The Arches decision was upheld in the Queen's Bench and in the Exchequer Chamber, but Lushington's decision was restored by the House of Lords. All the judges were summoned to give their opinion to the House of Lords; ten attended, dividing five to five. In the end, after fifteen separate judgments had been given by nineteen judges (not to mention the judgments in three courts in the first case) the issue was – according to the bizarre appellate practice of the House of Lords – decided by two members of the House (Lords Truro and Brougham), one of whom (Lord Truro) had dissented in the court below, both retired Whig politicians and both, as it happens, former close associates of Lushington and fellow counsel with him in the defence of Queen Caroline in 1820.

Church rates continued to be a fruitful source of litigation until their abolition in 1868. During the nine years during which Lushington sat as Dean of the Arches (1858–67) church rate cases formed the largest class of cases in the court (probate, matrimonial and defamation litigation having then ceased). Most of Lushington's reported decisions were in favour of church-wardens, suggesting that he was doing his best at this stage to adhere to the principle of setting aside his personal opinion and administering the law as he found it. His opposite decisions in the two *Braintree* cases, however, show that this is not a simple or mechanical task. His varying roles in this prolonged controversy demonstrate the interaction of law, religion and politics. Church

53 *Veley v. Gosling* (1842) 3 Curt 253, 301–2.

rates were seen, by both sides, as a test of whether the national Church could impose burdens on the whole population. In the end the burden proved intolerable to the liberal and individualistic spirit of the time. Lushington might be thought to have been predisposed, both by personal attachment and by professional connections, to favour the Established Church. Yet the force of political liberalism prevailed in his mind, as, ultimately, it did in the national polity.

Gorham

The *Gorham* case involved a fierce controversy about the theology of baptism, the Christian rite of initiation. The dispute was essentially between a Catholic and a Protestant view of the sacrament. There were many shades of opinion on both sides of this controversy, but its general nature can be sufficiently indicated by saying that the Catholic view tended to emphasise the objective effect of the ceremony duly administered, whereas the Protestant view tended to insist on the need for faith on the part of the recipient (afterwards, in the case of infant baptism), or emphasised the autonomy of God's grace, independent of human acts. The case was perceived to have important effects for the Church of England, and the public interest was enormous. More than 140 pamphlets were published. Dire consequences were anticipated regardless of the outcome: if Gorham lost, the evangelicals would be driven out of the Church; if he won, widespread defections to Rome were predicted. The final decision of the Privy Council did in fact lead to the exodus from the Church of England of many Anglo-Catholics, the most prominent of whom was Archdeacon (later Cardinal) Henry Manning.

Gorham, a clergyman of forty years' standing and a holder of Protestant views, had incurred the displeasure of his bishop (Phillpotts, of Exeter) by (among other things) advertising for a curate who should be 'free from Tractarian error'. When, in 1847, Gorham was presented to another benefice in the same diocese, Phillpotts refused to institute him without an examination of the soundness of his view of baptism. The Canons of 1603 entitled the bishop to examine those presented to benefices, but extensive examinations were highly unusual, especially in the case of a clergyman of Gorham's age and standing. Gorham hinted that he had a right to be instituted, but Phillpotts was an aggressive litigant, caricatured by Trollope as a pugnacious schoolboy who would continue to fight even when he had no leg to stand on.[54] The bishop's examination lasted for fifty-two hours over eight days and

[54] A Trollope, *The Warden*, ch. 8.

involved Gorham's written answers to 149 questions – an examination, as Sir John Baker has remarked, that Gorham was doubtless intended to fail.[55] The bishop, predictably, found Gorham's theology wanting and refused to institute him. Gorham commenced proceedings against the bishop in the Court of the Arches. So rare were such cases that 'for some time no precedent could be found for the forms of pleading', but at last one was discovered in a proctor's office. Gorham failed in the Arches Court but appealed successfully to the Judicial Committee of the Privy Council. Lushington sat as a member of the Judicial Committee. He was the only civilian member of the committee and so the only member with a professional expertise in ecclesiastical law. The Dean of the Arches (Jenner Fust), who gave the judgment in favour of the bishop at first instance, indicated that he would himself have sought Lushington's assistance had it not been anticipated that he would be hearing the appeal.

The extensive nature of the theological arguments addressed to the courts was extraordinary. The arguments before the Privy Council took four days and occupy 277 pages in Moore's report. The nature of the question in issue might be said, without offence to either side, to be inherently mysterious, and Gorham had carefully avoided, in his examination, any statements that conflicted on their face with the official formularies. It is not surprising that the Privy Council sought to decide the case on grounds other than theological. Greville, the clerk of the Privy Council, records that when, at a conference of the judges after argument, the Bishop of London (present during argument but not an actual member of the Committee) said he hoped that the judgment would not condemn Phillpotts' doctrine,

> they all exclaimed that they would take care that nothing of the kind was done; they would steer as clear as possible of any declaration as to doctrine, and found their judgment on this, that it had not been proved to them that Gorham had put forth any doctrine so clearly and undoubtedly at variance with the Articles and formularies as to warrant the bishop's refusal to induct him.[56]

At the end of the judgment, Lord Langdale said that 'the case not requiring it, we have abstained from expressing any opinion of our own upon the theological correctness or error of the doctrine held by Mr Gorham, which was discussed before us at such great length and with so much learning'.

55 J. H. Baker, *Monuments of Endlesse Labours* (London: Hambledon Press, 1998), 137.

56 L. Strachey and R. Fulford, eds., *The Greville Memoirs*, 8 vols. (London: Macmillan & Co., 1938), 6:193.

Lushington was influential. Greville records that, at the judicial conference,

> Lushington said he had written out his opinion, but had not brought his paper with him. He made, however, a short speech, very good indeed, in which he pronounced a strong opinion against the bishop, commenting in severe terms upon the nature of the examination, and setting forth the great danger to the peace of the Church which would result from a judicial declaration on their part that Gorham's opinions were clearly proved to be heretical.

This suggests that, in the privacy of the judicial conference room, Lushington did not think first of a strict and neutral interpretation of words, but paid primary attention to what he perceived to be the likely practical consequences of upholding Jenner Fust's decision, which was that many respectable clergymen, holding views that had been perfectly acceptable within the Church of England for 300 years, would be subjected to an Anglo-Catholic witch-hunt. For Lushington to set aside his own theological inclinations on an issue of this sort was more easily said than done.

Denison

A few years later, Lushington was called upon to consider the other principal sacrament of the Church of England, called, in the Articles, the Supper of the Lord. Bread and wine consumed by the faithful represented, in some sense, the body and blood of Christ. But in what sense? This was an issue that had divided Catholics and Protestants for centuries and, in the sixteenth century, had been a matter of life and death. As with baptism there were various shades of Catholic and Protestant opinion. In general, the Catholic view stressed the objective operation of the sacrament, while the Protestant view emphasised the faith of the recipient and the overriding unfettered nature of God's gift of grace.

The Articles, drawn up in the sixteenth century to accommodate a variety of views, were, not surprisingly, ambiguous in respect of both sacraments. Though Protestant in tone, they stopped short of condemning unequivocally an objective view of the sacraments. The Article at issue in the *Denison* case, entitled 'Of the wicked which eat not the body of Christ in the use of the Lord's Supper', read:

> The wicked, and such as be void of a lively faith, although they do carnally and visibly press with their teeth (as Saint Augustine saith) the Sacrament of the Body and Blood of Christ, yet in no wise are they partakers of Christ: but rather, to their condemnation, do eat and drink the sign or sacrament of so great a thing.

George Anthony Denison was an aggressive Anglo-Catholic, who, along with Manning and others, had signed a protest against the decision of the Privy

Council in the *Gorham* case. Unlike Manning, Denison remained to fight his battles within the Church of England. In 1852, acting as examining chaplain to the Bishop of Bath and Wells, Denison had insisted that ordinands should assent to the proposition that an unfaithful communicant would, despite lack of faith, truly receive the body and blood of Christ.

Not surprisingly, objections were raised to Denison's conduct and his opponents were alerted. He repeated his views in a series of sermons preached in Wells Cathedral, and legal proceedings were instituted by an evangelical clergyman, Ditcher. Because Denison's bishop also happened to be the patron of his living (and therefore might be supposed to have an interest in causing a vacancy), the archbishop (Sumner) was designated as the proper person to hear the case. Lushington sat with him in hearings in Bath, nominally as assessor, but in reality in a judicial role.

Unlike Gorham, Denison had made no effort to reconcile his statements with the wording of the Articles, and Lushington delivered a judgment condemning Denison and depriving him of his benefice. Unlike the *Gorham* case, which was permissive, the decision in the *Denison* case was exclusory in that, if the decision stood, clergy expressing Denison's views could be driven out of the Church. Public interest in the case was considerable. Trollope, as an indication that his heroine, Eleanor, has some sympathy with Anglo-Catholic opinion, wrote that 'she sent a handsome subscription toward certain very heavy legal expenses which had lately been incurred at Bath',[57] the indirect allusion evidently being thought sufficient indication for his readers.

Lushington's decision was very harshly criticised by commentators sympathetic with the Anglo-Catholic position. It was eventually reversed on a technicality (that the proceedings were brought too late). Lushington himself said that his task was simply to compare the words used by Denison with the terms of the relevant Article: '[T]his tribunal is a court of justice and of ecclesiastical law, not a school of theology, and, as a court of justice, bound to administer the law as we find it.' The suggestions that Lushington was guilty of crude bias or impropriety can be rebutted, but it would be harder to show that his interpretation of the Article, and his certainty that the words were clearly incompatible with Denison's view, could have been wholly dissociated from Lushington's own assumptions about the Church of England.

Other Decisions of Theological Significance

Lushington had to make various other decisions on controversial matters, including the practice of confession, ceremonial and church ornaments.

[57] A. Trollope, *Barchester Towers*, ch. 53.

In these cases, as in the *Denison* case, he stated his intention to act strictly in a judicial capacity and to set aside his own religious opinions: 'my present task is ... to institute a dry and tedious inquiry into doubtful propositions of positive law',[58] but the decisions – and the reasons given for them – demonstrate a marked lack of sympathy with the Anglo-Catholic perspective. 'What is this', he asked rhetorically, referring to the practice of changing the colours of altar coverings according to the liturgical seasons, 'but a servile imitation of the Church of Rome?'[59] In the important case of *Essays and Reviews*, mentioned at the beginning of this chapter, Lushington was called upon to determine the scope that would be allowed in the Church of England to liberal theological thought. His decision, condemning two of the contributors to *Essays and Reviews*, was reversed by the Privy Council, whose judgment established a wide freedom of thought and expression for liberal theological opinion and opened the door to virtually unrestricted scope for academic theology. As mentioned earlier, Lushington's journey to Oxford at the age of nearly ninety-one in order to vote in favour of Stanley (Dean of Westminster and *doyen* of theological liberalism) may suggest that Lushington had modified his views since his decision in the *Essays and Reviews* case. Overall, it cannot be said that Lushington's theological decisions were free of the influence of his own opinions, but it is not realistic, given his religious background, to suppose that they could be, for it is doubtful that perfect neutrality on questions of high religious and political controversy, even if desirable, is attainable.

OCKHAM

For the last twenty-six years of his life, Lushington resided in the village of Ockham in Surrey, occupying the principal house, Ockham Park, owned by Lord Lovelace, son-in-law of Lady Byron. The distinguished theologian F. D. Maurice, temporarily performing clerical duties at Ockham, wrote that 'the squire is Dr Lushington, the freshest and heartiest as well as the kindest of old gentlemen. His family has been all that we could desire for friendliness and parish activity.' On the marriage of Lushington's son, Vernon, in 1865, the poor of the village received gifts of food and clothing.

58 A. F. Bayford, ed., *The Judgment of the Right Honourable Stephen Lushington ... in the Cases of Westerton against Liddell* (London: Butterworths, 1855), 10.

59 Ibid., 59. Setting aside the disparaging adjective and the indignant tone of the question, Lushington was, as a matter of liturgical history, correct, but the practice was not expressly prohibited by the canon in question. Lushington was upheld by the Arches Court but summarily reversed on this point by the Privy Council.

There is other evidence of Lushington's sense of duty to the poor of the village, and of the link between duty and religion. In 1856 he wrote to his daughter, 'You have now sole charge of Ockham. Should the weather continue severe remember you have the command of my purse & God has blessed me with great prosperity & I ought not to be niggardly.'[60] In 1867 he wrote, to another of his daughters:

> I fear the poor must suffer. You will, I doubt not, do all you can to mitigate their suffering. What say you to ordering a supply of *soup*? ... If this frost should last I fear for our poor people. What think you of asking Mr Onslow[61] *in our absence in urgent* cases to give relief at my expense? Use your own discretion in this matter.[62]

These letters show that Lushington's concern for the poor sprang from genuine concern, that it was linked with his religious beliefs and that it was far more than a perfunctory performance of the duties of a village squire. He also established a convalescent hospital in the grounds of Ockham Park.

CONCLUSION

Ecclesiastical court judges were required, by one of the Canons of 1603, to be 'zealously bent to religion'.[63] It is doubtful that religious zeal was much valued in the Doctors' Commons of the nineteenth century, the proceedings of which Dickens, who had been a shorthand reporter there, described as a 'cosey, dosey, old-fashioned, time forgotten, sleepy headed little family party'.[64] Yet Lushington was certainly influenced, at many points in his career, public and private, by his religious views. More than any other judge of his time – perhaps of any time – he was called upon to determine disputes on varied points of acute religious controversy. Here he sought to set aside his own religious opinions, portraying his role as strictly judicial rather than theological, but he did not entirely succeed in this objective. In the campaign against slavery, on the other hand, religious considerations were openly and often avowed, and there, as in Lushington's private life, it cannot be doubted that they motivated his actions.

60 Lushington to Alice Lushington, 3 December 1856, Lushington Papers, 7854/1/8/8.

61 Probably Pitcairn Onslow, Justice of the Peace, occupying a large property in the adjacent village of Ripley (*Debrett's Peerage* [1884], s.n. Onslow). There was a distant family connection, Lushington's sister having married an Onslow in 1800 (Debrett's *Baronetage of England* [1835], s.n. Lushington).

62 Lushington to Fanny Lushington, 13 January 1867. Lushington Papers, 7854/1/7/40a–c (punctuation added).

63 Canon 127 (1603).

64 C. Dickens, *David Copperfield*, ch. 23.

Portrait of Roundell Palmer / Universal History Archive / UIG / Bridgeman Images

13

Roundell Palmer, Earl of Selborne

Charlotte Smith

INTRODUCTION

Born in 1812 to the Reverend William Jocelyn Palmer, Rector of Mixbury and Finmere in Oxfordshire, and Dorothea Richardson, Roundell Palmer, first Earl of Selborne, was the son of a typical English country rectory. His family had both landed and mercantile wealth and standing, and possessed impeccable and extensive connections within the Anglican ecclesiastical establishment. His subsequent life and career exemplified the values of public service, professional and political prowess as a lawyer and statesman, and deep personal piety and faith.

This chapter makes no attempt to chart in detail the twists and turns of Selborne's long life on the public stage. Others, including Selborne himself in his voluminous and discursive *Memorials*, have already performed that task.[1] Instead, it seeks to explore key aspects of Selborne's faith, his spiritual life and his churchmanship. It sets out to examine how these impacted upon his legal and political career and legacy. Most importantly, it analyses the contribution which Selborne, through his public standing, his reputation and his personal commitment, made to attempts to defend, to rearticulate and to reimagine the constitutional position and role of the Church of England in the high Victorian period. In doing so it reveals a man whose life and faith reflected much of the theological, social and political maelstrom of his time and of the personal and individual

[1] Roundell Palmer, first Earl of Selborne, *Memorials. Part I: Family and Personal, 1766–1865*, ed. S. M. Palmer, 2 vols. (London: MacMillan and Co., 1896); Roundell Palmer, first Earl of Selborne, *Memorials. Part II: Personal and Political, 1865–1895*, ed. S. M. Palmer, 2 vols. (London: Macmillan and Co.,1898); David Steele, 'Palmer, Roundell, First Earl of Selborne (1812–1895)', *Oxford Dictionary of National Biography*, Oxford University Press, 2004; online edn, January 2008, www.oxforddnb.com.idpproxy.reading.ac.uk/view/article/21210, accessed 3 January 2016; Edmund Heward, *A Victorian Law Reformer: A Life of Lord Selborne* (Chichester: Barry Rose Law Publishers Ltd, 1997). All biographical details are derived from these sources.

experiences of those who lived through it.[2] It illuminates the figure of a man who was, in every meaningful sense, one of the great Christian jurists of his age.

This is a claim made for Selborne, not on the basis that he caused his faith to determine the direction of specific legal judgments, but because he steadfastly and self-consciously stood firm against any tendency or temptation to confine his faith to the private sphere. It was, it will be argued, from the very public and sacrificial living out of his faith, as well as from his very real professional acumen, that his greatest legacy as a Christian jurist was derived.

SELBORNE'S LEGAL AND POLITICAL CAREER

Having been educated successively at Rugby, Winchester and Trinity College Oxford, where he gained high honours, Roundell Palmer was elected to a fellowship at Magdalen, which he held from 1834 until 1848. He became a member of Lincoln's Inn in 1836, intending, as his father had planned for him, to pursue a career at the Chancery Bar. This course, commencing as it did with a year's pupillage in conveyancing chambers and a further period learning the skills of an equity draftsman, caused him later to remark that '[t]he descent, from the flowers of history, poetry, and philosophy, to those dry bones of technical systems, and especially to the dull copying-clerk's work and mechanical processes of conveyancing, was dispiriting enough'.[3] Like many men in his position, he initially struggled to make his way at the bar but, through the kind offices of his uncle, a leading figure in the city and the Bank of England, he secured a number of briefs from Freshfields, solicitors to the Bank of England. From those beginnings his reputation and business grew slowly but surely, so that by 1843 he had sufficient income to accede to his father's urging to cease writing leaders for *The Times*.

Like other men of the law before and since, Selborne soon came to combine his legal practice with membership of the House of Commons, setting himself upon the path which saw him attain the highest offices of his profession. Sitting first as a Peelite and then as a Liberal, Selborne first entered the House of Commons as the member for Plymouth in 1847. Having lost that seat in the general election of 1852, he regained it in a by-election in 1853 and held it until 1859. He then had a spell out of Parliament before accepting the safe seat of Richmond in Yorkshire, along with the office of Solicitor General in

[2] The best-known and most accessible account of these is provided by Owen Chadwick, *The Victorian Church: Part I, 1829–1859* (London: A. and C. Black, 1966) and *Part II, 1860–1901* (London: A. and C. Black, 1970). See also Frances Knight, *The Nineteenth Century Church and Society* (Cambridge: Cambridge University Press, 1995).

[3] Selborne, *Memorials I*, 1: 199–200.

Palmerston's second administration, in June 1861. Thus began his ascent to the height of his profession. He was knighted on 5 August 1861 and transferred to the more senior office of Attorney General in October 1863. Though he later broke with him over Irish Home Rule,[4] Selborne was at this time, as for much of his career, an ardent disciple of William Gladstone, and his political fortunes mirrored those of that great statesman. Having taken a prominent role in the arbitrations which followed the end of the American Civil War, Selborne followed Lord Hatherley as Lord Chancellor under Gladstone between 15 October 1872 and 17 February 1874. He was then out of office for six years before resuming the office of Lord Chancellor under Gladstone's second administration, between 28 April 1880 and 9 June 1885. He was promoted to an earldom on 29 December 1882, on the opening of the Royal Courts of Justice on the Strand, towards the building of which he had made a decisive contribution.

It is as a statesman that Selborne is probably best known today – a view of him reinforced by his intense political activism in opposition to Irish Home Rule and Disestablishment. Yet Selborne himself, despite his initial lack of enthusiasm for the mundanities of legal practice, clearly identified himself as a lawyer and saw this as being his calling. So, for example, in explaining why he did not challenge Gladstone for the Liberal leadership in 1867, he identified not only ties of friendship to Gladstone and a sense of unworthiness as precluding this, but also the claims of his profession – saying that this was 'too plainly a real vocation to be give way to any other, without some very urgent cause'.[5]

It is obvious, too, that he was held in great esteem as a lawyer by his contemporaries. Upon his first appointment to the woolsack, *The Times* opined that '[p]robably no man better qualified by gifts of intellect and character, by legal attainments and by political expertise has ever filled that high office'.[6] Some allowance might be made for a tendency towards hyperbole or an excess of enthusiasm, but *The Times'* conviction of Selborne's skills and standing as a lawyer was consistent, and untarnished by the passage of time. Upon his return to the woolsack in 1880, it reported:

> Lord Selborne's return to the Lord Chancellorship will give general satisfaction. In none of the other lawyers who were in any way eligible for the office would the public repose so much confidence as they will in him. He quitted the bar with an almost unequalled reputation for ability and industry. He was

[4] Selborne to Gladstone (22 January 1886), Lambeth Palace Library [hereafter LPL], MS 1869, ff. 139–41.

[5] Selborne, *Memorials II*, 2: 160–2.

[6] *The Times*, 6 October 1872, 9.

> not sufficiently long as Lord Chancellor to satisfy as a Judge the expectations formed of him ... But during the short time he sat on the wool sack he did excellent work as a law reformer.[7]

Similarly, in a leader on the death of Lord Cairns, *The Times* described Selborne as being pre-eminent among the leaders of the Chancery Bar and the statesmen of the time.[8]

Upon his death it was evident that, despite his growing partisanship and absorption into the world of the statesman, Selborne had continued to be held in affection and esteem by his legal brethren. They spoke consistently of his courtesy and sense of honour, and repeatedly identified him as being in the first rank of Chancery lawyers. So, for example, Lord Davey wrote of him:

> Palmer's mind was as quick and acute as that of either of his great competitors [Rolt and Cairns]. He had, I think, an even greater knowledge of case law and greater subtlety. If he could not meet his opponent's arguments on principle or authority in front, he had an extraordinary power of subtle distinction and refinement which enabled him to walk around the argument and attack it, as it were, on flank.[9]

However, while his claims to greatness as a practitioner were universally acknowledged, even his greatest admirers admitted that he had been, though solid and consistent, somewhat less successful as a judge. Thus, *The Times*, in its obituary repeated a remark of Lord Westbury to the effect that his reasoning was 'impaired' by his inability to "get rid of the habit" of pursuing a fine train of thought on matters collateral to the main issues before him'.[10] This was a habit which it ascribed to both the strength of his intellect and its development in the Oxford of Newman and of Gladstone. It nevertheless gave rise to unnecessarily complex and involved judgments; or, as Lord Herschell more kindly put it, he 'used his utmost endeavours to arrive at a right conclusion, and his judgments are as remarkable for their thoroughness and solidity as for the clearness of their expression'.[11]

Yet it is neither to his skills and learning as an advocate, nor as a judge, which Selborne's claims to legal greatness are best ascribed. Rather, it is to Selborne as a law reformer that we owe the greatest debt. Having played a decisive part in the deliberations and work of the first Judicature Commission of 1867, building on the efforts of his predecessors and mobilising the forces of the leaders of his profession, he succeeded where Lord Hatherley had failed. In 1873 he successfully piloted the Supreme Court of Judicature

[7] *The Times*, 29 April 1880, 11. [8] *The Times*, 3 April 1885, 7.
[9] Selborne, *Memorials II*, 2: 441. [10] *The Times*, 6 May 1895, 9.
[11] *The Times*, 8 May 1895, 9.

Act through Parliament. Though he ultimately failed in his efforts to abolish the Judicial Committee of the House of Lords or to rid the English legal system of the inconveniences of two layers of appeals (these sections of the Judicature Act were initially suspended and then repealed by the Appellate Jurisdiction Act 1876), the 1873 act succeeded in sweeping away the jurisdictional and procedural clutter of ages, leaving in its place a system of judicature which remains to a large extent familiar to the modern lawyer. It was in this act, which he claimed as being largely the work of his own hand and which he succeeded in getting through Parliament substantially unscathed, that Selborne saw his greatest legacy as a lawyer. Of it he wrote, 'If I leave any monument behind me which will bear the test of time, it may be this.'[12] It was a legacy bolstered and reinforced by the successful scheme, of which he was one of the most active proponents, to concentrate all of the courts within one purpose-built building, the Royal Courts of Justice on the Strand.[13]

If the Judicature Act 1873 was Selborne's greatest tangible contribution to the English legal system, then so too did it mark probably his most decisive contribution to the enduring perplexities surrounding the appellate jurisdiction of the Church of England. For during the course of its passage his interests as a churchman and as a reforming lawyer collided. It was a collision which he resolved with characteristic pragmatism. Just as he advocated the Strand as the site of the new Royal Courts of Justice because it was equidistant between Lincoln's Inn and the Temple; just as he advocated the creation of a university of law in London and the unification of the education of barristers and solicitors as being the most expedient and useful course; in 1873 he brokered a settlement regarding ecclesiastical appeals prompted rather less by personal conviction or ideology than by the pressing need to avert the potential ship wreck of his bill upon the shoals of ecclesiastical controversy.[14]

In 1873, as for several decades before, the question of ecclesiastical appellate jurisdiction was a vexed one. Lord Brougham's Privy Council Appeals Act 1832 had transferred ecclesiastical appeals from the High Court of Delegates, the mixed court of civilians, common lawyers and (in theory) bishops to which appeals to Rome had been transferred at the Reformation, to the Judicial Committee of the Privy Council in the last resort. The act made no legal provision for the representation of bishops on the panel of a court composed entirely of laymen and lawyers, though by convention the president of the

12 Selborne, *Memorials II*, 2: 300. 13 Lord Herschell in *The Times*, 8 May 1895, 9.

14 On this aspect of the bill's history, see C. L. Smith, 'The Quest for an Authoritative Court of Final Appeal in Ecclesiastical Causes: A Study of the Difficulties, c. 1830–1876', *Journal of Legal History* 32 (2011): 189–213.

Council was to appoint one or more episcopal privy councillors to act as assessors to advise the court on theological issues. This situation was remedied to some extent by the Church Discipline Act 1840, section 16 of which provided that in appeals brought under it at least one bishop was to sit as a judge. However that provision did not apply to appeals brought by other means. In an era which witnessed the advent of a number of theologically contentious appeals, an increase in the partisan spirit within the Church of England and strident calls from some within its High Church community for the Church to stand firm upon its claims to spiritual authority, the substitution by act of Parliament for the mixed court of the Reformation with one having potentially no ecclesiastical element was profoundly unsatisfactory and problematic. No easy remedy was, however, to be found. Divisions within the Church itself ensured an enduring lack of consensus regarding the authority upon which the court of final ecclesiastical appeal should be based, and also as to the nature of its work and thus the necessary attributes of its judges.

Selborne was fully awake to these controversies and, though he himself had in the past sought to achieve reform of the final court of ecclesiastical appeal,[15] he initially resolved to exclude their treatment from the scope of the 1873 bill.[16] His hand was forced, though, when the Conservative front bencher Gathorne Hardy introduced an amendment by which ecclesiastical appeals were to be transferred to Selborne's newly formulated court of appeal for secular causes. Gladstone, a committed High Churchman who was personally in sympathy with it, swiftly threw the weight of the government's support behind Hardy's amendment.[17] This placed Selborne upon the horns of a dilemma. Not only was there some suspicion that the amendment was a ploy to enable High Church litigants to deny the authority of a purely lay and secular court of appeal, but Archbishop Tait of Canterbury was as implacably opposed to it as Gladstone was in favour.[18] Selborne perceived that his major law reform bill, beset as it already was by opposition from elements of the Chancery Bar and by controversies surrounding the appellate jurisdiction of the House of Lords, was in grave peril.

His solution was of the sort which characterised his consistent approach in navigating the currents of the turbulent relationship between Church and state. In short, he acted as any common sense lawyer and statesman would

15 Selborne, *Memorials I*, 2: 64–84.

16 HL Deb., 13 February 1873, vol. 214, cols. 357–8.

17 See HL Deb., 4 July 1873, vol. 216, cols. 1793–4; Gladstone to Tait, 4 July 1873, LPL, MS 1866, ff. 3–4. Selborne had previously stated, in response to a similar proposal by Lord Salisbury, that the government had no objection to the inclusion of such a provision if it was shown to have the support of the House: HL Deb., 11 March 1873, vol. 214, cols 1737–8.

18 Tait to Gathorne Hardy, 7 July 1873, LPL, Tait 92, ff. 186–7; Tait to Gladstone, 5 July 1873, LPL, Tait 92, ff. 178–9.

have done and formulated a compromise amendment to which Archbishop Tait, Gladstone and the House could agree.[19] Thus he provided that his Court of Appeal would be assisted in ecclesiastical appeals, at its discretion, by three episcopal assessors. This formulation of the final court of ecclesiastical appeal was retained by the Appellate Jurisdiction Act 1876, which, with almost no debate upon the issue, confirmed the jurisdiction of the Judicial Committee of the Privy Council in ecclesiastical causes.[20]

SELBORNE AS CHRISTIAN, CHURCHMAN AND LAWYER

Selborne's role in formulating the court of final ecclesiastical appeal provides us with a link between his life and legacy as a lawyer and his life and legacy as a Christian and churchman.

There can be no doubt that, by virtue of his birth, education, social and professional standing, Lord Selborne possessed all of the trappings and attributes of a great churchman of his era. He was born the son of a well-respected and devoted country clergyman who he himself described as being 'one of the best examples of an English Churchman of the old school',[21] and who was a deeply influential figure throughout his life. Three of his brothers took orders within the Church of England, and his wider family included a number of eminent clergymen. Following his school days at Rugby and Winchester, his career at Oxford served only to deepen his faith, his political and religious interests and his ties to the political and ecclesiastical establishments. In his time there he nurtured enduring friendships with men, such as Gladstone and Cardwell, who would go on to become eminent statesmen. So, too, he rubbed shoulders with men such as Archibald Tait, who would later become Bishop of London and Archbishop of Canterbury. No less importantly, he became close friends with many of the same High Churchmen, such as F. W. Faber and W. G. Ward, whose life and faith in the Church of England would be so disastrously shaken by the theological controversies which beset the Church in the first half of the nineteenth century. Such men, along with one of his own brothers, were among the many who ultimately seceded from the Church of England and found their spiritual home in the Church of Rome.

19 Selborne to Cairns, 23 July 1873, The National Archives, Public Record Office [hereafter TNA, PRO], 30/51/9 ff. 92–3; Selborne to Tait, 23 July 1873, LPL, Tait 92, ff. 213–14.

20 The jurisdiction, though arcane, is not yet entirely obsolete: in 2015 two cross-petitions were lodged for leave to appeal to the Judicial Committee of the Privy Council from the Court of Arches exercising the faculty jurisdiction. Both were refused: see *Victorian Society v. Dennard and another*, case nos. JCPC 2015/0049 and JCPC 2015/0052.

21 Selborne, *Memorials I*, 1: 207.

Selborne's time at Oxford as an undergraduate, and his continuing ties to it as a fellow of Magdalen until 1848, were decisive forces in shaping his character, ideologies and abiding interests and concerns. It is clear that he viewed the period of his life there with affection. He later wrote that arriving in Oxford from Winchester was 'like a new beginning of life'. He remarked that the 'liberty and independence, the refinement amounting to luxury, the society, the intellectual atmosphere, the higher tone of opinion and feeling, were all delightful'.[22] It was in this intellectual and spiritual atmosphere that Selborne first formed his own views as both a High Churchman and a politician. In his memoirs he acknowledged that prior to becoming active in the Oxford Union he 'had no political opinions beyond the hereditary Toryism of my Father and other members of my family'.[23] Similarly, in its obituary upon his death, *The Times* noted that:

> It was in the Oxford of Newman that his ideas assumed the shape from which they never afterwards substantially departed. It was there that the affection to the Anglican Church which he brought with him from his home was confirmed, there that his grave and serious conception of the duties of life from a religious standpoint was finally formed, and there that the foundations of his political creed were laid.[24]

While his own family and Oxford connections tied Selborne's spiritual sympathies to the High Church element within the Church of England, his marriage ties brought him into close connection with its evangelical component, as well as further cementing his links to the political and ecclesiastical establishments. In 1848 he married Lady Laura Waldegrave, the second daughter of the eighth Earl Waldegrave, and the sister of Samuel Waldegrave (later Bishop of Carlisle), who was one of his closest friends. His wife's family were staunch evangelicals, and upon their marriage they made All Souls Langham Place, a centre of Anglican evangelicalism, their family's place of worship.

Surveying the ecclesiastical controversies through which he had lived, Selborne – despite very real reservations about aspects of evangelical theology – ascribed great importance to the role played by his knowledge of, and connections to, evangelical churchmen in safeguarding both his own faith and his own adherence to the Church of England. Reflecting on this, he wrote:

> Next to the home influence which surrounded me, none contributed more to preserve the balance of my mind than that of the excellent representatives of 'Evangelical' opinion, with whom I had been brought into contact. There were many things in that system, particularly the Calvinistic tenets . . . with

[22] Ibid., 1: 114. [23] Ibid., 1: 130. [24] *The Times*, 6 May 1895, 9.

which I have never agreed; and it always seemed to me defective, as having too much out of sight the organic side of Christianity. But in its spirituality, in its constant representation of Christ and His work as the foundation of faith and practice, and in its reverence for the Scriptures, I thought it set an example which all might have done well to follow.[25]

He spoke somewhat pompously of his conviction that, when he first became actively concerned with theological controversies during his early professional years in London, it was only his exposure to a wide and varied range of views and opinions which saved him from the danger of 'surrendering too much of my own perceptions of truth, and my consciousness of moral responsibility, to the government of other men'.[26]

Selborne's place at the heart of a wide network of ecclesiastical contacts was not solely significant in safeguarding his faith and attachment to the Church of England. Along with his social and political standing, his natural interests and his growing professional reputation, it also ensured that he had a prominent role in many of the foremost ecclesiastical controversies and practical conundrums of his time. Only a flavour of these activities can be conveyed within the confines of this chapter.

In some instances he threw himself into the fray upon his own initiative. So, for example, as a practitioner and backbencher he was among the men who signed a remonstrance against the *Gorham Judgment*,[27] in which the Judicial Committee of the Privy Council appeared to confirm that an Anglican clergyman could legally hold preferment while denying the doctrine of baptismal regeneration – a doctrine which many in the Church saw as a logical concomitant of the Articles of Religion. Participating in a wave of High Church dissatisfaction with the Judicial Committee of the Privy Council, he was among those in Parliament who sought to induce Bishop Blomfield of London to introduce a bill on ecclesiastical appeals.[28] His espousal of this cause marked the commencement of a long career during the course of which he absolutely refused to permit his faith and personal convictions to be swayed by consideration of the interests of his political masters. So, for example, he was a vociferous opponent of legislation to legalise marriage with a deceased wife's sister and, more importantly, was a steadfast supporter of the Anglican Establishment and an unswerving opponent of initiatives towards disestablishment and disendowment.

Lord Selborne was marked out by his espousal of a moderate High Church position, by his connections and by his professional prowess. He early became

25 Selborne, *Memorials I*, 1: 211. 26 Ibid., 1: 207.

27 *Gorham v. Bishop of Exeter* (1849–50) 163 English Reports 1221.

28 Selborne, *Memorials I*, 2: 64–83.

a figure to whom Church leaders might refer knotty problems or pleas for action. So, for example, in 1850 Bishop Blomfield appealed to him for advice on how best to deal with the Papal Aggression, by which Pius IX had reasserted the full Roman Catholic hierarchy in England. Selborne's response demonstrated both his instinctive pragmatism, expediency and liberalism and his refusal to succumb to the political passions of the day. He refused to espouse the popular cause of anti-Catholic legislation, writing instead:

> No man can be more opposed, than I am, to the corrupt doctrines, and uncatholic usurpations, of the Church of Rome: but I think the true way of resisting the encroachments of that Church is by strengthening the hand of the Church of England ... and not by the enactment or extension of penal laws against the Roman Catholics ... The longer I have lived, the more attached I have become to the principle of religious liberty, and the more sincerely I have learned to see the interest which every man, who is in earnest about his own religion, has in the maintenance of the principle. ... [A]nd I think it is a sound and right policy for a Christian State to be tolerant towards every form of religious belief, which, not inculcating disloyalty or immorality, is seriously professed by numbers of its subjects.[29]

The habit, acquired by both government and senior clerics, of using Selborne as a conduit of communication between the two sides, became entrenched during his years first as a law officer and then as Lord Chancellor. The examples are myriad of his role in negotiating settlements and communicating the lines taken on issues touching the constitutional and legal position of the Church. They fill the volumes of his correspondence in Lambeth Palace Library and the papers of Archbishop Tait and others. So, for example, despite his opposition to Irish Disestablishment, he took a leading role in securing the necessary communications and negotiations between the Liberal government and the Church of Ireland bishops. He was thereby enabled to advise Gladstone upon how best to achieve his ends in Parliament and to secure the grudging acquiescence of the Irish bishops to Gladstone's schemes.[30] This was not an isolated example of Selborne's role as a go-between and 'fixer'. In 1880, for example, Gladstone used him to sound out Archbishop Tait on the question of burials legislation, giving nonconformists the right to be buried in their parish churchyard without the rites of the Church of England. He sought information upon what protections and amendments the bishops might wish to see introduced to the scheme, and

29 Selborne to Blomfield, Lincoln's Inn, 1850, LPL, MS 1861, f. 216.

30 Memorandum to Gladstone following meeting between Palmer, Lord Carnarvon, and the Archbishop of Dublin, 11 February 1869, LPL, MS 1863, ff. 206–9.

the likely attitude of the bishops to what was proposed. This information was solicited in order to assist Gladstone in determining whether the bill was to be introduced in the House of Commons or the House of Lords.[31]

Archbishop Tait also often used Selborne as his intermediary when approaching Gladstone, particularly on the question of legislation to address the vexed question of clergy discipline and ritualist liturgical practices. In response, Selborne not only approached Gladstone and represented Tait's views to the bishops, but he also freely offered his own advice on how the bishops might best remedy the difficulties in which they found themselves. His suggestions were typically pragmatic, expedient and common sense in character. In a protracted correspondence in 1880, for example, he advised Archbishop Tait that it was both impossible for Gladstone to undertake to introduce a government bill on clergy discipline and to ask Parliament or the government to authorise the Church's Convocations to take remedial action. This latter course, he warned, could not be dissociated from the presumption by a large body of clergy that the actions of Parliament were not binding on their consciences in these matters. Writing in robust terms, he continued:

> They seek nothing less than to reduce the Royal Supremacy within limits utterly unknown in this country since the Reformation . . . In the face of such a movement, to ask Parliament to abate one iota of its present legislative powers in ecclesiastical matters, or to concede any degree of power beyond what they now possess in the Convocations, seems to me not only impracticable, but very difficult to defend in Parliament.[32]

Quite apart from any question of high constitutional principle concerning the relationship between Church and state, it was, he advised, impossible in the current democratic day and age to reformulate that relationship in a way which gave more power to the clergy and less to the laity. All practicable solutions tended in the opposing direction.

Lord Selborne, then, plainly has a claim to greatness, if not as a Christian jurist, then certainly as a Christian statesman. This did not, though, mean that his advice or solutions were necessarily palatable or acceptable to those who sought them, nor that they were inevitably successful. The compromise package which he recommended in respect of Irish Disestablishment and Disendowment in 1868 in large part failed to materialise. Similarly, his provision for episcopal assessors to assist the final court of appeal, which he made in

[31] Selborne to Tait, 7 May 1880, LPL, MS 1867, ff. 94–5.

[32] Selborne to Tait, December 1880, LPL, Tait MS 100, ff. 193–6. See also ff. 169–78, where Selborne advises, among other things, that there should be an indemnity and amnesty regarding past offences, a dispensing power for the bishops in relation to established practices and the removal of the punishment of imprisonment for contempt.

respect of the Judicature Act 1873, was long the cause of continuing dissatisfaction and controversy regarding the nature, work and authority of that court. Nor were Lord Selborne's actions as a judge universally pleasing to the contestants in the increasingly acrimonious legal battle over High Church ceremonial, ritual and ornaments. In respect of one case in particular, that of *Ridsdale v. Clifton*,[33] his role as one of the judges sitting in the Judicial Committee of the Privy Council attracted particular obloquy from many High Church Anglicans.

The fracas surrounding *Ridsdale v. Clifton*, and the treatment and actions of Lord Selborne and others involved in hearing the appeal before the Judicial Committee of the Privy Council, encapsulates in one episode many of the aspects of his life and career which this chapter is concerned to tease out. It illustrates the febrile atmosphere prevailing within certain sections of the Church of England, during the second half of the nineteenth century, with respect to questions of ceremonial and ornaments in public worship and the theology which underpinned them. So, too, it highlights the internal conflicts played out within the Church over the nature of the relationship between Church and state, and the balance between secular and spiritual authority in an established church. Most importantly, it brings us to a consideration of Lord Selborne's relationship with the combatants in those controversies, his perceived standing in relation to the legal judgments through which their resolution was sought and his own attitudes with regards to the constitutional settlement between Church and state.[34]

Ridsdale v. Clifton, like many of the so-called ritual cases of the nineteenth century, attracted great publicity and comment. The appeal to the Judicial Committee was viewed as being particularly significant, first because it was anticipated that it would settle longstanding questions about the legality of Eucharistic vestments and the adoption of the eastward position (in which the priest stands with his back to the congregation) during the Eucharistic prayer, and second because it was the first ecclesiastical appeal to be heard by the Judicial Committee of the Privy Council as composed under the Appellate Jurisdiction Act 1876.

When the Judicial Committee of the Privy Council, which included Selborne among its number, finally delivered its much anticipated judgment, it partially retreated from its previous decision[35] which had condemned both

33 (1876) 1 PD 316; (1877) 2 PD 276.

34 For a fuller examination of this case, see C. L. Smith, '*Ridsdale v. Clifton*: Representations of the Judicial Committee of the Privy Council in Ecclesiastical Appeals', *King's Law Journal* 19 (2008): 551–74.

35 *Hebbert v. Purchas* (1871) LR 3 PC 605.

vestments and the eastward position. The Judicial Committee, though it confirmed the illegality of vestments, held that the eastward position was legally permissible. It might have been hoped that this judgment would have been welcomed with at least a degree of satisfaction by many of those who most keenly awaited it. The eastward position was adopted by many moderate High Churchmen who had no sympathy with the elaborate vestments worn by their more advanced ritualist brethren. Equally, the condemnation of such vestments was pleasing to evangelical churchmen who so vehemently opposed their use as being redolent of the theology of Rome. Any hopes, however, of a peaceful acquiescence in the judgment were soon dashed. The ritualists, whose beloved vestments were declared to be illegal, heaped calumnies upon the heads of the members of the Judicial Committee.

In particular, in denying the Privy Council's authority and claims to their obedience, they characterised the judgment as being driven by policy considerations rather than by law, and of being concocted by Lords Cairns and Selborne in concert with Archbishop Tait.[36] Such allegations were propagated in fertile soil, since rumours about the deliberations of the judicial panel and the opinions of the various judges and assessors had been rife for some time.[37] These rumours were given further substance by the failure, in breach of settled convention, of three members of the judicial panel to attend the delivery of the judgment.[38]

The *Church Times* cast aspersions freely upon assessors and judges alike. It accused the episcopal assessors of yielding to Archbishop Tait and not upholding their proper view of the matter in the face of policy considerations. It further claimed that the majority of the judges believed in the legality of the vestments they condemned, but lacked 'the moral courage to say so in the face of the supposed popular hostility to them, and the possible vindictive action of

36 See e.g. 'More about the Privy Council', *Church Times*, 23 March 1877; 'The Coming Decision', *Church Times*, 29 March 1877. See also W. F. Finlason, *The Judgment of the Judicial Committee in the Folkestone Ritual Case with an Historical Introduction and Brief Notes* (London: Stevens and Sons, 1877), 39.

37 See e.g. 'Judgment in the Ridsdale Case', *Church Times*, 16 March 1877; Letter from 'One on the Watch', *Church Times*, 29 March 1877. The source was The Chief Baron, Fitzroy Kelly, and, following a long and very public exchange of letters between him and Lord Cairns, his indiscretion led to Cairns re-issuing the Order of Secrecy in relation to the proceedings of the Judicial Committee of the Privy Council.

38 Sir Robert Phillimore, Sir Fitzroy Kelly and Sir Richard Amphlett did not attend, and Archbishop Tait was the only assessor present. That the three judges were likely to make known their dissent from the judgment was first reported in 'More about the Privy Council' and confirmed in a report on the delivery of the judgment, 'The Privy Council Judgment', *Church Times*, 18 May 1877.

the Evangelical party'.[39] It even alleged that one of the judges had only concurred in the judgment upon being threatened with not being given his long-awaited peerage unless he did so.[40]

The *Church Times* singled Selborne out for personal attack. It accused both him and Lord Cairns of being 'embittered opponents of the High Church School'. They expected nothing better of Cairns, who as an Orangeman was 'anti-catholic by heredity descent and early association'. In Selborne's case, in respect of one whom they had once counted as an ally, they blamed this apostasy on his marriage into a family 'which has long been in active conflict of religious opinion with the formularies of the Church of England'.[41]

This reference to Selborne's churchmanship brings us to a consideration of the precise nature of his place within the Church and the various shades of opinion and practice accommodated by it. He was, as we have seen, the scion of an old-fashioned High Church rectory, but had also been influenced both by the High Church revival in the Oxford of his youth and by the evangelical connections which came with his marriage. The truth was that, though he was a convinced High Churchman of a very Victorian kind, and though he had been involved in almost all of the great controversies of the Tractarian era at Oxford, he instinctively recoiled from the course taken by the ritualist heirs of the High Church revival. He could never follow them in their love of ritual, nor in their denial of earthly authority.

In part he ascribed this to his father's powerful and abiding influence, and to a resulting distrust of all 'emotional forms of religious enthusiasm'.[42] No less important, however, was his conviction that uniformity of worship had a valuable place in a broad national church, in which acts of worship provided a common ground upon which churchmen of differing opinions and temperaments could meet in fellowship. He was evidently willing to sacrifice this in the interests of the peace of the Church or in order to avert what he saw as being the evils of disestablishment, but such a sacrifice would have been grudging on his part. He had no love of liturgical innovation, and as he somewhat acerbically commented to Archbishop Tait:

> I must ... express my inability to understand how the very same men, who insist upon these things [High Church liturgical practices] ... can pretend, with even a moderate degree of good faith, to take their stand on the settlement of 1662; which established the Act of Uniformity and bore out of the

39 'Judgment in the Ridsdale Case'. 40 'The Privy Council Judgment'. 41 Ibid.
42 Selborne, *Memorials I*, 1: 207.

> Church, for the sake of the sacrifice and one or more other such matters, almost as many ministers as now belong to [the High Church] English Church Union.[43]

Also significant was the fact that the controversies to which the High Church revival gave rise, together with other theological controversies, carried out of the Church many of those High Churchmen to whom he had been closest. He himself noted that he was 'more detached' from the Tractarian party by virtue of those secessions than he had ever been before.[44]

The ultimate point of breach between Selborne and the more extreme proponents of the High Church was, however, found in their attitude to authority in matters of church government. He explained his own position as follows:

> I had always maintained the duty of obedience, in things which it is within the province of human authority to regulate, to those particular authorities, whether in Church or in State, under whose government a man was actually living; I had always acknowledged the principle involved in an answer of Bishop Blomfield to a clergyman of his diocese, who quoted St. Ambrose to him on some matters of that kind: 'St. Ambrose is not your Bishop'.[45]

He took his stand on the Reformation Settlement and he argued that many within the High Church were both departing from this and endangering its continued existence. Writing to Archbishop Tait, he stated:

> I have always gone so far as this (and no further) with the opponents of (so called) Erastianism; that I, like them, would consider a mere State or Parliamentary Church unendurable: and that I should dispute any exercise of the undoubted powers of powers of Parliament to impose doctrine or ritual on the Church without the concurrence of ecclesiastical authority, as inviting a unilateral change in the practical relations between Church and State, of such great importance, as to make it possible that even I might regard disestablishment as a less evil ....
>
> But, on the other hand, I regard the resistance offered by so many of the clergy to the judicial [influence] of the Crown, and the pretension that the authority of Ecclesiastical Courts, and of Bishops acting upon their decisions, as vitiated by Parliamentary legislation (without the concurrence of Convocation), as to the constitution and powers of these Courts, as inviting a change in the settlement of the relations between Church and State which has existed since the Reformation.

43 Selborne to Tait, December 1880, LPL, Tait 100, ff. 207–15.

44 Selborne, *Memorials I*, 1: 400.

45 Ibid.

Selborne had no sympathy with ritualists' underlying arguments that the ecclesiastical courts as formulated by the Public Worship Regulation Act 1874 and other such legislation lacked spiritual authority, or that ecclesiastical courts could not be authoritative or appropriately staffed unless they were appointed by spiritual authority and staffed by persons with theological knowledge. He roundly stated that the result of the previous three centuries was that all questions of doctrine, discipline and ritual had come to depend upon the interpretation of parliamentary legislation. He concluded in a characteristically pragmatic manner saying, 'Whether this is . . . a desirable state of affairs, or not, I do not care to inquire: but it is, at least (in my opinion), an endurable state of things: and of one thing I am perfectly sure, viz. that the demand for its reversal means disestablishment, and nothing else.'[46]

It is in this letter to Archbishop Tait, and especially in this last statement, that we find the most fundamental reason why Selborne could never unreservedly throw his lot in with the more advanced of his High Church contemporaries (including Gladstone). He could never condone anything which might endanger that relationship of the Church of England with the state which was found in Establishment.

SELBORNE AS DEFENDER OF ESTABLISHMENT

Ultimately Selborne could never have an uncomplicated relationship with the advanced High Churchmen and ritualists. Even as many of them turned away from the earthly authority granted to the Church by virtue of Establishment and increasingly sought to loosen the ties between Church and state, he remained self-consciously a churchman of the national church. In the words of *The Times*' obituary of Lord Selborne:

> To the last he remained true to the convictions of his youth; to the last he remained, first and above all things, a devoted son of the Church of England, a powerful but sober defender of her doctrines, an ardent champion of her rights and privileges, an illustrious example of the high type of layman which she abundantly produces.[47]

This was the identity that he chose for himself and which dictated his course on numerous occasions throughout his life. So, for example, explaining to Gladstone why he could not lend his support to the Irish Church Bill of 1868, he wrote:

46 Selborne to Tait, December 1880, LPL, Tait 100, ff. 207–15. 47 *The Times*, 6 May 1895, 9.

> I have been through my whole life . . . a Churchman by conviction. I have no object in life dearer, no conception of public duty higher, than those which are connected with my attachment to the Church, and which would be violated by any act on my part, which might tend to diminish its moral power, and means of influence in this country. If the dangers which I apprehend are really impending, I wish to be free from the responsibility, even in appearance, of accelerating or increasing them.[48]

Following the disestablishment of the Church of Ireland, and as Gladstone flirted with disestablishment in Wales and even in England, Selborne found his mission in defending the Establishment and endowments of the Church of England from attack. In this he found a way of turning his increasing estrangement from the High Church to good effect. Thus, reflecting on a request from a 'Liberal Churchman' to write a book in defence of Establishment, he wrote:

> To give the world my views on that question could not be the work of a day. But the wish so conveyed sounded to my inner ear like a call to that work. My differences from party of the [High Church] English Church Union had cut me off from some opportunities of usefulness, which might otherwise have been open to me: might not that involuntary isolation give me a better opportunity of gaining the ear of men of various ways of thinking, if I endeavoured to serve the Church in the way suggested?[49]

He spent many of the later years of his life campaigning and writing tirelessly against disestablishment and disendowment. He combined this with his implacable opposition to Irish Home Rule, the issue which had led to an irreparable rupture between himself and Gladstone.

Selborne was, as we have already seen, in many respects a true liberal in his commitment to the principle of religious liberty. He could not countenance any return to the penal laws under which Roman Catholics and Protestant dissenters were barred from participation in the full civic life of the nation. In 1847, for example, he renounced popular calls to subject Roman Catholicism to penal laws, writing to his brother-in-law:

> [I]f anyone thinks that the profession of their [Roman Catholic] religion ought in all Christian countries, or particularly in this country, to be repressed by penal laws, or to be treated as a disqualification for civil rights, – or that public faith is not to be scrupulously kept by Roman Catholics in matters connected with their religion and religious interests, – from such an

48 Memorandum on the Irish Church Question, LPL, MS 1863, f. 72.

49 Selborne, *Memorials II*, 2: 246.

one I shall differ, and I must expect to incur his disapprobation sometimes by my conduct in Parliament.[50]

This stance led to him losing his seat at Plymouth. His attachment to the principle of religious liberty also caused him to vote in support of the admission of Jews to Parliament and to acquiesce in the admission to Parliament of an avowed atheist who would not take an oath.

If an attachment to the principle of religious liberty was one aspect of Selborne's approach to church defence, then another equally strong strand was a pragmatic willingness to embrace necessary change in the light of social and constitutional developments. Thus, he took charge of the bill for the abolition of church rates and eventually acquiesced in the abolition of religious tests in the ancient universities. Equally, in his writing on church defence, he faced the reality that churchmanship and citizenship were not synonymous,[51] and he took a key role in helping the Church to define its membership in ways that reflected that reality, and to develop governance structures which reflected its changed context. His efforts in this respect were recognised by his appointment, in 1886, as the first chairman of the House of Laymen for the Canterbury Convocation.

In many respects, however, Selborne's contribution to church defence was a profoundly conservative one. His three most notable contributions to the voluminous nineteenth-century literature on the relationship between Church and state were *Disestablishment* (1878), *A Defence of the Church of England Against Disestablishment* (1886) and *The Endowment and Establishment of the Church of England* (1886).[52] To these might be added *The Catholic and Apostolic Church* (1899), which constituted a final and posthumously printed restatement of his churchmanship.[53] None of these works was startling or novel in the content articulated or the position adopted. They were remarkable only for Selborne's meticulous and lawyerly approach, and for the conservatism of his position vis-à-vis many of his High Church and liberal fellows. They encapsulated his attachment to old ideals, the pragmatism and common sense with which he

[50] Palmer to Bishop Waldegrave of Carlisle, 6 August 1847, LPL, MS 1861, ff. 141–3.

[51] Roundell Palmer, first Earl of Selborne, *A Defence of the Church of England Against Disestablishment* (London: Macmillan, 1886), ch. 4.

[52] Roundell Palmer, first Earl of Selborne, *Disestablishment. A Paper Read at Winchester Diocesan Conference, on Friday, October 11, 1878* (London: Church Defence Association, 1878); Selborne, *A Defence of the Church of England*; Roundell Palmer, first Earl of Selborne, *The Endowment and Establishment of the Church of England: An Address Delivered at Blackmoor on Monday, January 11, 1866* (London: Cassell and Co., 1886).

[53] Roundell Palmer, first Earl of Selborne, *The Catholic and Apostolic Church: Letters to His Son* (London: Macmillan and Co., 1899).

approached questions of Church and state, and above all his continuing commitment to the ideal of a national church.

The conservatism of Selborne's defence of Establishment was found in his conviction that religion underpinned the moral sense that was a necessary corollary of the ability to be a good citizen. It was found, too, in his restatement of a familiar justification of the connection between Church and state. Echoing the likes of Thomas Arnold and Samuel Taylor Coleridge, he argued that Church and state each had its own divinely ordered and distinctive sphere of knowledge and action, and that each worked best when in harmony with the other. So, for example, in *A Defence of the Church of England* he wrote:

> The mainstay of all law ... is ... the moral sense of mankind; religion, wherever it is truly professed, is ... powerful in the direction and reinforcement of that moral sense. Both powers, the Ecclesiastical and the Civil, are ... in their origin divine; each has its proper province; the persons over which exercises its authority are to a great extent the same; and there is, by the unchangeable laws of nature and Providence, a middle or common ground between them. Each will best perform its proper work within its own province when it works in harmony with the other.[54]

His conservatism also reverberated in his warning that the particulars of the relationship between Church and state were 'in their true nature securities taken by the State against possible excesses of uncontrolled ecclesiastical power, rather than privileges conferred upon the Church by the State'.[55] More stridently still was it articulated in his warning to the supporters of disestablishment:

> I do not believe it to be possible that Church property, generally, could be secularized, and all formal relations between Church and State dissolved in this country, without giving a formidable impulse to other revolutionary movements, and weakening very much the social bond which now gives strength to law, and unites honest men of all classes in a common sense of public duty.[56]

Selborne strove, where possible, to preserve the status quo and to avert revolutionary change. Thus one great strand running through his various publications was, as we have seen, a warning to the liberationists of the consequences of disestablishment. Another and no less important refrain addressed those within the High Church faction whose actions he saw as

[54] Selborne, *A Defence of the Church of England*, 73. [55] Ibid., 74.
[56] Selborne, *Disestablishment*, 3.

tending to loosen the ties between Church and state. Characteristic of this was his warning that

> [t]he legislative and judicial supremacy of the Crown is the keystone of the whole existing relations between Church and State in this country; and it would be blindest self-delusion to suppose that it can ever be got rid of, or for any long time practically resisted, without leading, as an inevitable consequence, to Disestablishment and Disendowment.[57]

Selborne's arguments were not striking, nor were they novel. Further, he himself denied that they had ideological foundations, writing to one correspondent on the Irish Church question, 'I value Church Establishments simply and solely for the good they do.'[58] His most important task, however, was to refrain from engaging in the familiar rhetoric of the debate about Establishment, which was well trodden ground, but rather to write a lawyer's defence of the Church's property against any attempt by the state to remove it by the process of disendowment. This was his distinctive contribution to the controversies which raged at that time.[59] It was a significant and practically useful one in an era which had witnessed the partial disendowment of the Church of Ireland and in which public and political conceptualisations of Church property as a species of national property abounded.[60] Its importance was reflected in the memorials published after Selborne's death, which frequently refer to his stature and significance as a contributor on the side of church defence.[61]

Selborne could never countenance the appropriation of Church endowments to secular purposes, and he was vociferous in rejecting the legal foundations of any claim by the state to do so. So, for example, he asserted:

> There is, no doubt, a true sense, in which the Church of England may be called a National Institution … But this does not make its property national property.
>
> The argument which I am controverting assumes the revenues derived from Church endowments to be funds at present belonging, in point of right and title, to the public treasury, and their appropriation to Church purposes to be the same thing in substance as if they were monies voted by Parliament.

57 Ibid., 5. 58 Palmer to Stanley, 2 May 1868, LPL, MS, 1863, ff. 85–6.
59 See e.g. *The Times*, 1 December 1886, 9.
60 This idea was a central theme in Samuel Taylor Coleridge, *On the Constitution of Church and State According to the Idea of Each* (London, 1829). It was repeated numerous times in justifications of state control of the Church.
61 See Selborne, *Memorials II*, 2: 'In Memoriam'.

Both assumptions are legally, historically, practically, and absolutely, in every sense, untrue.[62]

Above all, however, whether he was espousing religious liberty, defending the status quo or embracing necessary change, Selborne was sustained by a deep personal faith. As he wrote to Bishop Blomfield in the wake of the Papal Aggression, 'I have sufficient faith in the power of truth and in the truth of our own religion, to believe that we can afford to be tolerant even towards those who would not tolerate us'.[63] His faith in the Church of England was no less convicted than his faith in Christ. It reverberated through his declaration, in one of his pamphlets, that 'our Church, as an element of the national life, has struck her roots very deep and wide, and, whatever other institutions might be shaken by her fall, no possible process of disestablishment could make her cease to be a great moral and political power'.[64]

Arguably, it was his reputation as a man of sacrificial faith and of unswerving integrity which was his greatest gift to the Church of his time and to its defence. It was in this aspect of his life, which is given prominence in all the published obituaries following his death,[65] that he might truly be said to have been formidable. For it was evident that, whatever might have been his inner struggles,[66] he had always acted in a manner consistent with his faith and convictions. He had been a Christian and a churchman in all things, whether in the public or the private sphere. He was honoured, not only for his legal and political acumen, but above all for his self-denying faith and utter integrity. His fellows knew that when he had been on the path to legal and political greatness, he had declined offers of both a lord justiceship and the Privy Seal in order to fight Gladstone's Irish Church bill as a private member. It was for this reason, no less than for his legal learning and status, that he was repeatedly identified as being 'one of those who are eminently entitled to be heard'.[67]

THE ANATOMY OF A GREAT CHRISTIAN JURIST

Selborne, the statesman and the lawyer, lived his life in the thick of the constitutional and theological upheavals of the nineteenth century, and of efforts on the part of both the Church and the state to respond to them. As the

62 Selborne, *A Defence of the Church of England*, 179.

63 Selborne to Palmer, Lincoln's Inn, 1850, LPL, MS 1861, ff. 216–18.

64 Selborne, *Disestablishment*, 4.

65 See e.g. Selborne, *Memorials II*, 2: 427 (Herschell LC), 431–2 (Bishop of London). See also *The Times*, 6 May 1895, 9.

66 Selborne, *Memorials I*, 1: 233.

67 *The Times*, 1 December 1886, 9.

Reformation Settlement was challenged by external forces, and as it was disputed by sections of the Church of England, he steadfastly sought to uphold and remould the relationship between Church and state. In this capacity he was a crucial tool of communication between the Church and reforming – and increasingly radical – Liberal governments; but he was also an unfailing source of sage and pragmatic advice to the Church. One of his great gifts to the Church, of which he was a devoted son, was the willingness to advocate its cause and to defend its position. A no less great gift was his ability to recognise indefensible aspects of the status quo and to cede ground in the interests of the larger picture. It might be said that his actions were those of a statesman, rather than of a lawyer, but they were underpinned by a practitioner's pragmatism and by his own determination that constitutional reform was one of those areas to which lawyer members of Parliament should most properly devote their attention.

Turning to Selborne's more strictly legal endeavours, no one would contest his claim to greatness as the architect of the modern system of judicature in England. Yet his claim to any degree of approbation in the realms of ecclesiastical court reform would have been vehemently contested by many within the High Church section of the Church of England to which he himself belonged. Further, many within that same section of the Church were at best disappointed by his activities as a judge in ecclesiastical causes. Nor was he particularly noteworthy, in juristic terms, as a defender of the constitutional relationship between Church and state – though his legal defence of the Church's endowments was a practically useful one. But to look at Selborne's specific attributes and contributions is to miss the point of a man whose truly great contribution to the life of his Church and nation was greater than the sum of its parts.

Selborne can be accounted a great Christian jurist, not because we can trace examples of when his faith determined the shape of his judgments, nor because he was the exponent of a great and theoretically informed ideological position. He was horrified at any suspicion that he might have permitted the former to happen,[68] and he expressly disavowed any attempt to do the latter.[69] Nor, really, does his claim to greatness lie in his participation in the great ecclesiastical, legal and political events of his time – though his historical significance is hard to deny. His real claim to be a great Christian jurist rests in his lived experience and reputation as a man whose faith ruled and determined every aspect of his life and behaviour, and whose churchmanship was an inescapable and dominant force in moulding his character, his behaviour

68 Selborne to Pusey, 19 February 1877, LPL, MS 1866, ff. 234–5.

69 Memorandum on the Irish Church Question, 22 April 1868, LPL, MS 1863, ff. 71–2.

and his actions in public and private life. It is impossible to have any understanding of Selborne, as a man or as a lawyer, without first understanding Selborne as a Christian and as a churchman. As *The Times* put it, '[T]o the depth and sincerity of his religious convictions he in no small measure owed the solidity and the consistency of judgment which made him a moral force in wide classes of English society.'[70]

70 *The Times*, 6 May 1895, 9.

Portrait of Frederic William Maitland (1906), oil on canvas, Beatrice Lock (Mrs Fripp) / National Portrait Gallery, London

14

F. W. Maitland
Faithful Dissenter

Russell Sandberg

Such is the worth and unity of Maitland's work that anyone who endeavours to tell a piece of it risks tearing a seamless web.[1] Variably hailed as a 'patron saint' and 'the master',[2] with revisions to his views regarded as 'heresies',[3] it is clear that Maitland was and is a classic: he is one of those rare figures who 'still speak[s] to us in a voice which is held to be relevant' and with whom 'a continuing dialogue is carried on'.[4] As Milsom eulogised, Maitland's work remains 'a still living authority' providing 'the foundation of all we know about the history of common law': Maitland's work 'established both the subject and the assumptions on which historians have worked ever since', so much so that those interested in the history of English law still invariably begin with Maitland: 'Their questions still take the form: was Maitland right?'[5] This chapter will contend that this is as true in relation to the history of ecclesiastical law as it is for the history of the common law. It will argue that Maitland's picture of the historical development of the relations between Church and state, as found mainly in his essays collected in *Roman Canon*

I am grateful to Carrie Gwyther and Scarlet Thomas-Perry for their invaluable research assistance and to the Research Committee at the Cardiff School of Law and Politics for funding their work.

1 See F. Pollock and F. W. Maitland, *The History of English Law before the Time of Edward I*, 2d ed., 2 vols. (Cambridge: Cambridge University Press, 1968, first published 1898), 1:1.

2 T. G. Watkin, 'Feudal Theory, Social Needs and the Rise of the Heritable Fee', *Cambrian Law Review* 10 (1979): 41.

3 S. F. C. Milsom, 'Introduction', in Pollock and Maitland, *History of English Law*, 1: xxiii, xxv.

4 A. Giddens, *Politics, Sociology and Social Theory* (Stanford: Polity Press, 1995) 5–6.

5 Milsom, 'Introduction', xxiii, xxi, xxiv; S. F. C. Milsom, *A Natural History of the Common Law* (New York: Columbia University Press, 2003), xiv. Some accounts now begin with Milsom's heretical criticisms of Maitland: R. V. Turner, 'Henry II's Aims in Reforming England's Land Law: Feudal or Royalist', in E. B. King and S. J. Ridyard, eds., *Law in Mediaeval Life and Thought* (Sewanee, TN: University of the South, 1990), 121, 122.

Law in the Church of England,[6] continue to provide the starting point for studies today.

Maitland was incontrovertibly a great jurist, but what of his religiosity? There may be some doubt as to whether he was a great *Christian* jurist. Such dubiety relates to his supposed agnosticism, or even atheism, and originates in his comment in the preface to *Roman Canon Law in the Church of England*, which merits quoting in full:

> At a time when the perennial stream of Anglo-Roman controversy has burst its accustomed channels and invaded the daily papers, the assumption will be readily made that anyone who writes about these matters of which I have here written is an advocate of one of two churches, the English or the Roman. Therefore it may be expedient for me to say that I am a dissenter from both, and from other churches. Probably that fact will be, and I think it ought to be, of no interest to the readers of this book but I have reason to fear the repetition of a mistake.[7]

At the risk of appropriating Milsom's reputation as chief heretic, it may be asserted that Maitland was wrong here. He was certainly wrong to assume that this would be of little interest to his readers. It has proved to be a much quoted passage and has informed the depiction of Maitland as being the cold agnostic/atheist academic who debated with the bishop and man of faith William Stubbs. Yet this passage, especially when placed in the context of the preface as a whole which spoke of undertaking a 'study, which must not be called prolonged or profound, but none the less was unprejudiced', was clearly intended to show Maitland's modesty and independence of mind rather than constitute a declaration of atheism. Maitland was simply saying that he was not an apologist for either Church. His statement that he was a 'dissenter from both, and from other churches' does not detract from his status as a great Christian jurist. It does not exclude the possibility that Maitland remained a man of faith – a believer but not a belonger, to use the language of a modern sociologist of religion[8] – and even if Maitland's dissent from institutional churches led him to abandon his Christian faith, that does not mean that his work was still not influenced by the Christian values of the society in which he lived and his own experiences of Christianity before his dissent began. Moreover, and perhaps most importantly, Maitland's own lack of belief (if that is established) does not mean that his work has not had a profound influence upon how believers see the law and are regulated by it. This chapter, therefore,

6 F. W. Maitland, *Roman Canon Law in the Church of England* (London: Methuen & Co, 1898).

7 Ibid., vi. 8 G. Davie, *Religion in Britain since 1945* (Oxford: Blackwell, 1994).

falls into three parts. It begins with a brief biographical account focusing on Maitland as a Christian. The second part then explores the importance and impact of *Roman Canon Law in the Church of England*. The final part examines his influence more widely, contending that all who are engaged with the academic study of law are indebted to and influenced by 'the sainted Maitland'.[9]

THE MAN AND HIS FAITH

Much has been written about the life and work of Frederic William Maitland, and so the focus of this brief biography is the religious dimension of his life.[10] He was born on 28 May 1850. His mother, Emma Daniel, died just one year after his birth and his father, John Gorham Maitland, died thirteen years later, so he was brought up by his mother's sister, Louisa, and a series of German governesses. His aunt Louisa ensured that Maitland grew up in a Christian household, and it was only after her death in 1880, when Maitland was thirty, that he ceased regular church attendance. Religion was part of the fabric of the Maitland family. His grandfather, the Reverend Samuel Roffey Maitland, had been an erudite, controversial historian of the Church and Christianity, specialising in the medieval period. Although there are similarities between grandfather and grandson as historians in terms of their power of visualisation and critical independence, the grandson showed no early inclination to history. Although he paid visits to his grandfather, for the most part Maitland was brought up by the women in his life. This changed, of course, during formal education. Maitland started at Eton College in 1863, which developed in him a strong love of music, some enthusiasm for rowing and a hatred of Greek. Here, too, Christianity was ever-present: his housemasters were clerics and Maitland is said to

9 J. P. Kenyon, in *Times Literary Supplement*, 2 March 1984, 222, quoted in G. R. Elton, *F. W. Maitland* (New Haven: Yale University Press, 1985), 5.

10 This biographical sketch draws upon the following sources: H. E. Bell, *Maitland: A Critical Examination and Assessment* (Cambridge, MA: Harvard University Press, 1965); Elton, *F. W. Maitland*; J. G. H. Hudson, *F. W. Maitland and the Englishness of English Law* (London: Selden Society, 2007); H. A. L. Fisher, *Frederick William Maitland, Downing Professor of the Laws of England: A Biographical Sketch* (Cambridge: Cambridge University Press, 1910), 2; C. H. S. Fifoot, *Frederic William Maitland: A Life* (Cambridge, MA: Harvard University Press 1971); Mrs Reynell, 'Frederic William Maitland', *Cambridge Law Journal* 6 (1951): 67–73; R. L. Schuyler, 'The Historical Spirit Incarnate: Frederic William Maitland', *American Historical Review* 57 (1952): 303–22; M. Shotwell and J. T. Shotwell, 'Frederic William Maitland', *Political Science Quarterly* 22 (1907): 282–96 ; and A. L. Smith, *Frederick William Maitland: Two Lectures and a Bibliography* (Oxford: Clarendon Press, 1908).

have spent Sunday afternoons running to St George's Chapel to hear the anthem.

The same religious background was present at Cambridge, where he entered Trinity College in 1869. Maitland had a number of accomplishments while at Cambridge, winning the three-mile race in the Oxford and Cambridge match and becoming a memorable president of the Union Society, renowned for his debating skills, but his academic achievements were at first far from accomplished. He began reading maths but his poor performance led him to switch to philosophy, studying the recently introduced Moral Sciences Tripos and graduating in 1872 with a first-class degree. The influence of his philosophy professor, Henry Sidgwick, was to prove pivotal, not just upon Maitland's education but also upon his religious outlook. Maitland was not immune to the wider intellectual climate which was setting against orthodoxy, and Sidgwick provided an important influence in this respect. This wider critical and rational intellectual environment produced sceptics rather than atheists. This is shown by a letter written by Sidgwick in 1870 that shows his inner tensions:

> I can neither adequately rationalise faith nor reconcile faith and reason nor suppress reason ... But in an irreligious age one must not let oneself drift, or else the rational element is disproportionately expressed and developed by the influence of the environment, and one loses the fidelity to one's true self ... My true self is a Theist, but I believe that many persons are really faithful to themselves in being irreligious, and I do not feel able to prophesy to them.[11]

A further important influence upon Maitland came in the next chapter of his life. Although he had wanted to continue his philosophical studies, his failure to obtain a fellowship at Cambridge led him to follow his father and grandfather to the bar. Though called to the bar, Maitland actually sat idle in chambers, and as his practice in Lincoln's Inn failed to grow, his intellectual curiosity blossomed. While in London he became a member of the Tramps, a typical Victorian society dedicated to regular Sunday walks around the city and some activities that displayed a certain juvenile facetiousness, but also, more importantly, he developed a number of life-long friendships, including one with Leslie Stephen, who was to become the founder of the Dictionary of National Biography. Stephen, though ordained in the Church of England, had renounced his orders, and in an 1876 essay, he put the word 'agnosticism'

[11] Quoted in Fifoot, *Frederic William Maitland*, 179. See also B. Schultz, *Henry Sidgwick: Eye of the Universe: An Intellectual Biography* (Cambridge: Cambridge University Press, 2004), 4.

into wide circulation. It is possible that Maitland's friendship with Stephen provided a reason for this departure from the Church at the time of his aunt Louisa's death in 1880.

It is clear that a number of changes were occurring in Maitland's life at this time. This included an eventual return to academia. In 1883 he was unsuccessful in an application for the Readership in English Law at Oxford, but in 1884 he succeeded in gaining a Readership in Cambridge, largely due to Sidgwick, who had 'personally endowed the readership in order to bring his most brilliant pupil back to the university'.[12] In 1888 a professorship followed, but so did a spate of ill health that would plague him for the remainder of his life. Cambridge accommodated his illness by allowing him to encamp to warmer climes in winter months while compressing his teaching and other academic duties at other times of the year. When he was at Cambridge, his lecturing style was regarded as distinctive. Sir Cecil Carr commented that Maitland's 'style was like that of no one else, compact of extraordinary Biblical and other archaisms, intensely individual, vivid and striking, packed with allusion, sparkling with humour and suggesting even more than it stated'.[13] It was not only the invocation of biblical quotations and notions that gave his lecturing style a religious aura: one of his frequent lecture halls was described as 'something between a monastic refectory and a Quaker meeting-house' and this 'ecclesiastical atmosphere' was revelled in by the lecturer:

> Maitland lectured on English law, at least when I heard him, as though he were some saintly medieval monk reciting the miracles of his order. His tall gaunt figure was restless with animation; his voice would throw off the huskiness due to his physical weakness, and pass into a sort of liturgic rhythm as he completed his outline of some large cycle of legal development.[14]

The year 1886 proved to be pivotal in that it saw the foundation of the Selden Society and, whether it was his original idea or not, Maitland became its lasting inspiration. As literary director of the Society until the end of his life, Maitland contributed a number of important volumes, and the Society has been described as a 'living memorial which perpetuates not only the work but also the spirit of Maitland'.[15] In addition to his role with the Selden Society and despite his ill health, Maitland produced a body of work the quality and

12 Elton, *F. W. Maitland*, 8. 13 Quoted in Fifoot, *Frederic William Maitland*, 98.

14 Shotwell and Shotwell, 'Frederic William Maitland', 288.

15 T. F. T. Plucknett, 'Frederic William Maitland', *New York University Law Review* 26 (1951): 10.

quantity of which was impressive, almost superhuman, drawing upon mostly original sources to produce authoritative accounts that were accessible, and he also demonstrated an eye to detail. Space here does not permit even a summary of his prodigious output. It is important to note, however, two things. First, the extent to which biblical words and images permeated his writings is telling. Such language is especially present in his personal communications: his letters include references, for example, to 'my Protestant mind', the reflection that 'Quakerism is the best form of Christianity' and acting 'like a Christian and an ordinary man'.[16] Maitland was clearly influenced and infused by Christian ideas, though he had a detachment and perhaps disdain for the institutional churches. Indeed, the letters also tellingly refer to 'the Christians', suggesting a group to which he was not aligned.[17] Second, it is also revealing how often Maitland discussed matters of Church and state: leaving aside the various articles on Church–State issues which were collectively published as *Roman Canon Law in the Church of England*, it is striking that in his *History of English Law* and his lectures on constitutional history, Maitland sketched the relationship between Church and state in medieval England and that the penultimate section of his lectures was dedicated to 'The Church'.[18] Maitland's view of the centrality of religion in the historical understanding of English law was underpinned by the preface to *Roman Canon Law in the Church of England*, which presented that book as a necessary spin-off from *Pollock and Maitland*:

> When, in co-operation with Sir Fredrick Pollock, I was at work upon certain chapters in a History of English Law, and, in particular a chapter on marriage, I found that, on pain of leaving the book shamefully incomplete, I was compelled to make an inclusion into a region that was unfamiliar to me, namely that of ecclesiastical jurisprudence.[19]

The year 1886 also saw Maitland's marriage to Florence Henrietta Fisher with whom he would later have two daughters, Ermengard and Fredegond. Reference to his family life sheds a little further light on what being a dissenter from churches actually meant to Maitland. His Cambridge environment allowed Maitland to express a distance from institutional

16 C. H. S. Fifoot, ed., *The Letters of Frederic William Maitland* (London: Selden Society 1965), 103, 191, 26.

17 Ibid., 148.

18 Pollock and Maitland, *History of English Law*; F. W. Maitland, *The Constitutional History of England* (Cambridge: Cambridge University Press, 1941, first published 1908), 506–26.

19 Maitland, *Roman Canon Law*, v.

churches, which was unusual and perhaps even scandalous in Victorian England. The fact that his wife came from a home where church attendance was at least irregular meant that the Maitland family were non-churchgoers. The Maitland girls were apparently mocked by fellow schoolchildren for not going to church: 'I suppose you hold a service in your little dining-room.' However, Maitland brought up his daughters to be religiously literate: they received biblical readings from Maitland himself, who apparently

> wished his children to know something of Christ's teaching so that they might have the material upon which, as they grew up, they could make their own decisions and perhaps find their own faith. He read to them the Gospel of St Mark which he thought the most helpful to young minds.[20]

This tolerance was demonstrated when Fredegond asked her father if she could become a Catholic: her elder sister recounted that 'there was no protest, only the statement that when she was twenty-one she could do as she thought best'. Ermengard would later say that her father could be described as 'a very Protestant agnostic, I might almost say as Low Church agnostic'.[21] Although Fifoot argued that the 'Protestant agnostic' label gave 'too sharp an outline to Maitland's position', it was clear that 'though he was anticlerical, he was not anti-Christian'. Maitland adopted a critical, sceptical but open perspective. This is reflected in the fact that following his death on 17 December 1906 Maitland became the only university historian to be commemorated by a monument in Westminster Abbey. Maitland's monument, like that of Darwin's, appears ironic given his reputation as the agnostic academic dissenter. However, it is clear that this reputation is a simplification. Maitland's absence from church pews should not be confused as a sign of militant atheism. Christianity was influential upon Maitland, both culturally and individually. For Elton, Maitland's religious outlook was one 'increasingly typical during the last hundred years – Protestant by upbringing who had turned agnostic but retained a barely conscious Christian essence in his conduct and beliefs'.[22]

It is therefore possible to refer to Maitland as a Christian, not least because of the lack of definitional clarity concerning that term. However, even if we ignore the Christian influence implicitly and explicitly present in his work and if his clearly Christian upbringing is ignored or counterbalanced by his self-description in the preface as dissenter, Maitland's status as

[20] Fifoot, *Frederic William Maitland*, 181.

[21] Quoted in Fifoot, *Frederic William Maitland*, 180.

[22] Elton, *F. W. Maitland*, 15.

a great Christian jurist lies in the contribution his work has had in developing understandings of the relationship between law and religion in a way that has stimulated later commentators and thinkers, including those who overtly align themselves to an institutional church or a particular creed as well as those who do not.

THE GRAND ARCHITECT

There is a startling different conclusion that can be reached about Maitland's religiosity by reference to his work. Cam contended that 'whatever his personal predilections were, his passion for historical truth and legal exactness made him a papalist when determining an issue long obscured by ecclesiastical controversy'.[23] This is a reference to the so-called Stubbs–Maitland debate, the work for which Maitland is perhaps best known today by ecclesiastical lawyers. This debate concerns the status of Catholic canon law prior to the Reformation. The argument attributed to Stubbs was that the papal law of Rome, though of great authority in the medieval period, was not binding upon the English Church and that ecclesiastical courts applied the native law even where it was in conflict with the papal law. The argument attributed to Maitland was that the ecclesiastical courts accepted and applied Roman canon law as 'binding statute law', only refusing to follow it in situations where royal law forced ecclesiastical practice to depart from canon law. Three of the six essays in *Roman Canon Law in the Church of England* concerned the Stubbs–Maitland debate.[24] As Smith has noted, the genius of Maitland was 'to treat this one controversial point in such a way as not merely to elevate controversy into dispassionateness, but he also . . . as the thread on which to build up a review of relations of Church and State and Papacy'.[25] Maitland's writings on this topic therefore not only constitute a starting point for the study of ecclesiastical authority both before and

[23] H. Cam, *Law-Finders and Law-Makers in Medieval England: Collected Studies in Legal and Constitutional History* (New York: Barnes and Noble, 1963), 224.

[24] The volume comprised six essays previously published in the *English Historical Review* and *Law Quarterly Review*: the first, 'William Lyndwood', set out Maitland's argument by detailed discussion of the *Provinciale* and other sources. See Chapter 3 on Lyndwood in this volume. The second essay, 'Church, State, and Decretals', explored the space between the lay and spiritual jurisdictions. Of the third, 'William of Drogheda and the Universal Ordinary', Elton wrote that this 'hammered down the coffin lid on the false doctrine by demonstrating that William Drogheda, a leading English canonist of the early fourteenth century, totally accepted the "Hilderbrandine" view of the Church according to which it was single-empire ruled by the pope and not a federation of practically independent local Churches': Elton, *F. W. Maitland*, 72.

[25] Smith, *Frederick William Maitland*, 48–9.

after the English Reformation, but also provide an inspiration of how scholarship into Church–State affairs can be achieved in an academic manner. Perhaps we can trace in his work the seeds of the modern academic study of ecclesiastical law (and perhaps even law and religion). This possibility will be discussed in the concluding section of this chapter, while this section focuses on the importance and significance of the Stubbs–Maitland debate.

The label 'Stubbs–Maitland debate' may be misleading, given that the name of Maitland's apparent adversary (William Stubbs, then Bishop of Oxford and a distinguished historian) appears only twice in the index to *Roman Canon Law in the Church of England*. As the title of the first essay suggests, Maitland's primary concern was the work of the fifteenth-century canonist, William Lyndwood.[26] Yet Stubbs is the elephant in the room. As Cameron has noted, Stubbs' view was the orthodox view: 'When Maitland began to work on the subject of canon law in England, Bishop Stubbs, having both lectured on it at Oxford and compiled a memorandum for the Royal Commission on Ecclesiastical Courts, was the only authority in the field.'[27] In one of his two mentions of Stubbs, Maitland notes that Stubbs was the author of the 'Historical Appendix' added to the 1883 Report of the Ecclesiastical Courts Commission, noting that he need not 'say that I regard that discourse with reverence and admiration'.[28] It is this Report which motivated Maitland's attack – although *Roman Canon Law in the Church of England* does not provide a close analysis or dialogue with the report. Rather, Maitland's concern is with its underpinning assumptions,[29] and one

26 Cam noted that Maitland's study of Lyndwood's *Provinciale*, during 'the summer of 1895, while working on a course of lectures on Canon Law for law students', was the catalyst for his interest in the issue: Cam, *Law-Finders and Law-Makers*, 224. Lyndwood, another great Christian jurist, is Professor Helmholz's subject in Chapter 3 in this volume. It is worth noting that Maitland, like Helmholz, advocated further study of Lyndwood's *Provinciale*, opining that 'I cannot think that it has yet done all the work that it is capable of doing for the history of the English Church during "the conciliar period" or that it will do that work until it falls into the hands of one who is deeply read in foreign law-books': Maitland, *Roman Canon Law*, 6.

27 J. R. Cameron, *Frederick William Maitland and the History of English Law* (Norman: University of Oklahoma Press, 1961), 81.

28 Maitland, *Roman Canon Law*, 59.

29 Stubbs's argument had a political and religious motive. In claiming that the English ecclesiastical courts had been able to follow an independent line in the Middle Ages, he was able to argue that the Reformation was no true innovation: R. H. Helmholz, *Roman Canon Law in Reformation England* (Cambridge: Cambridge University Press, 1990), 4. This political/religious motive was still alive at the time of debates concerning disestablishment in Wales. As Ogle noted: 'If it can be shown that the Church as a spiritual body has had a continuous existence from the time of Augustine; that the four Welsh dioceses are its most ancient

sentence in particular: 'But the canon law of Rome, although always regarded as of great authority in England, was not held to be binding on the courts.'[30]

As Maitland stated, the reference to 'the courts' here meant the ecclesiastical courts in the three centuries immediately prior to the Reformation.[31] He contended that, although 'the difference between "great authority" and binding force is somewhat fine', nevertheless, that sentence, 'carefully worded though it be, is questionable and should be questioned'. It implied a relationship between domestic ecclesiastical courts and Rome as being based on 'respect, not of obedience', a relationship similar to the way in which English courts treat foreign law today: Roman canon law 'was not regarded as statute law by the English ecclesiastical courts; they did not conceive that it proceeded from a legislator whose commands they were bound to obey'. Maitland disagreed with this. For Maitland, this view was 'not yet beyond dispute' given that 'in all probability large proportions (to say the least) of the "canon law of Rome" were regarded by the courts Christian in this country as absolutely binding statute law'. Maitland wrote that there had been a tendency to confuse two propositions:

> The first is this: that in England the state did not suffer the church to appropriate considerable portions of that wide field of jurisdiction which the canonists claimed as heritage of ecclesiastical law. The second is this: the English courts Christian held themselves free to accept or reject, and did in some cases reject 'the canon law of Rome'.[32]

For Maitland, the truth of the first statement was beyond doubt: 'there are large portions of the canon law which, as a matter of fact, are not being enforced in England, because the temporal power will not suffer this enforcement'.[33] However, by contrast, Maitland found the second statement to be 'exceedingly dubious' asserting that he had looked 'in vain for any suggestion that an English judge or advocate ever called in question the statutory power of a text that was contained in any of the three papal lawbooks'.[34] As Elton noted, Maitland's distinction was very helpful in that it

dioceses; and that it has not only taught substantially the same doctrine, but maintained the same relation to the State throughout that long period; it has a right to retain the endowments which originated in medieval times that cannot be successfully challenged on the ground either of law or of ethics': A. Ogle, *The Canon Law in Medieval England an Examination of William Lyndwood's 'Provinciale,' in Reply to the late Professor F. W. Maitland* (London: John Murray, 1912), ix.

30 *Ecclesiastical Courts Commission: Report of the Commissioners*, 2 vols. (London: Eyre & Spottiswoode, 1883), 1:xviii.

31 Maitland, *Roman Canon Law*, 2. 32 Ibid., 51. 33 Ibid., 9. 34 Ibid., 51.

'cleared up an extraordinary confusion in part accepted and in part created by Stubbs' and showed that while there was 'much disputing between the king and Church', there was 'none between the Church and Rome'.[35] There seems to be some inconsistency, however, with the way in which Maitland describes the argument that he is debunking. His second proposition that the English courts were 'free' seems much wider than the Commission's carefully worded statement that canon law was 'regarded as of great authority in England' but 'not held to be binding on the courts'. As Helmholz has warned, we need to be wary of the 'argument that the English Church considered itself "independent" of papal law during the Middle Ages' since expressed that way the argument is more extreme than that expressed by Stubbs and is 'anachronistic and even silly'.[36] However, these inconsistencies do not pollute Maitland's conclusions.

Maitland's important contribution was the way that he 'was not content to rest his case on this negative note, but proceeded to positive arguments in support of his interpretation'.[37] He did not look for evidence of independence per se; rather he sought evidence of any 'situation where the ecclesiastical courts acted contrary to the formal canon law and where they were not constrained to do so by royal writs of prohibition or the threat of Praemunire'.[38] Maitland used Lyndwood's *Provinciale* (and other sources) not only to show the absence of native canonists following a 'national' line but to underline how doubting the Pope's legislative power or the binding force decretals was heretical. As Elton noted:

> He left no doubt at all that to those canonists the papal edicts constituted the source binding law; such provinces of the Universal Church as Canterbury and York could legislate as best by what Maitland called 'bye-laws' – local edicts which could only clarify or elaborate in detail where Rome had laid done general rule.[39]

Generally, *Roman Canon Law in the Church of England* was very well received: the immediate reaction was apparently one of 'stunned amazement' and 'even Stubbs, no longer active as a historian, slightly amended some things he had said when a new edition of his lectures came out'.[40] It was suggested that 'the history of our medieval church would have to be rewritten in its light'.[41] As Cameron has noted, all writers on the subject since 'have either begun or assumed the general conclusions at which Maitland arrived'.[42]

35 Elton, *F. W. Maitland*, 71, 72. 36 Helmholz, *Roman Canon Law*, 5.
37 Cameron, *Frederick William Maitland*, 79. 38 Bell, *Maitland*, 4–5.
39 Elton, *F. W. Maitland*, 70–1. 40 Ibid., 74. 41 Bell, *Maitland*, 123.
42 Cameron, *Frederick William Maitland*, 81.

However, although modern scholarship has broadly supported the view of Maitland, scholars such as Helmholz and Donahue, who have examined primary materials, have concluded that Maitland's work needs to be qualified in certain respects.[43] Helmholz stressed how both Stubbs and Maitland thought in positivist terms which were not shared by medieval litigants and court personnel. The Stubbs–Maitland choice, that either Western canon law was binding statute law or the English Church enjoyed an unfettered discretion, does not need to be made since in most cases there was no conflict between the canon and common law in relation to principle; the difference was to be found in the detail. In his study of the records of the Consistory Court of York 1300–1399, Donahue concluded that there were three important variables (the institution, the time and the type of case) which needed to be taken into account, but overall the relationship between the English courts and Rome could be characterised as one of great deference but not of blind adherence.[44] He endorsed what he called a 'Yes but' school, concluding that Maitland's view was to be preferred to Stubbs' but that a number of qualifications were needed to be made. This was especially true in relation to Maitland's second chapter, 'Church, State, and Decretals', where his assumption that the writs of prohibition constituted an example where the king's 'strong hand' tied the hands of the English judges has proved questionable given the absence of attempts to enforce this jurisdiction and the fact that courts had their own means by which to counter the writs.

Overall, as with Milsom's supposedly heretical comments on Maitland's account of the development of the common law, recent scholarship has only provided slight modifications to Maitland's account. As Ibbetson has noted in a different context, 'Maitland was, as always, more or less right'.[45] Of *Roman*

43 Helmholz, *Roman Canon Law*, ch. 1; C. Donahue Jr., 'Roman Canon Law in the Medieval English Church: Stubbs vs. Maitland Re-Examined after 75 Years in the Light of Some Records from the Church Courts', *Michigan Law Review* 72 (1974): 647–708.

44 Donahue contended that the records tell us nothing about the king–pope relationship but do tell us about (a) the king–English Church relationship and (b) the English Church–pope relationship. In respect of the king–English Church relationship, the records indicate that the church courts were quite independent of the king. The church courts turned to canon law as authority, not the king's law. However, the church courts depended on the king to support jurisdiction and sanctions. Litigants did not regard the choice of one forum as precluding the choice of the other. In respect of the English Church–pope relationship, Donahue found that the courts in Rome took most important cases themselves, meaning that the English church courts exercised a filtering function.

45 D. Ibbetson, 'The Challenges of Comparative Legal History', *Comparative Legal History* 1:1 (2013): 2.

Canon Law in the Church of England in particular, Elton has commented that it is 'astonishing how well Maitland's book stood up through decades of quite intensive efforts to assail him on a front which he himself regarded as less well defended than it should have been'.[46] Indeed, Maitland's account has now itself become the orthodox view as shown not only by Stubbs' revisions but also the report of the Archbishops' Commission on Canon Law, which rejected the view of the Ecclesiastical Courts Commission, noting that 'Maitland's point of view, for which support is abundant, whether in the text of legal treatises or in historical practice, has won general acceptance, and such opposition as it has met has been curiously ineffective.'[47] As Cameron noted, Maitland's work was so foundational that 'it opened a whole new field of study which other scholars have for the past half-century been exploring and explaining'.[48]

As with his work on the medieval land law, Maitland proved to be an architect designing and building the foundations upon which all subsequent work exists. The difference, here, is that there was a process of demolition before the building could begin. Maitland's success as an architect of knowledge arose from his ability to take a broad approach, and so, in the words of Milsom, his work 'established both the subject and the assumptions on which historians have worked ever since'.[49] Indeed, so foundational is his work that it is taken for granted and its controversial nature is overlooked. This is unfortunate since this context sheds a little more light upon both the question that we have previously explored and the question to which the next section will explore. Looking backwards, the controversial nature of the work sheds some further light upon Maitland the man and his religious background. Elton asserted that Maitland 'enjoyed the rumpus he had caused' and questioned the purity of his intentions:

> The delight and bubbling irony which spring from the pages of the book did not come from nowhere: at the task Maitland ever went with a degree of mild malice that is not to be found elsewhere in his writings. When all has been said, and true as his disavowal of any religious allegiance unquestionably was, Maitland belonged to that not unfamiliar brand of historian who, brought up as a Protestant retains for the rest of his agnostic

46 Elton, *F. W. Maitland*, 75–6.

47 *The Canon Law of the Church of England being the Report of the Archbishop's Commission on Canon Law* (London: Society for Promoting Christian Knowledge, 1947), 36. That reference to opposition presumably refers to the one attempt to support the contrary view by Ogle: *Canon Law in Medieval England*.

48 Cameron, *Frederick William Maitland*, 63.

49 Milsom, *Natural History of the Common Law*, xiv; Milsom, 'Introduction', xxi.

days a sympathy for the Reformation as the punishment of clerical arrogance.[50]

Looking forwards, *Roman Canon Law in the Church of England* also provides an illustration of Maitland's wider influence. Maitland's great achievement was to show how matters of ecclesiastic legal history could be explored dispassionately. As Donahue has noted, although today Maitland's work may still have 'some relevance for the ecclesiological debates of our own time, modern scholarship has seen an importance in the question beyond the polemical purposes to which its answer might be put'.[51] Maitland's genius was to ground the debate in a broader understanding of the interrelationship between the papacy, the state and the national churches in the Middle Ages. As Donahue argued, legal historians and lawyers are indebted to Maitland since his work may enable us to explore 'two separate groups of questions':

> First, is it possible for two different legal systems – canon law and common law – to operate simultaneously in the same geographic area, particularly when those two legal systems make overlapping jurisdictional claims?
>
> Second, putting to one side the potential institutional conflicts, to what extent is any body of law 'binding' on a judge called upon to decide a given case? To what extent and in what way does a judge use law to decide a case?[52]

These questions continue to be of great interest, especially in recent years given the focus on religious legal pluralism – or the fear of sharia – that was reflected in and perpetuated by the 2008 lecture by the then Archbishop of Canterbury Dr Rowan Williams.[53] However, it is not only the substance that is of importance and influence today. Legal scholars are also influenced often implicitly by Maitland's style.

A LASTING INSPIRATION

Maitland seldom spoke about his methodology or his approach to legal history, save his very pessimistic inaugural lecture when elected to the

[50] Elton, *F. W. Maitland*, 73.

[51] Donahue, 'Roman Canon Law in the Medieval English Church', 655. [52] Ibid., 655–6.

[53] R. Williams, 'Civil and Religious Law in England: A Religious Perspective', *Ecclesiastical Law Journal* 10 (2008): 262–82. For an analysis, see e.g. the essays in R. Sandberg, ed., *Religion and Legal Pluralism* (Farnham: Ashgate, 2015) and R. Sandberg and S. Thompson, 'Relational Autonomy and Religious Tribunals' (2017) 6 *Oxford Journal of Law and Religion* 137–161.

Downing Chair of English Law in 1888, which was entitled 'Why the History of English Law Is Not Written'. Plucknett has attempted to explain Maitland's 'mood of deep depression' by suggesting that the title that plagued Maitland's mind was actually 'Why the Selden Society Cannot Find Editors'.[54] Moreover, he has argued convincingly that Maitland's subsequent career can be 'read as the gradual abandonment of the propositions laid down in 1888'. This included the proposition that 'we should not wish to see a professor of law breaking and entering the close of the professor of history'. Maitland's work is now seen as a forerunner of interdisciplinary work which is so prevalent today, and which is often labelled as the 'new', 'external' or 'critical' legal history.[55] It has been noted that:

> Maitland is the founder of modern legal history, and all legal historians, no matter what kind of legal history they pursue, are in his debt. Although his best-known work, *The History of English Law before the Time of Edward I*, focuses on institutional and doctrinal development, it is not purely legal, as he understands the relationship of law to a broader social and political context. Moreover, his work is extensive, varied, and eclectic, abounding in ideas, insights, and concepts . . . Thus, Maitland is both the discipline's most important pioneer and one whose work connects with legal history's more recent manifestations.[56]

Maitland practised legal history as an interdisciplinary endeavour requiring detailed historical study alongside legal analysis. His work, therefore, provides a template for those interested in the study of law today. Doctrinal legal study is now seen as being insufficient on its own: even in trying to understand the narrowest of legal rules, doctrinal lawyers have constantly felt it necessary to ask questions which could not be answered by their own methodology.[57] Insights from other disciplines need to be added to the doctrinal analysis, but it is vital that each discipline brings together the insights that they would normally reach separately being aware, reflective and critical of their respective insights and the limitations, biases and

54 T. F. T. Plucknett, *Early English Legal Literature* (Cambridge: Cambridge University Press, 1958), 11, 13.

55 For 'new' see e.g. A. Hunt, 'The New Legal History: Prospects and Perspectives', *Contemporary Crises* 10 (1986): 201–8 (a review of G. R. Rubin and D. Sugarman, eds., *Law, Economy and Society: Essays in the History of English Law 1750–1914* [Abingdon: Professional Books, 1984]). For 'external' see e.g. J. Webber 'The Past and Foreign Countries', *Legal History* 10 (2006): 2. For 'critical' see e.g. R. W. Gordon, 'Critical Legal Histories', *Stanford Law Review* 36 (1984): 57–125.

56 J. Rose, 'Studying the Past: The Nature and Development of Legal History as an Academic Discipline', *Journal of Legal History* 31:2 (2010): 114, 115.

57 A. Bradney, 'Law as a Parasitic Discipline', *Journal of Law and Society* 25:1 (1998): 72.

implications of the way in which they see (and do not see) the subject studied.[58] In addition to being an inspiration to interdisciplinary work generally, Maitland can be seen (and should be reclaimed) as an inspiration for law and religion scholars in particular. As Cameron has argued, Maitland 'was one of the first scholars to become interested in the history of the law for its own sake rather than as a mere adjunct to some other dominant concern'.[59] It is possible to be even bolder: Maitland was one of the first scholars to be interested in ecclesiastical law as law from an academic perspective. A claim could be made that *Roman Canon Law in the Church of England* is the first work of law and religion scholarship. The influence of Maitland's approach can still be found today: the works of Richard Helmholz and John Witte Jr., among others, carry on the Maitland legacy, providing lucid historical accounts of ecclesiastical matters, while the forensic legal analysis of Norman Doe and Mark Hill QC follow Maitland's example of subjecting the law of the Church to the same if not higher academic scrutiny as that afforded to the law of the land.

Maitland, in short, is an inspiration to all legal writers, not only in substance and in style but also in spirit. As Bell has noted, Maitland's work 'was never channelled in a single groove or pointed to a single end; he had a lively, flexible mind that was always ready to follow a hint from the data that it happened to be processing'.[60] This included the questioning of received wisdoms. For Cameron, '[f]ew English historians seemed to have had the polemic spirit which causes one to go around looking for skeletons in closets which might be exposed'.[61] When Maitland 'became suspicious of the validity of any piece of received and traditionally accepted matter', he was always able to state his own conclusions 'with an admirable mixture of modesty and courage'.[62] This chapter has attempted to do a little of the same, questioning what Maitland really intended by once styling himself a dissenter from all churches. Maitland's religiosity was more complicated than the expedient phrase in the preface to *Roman Canon Law in the Church of England* might suggest. The nature and content of those essays show that Maitland deserves the same reputation in the history of ecclesiastical law (and law and religion more generally) as he is unquestioningly afforded in

58 See, further, R. Sandberg, *Religion, Law and Society* (Cambridge: Cambridge University Press, 2014), ch. 6.

59 Cameron, *Frederick William Maitland*, 62–3.

60 Bell, *Maitland*, 108.

61 He added, 'Perhaps it is putting it too strongly to imply that Maitland had a polemic spirit, but there is no doubt that when he thought he saw a historical truth, he hewed to the line and let the chips fall where they might': Cameron, *Frederick William Maitland*, 65.

62 Bell, *Maitland*, 108.

relation to the history of the common law. He remains a 'living authority' for ecclesiastical lawyers too. Maitland is not only the architect of the way in which we continue to see the subject today,[63] he is also an inspiration in both style and spirit, and that is ample evidence of his undoubted status as a great Christian jurist.

63 For a contemporary evaluation of the breadth and depth of the subject, see Frank Cranmer, Mark Hill, Celia Kenny and Russell Sandberg, eds., *The Confluence of Law and Religion* (Cambridge: Cambridge University Press, 2016).

Lord Denning, photograph © Bridgeman Images

15

A Passion for Justice
Lord Denning, Christianity and the Law

Andrew Phang

INTRODUCTION

Among the English judges of the twentieth century, there was perhaps none more candid about his religious beliefs than Lord Denning, who took silk in 1938, served as a judge of first instance from 1944 to 1948, as a Lord Justice of Appeal in the Court of Appeal from 1948 to 1957, as a Law Lord in the House of Lords from 1957 and as Master of the Rolls presiding over the Civil Division of the Court of Appeal from 1962 until his retirement in 1982. His views in this regard were confined, in the main, to the extra-judicial sphere and constitute the theme of the first part of this essay, which is more descriptive and informative in nature. The second part of this essay focuses on Denning's judgments and is more theoretical and normative. This latter theme arises from the popular perception that, notwithstanding his brilliance as a judge, Denning often relied on his subjective sense of the justice of the particular case in hand to arrive at a specific result and that this was the antithesis of the objectivity that ought to inform the judicial function. Indeed, it has been observed more than once that, in order to achieve justice in a specific case, Denning often circumvented (or even abrogated) existing legal principle. This objection, I suggest, never really bothered Denning as his vision of the law was premised on a unified and objective basis rooted in his Christian faith. Put simply, to him, religion and law were inextricably connected in a symbiotic relationship: there

This chapter draws liberally from the author's earlier work, including A. Phang, 'The Natural Law Foundations of Lord Denning's Thought and Work', *Denning Law Journal* 14 (1999): 159–77. A lengthier paper (originally delivered at the University of Buckingham at a symposium to mark Lord Denning's one-hundredth birthday in 1999) was subsequently published in two parts: A. Phang, 'A Passion for Justice: The Natural Law Foundations of Lord Denning's Thought and Work', *Global Journal of Classical Theology* 5(1) (2005) and 5(2) (2006). The author would like to express his gratitude to Prof. Mark Hill QC and Mr Justin Yeo, Assistant Registrar, Supreme Court of Singapore, for their helpful comments and suggestions. All views expressed are personal to the author and do not represent those of the Supreme Court of Singapore.

was a higher (and objective) law against which all legal rules and principles ought to be measured, especially in relation to the spirit of justice and fairness for which Denning had a discernible passion. As a result, Denning set out not only to achieve a just and fair result in individual cases but also to develop the law in a more general sense. Contrary to his critics' view that he was arbitrary (especially in so-called hard cases),[1] Denning's approach was that hard cases not only resulted in just and fair results in the specific cases themselves but also at the same time created sound law of general application for future cases as well.

DENNING AND HIS FAITH

It is significant that Denning never, at least expressly, espoused his religious beliefs in his judgments. Such views are to be found, instead, in his extra-judicial writings. This is only right as the law applies to everyone, regardless of his or her religious persuasion. Legal rules and principles are not – and cannot be – coterminous or in any way linked with a single religious belief or view-point, especially in common law countries which are multi-cultural and religiously plural in their nature. However, personal religious and ethical beliefs are not necessarily inconsistent with the general sense of justice and fairness that is embodied in the general rules and principles of the law itself; indeed, there is every reason to believe that the converse would be the case. Even when viewed from a Christian perspective, it cannot be said that courts which do not subscribe to a Christian natural law theory do not dispense justice. Indeed, the Christian faith itself acknowledges that God can ensure that justice is dispensed by common grace, consistently with what the apostle Paul has termed (in Romans 2:14–15) 'the law written on the heart'.

It is important to emphasise that Denning's approach was consistent with his attitude towards other religions and religious groups. His basic philosophy in this regard was straightforward: there ought always to be freedom of religion.[2] Indeed, his openness towards other religions is displayed, for instance, in his exhortation that 'Christians and Jews should come together in the search for truth'[3] – all this despite the clear and distinct differences between Jewish and Christian beliefs which Denning frankly and matter-of-factly acknowledges.

1 See generally P. Robson and P. Watchman, eds., *Justice, Lord Denning and the Constitution* (Farnborough, Hampshire: Gower, 1981) and J. L. Jowell and J. P. W. B. McAuslan, eds., *Lord Denning: The Judge and the Law* (London: Sweet & Maxwell, 1985).

2 See generally A. T. Denning, *Freedom under the Law* (London: Stevens & Sons Limited, 1949), 35 and 45–8; A. T. Denning, *The Road to Justice* (London: Stevens & Sons Limited, 1955), 116–17; A. T. Denning, *Freedom of Religion*, William Ainslie Memorial Lecture, delivered at the church of St Martin-in-the-Fields on 17 November 1955 (London: Cranbourn Press, 1955).

3 A. T. Denning, *Landmarks in the Law* (London: Butterworths, 1984), 328.

Indeed, in *Landmarks in the Law*, he devotes a significant portion of his book to the Jews. Insofar as Christianity is concerned, Denning is firmly of the view that 'we have reached the point ... that whilst the Christian beliefs still form the foundation of our way of life, as I trust they always will, they are not to be enforced by law but by teaching and example'.[4]

Family Background

Alfred Thompson Denning was born just before the turn of the twentieth century – on 23 January 1899.[5] His was a humble background. His family was not only the source of much love but was also an important and significant influence from a religious (in particular, Christian) context. As Denning himself observed in his Preface to *The Family Story* on what went into the making of his family: 'Religion – perhaps the chiefest influence of all. Not talked of much. Yet very present in our family. Faith in God handed down from generation to generation.'[6] And, as Denning's biographer, Iris Freeman, pertinently observed:

> Both Charles and Clara [Denning's parents] had grown up in homes where the Church of England played an important part, at a time when the evangelical movement placed great emphasis upon the scriptures. By the start of the twentieth century religious observance was becoming more relaxed and in some homes it was beginning to have a social rather than a morally compulsive foundation. In the Denning home belief in God's goodness was of fundamental importance and was to remain a mainspring of Tom's [Denning's] life.[7]

The Influence of William Temple

Denning was also influenced by the work of the late Archbishop of Canterbury, William Temple, who studied at Balliol College, Oxford, was a Fellow in Philosophy at the University of Oxford, Bishop of Manchester and Archbishop of York, before his translation to Archbishop of

[4] Denning, *Freedom under the Law*, 47. See also Denning, *Road to Justice*, 117–18.

[5] Denning had expressed the hope that he would live to see three centuries. Sadly, this was not to be as he passed away six weeks after his hundredth birthday, on 6 March 1999. On his life, see generally, A. T. Denning, *The Family Story* (London: Butterworths, 1981), book 1; I. Freeman, *Lord Denning: A Life* (London: Hutchinson, 1993), part 1.

[6] Denning, *Family Story*, vi.

[7] Freeman, *Lord Denning*, 14–15. Denning was confirmed as a member of the Church of England on 25 October 1914; one of the family's most prized books was an early edition of John Bunyan's *Pilgrim's Progress* (see Denning, *Family Story*, 11–12).

Canterbury.[8] Denning once described Temple as 'one of the greatest thinkers of the present century'.[9] It is no surprise, therefore, that he constantly cited Temple's work and philosophy.

In one instance, Denning recounts how Temple, in an address at the Inns of Court, opened his remarks by saying, 'I cannot say that I know much about the law, having been far more interested in justice.'[10] Denning opines that 'the rebuke was well merited', as the hearers, all lawyers, 'had been brought up in the philosophy of John Austin' and '[t]hose who believe in that philosophy regard the law as something separate and apart from justice'. Denning challenges what he terms 'this facile assumption', not least because lawyers are responsible for the law and, hence, any injustice that occurs. Further, he is of the view that it is a great mistake because 'it overlooks the reason why people obey the law': 'they obey the law because they know it is a thing they ought to do'; in other words, they 'obey the law simply because they recognise it to be obligatory on them'; the 'sense of obligation' arising 'from the habits of the people which have grown up in their history'. Above all, however, is 'moral obligation', which goes beyond mere habit and arises because of 'the moral quality of the law itself': 'people will respect rules of law which are intrinsically right and just and will expect their neighbours to obey them, as well as obeying the rules themselves'. The law must therefore 'correspond with what they think to be right and just, or, at any rate, must not unduly diverge from it. In other words, it must correspond, as near as may be, with justice'. Denning then proceeds to define 'justice' as 'what the right-minded members of the community – those who have the right spirit within them – believe to be fair'. Another instance of citing Temple occurs in the following, very similar, passage: 'It is axiomatic that love should be the predominant Christian impulse, and that the primary form of love in social organisation is justice.'[11]

Concerning the duties of lawyers, Denning cited Temple in *Christianity and Social Order* as follows:

> Love, in fact, finds its primary expression through Justice – which . . . means in practice that each side should state its case as strongly as it can, before the most impartial tribunal available, with determination to accept the award of

[8] See A. T. Denning, 'The Traditions of the Bar', *South Africa Law Journal* 72 (1955): 43; Denning, *Road to Justice*, 1 and 34.

[9] See A. T. Denning, 'The Influence of Religion', in *The Changing Law* (London: Steven & Sons Limited, 1953), 99 at 107.

[10] Denning, *Road to Justice*, 1–3, from which all the following quotations in this paragraph derive.

[11] W. Temple, *Christianity and Social Order* (Harmondsworth: Penguin, 1942, repr. 1956), 55, cited in Denning, 'Influence of Religion', 107.

> the tribunal. At least that puts the two parties on a level and is to that extent in accord with the command 'Thou shalt love thy neighbour as thyself'.[12]

There were numerous other instances of Denning quoting directly from Temple. In the context of freedom of religion, Denning stated that 'it was William Temple who pointed out that there is a tendency for religions and for religious denominations to claim to have a monopoly of light, when in fact each has only a few rays of that light'.[13] In advocating a welfare state governed by Christian principles, Denning observed that Temple 'pointed out time after time the troubles and difficulties which arise in a society which is excessively capitalistic'.[14] With regard to the importance of respect for the individual, Denning again quoted Temple, in particular the fact that '[t]he person is primary, not the society; the State exists for the citizen, not the citizen for the State'.[15]

Denning's Religious Beliefs

Denning's religious and ethical beliefs were clear and express, albeit articulated, in the main, extra-judicially. It might have been thought that Denning's interest would be somewhat theoretical, not least because of the influence of Temple, a trained philosopher; but Denning always claimed to be wary of theory and endorsed experience and practice instead.[16] Indeed, he once remarked:

> Jurisprudence was too abstract a subject for my liking. All about ideologies, legal norms and basic norms, 'ought' and 'is', realism and behaviourism: and goodness knows what else. The jargon of the philosophers of law has always been beyond me. I like to get down to the practical problems which come up for decision.[17]

12 Address Delivered by the Rt Hon. The Lord Denning, Master of the Rolls, at the Annual Service of the Lawyers Christian Fellowship on 6 October 1977 [hereafter LCF Address, 1977], on file at the Hampshire Record Office.

13 Denning, *Freedom of Religion*, 16.

14 A. T. Denning, *The Christian Approach to the Welfare State*, 17th Shaftesbury Lecture (London: H. Williams & Son, 1953), 10. See also Denning, 'Influence of Religion', 120.

15 Denning, 'Influence of Religion', 116–17.

16 See, by way of example, A. T. Denning, 'The Independence of the Judges', in B. W. Harvey, ed., *The Lawyer and Justice: A Collection of Addresses by Judges and Jurists to the Holdsworth Club of The University of Birmingham* (London: Sweet & Maxwell, 1978), 55–69; and Denning, *Changing Law*, 15–16. On Denning's application of biblical Scripture to judicial administration, see A. T. Denning, *The Closing Chapter* (London: Butterworths, 1983), 32–3, which includes a reference to Exodus 18:13–27 on the appointment of judges to help Moses in clearing the backlog of work.

17 Denning, *Family Story*, 240.

On another occasion, Denning summarised his judicial philosophy thus: 'my philosophy can be summarised under three headings: (i) let justice be done; (ii) freedom under the law; (iii) put your trust in God'.[18]

Turning to Denning's specific enunciations of his beliefs, in a brief typescript entitled 'What Life Has Taught Me', Denning commenced by stating 'the most important thing that life has taught me is to believe in God'.[19] He then declared that this belief was due both to his upbringing as well as to his experience 'in going through life'.[20] On this latter aspect, he said, 'My experience as a lawyer and as a judge has verified what I was taught about God.' To Denning, law and religion are inextricably connected: 'The aim of the law is to see that truth is observed and that justice is done between man and man'.[21] On another occasion, Denning observed that 'without religion there can be no morality and without morality there can be no law'.[22] As to what constitutes 'truth' and 'justice', Denning said that '[t]he spirit of truth and justice is not something you can see. It is not temporal but eternal. How does man know what is truth or justice? It is not the product of his intellect, but of his spirit.'[23]

As to how the 'right spirit' is created in man, Denning was of the view that such 'is the province of religion' and, in particular, the Christian religion. He developed his argument as follows: 'Religion concerns the spirit in man whereby he is able to recognise what is truth and what is justice: whereas law is only the application, however imperfectly, of truth and justice in our everyday affairs.'[24] In a passage notable for its candour, Denning stated:

18 Ibid., 172.

19 A. T. Denning, 'What Life Has Taught Me', on file with the Hampshire Record Office.

20 See also A. T. Denning, 'Why I Believe in God', transcript of a talk delivered on the BBC Home Service, 14 September 1943 (on file with the Hampshire Record Office). References hereafter are to page numbers of the transcript. See also Lord Edmund-Davies, 'Lord Denning: Christian Advocate and Judge', *Denning Law Journal* 1 (1986): 41, which refers to Denning's service as a churchwarden as well as member of the Parochial Church Council. Denning was also for many years President of the Lawyers Christian Fellowship. See further, Denning's Address at the Annual Service of the Lawyers Christian Fellowship, 8 October 1970, on file with the Hampshire Record Office [hereafter LCF Address, 1970].

21 Denning, 'Why I Believe in God'.

22 A. T. Denning, 'The Right Standards of Conduct', *Law Society Gazette* (1957): 609. See also LCF Addresses, 1970 and 1977; and 'Denning and Scarman: A Conversation between Lord Denning, Master of the Rolls, and Lord Justice Scarman', BBC Transcript, Radio 3, Talks and Documentaries Department, transmission 3 March 1977, 12 (on file with the Hampshire Record Office).

23 Denning, 'What Life Has Taught Me'. See also Denning, 'Why I Believe in God', 2.

24 Denning, 'What Life Has Taught Me'. See also Denning, 'Why I Believe in God', 3.

> I do know that in the great experiences of life, and indeed in the small ones too, such strength as I have is of God, and the weakness is mine. Need I enumerate the experiences? Take the hard things. When faced with a task on which great issues depend; when high hopes lie shattered; when anxiety gnaws deep; or when overwhelmed by grief; where can I turn for help but to God? Or take the joyful things: a hard task attempted or done; the happiness of family life; or the beauty of nature; where can I turn for thankfulness but to God? All experiences convince me, not only that God is ever-present, but also that it is by contact with the spirit of God that the spirit in Man reaches its highest and wisest plane.[25]

It is suggested that the 'spirit of God' Denning referred to is probably the Holy Spirit, who is described in the Bible, among other things, as a 'counsellor'.[26]

In another address, Denning elaborated on the concept of justice as follows:

> Justice is not a temporal thing; it is eternal; a thing of the spirit; and the nearest approach to a definition that I could give is that justice is what the right-thinking members of the community believe to be fair. Simply that. You and I, representing the right-thinking members of the community, doing, as best we can, what is fair – and, in these days, fair not only between man and man but between man and the state.[27]

In yet another address, Denning again linked the concept of justice to the eternal realm: 'Surely we ought to go back two thousand years and say, "What doth it profit a man if he gain the whole world and lose his own soul?" In organised society the soul of man finds its expression in justice.'[28]

The upshot of all this, insofar as lawyers are concerned, is that:

> Lawyers should be men of religion: and speaking generally that has always been the case in this country. It is the reason why the common law of England

[25] Denning, 'What Life Has Taught Me' (part of the passage is handwritten). See also Denning, 'Why I Believe in God', 4.

[26] See John 14:16, 26; 15:26 and 16:7. See also LCF Address, 1977, where Denning observes, 'The whole world today, so far as spiritual values are concerned, is a valley of bones . . . A valley of dry bones dead to the things of the spirit. Would that I could prophesy with Ezekiel – "Come from the four winds O Lord and breathe on them that they may live. So I prophesied as he commanded me, and the breath came into them, and they lived, and stood upon their feet, an exceeding great army." Can we put this spirit back into the soul of man and bring it back into a world which is so dead to it?' The reference is to Ezekiel 37:9–10.

[27] See A. T. Denning, 'The Freedom of the Individual To-day', *Medico-Legal Journal* 45 (1977): 49 at 55. See also Denning, 'Why I Believe in God', 3; Denning, 'Right Standards of Conduct', 614; Denning, *Road to Justice*, 4; A. T. Denning, 'Law and Life in Our Time', *Manitoba Law Journal* 2 (1966): 3 at 13; and A. T. Denning, 'Recent Changes in the Law', *New Zealand Law Journal* (1966): 167 at 174.

[28] See A. T. Denning, 'Let Justice Be Done', *Manitoba Law Journal* 6 (1975): 227 at 228. The quotation is from Matthew 16:26. See also Denning, *Road to Justice*, 5, where Micah 6:6–8 is quoted.

> is so great. The law has been moulded for centuries by judges who have been brought up in the Christian faith. The precepts of religion, consciously or unconsciously, have been their guide in the administration of justice.[29]

In a message given to the Quarterly Meeting of the Lawyers Christian Fellowship entitled 'The Influence of Religion on Law', Denning observed that 'in the days when the Bible was first put into English the Judges laid down rules which were undoubtedly influenced by Bible teaching'.[30] More importantly, perhaps, he pointed to 'the more fundamental teaching of our Lord': 'the Gospel of Love', that is, that one is to love God first and then our neighbour as ourselves.[31] Although 'this is a precept of religion, not of morals nor of law', Denning was of the view that 'it is not unrelated to them', for 'in social organisation, love finds its primary expression through justice': 'the two – love and justice – are interdependent'.[32] And, as already seen, Denning proceeds to point out that justice 'is not the product of [a man's] intellect, but of his spirit'. He also reiterates the point that the Christian 'religion concerns the spirit in man whereby he is able to recognise what is truth and what is justice; whereas law is only the application, however imperfectly, of truth and justice in our everyday affairs'.[33]

Insofar as societal welfare is concerned, Denning argued that 'the Welfare State has come into being by a true application of Christian principles, but . . . there is a danger of its being mishandled and abused by people who have no knowledge of those principles and seek only their own advantage'.[34] Indeed, this is the Christian distinction between *agape* (self-sacrificial love) on the one hand and overweening self-interest on the other. To the extent that the latter is increasingly predominant, there are particular problems with the capitalist system, which are, in turn, reflected in existing contract law, as will be discussed. Denning's views in this lecture were that 'it is plainly wrong in a Christian society, where each should love his neighbour, that some people should be sick and in need, and that nothing should be done about it'; he then observed that 'it cannot all be left to the few good Samaritans' and that 'the Welfare State came into being as a consequence of the application of Christian principles to the existing social order'. One major problem which subsequently arose, however, was that state-provided social security, which was

[29] See Denning, 'Why I Believe in God', 3; Denning, 'Influence of Religion', 109.

[30] A. T. Denning, *The Influence of Religion on Law* (Bletchley Printers Ltd, 1950), 2–3, from where the following quotations are all derived.

[31] Citing Luke 10:25–8. [32] Citing Temple, *Christianity and Social Order*.

[33] See also Denning, 'Influence of Religion', 122.

[34] See Denning, *Christian Approach*, 3. The quotations in the remainder of this paragraph are also from this lecture.

not animated by true Christian principles mandating love for fellow human beings, soon degenerated into selfish abuse. Denning argued that the recapture of love and service through Christian doctrine is essential to combat such abuse, but added: 'If these principles are to guide the people of the Welfare State, then it is important that the State itself should show that it is religious. You cannot expect the people to be faithful to Christian principles if the State itself is not so.'[35] As Lord Denning had poignantly observed elsewhere: 'In coming upon legal obstacles, it is not enough to keep your law books dry. It is as well to have a Bible ready to hand too. It is the most tattered book in my library. I have drawn upon it constantly.'[36]

Summary

Denning could not have been clearer about his Christian faith, which he received in his childhood and which continued throughout his life. In addition to his family, Denning was also influenced by the views of William Temple. However, his expression of faith is mainly to be found in the extra-judicial sphere. It is in the exploration of the interaction, if any, between Denning's Christian beliefs and his considerable judicial output, that the second part of this chapter is devoted.

DENNING AND THE LAW

There is a perennial tension in the law between certainty and fairness. While there is no necessary incompatibility between them, conflicts do occur. The paradigm example is where the existing doctrine mandates a certain result which the judge considers to be unfair. What, then, is the judge to do? The popular perception is that Denning often circumvented (or even abrogated) existing doctrine in order to achieve a fair outcome in a specific case. But could it not be said that Denning, instead, developed existing doctrine to achieve such an outcome, especially since, as already discussed, Denning clearly acknowledged that 'law is only the application, however imperfectly, of truth and justice in our everyday affairs'?[37] After all, legal doctrine is not static and has to be incrementally developed in order to meet changing needs and circumstances. The rigid and mechanistic preoccupation with legal doctrine that results in unfairness in any given case is the antithesis of the ideal of the law, certainty notwithstanding. However, the opposite extreme is equally

35 Ibid., 14. 36 Denning, *Family Story*, 181.
37 Denning, *Influence of Religion on Law*, 4.

undesirable inasmuch as the court cannot be said to have arrived at an objectively fair decision if it disregards existing legal principle.[38] As I have observed elsewhere, 'the rules and principles which constitute the doctrine of the law are not ends in themselves but are, rather, the means through which the courts arrive at substantively fair outcomes in the cases before them in every area of the law'.[39] Neither is more important than the other, as both are to be viewed as an interactive process.

Denning's judgments reveal his constant concern to achieve a fair result or outcome in every case. This passion for justice finds its source in his religious faith and beliefs that prevented legal doctrine from becoming ossified and therefore an instrument of injustice. For Denning, that passionate spirit of justice would enable the existing doctrine to be applied in a fashion that achieved a just and fair result in the case at hand. And if the existing doctrine could not achieve such a result, he was prepared to change it in order to achieve such a result, not only in the case at hand but also in future cases. Passion for justice infused every aspect of Denning's judgments, and such passion was not based on purely subjective preferences but also manifested itself in the objective development and, on occasion, somewhat radical reform, of the law itself.

Denning was of the view that his faith and beliefs (which were more akin to a natural law approach that had its root source in the Christian faith) were more productive of justice and fairness than, for example, the legal positivism found in the jurisprudential theories of scholars such as John Austin and H. L. A. Hart, which posited that there was no necessary connection between law and morality.[40] Whether Denning's faith and beliefs can be justified engages a sphere of Christian apologetics which is beyond the scope of this chapter. The existence of God, including the creation–evolution debate, the claims of Christ by His death and resurrection, the authenticity and veracity of the Bible and the concept of the Holy Spirit, may well form part of a larger Christian natural law theory.[41] There is also a threshold issue which relates to the inevitability of, and necessity for, objective standards.[42] Any rational

38 This judicial approach is reminiscent of that of Lord Mansfield, discussed in Chapter 9.

39 A. Phang, 'Doctrine and Fairness in the Law of Contract', *Legal Studies* 29 (2009): 534 at 535.

40 See generally H. L. A. Hart, 'Positivism and the Separation of Law and Morals', *Harvard Law Review* 71 (1958): 593; H. L. A. Hart, *The Concept of Law*, 2d ed. (Oxford: Clarendon Press, 1994); L. Fuller, 'Positivism and Fidelity to Law: A Reply to Hart', *Harvard Law Review* 71 (1958): 630.

41 For a provisional and cursory discussion, see Phang, 'Natural Law Foundations', 174–6; A. Phang, 'American Jurisprudence through Christian Eyes: Beyond the Nightmare and the Noble Dream', *University of Detroit Mercy Law Review*, 81 (2004): 867 at 902–18.

42 Phang, 'American Jurisprudence': 870–5; A. Phang, 'Security of Contract and the Pursuit of Fairness', *Journal of Contract Law* 16 (2000): 158 at 166–8.

argument that is seriously made necessarily implies a truth-claim, so that even the argument that there is no objective standard (that is, that everything is relative or subjective) is itself self-refuting.

The content of Denning's judgments serves to illustrate the two main themes of this chapter: Denning's passion for justice in particular cases, together with his development of the law more generally. Denning did not circumvent, distort or abrogate existing legal doctrine in his pursuit of the individual justice of the case before him but rather, for the most part at least, he developed principles of law in a coherent and systemic manner. A further point ought also to be made, which Denning could not have known and which I could not myself have known when I wrote my original paper on Denning a decade and a half ago. It is that subsequent developments (in both common law and statute) have vindicated many of the changes which Denning had propounded. This underscores the immense vision and fairness of Denning's approach towards the moulding of the law itself.

The Law of Contract

Denning's contributions to the law of contract are far too many to do justice to in this chapter, so a discussion of a few of the more significant will have to suffice. A general observation by Denning himself on the law of contract is apposite before turning to certain specific areas of contract law:

> The influence of the Church was immense: because the Church courts assumed jurisdiction in matters of conscience. Originally in English law a promise was not enforceable unless it was hedged about with the formality of a seal. But the teaching of the Church was in favour of rejecting formalities and insisting on good faith. The just man is 'he that sweareth not his neighbour and disappointeth him not, though it were to his own hindrance'. If a man made a promise and did not keep it, the ecclesiastical courts would punish him for breach of faith.[43]

Contract law today has been secularised, with an emphasis on rationalism and individualism,[44] and this may well explain why courts have been unable to mediate objectively the tension between certainty and fairness. Denning would surely agree with Professor Berman's pertinent suggestion that

[43] Denning, *Influence of Religion on Law*, 7, citing Psalm 15:4.

[44] See, generally, H. Berman, 'The Religious Sources of General Contract Law: An Historical Perspective', *Journal of Law and Religion*, 4 (1986): 103–24, reprinted in H. Berman, *Faith and Order: The Reconciliation of Law and Religion* (Atlanta: Scholars Press, 1993), ch. 7.

a return to objective religious foundations will enable a new and more coherent theory of contract law to be developed.

In relation to specific aspects of contract law, the doctrine of consideration is familiar to all law students, yet it is not without its problems.[45] It was traditionally held that a promise to take part-payment in full discharge of a debt did not constitute valid consideration.[46] The harshness of this approach has been mitigated somewhat by the recognition that some other actual benefit or indeed detriment might constitute valid consideration.[47] However, prior to that, the courts had to rely on various exceptions to avoid the possible injustice that might result from a rigid application of the doctrine of consideration. One of the most important exceptions is the doctrine of promissory estoppel, which finds its genesis in the seminal judgment of Denning J (as he then was) in the English High Court decision of *Central London Property Trust Ltd v. High Trees House Limited*.[48] Put shortly, if one person makes to another an unambiguous representation that he will not enforce his strict legal rights, intending that other party to act on it, and that party does act on it, then the representor/promisor will not be allowed to resile from his promise if it would be inequitable for him to do so.

The *High Trees* case is commonly hailed as a landmark in the common law of contract and was perceived as a somewhat radical development of the law.[49] To Denning, though, the case 'helped to narrow [the] gap' between the 'strict rules and the social necessities of the 20th century', thus achieving justice and fairness in the process. He also recounted that 'it was not a reserved judgment. I decided it at first instance straightaway at the end of the argument'.[50] He observed:

> Its importance was in getting rid of the old notion that estoppels were confined to representations of fact and did not extend to representations as to the future. It brought in a new species of estoppel called promissory

45 See, for instance, the calls for its abolition by the Law Revision Committee of England and Wales almost eight decades ago in *Sixth Interim Report (Statute of Frauds and the Doctrine of Consideration)* (Cmnd 5449, 1937).

46 *Foakes v. Beer* (1884) 9 App Cas 605.

47 See *Williams v. Roffey Bros & Nicholls (Contractors) Ltd* [1991] 1 QB 1; cf. *Re Selectmove* [1995] 1 WLR 474.

48 [1947] KB 180. See A. T. Denning, *The Discipline of Law* (London: Butterworths, 1979), 197–223, for his own account.

49 See A. Mason, 'The Impact of Equitable Doctrine on the Law of Contract', *Anglo-American Law Review*, 27 (1998): 1 at 18; and Lord Devlin's foreword in Jowell and McAuslan, *Lord Denning*, vi.

50 Denning, *Discipline of Law*, 197. Denning's foreword to the inaugural issue of the *Denning Law Journal* 1 (1986): 1 at 2.

> estoppel. Many were the doubts cast upon it, notably by the House of Lords, but it became and is well established.[51]

Leaving aside certain problematic aspects of the doctrine, Denning emphasises that the law in general and promissory estoppel in particular are premised on moral foundations – aiding in the attainment of justice and fairness while simultaneously avoiding the technicality and injustice engendered by the strict doctrine of consideration which, he observed, 'has been replaced by the better precept: "my word is my bond", irrespective of whether there is consideration to support it'. More significantly, perhaps, there are resonances of Christian principles when Denning continues:

> Once a man gives a promise or assurance to his neighbour – on which his neighbour relies – he should not be allowed to go back on it. In stating the principle, and its extensions, the lawyers use the archaic word 'estoppel'. I would prefer to put it in language which the ordinary man understands: It is a principle of justice and of equity.[52]

However, Denning was also cognisant of the need for the law to be developed in a *principled* fashion. In this regard, he realised the very real danger that a logical extension of the doctrine of promissory estoppel posed to the doctrine of consideration itself. So, for example, in *Combe v. Combe*,[53] he took the view that promissory estoppel could only be used as a shield and not a sword. Interestingly, in a subsequent videotaped interview, it appears that 'Lord Denning withdraws his reservations in *Combe v. Combe* ... about the defensive nature or estoppel and "is quite happy to see the doctrine of consideration go" in favour of a more fundamental principle that a man should stand by his word.'[54] This view was prophetic – the High Court of Australia subsequently permitted promissory estoppel to be utilised as a sword, although this issue remains open in English law.[55]

Denning was also an activist in the sphere of implied terms, which he viewed as centring on the demands of what he termed 'simple justice'. He made no secret that in implying terms, courts were, in effect, 'filling in the gaps'.[56] He thus asserted, in *Liverpool City Council v. Irwin*,[57] that courts could imply terms where it was 'reasonable' to do so. Although this was subsequently rejected on a further appeal to the House of Lords,[58] Denning won a victory of sorts, for the Law Lords drew a distinction between 'terms implied in fact' and

[51] Denning, 'Foreword', 2. [52] Denning, *Discipline of Law*, 223. [53] [1951] 2 KB 215.

[54] Dockray et al., *Review of The Denning Interviews*, *Law Quarterly Review* 101 (1985): 137 at 140.

[55] See *Walton Stores (Interstate) Ltd v. Maher* (1988) 164 CLR 387. See also *Commonwealth v. Verwayen* (1990) 170 CLR 394.

[56] Denning, *Discipline of Law*, 34. [57] [1976] QB 319. [58] [1977] AC 239.

'terms implied in law',[59] the test of reasonableness and public policy applying to the latter, which constituted a broader category of terms implied in a particular class of contracts, even if this were contrary to the actual or presumed intentions of the parties concerned. Denning was quick to seize upon this distinction and, naturally, he endorsed it fully.[60]

Denning is also well known for judgments that were geared towards aiding consumers vis-à-vis contractual terms purporting to exclude or limit liability. This had not always been the case. He lamented his involvement, as counsel, in the decision of *L'Estrange v. Graucob*,[61] which held that a contracting party is, in the absence of fraud or misrepresentation, bound by exception clauses in a signed contract.[62] But things had radically changed by the time Denning was appointed to the bench. The famous doctrine of fundamental breach finds its genesis with Denning himself.[63] It may, in fact, be said that the underlying impetus for Denning's approach towards exemption clauses stemmed from the perception of the need to prevent abuse which, in turn, is embodied in Christian doctrine. While this doctrine was rejected by the House of Lords in *Photo Production Limited v. Securicor Transport Limited*,[64] Denning could take some consolation in the subsequent enactment of the Unfair Contract Terms Act 1977, which amounted to vindication of his views, albeit indirectly. As Denning himself put it:

> It has been put right now. We can look to see whether a clause is reasonable or not. If it is not reasonable, we can hold it to be bad or not reasonable to apply. So all's well now, after all these years. At all events I hope that you will find it so.[65]

On an even broader level is Denning's controversial statement of principle in *Lloyd's Bank Limited v. Bundy*[66] with respect to inequality of bargaining power. It is frequently read as embodying too general and vague a standard that obviates the need for showing some wrongdoing on the defendant's part,

59 Not explicitly, but the point has been since reaffirmed: see A. Phang, 'The Challenge of Principled Gap-Filling: A Study of Implied Terms in a Comparative Context', *Journal of Business Law* 4 (2014): 263 at 295–307.

60 *Shell UK Ltd v. Lostock Garage Limited* [1976] 1 WLR 1187 at 1196–7.

61 [1934] 2 KB 394.

62 See e.g. Denning, 'Right Standards of Conduct', 610; Denning, *Family Story*, 99 and 174–5.

63 See e.g. *Karsales (Harrow) Ltd v. Wallis* [1956] 1 WLR 938; *Sze Hai Tong Bank Ltd v. Rambler Cycle Co* [1959] AC 576; *Harbutt's Plasticine Ltd v. Wayne Tank and Pump Co Ltd* [1970] 1 QB 447; *Levison v. Patent Steam Carpet Cleaning Co Ltd* [1978] QB 69; and *Photo Production Ltd v. Securicor Transport Ltd* [1978] 1 WLR 856.

64 [1980] AC 827.

65 See A. T. Denning, 'This Is My Life', *Denning Law Journal* 1 (1986): 17 at 25.

66 [1975] 1 QB 326 at 339.

and has been roundly rejected by the courts.[67] However, it should be noted that prior to enunciating the principle, Denning embarked on a detailed survey of the existing law which involved some form of wrongdoing.[68] While Denning stated that there is no real need for proof of any wrongdoing, this might be inconclusive because he utilised the concept in the sense of an intention to bring distress to the other party, as opposed to an independent standard embodied in the law itself. Denning's broader approach might still find vindication, at least in part, in the possible introduction and development of the broader doctrines of unconscionability[69] or good faith.[70]

With regard to the doctrine of privity of contract, Denning believed that justice might be done by recognising an exception to the rule against conferring benefits on third parties. He argued extra-judicially that a departure from the Christian ethic current in the nineteenth century in favour of a philosophy giving untrammelled reign to freewill had been discredited, such that 'it is to be hoped that soon there will be restored the principle that person who makes a solemn promise must keep it' and that contracts for the benefit of third parties should be recognised in law.[71] Denning strenuously attempted to effect a change in the law, but to no avail. However, recent (and not so recent) developments in both case law and statute appear to have vindicated Denning's views.[72]

Finally, Denning is also notable for his contribution to the doctrine of mistake. In particular, he can be credited with the creation of the doctrine of common mistake in equity, which is traceable to the English Court of

67 See the House of Lords' decision of *National Westminster Bank plc v. Morgan* [1985] AC 686 at 707–8.

68 Duress of goods, unconscionable transactions, undue influence, undue pressure and salvage agreements.

69 See A. Phang, 'Undue Influence: Methodology, Sources, Linkages', *Journal of Business Law* (1995): 552 at 570–4.

70 See Phang, 'Challenge of Principled Gap-Filling', 298–307; M. Arden, 'Coming to Terms with Good Faith', *Journal of Contract Law* 30 (2013): 199.

71 See A. T. Denning, 'The Universities and Law Reform', *Journal of the Society of Public Teachers of Law*, n.s. 1 (1949): 258 at 261–2.

72 See Denning's dissent in *Scruttons Limited v. Midland Silicones Limited* [1962] AC 446 and his judgment in *Beswick v. Beswick* [1966] 1 Ch 538, an approach that was rejected by the House of Lords: see [1968] AC 58. For recent examples, see *The Eurymedon* [1975] AC 446 and *The New York Star* [1980] 3 All ER 257. Outside the UK, see the High Court of Australia's decision in *Trident General Insurance Co Limited v. McNiece Bros Pty Limited* (1988) 165 CLR 107 and the Supreme Court of Canada's decision in *London Drugs Limited v. Kuehne & Nagel International Limited* [1993] 1 WWR 1. In addition, the UK Parliament enacted the Contracts (Rights of Third Parties) Act 1999, which constitutes a wide-ranging statutory exception to the doctrine of privity of contract: see C. MacMillan, 'A Birthday Present for Lord Denning: The Contracts (Rights of Third Parties) Act 1999', *Modern Law Review*, 63 (2000): 721.

Appeal decision in *Solle v. Butcher*.[73] Denning was of the view that there was no doctrine of common mistake at common law, but that the doctrine of common mistake in equity is much more flexible and, unlike the corresponding doctrine at common law, accommodates rights of innocent third parties. The English Court of Appeal, in *Great Peace Shipping Limited v. Tsavliris Salvage (International) Limited*,[74] refused to follow *Solle*. However, it is significant that the Singapore courts have not followed the latest English approach and continue to endorse the doctrine of common mistake in equity.[75] Put simply, Denning's approach, while rejected in England, has been vindicated and endorsed overseas.

The Law of Negligence

Perhaps Denning's best remembered judgment in the law of negligence is his dissent in the English Court of Appeal decision in *Candler v. Crane, Christmas & Co*.[76] His approach was ultimately adopted by the House of Lords in the landmark decision of *Hedley Byrne & Co Limited v. Heller & Partners Limited*,[77] which established liability for negligent misstatements. Significantly, Denning himself refers to the *Candler* case as his 'most important judgment'.[78] It is also apposite to note Denning's observation that insofar as the law of negligence is concerned, 'the moral element does come in', and that

> [t]he sufferer will not recover any damages from anyone except when it is that person's fault. It is only by retaining that moral element that society can be kept solvent. To award compensation without fault would make society bankrupt. No one could pay the [insurance] premium needed to get cover.[79]

Even when he expounds on morality, Denning is equally alive to the needs of the wider society.

Mention should be made of Denning's explicit reference to Christianity in the context of Lord Atkin's seminal 'neighbour principle' as enunciated in *Donoghue v. Stevenson*.[80] Denning observes that 'Lord Atkin took the

73 [1950] 1 KB 671. 74 [2003] QB 679.
75 See the Singapore Court of Appeal decision of *Chwee Kin Keong v. Digilandmall.com Pte Limited* [2005] 1 SLR(R) 502.
76 [1951] 2 KB 164. For Denning's own extended analysis on the development of the law of negligence, see Denning, *Discipline of Law*, part 6.
77 [1964] AC 465. And see Denning, *The Discipline of Law*, 245 et seq.
78 Denning, 'Foreword', 1. 79 Denning, *Discipline of Law*, 280.
80 [1932] AC 562 at 580.

Christian precept as underlying the basis of his decision'.[81] While there is some truth in this, the analogy cannot be taken too far as the neighbour principle in law is somewhat different, and understandably so as we live in an imperfect world.[82]

Other Areas of Law

Denning's influence was extensive and pervasive: justice cannot be done to it in a single chapter. In both his judicial and extra-judicial observations in the law of restitution, Denning demonstrates once again not only his pioneering spirit but also the spirit of justice and fairness that undergirds all his judgments.[83] In the context of family law, there are references to the Bible and his view that 'the only basis for a sound family life is a Christian marriage – the personal union of one man with one woman, to the exclusion of all others on either side, for better or for worse, so long as both shall live'.[84] Denning cannot be accused of burying his head in the sand in relation to the practical difficulties concerned such as the rising divorce rate.[85] His views on sexual morality are also consistent with his Christian values[86] and have been subject, not surprisingly in this day and age, to some criticism.[87]

81 Denning, *Influence of Religion on Law*, 7; Denning, 'Influence of Religion', 108; Denning, *Family Story*, 181.

82 See E. Chamberlain, 'Lord Atkin's Opinion in *Donoghue v. Stevenson*: Perspectives from Biblical Hermeneutics', *Law and Humanities*, 4 (2010): 91 esp. at 98–9. See also R. Castle, 'Lord Atkin and the Neighbour Test', *Ecclesiastical Law Journal*, 7 (2003): 210.

83 For his judicial observations, see e.g. *Nelson v. Larholt* [1948] 1 KB 339. For extra-judicial observations, see A. T. Denning, 'The Recovery of Money', *Law Quarterly Review* 65 (1949): 37, and his review of the first edition of the seminal textbook, R. Goff and G. H. Jones, *The Law of Restitution* (London: Sweet & Maxwell Ltd, 1966) in *Law Quarterly Review* 83 (1967): 277. See also A. T. Denning, '*Quantum Meruit* and the Statute of Frauds', *Law Quarterly Review* 41 (1925): 79; A. T. Denning, '*Quantum Meruit*: The Case of *Craven-Ellis v. Canons Limited*', *Law Quarterly Review* 55 (1939): 54.

84 When first appointed to the High Court in 1944, Denning was allocated the Probate, Divorce and Admiralty Division where he remained for eighteen months until transferred to his more natural habitat in the King's Bench Division. For his use of the Bible in the context of family law, see A. T. Denning, *The Equality of Women*, Eleanor Rathbone Memorial Lecture (Liverpool: Liverpool University Press, 1960), 4–5, where he refers to Ephesians 5:22–24, 1 Peter 3:1 and Matthew 5:32; quotation from ibid., 16.

85 See e.g. Denning, 'Freedom of the Individual', 58, although he did observe that 'whilst accepting the principle of divorce when a marriage has irretrievably broken down, we should do all we can to maintain the Christian concept of marriage'. See also Denning, 'Law and Life in Our Time', 352.

86 See *Ward v. Bradford Corporation* (1972) 70 LGR 27, esp. at 35.

87 See e.g. R. Geary, 'Lord Denning and Morality', in Robson and Watchman, *Justice, Lord Denning and the Constitution*, 74–86; M. D. A. Freeman, 'Family Matters', in Jowell and

In the sphere of labour law, Denning's approach towards trade unions appears to have been particularly controversial.[88] It has been a common criticism that by his allegedly anti-union judgments, he represented an elite which had no thought for the working classes. However, Denning was concerned primarily with the abuse of power in whatever guise. He was, therefore, wary of the abuse of power by trade unions, which would not only adversely affect the rights of individual workers but also the very structure of the nation as a whole.[89] This is not, of course, to state that Denning was always right.[90] However, the other extreme should also be avoided, namely the argument that Denning was irretrievably (and, worse, irrationally) biased against trade unions.

Ecclesiastical Law

Brief mention should be made of Denning's involvement in the somewhat recondite field of ecclesiastical law. Mindful of the powerful influence of Christianity on his jurisprudence, it is surprising that relatively little is written about Denning's time as a judge of the ecclesiastical courts and his scholarly contribution to the law of the Church of England. Denning was appointed Chancellor of the Diocese of Southwark in 1937 and of the Diocese of London in 1942. He held both judicial posts in plurality, as was customary, until his appointment to the High Court Bench in 1944, when, by the convention prevailing at the time, he resigned both. Little is known of the faculty causes over which he presided. He wrote an article entitled 'The Meaning of Ecclesiastical Law' which was duly published in the *Law Quarterly Review*.[91] The article was precipitated by the decision of the House of Lords in *Representative Body of the Church in Wales v. Tithe Redemption Commission*.[92] It arose from the Welsh Church Act 1914, which had provided for the disestablishment of the Church in Wales. He noted that the Welsh

McAuslan, *Lord Denning*, ch. 4; and M. D. Kirby, 'Lord Denning: An Antipodean Appreciation', *Denning Law Journal* 1 (1986): 103 at 110–11.

88 See P. Davies and M. Freedland, 'Labour Law', in Jowell and McAuslan, *Lord Denning*, ch. 8. See also K. Miller, 'The Labours of Lord Denning', in Robson and Watchman, *Justice, Lord Denning and the Constitution*, 126–56.

89 See generally Davies and Freedland, 'Labour Law'. See also A. T. Denning, 'Restraining the Misuse of Power', in *Jubilee Lectures Celebrating the Foundation of the Faculty of Law, University of Birmingham* (London: Wildy & Sons, 1981), 11; Denning, *Road to Justice*, 104; A. T. Denning, 'Misuse of Power', *Australian Law Journal* 55 (1981): 720 at 724; Denning, 'Law and Life in Our Time', 12; and Denning, *Closing Chapter*, s. 6.

90 Davies and Freedland, 'Labour Law'.

91 A. T. Denning, 'The Meaning of Ecclesiastical Law', *Law Quarterly Review* 60 (1944): 235.

92 [1944] 1 All ER 710.

Church Act did not contain any definition of ecclesiastical law, nor did the Irish Church Act 1869, which effected the disestablishment of the Church of Ireland and provided the model for the Welsh Church Act.

Denning's article sought to differentiate between ecclesiastical law in its 'general' and 'technical' senses. In its technical meaning, ecclesiastical law is 'the law administered by ecclesiastical courts and persons, in the same way that "equity" in a technical sense meant the law administered by the Courts of Chancery'.[93] Denning's view was anachronistic at the time and seems even more so now, half a century later. It relied heavily on Lord Blackburn's analysis in *Mackonochie v. Lord Penzance*[94] and focused on the remedies available to an ecclesiastical court. In its general sense, on the other hand, ecclesiastical law is the law relating to any matter concerning the Church of England. The narrow, and technical, interpretation of the term 'ecclesiastical law' has not found favour with modern commentators.[95] Indeed, not long after Denning's article was published, Uthwatt J had occasion to consider the matter, concluding that ecclesiastical law is part of the law of the land, 'but jurisdiction as to its enforcement is divided between the ecclesiastical courts and the temporal courts'.[96]

CONCLUSION

Denning was consistently candid about his religious beliefs, and this is amply demonstrated from a wide variety of his extra-judicial writings. These beliefs necessarily entailed a view of morality as well as justice and fairness that was objective; it simultaneously constituted the source of the spirit of justice and fairness which motivated him to achieve a just and fair result in every case that came before him in a court of law. Indeed, so strong was that spirit of justice and fairness that I have termed it 'a passion for justice'.[97] That having been said, contrary to popular perception, it is evident through some of Denning's actual decisions that he never ignored legal doctrine. On the contrary, he was acutely aware of the frequently complex interaction between doctrine and

93 Denning, 'Meaning of Ecclesiastical Law', 236. 94 (1881) 6 App Cas 424.

95 See M. Hill, *Ecclesiastical Law*, 3d ed. (Cambridge: Cambridge University Press, 2007), para 1.20. It has been argued that 'the terms *canon law* and *ecclesiastical law* ought to be discarded in favour of the title "church law", to include both internal church-made law and external state-made law': see N. Doe, *The Legal Framework of the Church of England* (Oxford: Clarendon Press, 1996), 32.

96 *Attorney-General v. Dean and Chapter of Ripon Cathedral* [1945] Ch 239 at 245.

97 The same phrase was used by Lord Ackner, 'The Genius of the Common Law', *New Law Journal* 10 (1995): 525, and by Lord Goff of Chieveley, 'Lord Denning: A Memoir', *Denning Law Journal* (1999): xxiii at xxviii.

fairness in the law.[98] He always held the difficult balance between achieving a just and fair result in the specific case before him and the need at the same time to ensure that the law in general was also developed for the benefit of future cases as well. The following excerpts from the late Lord Bingham of Cornhill, himself an accomplished Law Lord and jurist, summarise this as well as many of the other themes addressed in this chapter:

> Lord Denning is the best-known and best-loved judge in the whole of our history ... He had something more: a unique gift of human warmth which endeared him to everyone who knew him and many who did not ... Throughout his long life he remained unfailingly true to the values, beliefs, habits and tastes of his early years. He was a devoted member of the Anglican Church, loving its worship, liturgy and language. He answered to an unbending sense of duty. He had an indefatigable capacity and inexhaustible relish for hard work. He had a love of his country both deep and proud ... He felt an instinctive respect for the continuity of our institutions and for authority, if not always for the authorities. He practised the virtues of thrift, sobriety and plain living. He had an unaffected simplicity of speech and bearing. He believed, profoundly, in the brotherhood of man and the worth of individual human beings. He was contemptuous of the fugitive, the trivial and the mean ... In the vast body of cases which he decided, two chords in particular are dominant. The first is fairness ... The second chord is freedom ... He saw the law not as a code of rules, but as a collection of human stories, each with a moral; not as a fetter, but as a source of freedom; not as an unwelcome but inescapable response to the ills of society, but as a means of providing that justice upon which good government and social harmony fundamentally depend.[99]

Perhaps, the last word ought to go to Denning himself. In his reply to the various valedictory speeches made upon his retirement as Master of the Rolls, Denning concluded: 'I wish I could say, as a great man did once, "I fought a good fight; I finished the course; I have kept the faith."'[100]

98 See Phang, 'Doctrine and Fairness'.

99 Lord Bingham of Cornhill, 'Address at the Service of Thanksgiving for the Rt Hon Lord Denning OM', in T. Bingham, *The Business of Judging* (Oxford: Oxford University Press, 2000), 409, 410 and 412–13.

100 'Valedictory Speeches upon the Impending Retirement of the Master of the Rolls', *Denning Law Journal* 1 (1986): 15, citing 2 Timothy 4:7.

Index

Lightning Source UK Ltd.
Milton Keynes UK
UKHW021537140520
363247UK00010B/84

9 781316 638019